THE PETER NORTON

PROGRAMMER'S GUIDE
TO THE IBM® PC

W9-CBH-843

THE PETER NORTON
PROGRAMMER'S GUIDE
TO THE IBM® PC

The ultimate reference
guide to the *entire*
family of IBM®
personal computers.

Microsoft®
PRESS

PUBLISHED BY
Microsoft Press
A Division of Microsoft Corporation
16011 N.E. 36th Way, Box 97017, Redmond, Washington 98073-9717

Library of Congress Cataloging in Publication Data
Norton, Peter, 1943–
        The Peter Norton Programmer's Guide to the IBM PC.
Includes index.
1. IBM Personal Computer—Programming. I. Title.
II. Title: Programmer's guide to the IBM PC.
QA76.8.I2594N68   1985   001.64'2   85-8872
ISBN 0-914845-46-2

Printed and bound in the United States of America.

            14 15   FGFG 8 9 0 9 8 7

Distributed to the book trade outside the United States of America
and Canada by Penguin Books Ltd.

Penguin Books Ltd., Harmondsworth, Middlesex, England
Penguin Books Australia Ltd., Ringwood, Victoria, Australia
Penguin Books N.Z. Ltd., 182-190 Wairau Road, Auckland 10,
New Zealand

Penguin ISBN 0-14-087-144-6

British Cataloging in Publication Data available

CONTENTS

ACKNOWLEDGMENTS

So many people have contributed to the making of this book that it would be impossible to list them all. There is one person, however, who has earned special mention and thanks for her efforts and dedication to this project: Suzanne Ropiequet.

INTRODUCTION

My goal in writing this book is a simple but an ambitious one: to help you master the principles of programming the IBM personal computer family. From the time that the first IBM Personal Computer (known to us as "the PC") was introduced in the fall of 1981, it was clear that it was going to be a very important computer. Later, as PC sales zoomed beyond the expectations of everyone, IBM included, and as the original model was joined by a sibling or two, the PC became recognized as *the* standard for serious desktop computers. From the original PC, a whole family of computers—a family with many branches—has evolved. And at the same time, the importance of the PC family has also grown.

The success and significance of the PC family has made the development of programs for it very important. However, the fact that each member of the family differs in its details and characteristics from its relatives has also made the development of programs for the family increasingly complex.

This book is about the knowledge, skills, and *concepts* that are needed to create programs for the PC family—not just for one member of the family, though we might perhaps cater to the peculiarities and quirks of one member, but for the family as a whole, in a way that is universal enough that our programs should work not only on all the present family members, but on future members as well.

I've written this book for anyone involved in the development of programs for the PC family. It is for programmers, but not *just* for programmers. It is for anyone who is involved in or needs to understand the technical details and working ideas that are the basis for PC program development, including anyone who manages programmers, anyone who plans or designs PC programs, and anyone who uses PC programs and wants to understand the details behind them.

SOME COMMENTS ON PHILOSOPHY

One of the most important elements of this book is the discussion of programming *philosophy*. You will find throughout this book explanations of the *ideas* underlying IBM's design of the PC family, and of the principles of sound PC programming, viewed from my own experience.

If this book were to provide you with only facts—tabulations of technical information—it would not serve you well. That's why I've interwoven with the technical discussion an explanation of what the PC family is all about, of the principles that tie the various family members together, and of the techniques and methods that help us produce programs that can endure and prosper along with the PC family.

HOW TO USE THIS BOOK

This book is both a reading book and a reference book, and there are at least two ways that you might approach it. You may wish to read it, like any other book, from front to back, digging in where the discussion is useful to you and quickly glancing through the material you don't yet need. This approach provides a grand overview of the workings and the ideas behind the workings of PC programs. You can also use this book as a pure reference, dipping into specific chapters for specific information. We've provided detailed tables of contents at the beginning of each chapter and an extensive index to help you find what you need.

When you use this book as a random-access reference to the details of PC programming, you'll find that much of the material is intricately interrelated. To help cope with the interrelationships, you'll see that I have repeated some details each time they came up where it was practical to duplicate information, and have used a ☞ symbol to refer you to other sections when it was not practical. I have also used the following self-explanatory symbols to help you zone in on material that is specific to a particular machine:

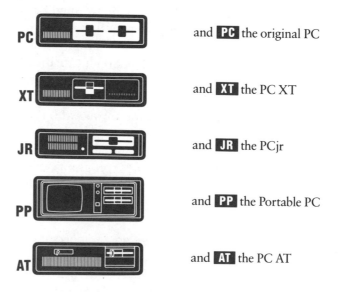

and **PC** the original PC

and **XT** the PC XT

and **JR** the PCjr

and **PP** the Portable PC

and **AT** the PC AT

The machine icons are displayed beside paragraphs and whole sections that apply to a specific machine, while the initials are used to draw your attention to machine-specific comments within a discussion that applies to the family as a whole. I hope this system will enable you to more easily zone in on the information you need for your programs.

OTHER RESOURCES

One book, of course, can't provide you with all the knowledge that you might possibly need. I've made this book as rich and complete as I reasonably can, but there will always be a need for other kinds of information. Here are some of the places you might look for material to supplement what you find here:

For detailed technical information about the PC family, the ultimate source is IBM's series of Technical Reference manuals. There are specific Technical Reference manuals for the original PC, for the XT, for the PCjr, for the AT, and for other specific models. The majority of the programming-related information in these manuals is essentially repeated, and any one manual could serve as a reference for the entire family. You should know a few things about these model-specific manuals: First, information that is specific to one model is not differentiated from general information for the whole PC family. To be sure of the differences, you should use common sense, compare the different manuals, and consult *this* book. Second, you should keep in mind that each new model of PC adds new features. If you turn to the manual for a later PC model, you will find information on a wide variety of features; if you turn to the manual for an earlier model, you'll avoid being distracted by features that do not apply to all models in the family.

There is also an IBM Options Adapters Technical Reference manual for the various options and adapters, such as different disk drives or display screens, used by the PC family. Technical information about this kind of equipment is gathered into that one book, which is updated periodically (the updates are available by subscription). Much of the information in this Technical Reference manual is not of use to programmers, but you'll find some parts that may be.

IBM also publishes Technical Reference manuals for special extensions to the PC, such as PC Network.

Perhaps *the* most important of the IBM Technical Reference manuals is the series for DOS. These manuals contain a wealth of detailed technical information, which I have summarized in this book. If you find that you need more specific details about the operation of DOS, you should turn to this manual.

Besides these IBM manuals, there is a host of other places to turn to for supplemental information. For a somewhat broader perspective on the IBM Personal Computer, one that is not focused on programming, see my *Inside the IBM Personal Computer,* published by Robert J. Brady Company. For a similarly broader perspective on DOS, see Van Wolverton's *Running MS-DOS,* published by Microsoft Press. For more details on the peculiarities and the ins and outs of the PCjr, see my *Exploring the PCjr,* also published by Microsoft Press.

Because this book covers the subject of PC programming in a broad fashion, it can't provide you with more than a few key details about individual programming languages. For any particular programming language, and for the many specific compilers for those languages, you will need more books than I could begin to list or recommend.

With these introductory remarks completed, it's time for us to plunge into our task of mastering the principles of programming the PC family!

1

Anatomy of the PC

From the programmer's point of view, all the members of the PC family consist of a processor, memory chips, and several smart, or programmable, circuit chips. All the main circuit components necessary to make the computer work are located on the system board; other important parts are located on expansion boards, which may be plugged into the system board.

The system board contains the microprocessor—either the 8088 or the 80286—which is tied to at least 64K bytes of memory, some built-in ROM programs, such as BASIC and the ROM-BIOS, and several very important support chips. Some of these chips control external devices, such as the disk drive or the display screen, and others help the microprocessor perform its tasks.

In this section, we discuss each major chip and give a few important technical specifications. The margin symbols tell which PCs use each chip. These chips are frequently known by more than one name. For example, some peripherals, such as the keyboard, are supervised by a chip known as the 8255. This chip is also referred to as the 8255A and the 8255A-5. The suffixes A and 5 refer to revision numbers and to parts rated for operation at different speeds. For programming purposes, any Intel chip part number that starts with 8255 is identical to any other chip whose part number starts with 8255, regardless of the suffix. However, when you replace one of these chips on a circuit board, note the suffix. If the suffixes are different, the part may not operate at the proper speed.

THE 8088 MICROPROCESSOR

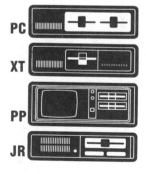

PC

XT

PP

JR

The 8088 is the 16-bit microprocessor that controls the standard IBM personal computers, including the original PC, the XT, the Portable PC, and the PCjr. It is the central processing unit (CPU) of the computer—the brains behind the machine. Almost every bit of data that enters or leaves the computer passes through the CPU to be processed or redirected.

The 8088 controls the computer's basic operation by sending and receiving control signals, memory addresses, and data from one part of the computer to another along a network of interconnecting electronic pathways called a bus. Located along the bus are input and output (I/O) ports that connect the various memory and support chips to the bus. Data passes through these I/O ports while it travels to and from the CPU and the other parts of the computer.

Inside the 8088, 14 registers provide a working area for data transfer and processing. These internal registers, forming an area 28 bytes in size, are able to temporarily store data, memory addresses, instruction pointers, and status and control flags. Through these registers, the 8088 can access over one million bytes of memory and up to 64K I/O ports. ☞ See Chapter 2 for an overview of the operating characteristics of the 8088.

8259A interrupt controller

8088 microprocessor

8087 math coprocessor plugs in here

8284A clock generator

ROM

RAM

8253 programmable timer

8255 programmable peripheral interface

8237A DMA controller

Figure 1-1. The PC system board

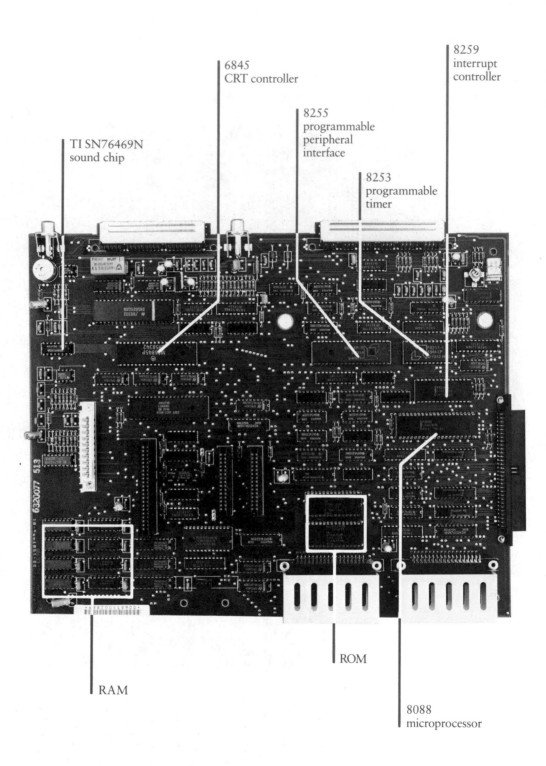

6845
CRT controller

8259
interrupt
controller

8255
programmable
peripheral
interface

TI SN76469N
sound chip

8253
programmable
timer

RAM

ROM

8088
microprocessor

Figure 1-2. The PCjr system board

80286
microprocessor

80287
math coprocessor
plugs in here

8254
programmable
timer

8259
interrupt
controllers

256/512 K
SYSTEM BOARD

8237
DMA controllers

RAM

ROM

8284
clock generator
(under shield)

Figure 1-3. The AT system board

The 8088's family tree. The 8088 is just one member of a closely related family of 16-bit microprocessors designed by Intel Corporation. The founding member of this microprocessor family is the 8086. The 8088 differs from the 8086 in only one minor respect: Although the 8088 is a 16-bit microprocessor, it uses an 8-bit data bus instead of the 16-bit bus that the 8086 uses. (☞ The difference between 8-bit and 16-bit buses is discussed on page 13.) Virtually anything that you read about the 8086 also applies to the 8088; for programming purposes, consider them identical.

Although the 8088 microprocessor has long been the main brain for the PC family, it isn't the only one available. Other Intel microprocessors are being used to power some of the PC family's distant cousins. For example, the 8086 is the brain of the Compaq Deskpro, a well-known portable PC-compatible computer. A pair of microprocessors known as the 80188 and 80186 (they're usually called the 188 and the 186), which are more advanced versions of the original 8088 and 8086 microprocessors, have been used in a variety of computers related to the IBM PC family, such as the Tandy 2000 computer. These two microprocessors have more computing power than their predecessors, but their chief asset is that they combine, in one chip, both a microprocessor and many important and necessary support operations—operations that are handled externally by older chips like the 8088 and the 8086. But in spite of their many improvements, the 186 and 188 are still not the last word as far as the 8086 family is concerned.

The 80286 Microprocessor

The most advanced Intel microprocessor currently used in the IBM personal computers is the 80286 (or 286). It is this chip that controls the operation of the AT. The 80286 is a true 16-bit microprocessor that uses a full 16-bit data bus and adds extra programming features to the 8086 design. Perhaps the 286's most important enhancements are its ability to allow multitasking and virtual memory storage—two concepts that are familiar to anyone experienced in mainframe computing.

Multitasking is the ability of a CPU to perform several tasks at a time—such as printing a document or calculating a spreadsheet—by quickly switching its attention among the controlling programs. A regular PC, which uses the 8088 microprocessor, can do a limited amount of multitasking with the help of very sophisticated software, such as IBM's Topview or Microsoft's Windows. But a true multitasking processor, like the 286, performs task switching internally—with some help from the operating system. Since the multitasking capabilities in the 286 are largely a part of the hardware design, they are much faster and more reliable than software-driven multitasking.

Virtual memory allows a computer to act as if it has much more memory than is physically present. Through an extremely sophisticated software and hardware design, a program may be led to believe that it has up to one gigabyte (one billion bytes) of memory at its disposal, even though the hardware memory chips account for only a fraction of that size. This deception is achieved through an elaborate memory addressing scheme that involves storing some parts of a program on disk and some parts in main memory. When particular instructions or program data are needed that are not in physical memory, they are loaded from the disk. The 286 and the operating system have the weighty task of figuring out where the information is and where it must go so that the program runs smoothly and efficiently, even though it is scattered throughout the computer system.

Virtual storage has been used in mini- and mainframe computers for a long time, but has only recently come of age in the microcomputer world. Its introduction through the 286 in the AT should have a profound effect on application programming since it allows us to write programs whose sizes are, for all practical purposes, limited only by the physical capacity of the disks.

The AT is often seen as just a faster, more powerful member of the 8086 family—able to run almost all the popular PC programs, including the DOS operating systems and most DOS programs. However, both multitasking and virtual memory storage change the operating characteristics of the 286. When we use these features, the AT actually becomes a different computer, requiring different programs and a different operating system. This makes the AT the first of an entirely new generation of personal computers, a generation apart from the original PC family.

With this in mind, it is best to leave the discussion of the AT's advanced capabilities to another book and focus in this one on the standard PC capabilities. You will find that most of the programming techniques discussed in this book focus on the 8088, with annotations on the 80286 where appropriate.

All members of the 8086 family are designed to work with additional processors. They also work with two special coprocessors: the 8087 math coprocessor and the 8089 I/O coprocessor. These optional chips can be wired together to help reduce the workload of the main CPU. IBM provides the circuitry to support only the 8087 math coprocessor, so we'll take a moment to discuss this chip in more detail.

The 8087 Math Coprocessor

The 8088 can work only with integers, or whole numbers. "Real" or floating-point numbers must be handled by special means. This is usually done with subroutines, which carry out the floating-point operations effectively enough, but at great cost to efficiency and speed.

The 8087 math coprocessor performs floating-point calculations in the neighborhood of 10 to 50 times faster than can be achieved with the 8088. In addition, it performs arithmetic with a much higher degree of precision than is usually achieved with the 8088 (or even with most multi-million-dollar mainframe computers). The 8087, besides doing simple add/subtract/multiply/divide arithmetic, has the built-in ability to perform trigonometric calculations (sine, cosine, tangent, etc.), which greatly simplify some complex programming. Furthermore, it can work with numbers that come in different formats, including integer, floating-point, and even decimal formats. Finally, it can do all this while the 8088 proceeds with other work.

Every 8088-based PC model except the PCjr can accommodate the 8087, though it does require special software support. (**AT** The AT uses the 80287 math coprocessor, a variation of the 8087 that is tailored to work with the 80286 microprocessor.) But though the 8087 greatly enhances the arithmetic performance of the IBM personal computers, relatively little software takes advantage of it. This unfortunate situation is due to a simple historical fact: Although provision for the use of the 8087

Data Type	Approximate Range (from)	(to)	Bits	Significant Digits (decimal)
Word integer	$-32{,}768$	$+32{,}767$	16	4
Short integer	$-2 \times 10E9$	$+2 \times 10E9$	32	9
Long integer	$-9 \times 10E18$	$+9 \times 10E18$	64	18
Packed decimal	$-99\ldots99$	$+99\ldots99$	80	18
Short real	$8.43 \times 10E-37$	$3.37 \times 10E38$	32	6–7
Long real	$4.19 \times 10E-307$	$1.67 \times 10E308$	64	15–16
Temporary real	$3.4 \times 10E-4932$	$1.2 \times 10E4932$	80	19

Figure 1-4. The range of numeric data types that can be operated on in the eight 80-bit registers of the 8087 or 80287 math coprocessors

was designed into the original model of the PC (and into most other models), IBM did not support the 8087—or even acknowledge its potential benefits—until the standards for PC hardware and software were well established. This meant that a large percentage of the original hardware and software developed for the PC family did not incorporate the use of the 8087, depriving us all of some remarkable computing power.

Although 8087 chips and software have so far sold in only limited numbers, we are beginning to see more programs, such as Ashton-Tate's Framework, that not only take advantage of the 8087, but also detect its presence and automatically use it or bypass it depending on the requirements of the program. Unfortunately, there are still only a handful of such programs available.

Since the use of the math coprocessor in the PC family is rare, we won't be covering the special problems of programming it in this book.

THE SUPPORT CHIPS

The microprocessor cannot control the entire computer without some help—nor should it. By delegating certain control functions to other chips, the CPU is free to attend to its own work. These support chips may be responsible for such processes as controlling the flow of information throughout the internal circuitry, as the interrupt controller and the DMA controller are, or for controlling the flow of information to or from a particular device attached to the computer, such as a video display or disk drive. These so-called *device controllers* are often housed on a separate board that is plugged into one of the PC's expansion slots.

Many of the support chips in the IBM PC are programmable, which means they can be manipulated to perform specialized tasks. For the most part, direct programming of these chips is not a good idea, but in the discussion of each chip that follows, I will point out which are safe to program and which aren't. Since this book does not cover direct hardware control, you should look in the IBM Technical Reference manual for details about programming individual chips.

The 8259 Interrupt Controller

The 8259 supervises the operation of interrupts. Interrupts are signals sent to the CPU by the hardware either to request attention or to request that some action be taken. The 8259 intercepts the signals, determines their level of importance in relation to the other signals it is receiving, and issues an interrupt to the CPU based on this determination. When the CPU receives the interrupt signal, it calls a specific program associated with that particular peripheral device. It is this program that actually performs the required action. ☛ We discuss interrupts more thoroughly in Chapters 2 and 3.

The 8259 can handle eight interrupt requests at a time, and can be linked to other 8259s for higher capacity. **AT** IBM has made use of this expansion capability by hooking two of them together in the AT so it can handle fifteen interrupts at a time.

Generally, we do not program the 8259, since any changes to it are likely to interfere with the computer's basic operation. However, it is possible to reconfigure the priority levels of the interrupts at any time during the execution of the main program. This means that the program can change the order in which the requests are processed by the 8259 to match its own needs.

Other names for the 8259 include the INTR and the PIC, for programmable interrupt controller.

The 8237 DMA Controller

To avoid harassing the microprocessor, some parts of the computer are able to transfer data to and from the computer's memory without passing through the CPU. This operation is called direct memory access, or DMA, and it is handled by a chip known as the 8237, or DMA controller. The main purpose of the DMA controller is to allow the disk drive to read or write data without involving the microprocessor. Since disk I/O is a relatively slow operation, DMA can speed up the computer's overall performance quite a bit.

All members of the PC family, with the important exception of the PCjr, use either the 8237 or its equivalent for direct memory access. **JR** The lack of DMA is one reason why the PCjr is slower than its cousins. Without a DMA controller to help out, the PCjr's 8088 has to take care of disk operations whenever they occur, which is indirectly why we cannot type on the Junior keyboard while the disk is in use.

The DMA controller contains four separate channels to carry data back and forth from memory, and 344 bits of internal memory to store the data that is in transit. Theoretically, it is possible for several DMA controllers to be connected to one another and, in fact, **AT** the AT uses two DMA controllers in its circuitry.

The 8284 Clock Generator

The clock generator supplies the multiphase clock signals that are needed to drive the microprocessor and the peripherals. Its base frequency is 14.3128 megahertz (MHz, or million cycles per second). The other chips generally divide the base frequency by a constant to obtain the frequency they need to accomplish their tasks. The standard PC family's 8088 is driven at 4.77 MHz, one-third of the base frequency. The new additions to the 8086 family can run faster. For example, the 8088-2, used on some variations of the PC, can be run at a clock speed of 8 MHz, providing nearly twice the raw computing power of the 8088, and the 80286 runs at 6 MHz, providing roughly one and a half times the computing power of the 8088. The internal bus and the 8253 programmable timer (☛ discussed shortly) use a frequency of 1.193 MHz, running at a quarter of the 8088 rate, and one-twelfth of the base rate.

The 8255 Programmable Peripheral Interface

The 8255 is used to connect some of the computer's peripheral devices to the bus. Information that is sent to or from devices such as the speaker and the cassette travels through the I/O ports via this chip.

The 8255 is also called the PPI (for programmable peripheral interface). It is normally programmed by the system software, so although possible, it is not necessary for us to program this chip.

The 8253 Programmable Timer

The 8253 (**AT** the 8254 in the AT) is a multipurpose timer and counter that can generate up to three accurate time delays under software control. It gets its signal from the 8284 clock generator and oscillates at a frequency of 1.193 MHz.

The 8253 is mainly used to generate sounds on the PC's internal speaker, but is also used for other frequency-dependent functions, such as cassette data I/O and timekeeping. ☛ See Chapter 7's discussion of sound for more information about this chip.

Other names for the 8253 include the timer, and sometimes the clock. Keep in mind that "clock" also refers to the 8284 chip, which generates the computer's 14.3-MHz heartbeat.

The 6845 CRT Controller

The 6845, also called the Motorola CRT chip, is generally located on an expansion board known as the video display adapter. It has 19 internal registers that are used to define and control a raster-scan CRT. Although we can program this chip ourselves, it is wisest by far to leave it under the control of the PC's BIOS. ☛ See Chapter 4 for more information on video displays and video display adapters.

The PD765 Diskette Controller

The PD765 supervises and controls the operation of the diskette drive. It is more commonly called the FDC (floppy-disk controller) or the NEC (Nippon Electric Company) controller. As with the 6845 CRT controller, we should leave this chip under the BIOS's control.

LINKING THE PARTS: THE BUS

As we mentioned, the PC family of computers links all internal control circuitry together by a circuit design known as a bus. A bus is simply a shared path on the main circuit board to which all the controlling parts of the computer are attached. When data is passed from one component to another it travels along this common path to reach its destination.

Every control chip and every byte of memory in the PC is connected directly or indirectly to the bus. When a new component is plugged into one of the expansion slots, it is actually plugged directly into the bus, making it an equal partner in the operation of the entire unit.

Any information that enters or leaves a computer system is temporarily stored in at least one of several locations along the bus. Most of the time data is placed in main memory, which in the PC family consists of thousands of 8-bit memory cells. But some data may end up in a port or register for a short time while it waits for the CPU to send it to its proper location. Generally, ports and registers hold only one or two bytes of information at a time and are usually used as stopover sites for data that is being sent from one place to another. (☛ Ports and registers are discussed in detail in Chapter 2.)

Whenever a memory cell or port is used as a storage site, its location is marked by an address that uniquely identifies it. When data is ready to be transferred, its destination address is first transmitted along the address bus; the data follows along behind on the data bus. So the bus carries more than just data. It carries power and control information, such as timing signals (from the system clock) and interrupt signals, as well as the addresses of the thousands of memory cells and the many devices attached to the bus. To accommodate these four different functions, the bus is divided into four parts: the *power lines,* the *control bus,* the *address bus,* and the *data bus.* We're going to delve deeper into the address and data buses because they conduct information in a way that helps to explain some of the unique properties of the PC family.

The Address Bus

The address bus in the standard PC family uses 20 signal lines to transmit the addresses of the memory cells and devices attached to the bus. (☛ Memory addressing is discussed more fully on page 14 and in Chapter 3.) Since there are two possible values (either 1 or 0) that can travel along each of the 20 address lines, the standard PC computers are able to specify 2^{20} addresses. This amounts to over a million possible addresses. **AT** The AT uses 24 address lines, allowing it to specify 2^{24} or over 16 million addresses.

The Data Bus

The data bus works in conjunction with the address bus to carry data throughout the computer. The PC's 8088-based system uses a data bus that has 8 signal lines, each of which carries a single binary digit (bit). This means that data is transmitted across the 8-line bus in 8-bit (1-byte) units. **AT** The 80286 microprocessor of the AT uses a 16-bit data bus, and therefore passes data in 16-bit (1-word) units.

The 8088, being a 16-bit microprocessor, can work with 16 bits of data at a time, just like its relative the 80286. Although the 8088 can work with 16-bit numbers internally, it passes data only 8 bits at a time when working with the circuitry around it because of the size of its data bus. This has led some people to comment that the 8088 is not a true 16-bit microprocessor. Rest assured that it is, even though it is less powerful than the 80286. The 16-bit data bus of the 80286 does help it move data around more efficiently than the 8088, but the real difference in speed between the 8088 and the AT comes from the AT's faster clock rate and its more powerful internal organization.

There is an important practical reason why so many computers, including the older members of the PC family, use the 8088 with its 8-bit data bus, rather than the 8086 with its 16-bit bus. The reason is simple economics. A host of 8-bit circuitry elements is available in large quantities at low prices. When the PC was being designed, 16-bit circuitry was more expensive and was less readily available. The use of the 8088, rather than the 8086, was important not only to hold down the cost of the PC, but also to avoid a shortage of parts. The price of 16-bit circuitry elements has decreased significantly since then, however, and it has become economically feasible to use the more efficient 80286 with its 16-bit bus. Furthermore, the 286 is able to use a mixture of 8-bit parts and 16-bit parts, thereby maintaining compatibility within the PC family.

THE MEMORY CHIPS

So far, we've discussed the CPU, the support chips, and the bus, but we've only touched on memory. We've left our discussion of memory to the end of this chapter because memory chips, unlike the other chips we have discussed, don't control or direct the flow of information through a computer system; they just store it until it is needed.

The number of memory chips that physically exist inside the computer determines the amount of memory we can use for programs and data. Although this may vary from one computer to another, a standard PC usually comes with around 40K of read-only memory (ROM)—with space for more—and from 128K to 256K of random-access memory (RAM). Since only 256K of RAM can be accommodated on the system board, it is possible to add memory cards of varying capacities via the PC's expansion slots. But this is just the physical view of the standard PC's memory. To the computer, the memory chips are nothing more than a few thousand 8-bit (1-byte) storage cells, each one with its own unique address.

Programmers must also think of memory in this way—not in terms of how much physical memory there is, but in terms of how much *addressable* memory there is. The 8088 can address up to 1,024K, or exactly 1,048,576 bytes of memory. In other words, that's the maximum number of addresses, and therefore the maximum number of individual bytes of information it can refer to. ☛ Memory addressing is discussed in more detail on page 24.

Each byte is referred to by a 20-bit numeric address. In the 8088's memory scheme, the addresses are 20 bits "wide" because they must travel along the 20-bit address bus. We tend to use hex notation rather than binary notation in determining memory locations, so we usually translate this 20-bit address into its 5-hex-digit equivalent. This allows address values to range from hex 00000 to hex FFFFF (0 to 1,048,576 in decimal notation). ☛ If you have trouble understanding hex notation, you might want to take a quick look at Appendix B.

When we discuss the PC's 1,024K-byte addressable memory space, we usually divide it into 16 blocks of 64K bytes each. We identify each 64K block by the first hex digit, or the high-order part, of all the memory addresses in the block. For example, the first 64K of memory is the 0 block, with bytes at addresses 00000 through 0FFFF; the last block of memory is the F block, at addresses F0000 through FFFFF.

For nearly all purposes, there is no functional boundary between blocks. We refer to memory in these blocks partly for convenience, and partly because the overall scheme for memory use in all the IBM personal computers assigns different uses block by block.

F 0 0 0 0	Permanent ROM area: ROM-BIOS, BASIC, diagnostics
E 0 0 0 0	Cartridge ROM area
D 0 0 0 0	Cartridge ROM area
C 0 0 0 0	BIOS extensions (XT Disk)
B 0 0 0 0	Conventional display memory (the PC, XT, and AT)
A 0 0 0 0	Display memory expansion
9 0 0 0 0	Working RAM, up to 640K
8 0 0 0 0	Working RAM, up to 576K
7 0 0 0 0	Working RAM, up to 512K
6 0 0 0 0	Working RAM, up to 448K
5 0 0 0 0	Working RAM, up to 384K
4 0 0 0 0	Working RAM, up to 320K
3 0 0 0 0	Working RAM, up to 256K
2 0 0 0 0	Working RAM, up to 192K
1 0 0 0 0	Working RAM, up to 128K; maximum allowed in PCjr
0 0 0 0 0	Working RAM, up to 64K; generally used by system software

*Figure 1-5. The memory block outline for
the PC family*

In theory, any area can contain either permanently recorded ROM, or changeable RAM. By convention, the first ten blocks (blocks 0 through 9), totaling 640K, are set aside for RAM in the IBM PCs and are used as ordinary working memory. Any memory that is installed in these computers is placed here, starting in the first block. Since RAM always occupies a contiguous space, no blocks are skipped. Any addresses in this 640K area with values larger than the actual memory installed are not ordinarily used. If a program tries to use an address where there is no actual memory, the results can vary. Usually no overt error is detected, and the program will continue running.

All IBM personal computers have memory installed in at least the first 64K block, block 0. Of course, 64K is a minimum amount of memory and it's rare for a PC to have only this amount. (At the time the PC was introduced, memory on the system board was expandable in 16K increments, and IBM offered a 16K minimum system; current boards are expandable in 64K minimum increments.) The lowest addresses in the 0 block are traditionally reserved for use by the system software. These addresses store such things as status information, address tables, character tables, and operating system routines. ☛ Chapter 3 explores these low-memory locations in greater detail.

The A block of memory is set aside for expansions to the video memory and is used by IBM's Enhanced Graphics Adapter (EGA) and the Professional Graphics Adapter. The use of the A block is rather special and also oddly quirky—so quirky, in fact, that there is little useful and reliable information that we'll be able to tell you about it. The best way to view the A block is as a provisional scratch pad that is used for brief instants in advanced video modes.

The B block is used for the ordinary video memory in every model except the PCjr. It is divided into two 32K halves, whose addresses begin at B0000 and B8000; for convenience, these areas are simply referred to as B0 and B8. The IBM Monochrome Adapter, the add-on circuit board that drives the IBM Monochrome Monitor, uses 4K of memory located at the beginning of the B0 area (the area's remaining 28K is unused). The IBM Color/Graphics Adapter, the add-on board that drives most other monitors, uses 16K of memory located at the beginning of the B8 area (the remaining 16K is unused).

Although the other IBM PC models can have either or both of these display adapters installed, the PCjr has the functional equivalent of the Color/Graphics Adapter built into it and cannot accommodate a monochrome adapter. The PCjr simulates the use of B8, but actually uses the high end of RAM (the 0 block for the entry-model PCjr and the 1 block for the 128K enhanced model) to support the video data. Through some special circuitry called a video gate array (VGA), the Junior manages to simulate the PC's video functions exactly, and makes our programs think it is using the B block, the standard location for PC video memory. The result is that a PCjr acts like a PC that has a Color/Graphics Adapter installed. Fortunately, the PCjr goes to great lengths to disguise its differences from the other members of the PC family. From a programming point of view, this means we can ignore the Junior's peculiarities and treat it just like a standard PC.

It is important to keep in mind that the use of the B block, and its division into the B0 half for monochrome use and the B8 half for color/graphics use, is a universal standard for the PC family. All models of the PC, including the PCjr, and all PC display adapters, including the Enhanced and Professional Graphics Adapters, either use or appear to use the standard B-block memory locations.

The C block is set aside for any additions that need to be made to permanently installed ROM programs. IBM first used this area to hold the ROM-BIOS routines for the fixed disk that comes with the XT model (and that can be added to the PC model). They did not place the routines at the beginning or end of the C block, as we might expect, but instead they placed them in the middle, starting at C8. We can probably assume most BIOS additions will also be placed in this general area, particularly those that support new hardware extensions.

The D and E blocks are set aside for ROM memory in software cartridges, which were introduced with the PCjr. Cartridge support can be added to nearly any model of PC, but cartridges are rarely used except in the Junior. Cartridge memory actually plugs into the beginning or middle of either of these blocks, at D0, D8, E0, or E8. In the PCjr *only,* cartridges can also plug into the next block, at either F0 or F8.

Normally, the F block is used for permanently installed ROM programs. These include the ROM "cassette" BASIC, the ROM-BIOS, and the test and diagnostic routines. ☞ See Chapter 3 for more details. **JR** The F block is used for a special purpose by the PCjr; plugging cartridges into the F block overrides the conventional ROM-BIOS programs that are placed there. ☞ There is more on cartridge use in the Junior in Chapter 3.

DESIGN PHILOSOPHY

Before we leap into the following chapters, we ought to discuss the control philosophy behind the PC family. This will help you understand what is (and what isn't) important or useful to you.

Part of the design philosophy of the IBM personal computer family centers around a set of BIOS service routines (☞ see Chapters 8 through 13) that provide essentially all the control functions and operations that IBM considers necessary. The basic philosophy of the PC family is: Let the BIOS do it; don't mess with direct control. In my judgment, this is a sound idea that has several beneficial results. Using the BIOS routines encourages good programming practices and it avoids some of the kludgy tricks that have been the curse of many other computers. It also increases the chances of our programs working on every member of the PC family. In addition, it gives IBM more flexibility in making improvements and additions to the line of PC computers. However, it would be naive for me to simply say to you, "Don't mess with direct control of the hardware." For good reasons or bad, you may wish or may need to have your programs work as directly with the computer hardware as possible, doing what is colorfully called *programming down to the bare metal.*

When you consider directly controlling the hardware with your programs, you should understand that the basic mechanism for doing this lies in the use of ports (☞ discussed in Chapter 2). With the single exception of sending output directly to the display screen (which is done through the use of memory), all direct control of the PC's hardware is done by sending data through hardware ports. With only a few exceptions, direct use of the ports to control the PC runs against IBM's design philosophy, and again I would urge you to avoid doing it. The exceptions to this rule involve those features that IBM did not provide BIOS control for, specifically sound generation (☞ see Chapter 7).

2

The Ins and Outs

Generally speaking, the more each of us learns about programming, the more we begin to realize the limitations of our programming languages. High-level programming languages, such as BASIC or C, are not designed to include every possible function that we might need while programming—though admittedly, some are better than others. At some point, we will want to go deeper into our system and use some of the routines the languages themselves use; or perhaps go even deeper and program at the hardware level.

Although some languages provide limited means to talk directly to memory (as with PEEK and POKE in BASIC) or even to some of the chips (as with BASIC's INP and OUT statements), most programmers eventually resort to assembly language, the basic language from which all other languages and operating systems are built. The 8088 assembly language, like all other assembly languages, is composed of a set of symbolic instruction codes as shown in Figure 2-1. Inside the 8088, these codes and the data that is associated with them are translated into a binary form, called machine language, so that they can reside in memory and move through the electronic circuitry to accomplish specific tasks.

The operations the 8088 instructions can perform break down into just a few categories. They can do simple, four-function arithmetic on 8- or 16-bit integers. They can move data around. They can, using only slightly clumsy methods, manipulate individual bits. They can test values and take logical action based on the results. And last but not least, they can interact with the circuitry around them. The size of each instruction varies from one byte to six bytes. By design, the most basic and often-used instructions are the shortest.

Assembly-language programming may be carried out on one of two levels: to create *interface routines* that will tie high-level programs to the lower-level DOS and ROM-BIOS routines; or to create full-fledged assembly-language programs that perform exotic tasks at the hardware level, perhaps accomplishing a feat that is accomplished nowhere else. Either way, in order to understand how to use assembly language, we must understand how the 8088 processes information and how it works with the rest of the computer. The focus of our discussion for the rest of this chapter will be the way the 8088 and the computer's other parts communicate.

Mnemonic	Full Name	Mnemonic	Full Name
AAA	ASCII adjust for addition	JNAE	Jump on not above or equal
AAD	ASCII adjust for division	JNB	Jump on not below
AAM	ASCII adjust for multiplication	JNBE	Jump on not below or equal
AAS	ASCII adjust for subtraction	JNC	Jump on no carry
ADC	Add with carry	JNE	Jump on not equal
ADD	Add	JNG	Jump on not greater
AND	AND	JNGE	Jump on not greater or equal
CALL	CALL	JNL	Jump on not less than
CBW	Convert byte to word	JNLE	Jump on not less than or equal
CLC	Clear carry flag	JNO	Jump on not overflow
CLD	Clear direction flag	JNP	Jump on not parity
CLI	Clear interrupt flag	JNS	Jump on not sign
CMC	Complement carry flag	JNZ	Jump on not zero
CMP	Compare	JO	Jump on overflow
CMPS	Compare byte or word (of string)	JP	Jump on parity
CMPSB	Compare byte string	JPE	Jump on parity even
CMPSW	Compare word string	JPO	Jump on parity odd
CWD	Convert word to double word	JS	Jump on sign
DAA	Decimal adjust for addition	JZ	Jump on zero
DAS	Decimal adjust for subtraction	LAHF	Load AH with flags
DEC	Decrement	LDS	Load pointer into DS
DIV	Divide	LEA	Load effective address
ESC	Escape	LES	Load pointer into ES
HLT	Halt	LOCK	LOCK bus
IDIV	Integer divide	LODS	Load byte or word (of string)
IMUL	Integer multiply	LODSB	Load byte (string)
IN	Input byte or word	LODSW	Load word (string)
INC	Increment	LOOP	LOOP
INT	Interrupt	LOOPE	LOOP while equal
INTO	Interrupt on overflow	LOOPNE	LOOP while not equal
IRET	Interrupt return	LOOPNZ	LOOP while not zero
JA	Jump on above	LOOPZ	LOOP while zero
JAE	Jump on above or equal	MOV	Move
JB	Jump on below	MOVS	Move byte or word (of string)
JBE	Jump on below or equal	MOVSB	Move byte (string)
JC	Jump on carry	MOVSW	Move word (string)
JCXZ	Jump on CX zero	MUL	Multiply
JE	Jump on equal	NEG	Negate
JG	Jump on greater	NOP	No operation
JGE	Jump on greater or equal	NOT	NOT
JL	Jump on less than	OR	OR
JLE	Jump on less than or equal	OUT	Output byte or word
JMP	Jump	POP	POP
JNA	Jump on not above	POPF	POP flags

(continued)

Figure 2-1. The 8088 instruction set

Mnemonic	Full Name	Mnemonic	Full Name
PUSH	PUSH	SCASB	Scan byte (string)
PUSHF	PUSH flags	SCASW	Scan word (string)
RCL	Rotate through carry left	SHL	Shift left
RCR	Rotate through carry right	SHR	Shift right
REP	Repeat	STC	Set carry flag
REPE	Repeat if equal	STD	Set direction flag
REPNE	Repeat if not equal	STI	Set interrupt flag
REPNZ	Repeat if not zero	STOS	Store byte or word (of string)
REPZ	Repeat if zero	STOSB	Store byte (string)
RET	Return	STOSW	Store word (string)
ROL	Rotate left	SUB	Subtract
ROR	Rotate right	TEST	TEST
SAHF	Store AH into flags	WAIT	WAIT
SAL	Shift arithmetic left	XCHG	Exchange
SAR	Shift arithmetic right	XLAT	Translate
SBB	Subtract with borrow	XOR	Exclusive OR
SCAS	Scan byte or word (of string)		

Figure 2-1. The 8088 instruction set
(continued)

HOW THE 8088 COMMUNICATES

The 8088 interacts with the circuitry world around it in three ways: via direct and indirect memory access, through ports, and with signals called interrupts.

Memory is used by reading or writing values that are stored in memory locations and identified with numeric addresses. The memory locations can be accessed in two ways: directly, through the 8237A chip, commonly known as the direct memory access (DMA) controller, or indirectly, through the 8088's internal registers. The disk drives and the serial communications ports can directly access memory through the DMA controller. All other devices transfer data to and from memory by way of the 8088's registers. ☛ For more information about the DMA controller, see page 10. For more on registers, see page 25.

Ports are the 8088's general means of communicating with any computer circuitry other than memory. Like memory locations, ports are identified by number, and data can be read from or written to any port. Port assignment is unique to the design of any particular computer. Generally, all members of the IBM PC family use the same port specifications, with just a few variations among the different models (☛ see page 38).

Interrupts are the means by which the circuitry outside the 8088 reports that something (such as a keystroke) has happened and requests that some action be taken. Although interrupts are essential to the 8088's interaction with the world around it, the concept of an interrupt is useful for other purposes as well. For example, the system BIOS or the operating system can produce software interrupts to request and execute special service programs. Interrupts will be quite important to us when programming the PC family, so we'll devote a special section to them at the end of this chapter.

The 8088 Data Formats

Numeric data. The 8088 is able to work with only four simple numeric data formats, all of which are integer values. The formats are founded on two building blocks: the 8-bit byte and the 16-bit (2-byte) word. Both of these basic units are derived from the 16-bit processing capacity of the 8088 and its 8-bit data bus. The byte is the more fundamental unit, and when the 8088 addresses memory, bytes are the basic unit addressed. In a single byte, the 8088 can work with unsigned positive numbers ranging in value from 0 through 255 (that is, 2^8 possibilities). If the number is a signed value, a byte can represent values ranging from -128 through $+127$. (see Figure 2-2.)

When we need integer values larger than one byte, the 8088 simply uses two adjacent bytes and treats them as a single unit. The 2-byte word is the most common format. A 2-byte word interpreted as an unsigned, positive number can have a value ranging from 0 through 65,535. As a signed number, the value can range from $-32,768$ through $+32,767$.

Character data. Character data is stored in the standard ASCII format, with each character occupying one byte. The 8088 knows nothing about ASCII characters and treats them as arbitrary bytes, with one partial exception: The 8088's instruction set accommodates decimal addition and subtraction performed on ASCII numeral characters. The actual arithmetic is done in binary, but the combination of the AF flag (see page 33) and a few special instructions makes it practical to work on decimal characters and get decimal results.

		Range	
Size	Signed?	Dec	Hex
8	No	0 to 255	00 to FF
8	Yes	-128 to 0 to $+127$	80 to 00 to 7F
16	No	0 to 65,535	0000 to FFFF
16	Yes	$-32,768$ to 0 to $+32,767$	8000 to 0000 to 7FFF

Figure 2-2. The four data formats used by the 8088

☛ See Appendix C for more information on ASCII and the PC family's extended ASCII character set.

HOW THE 8088 ADDRESSES MEMORY

The 8088 is a 16-bit microprocessor and cannot therefore work directly with numbers larger than 16 bits, the largest decimal value being 65,535 or 64K. Theoretically, this means that the 8088 should be able to access only 64K memory addresses. But, as we learned in the previous chapter, it can in fact access much more than that—1,024K to be exact. This is possible because of the 20-bit addressing scheme used with the 8088, which expands the full range of memory locations that the 8088 can work with from 2^{16} (65,535) to 2^{20} (1,048,576). But the 8088 is still limited by its 16-bit processing capacity. To access the 20-bit addresses, it must use an addressing method that fits into the 16-bit format.

Expanding Memory with Segmented Addresses

The 8088 divides the addressable memory space into an arbitrary number of *segments,* each containing no more than 64K bytes. Each segment begins at a location that is evenly divisible by 16 bytes, known as its *segment address* or *segment paragraph.* To access individual bytes or words, we use an additional address called an *offset address* that points to an exact byte location within the 64K segment designated by the segment paragraph. Because offset addresses are always measured relative to the beginning of a segment paragraph, they are also called *relative addresses* or *relative offsets.*

Addresses are created and manipulated by combining a 16-bit segment paragraph and a 16-bit relative offset. The segment paragraph is treated as if it were shifted to the left by four bits. When added to the relative offset, it yields a complete, 20-bit address, as we have shown in Figure 2-3. Together, the two 16-bit words are usually called a *segmented address;* they are also called a *vector,* particularly when referring to interrupts (☛ see page 39 for more on interrupt vectors).

Segment paragraphs are written as 5-digit hex values and always have a zero in the last place, such as FFE40 or B8120. The zero comes from multiplying the original 16-bit, 4-digit hex number by 16. (We get the same shifted effect when we multiply a decimal value by its base number 10, as in $23 \times 10 = 230$.) The fact that the segment part of a segmented address is shifted left by four bits (which is the same as if it were multiplied by 16) is the reason why the segment part alone can only point

1 0 1 1 1 0 1 1 1 0 1 0 0 0 1 1	0 0 0 0	◄— Segment paragraph address
1 0 1 1 1 0 1 0 0 1 1 0 0 1 1 1	◄— Relative offset address
1 1 0 0 0 1 1 1 0 1 0 0 1 0 0 1 0 1 1 1	◄— 20-bit segmented address

Figure 2-3. The segment paragraph, which points to the beginning of a 64K memory segment, and the relative offset, which points to a specific byte within the segment, are combined by the CPU to form a 20-bit physical address.

to actual memory addresses that are a multiple of 16, and why the relative offset is needed to define the precise location within the segment. Offset addresses are written as 4-digit hex values. When added together these two numbers form one 5-digit hex number which converts to the 20-bit address. For example, if we take a hex segment paragraph such as 1234 and multiply it by 16, we get 12340. Then if we add to this the relative offset of the byte we are looking for, such as 4321, we get our 5-digit hex result, as shown in the following example:

12340	The segment address in hex notation, shifted by four bits
+ 4321	The offset address in hex notation
16661	The 20-bit segmented address in hex notation

When we write a 20-bit address broken down into its segment and relative-offset parts, we use the notation 0000:0000, with the segment on the left side of the colon and the relative offset on the right. For example, a 20-bit address written as FFE6E could be written as FFE4:002E in segmented notation. As shown in Figure 2-4, we can express a single 20-bit address in a variety of ways using segmented notation, depending upon which segment paragraph we choose.

The 8088's Fourteen Registers

The 8088 was designed to execute instructions and perform arithmetic and logical operations at the same time it receives instructions and passes data to and from memory. To do this, it uses 16-bit registers.

There are fourteen registers in all, each with a special use. Four *scratch-pad registers* are used by programs to temporarily hold the intermediate results and operands of arithmetic and logical operations. Four

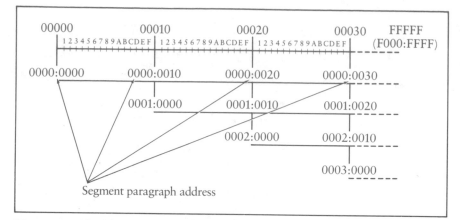

Figure 2-4. The offset address is always determined relative to the segment paragraph address. For this reason, there may be several different segmented addresses for exactly the same location in memory.

segment registers hold the starting addresses of certain segments in memory. Five *pointer and index registers* hold the offset addresses that are used with the segment paragraphs to pinpoint data in memory. Finally, there is one *flag register* containing nine 1-bit flags that are used to record 8088 status information and control 8088 operations. (☛ see Figure 2-5.)

The Scratch-Pad Registers

When a computer is processing data, a great deal of the microprocessor's time is spent fetching data back and forth from memory. This access time can be greatly reduced by keeping frequently used operands and results inside the 8088. Four 16-bit registers, usually called the scratch-pad or data registers, are designed for this purpose.

The scratch-pad registers are known as AX, BX, CX, and DX. Each of them can also be subdivided and separately addressed as two 8-bit half-registers. The high-order half-registers are known as AH, BH, CH, and DH and the low-order half-registers are known as AL, BL, CL, and DL. Use of the full- and half-registers can be freely intermixed, as needed.

The scratch-pad registers are used mostly as convenient temporary working areas, particularly for arithmetic operations. Addition and subtraction can be done in memory without using the registers, but the registers are faster.

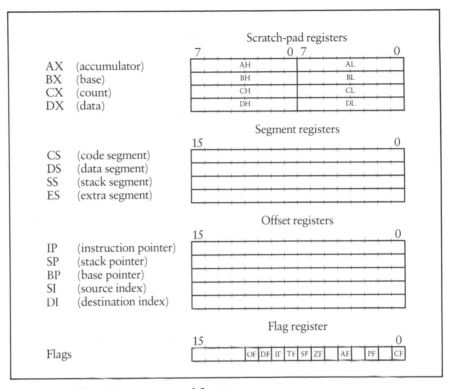

Figure 2-5. The 8088 registers and flags

Although these registers are available for any kind of scratch-pad work, each also has some special uses. For example:

- The AX register is an accumulator and is the main register used to perform arithmetic operations.

- The BX (base) register is often used to point to the beginning of a translation table in memory. It may also be used to hold the offset part of a segmented address.

- The CX (count) register is used as a repetition counter for loop control and repeated data moves. For example, the LOOP instruction in assembly language uses CX to store the count for the number of loop iterations. None of the other registers can perform this function.

- The DX register is used to store 16-bit data for general purposes.

Although the scratch-pad registers are used for temporary storage of data and operands, or for the specific tasks just mentioned, their "scratch-pad" nature opens them up for other uses as well. For example, all four are often used to house the relative offset addresses of data that are passed as parameters from a program.

Back-Words Storage

While the PC's memory is addressed in units of individual 8-bit bytes, many operations involve 16-bit words. In memory, a 16-bit word is stored in any two adjacent 8-bit bytes. The least-significant byte of the word is stored in the lower memory location and the most significant byte is stored in the higher memory location. From some points of view, storing a word this way is the opposite of what we might expect. Due to the backward appearance of this storage scheme, it is sometimes whimsically called "back-words" storage.

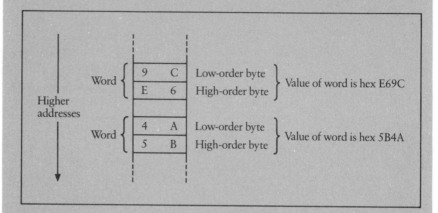

If you are working with bytes and words in memory, you should take care not to be confused by the back-words storage. The source of the confusion has mostly to do with how we write data. For example, if we are writing a word value in hex, we write it like this: ABCD. The order of significance is the same as if we are writing a decimal number: The most-significant digit is written first. But when we write a word the way it is stored in memory, we write the lowest address location first. So, in memory, we would write the number ABCD as CDAB, with the bytes switched.

The Segment Registers

As we discussed earlier, the complete address of a memory location consists of the address of a 64K segment and an offset address within the segment. Four registers, called CS, DS, SS, and ES, are used to identify four specific 64K segments of memory. Five offset registers, which we'll discuss shortly, are then used to store the relative offset address of the data within the 64K segment.

Of the four segment registers, the following three are dedicated to special purposes:

■ The CS register locates the code segment, which contains the program that is being executed.

- The DS register locates the data segment, the area of memory where the current data is stored.

- The SS register locates the stack segment, a temporary workplace that keeps track of the parameters and addresses currently in use by the active program (☞ see page 32 for more information about stacks).

The fourth segment register, the ES register, points to an extra segment that is normally used to supplement the data segment so that more than 64K of memory can be used to store data. It is also used for intersegment data transfers.

It is common for the four segments to overlap or even be identical. It is also common for only one part of a 64K segment to actually be used for its intended purpose; for example, a program may require only 16K of a 64K segment. Figure 2-6, below, illustrates how memory may actually be allocated.

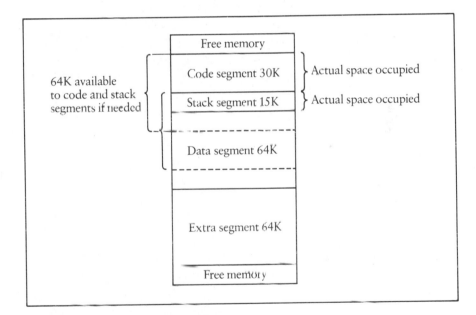

Figure 2-6. Segments may comprise a separate 64K area or they may overlap. We can indicate the starting paragraph of the stack, data, or extra segments by loading the appropriate segment register (either SS, DS, or ES) with the appropriate segment paragraph address.

All 8088 instructions that use memory have an implied use of the appropriate segment register for the operation being performed. For example, the MOV instruction, since it acts on data, uses the DS register. The JMP instruction, which affects the flow of a program, automatically uses the CS register. In most cases, we can, if we need to, override the implied segment register with another. In assembly language, this can be done with segment-override prefixes.

Understanding the segment registers and how they are used will give you insight into the practical limits of memory use in a 16-bit system. If your programs or data require blocks of memory larger than 64K, you will need to apply this knowledge to manipulate the segment registers. Here are a few hints.

If we leave the CS register alone, the maximum size of our programs is the 64K limit of an offset address. The 8088 was designed to retain control of a program, so it is not easy to *directly* manipulate the CS register and change the code-segment address if you need more memory. However, by using certain 8088 program-control instructions, such as far calls and far jumps, it is possible to *indirectly* update the CS register. This is how many programming languages allow programs to grow to any size. (Interpreted BASIC and Microsoft C, Version 1 do not allow such expansion; Pascal and Version 2 of C do.)

On the other hand, it is relatively easy to manipulate the DS register, or to use the ES register, to allow us to use more than 64K of data. But although, theoretically, this capability should allow for unlimited data size, in practice, most programming languages can only work with 64K of data in memory because of the way they're designed. For the most part, this does not present problems, since most programs can get by very comfortably within the 64K limit. Although the most sophisticated programs make good use of large amounts of memory, few programs need anywhere near 64K, and fewer still can use it.

❏ NOTE: *For interpreted BASIC, there are a few things worth noting about the segment registers. The CS register actually points to the BASIC interpreter. A BASIC program and its data are both considered data from the 8088's point of view and both use the DS register. For this reason, there is a 64K limit to the combined size of BASIC programs and their data.*

BASIC's DEF SEG statement lets us do the equivalent of setting the DS register for certain BASIC operations, such as PEEK and POKE, although it always maintains BASIC's original DS segment address. (PEEK and POKE are used to specify the offset address within the data segment.) ☛ *See page 57 for how to access BASIC's true DS value.*

The Offset Registers

Five offset registers are used to locate a precise byte or word within a specific 64K segment. One register, called the instruction pointer (IP), locates the current instruction in the code segment; two, called the stack registers, are intimately tied to the stack, a place in memory where the 8088 keeps a record of the addresses and data it needs to remember for later use (☞ for more on stacks see page 32); and the remaining two registers, called the index registers, are used to point to the current operands in the data segment.

The instruction pointer (IP), also called the program counter (PC), provides the offset address within the code segment where the current program is executing. It is used with the CS register to track the exact location of the next instruction to be executed.

Programs do not have direct access to the IP register, but there are a number of instructions, such as JMP and CALL, that change the IP setting indirectly or save and restore the setting to and from the stack.

The stack pointer registers, called the stack pointer (SP) and the base pointer (BP), provide offsets into the stack segment. The SP gives the location of the current top of the stack and is analogous to the IP. The BP is used to take a "snapshot" of a current top-of-the-stack location, so that later on we will know exactly where in the stack certain information is located. The BP is particularly important to assembly-language interface routines. We'll see it used quite often in the assembly-language examples that appear in Chapters 8 through 20.

The index registers, called the source index (SI) and the destination index (DI), are commonly used with another register (AX, BX, CX, or DX) or an instruction offset, which provides the relative offset to the beginning of a data field within the data segment. The SI and DI registers then provide relative offsets within the data field. They are used most often when transferring lengthy strings of data between memory locations. The string instructions that use the SI and DI registers transfer the string data one byte or word at a time. Both SI and DI usually increment their offset values automatically as each transfer occurs so that we don't have to add 1 to them each time we want to move on to the next byte.

The Flag Register

The fourteenth and last 8088 register, called the flag register, is really a collection of individual control bits called flags. The flags are available in the form of a register so they can either be saved and restored as a coordinated set or inspected as ordinary data. Normally, however, the flags are set and tested as independent items—not as a set.

The Stack

The stack is a built-in feature of the 8088. It provides programs with a place to store and keep track of work in progress. The most important use of the stack is to keep a record of where subroutines were invoked from and what parameters were passed to them. The stack can also be used for temporary working storage, though this is less fundamental and less common.

The stack gets its name from an analogy to a spring-loaded stack of plates in a cafeteria: New data is "pushed" onto the top of the stack and old data is "popped" off. A stack always operates in last-in-first-out (LIFO) order. This means that when the stack is used to keep track of where to return to a program, the most recent calling program is returned to first. This way, a stack maintains the orderly workings of programs, subroutines, and interrupt handlers, no matter how complex their operation.

A stack is used from the bottom (highest address) to the top (lowest address) so that when data is pushed onto the top of the stack, it is stored at the memory addresses just below the current top of the stack. The stack grows downward, so that as data is added, the location of the top of the stack moves to lower and lower addresses, decreasing the value of SP each time. This has the advantage of making displacements into old stack contents positive. We need to keep this in mind when we access the stack—as is commonly done in assembly-language interface routines.

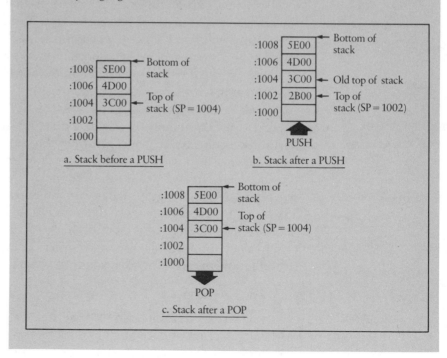

Any part of any program can create a new stack space at any time, but this is not usually done. Normally when a program is run, a single stack is created for it and that stack is used throughout the operation of the program—by the program itself, by its subroutines, and by any DOS and BIOS services that are invoked during program execution. When not running a program, DOS uses its own private stack.

There is no simple way to estimate the size of stack that a program might need, and the 8088's design does not provide any automatic way of detecting when stack space is in short supply or exhausted. This can make programmers nervous about the amount of space that should be set aside for a stack. It is common for programming languages to automatically use a stack size of 512 to 2K bytes, unless another amount is requested. You may safely assume that this size is ample, unless you have special reasons to expect otherwise.

There are nine 1-bit flags in the 16-bit flag register, leaving seven bits unused. The flags can be logically divided into two groups: six status flags, which are set to record processor status information (usually indicating what happened with a comparison or arithmetic), and three control flags, which direct some of the 8088 instructions. Be prepared to see a variety of notations for the flags, including distinct names for whether they are set (1) or clear (0). The terms used in Figures 2-7 and 2-8 are the most common.

Addressing Memory Through Registers

We've seen that memory is always addressed by a combination of a segment-paragraph value and a relative-offset value, and that the segment part of an address always comes from one of the four segment registers.

Code	Name	Use
CF	Carry flag	Indicates an arithmetic carry-out bit
OF	Overflow flag	Indicates arithmetic overflow
ZF	Zero flag	Indicates zero result, or equal comparison
SF	Sign flag	Indicates negative result/comparison
PF	Parity flag	Indicates even number of 1 bits
AF	Auxiliary carry flag	Indicates adjustment needed in binary-coded decimal (BCD) arithmetic operations

Figure 2-7. The six status flags in the 8088's flag register

Code	Name	Use
DF	Direction flag	Controls left/right direction in repeated operations (e.g. using SI and DI)
IF	Interrupt flag	Controls whether interrupts are enabled
TF	Trap flag	Controls single-step operation (used by DEBUG) by generating a software trap at the end of every instruction

Figure 2-8. The three control flags in the 8088's flag register

The offset part can come from any combination of one, two, or three of the following sources:

- A relative-offset value in the instruction itself.

- Register BX or BP.

- An index register, SI or DI.

You should be aware of the range of possibilities when you are either writing or reading assembly-language code. Not all instructions accommodate all possible ways of forming an offset address. One way to find out if a combination is allowed is to try it and see if it is accepted by either your assembler or DEBUG's A-assemble command.

You should also be aware of the notation conventions used for both memory addresses and for registers. Brackets, [ ], are used to indicate that the enclosed item is to be used as a relative-offset address. This is a key element of memory addressing: Without brackets, the actual value stored in the register is used in whatever operation is specified. Here are some examples:

ADD AX,BX	Adds the contents of BX into AX; no memory addressing
ADD AX,[BX]	Indirect addressing: Adds a value from memory into AX; BX gives the relative offset of the value
ADD [BX],AX	Adds the AX value into a memory location; BX gives the relative offset of the value to which the AX value will be added
ADD AX,123	Immediate addressing: Adds 123 to the value in AX

ADD AX,[123]	Adds the value located at relative offset 123 to the value in AX
ADD AX,[BX + SI + 123]	Indexed indirect addressing: Adds the value located at the relative offset generated by adding two registers and a number to the value in AX

Rules for Using Registers

It is important to know that various rules apply to the use of registers, and it is essential to be aware of these rules when writing assembly-language interface routines. The rules and conventions of usage vary by circumstance and by programming language, so unfortunately, exact guidelines are not always available, but here are some general rules that will apply in most cases. (☛ You will find additional guidance, and working models to copy, in the examples in Chapters 8 through 20.) Keep in mind, though, that the following rules are general, not absolute.

In an assembly-language interface routine, there are three general ways to use registers: Some registers can be freely changed; some registers can be changed, but should be restored at the end of the routine; and some registers should not be changed at all.

Generally, the scratch-pad registers (AX through DX) can be freely changed, with no harm to the calling program. Keep in mind that the AX register is commonly used to return results, and that under some circumstances parameters are passed via these registers and discarded after use.

Particular rules apply to the four segment registers (CS, DS, SS, and ES). The CS register should never be changed directly, although it may be changed indirectly through far and near subroutine calls. The DS register may be changed, but should usually be restored afterward. The original SS register value should be preserved whenever changes are made to the register. Normally, subroutines continue to use the stack that SS points to, but if they create their own stack, they should restore the original value of SS when they are through. Note that changing the SS value can interfere with the use of the base pointer (BP) to access parameters. The ES register can usually be changed at will.

The instruction pointer (IP/PC) should not be directly changed; as with the CS register, indirect changes occur automatically and correctly.

The stack pointer (SP) may be changed, but normally, all changes to the SP are made as the indirect result of using the stack. Cleaning up the stack (which implies resetting the SP) is an important part of the interface conventions for using subroutines; the rules for this vary (☛ see the examples in Chapters 8 through 20).

The base pointer (BP) is usually changed to gain access to parameters, and often it should be restored.

The index registers (SI and DI) can be freely changed as needed.

In the flag register, the status flags can also be routinely changed. Remember that some of the status flags are occasionally used to signal a result, so their setting can be important. The CF and ZF flags are most often used for this purpose. As for the control flags, the interrupt flag (IF) should be left set (interrupts enabled); it is probably also wise to leave the direction flag (DF) set; setting the trap flag (TF) is suicidal.

HOW THE 8088 USES PORTS

The 8088 communicates with and controls many parts of the computer through the use of input and output (I/O) ports. The I/O ports are doorways through which information passes as it travels to or from an I/O device, such as a keyboard or a printer. Most of the support chips we described in Chapter 1 use the I/O ports; in fact, each chip may use several port addresses for different purposes.

Each port is identified by a 16-bit port number, which can range from 0 through 65,535. The CPU sends data or control information to a particular port by specifying the port's number, and the port responds by passing data or status information back to the CPU.

As when accessing memory, the CPU uses the data and address buses as conduits for communication with the ports. To access a port, first the CPU sends a signal on the control bus which notifies all I/O devices that the address on the bus is that of a port, and then sends the port address. The device with the matching port address responds.

The port number addresses a memory location that is part of the I/O device but is not part of main memory. Special input/output instructions are used to signal a port access and send information back and forth to the I/O devices. Some I/O devices, such as the video controllers, also use the main memory addresses in addition to their I/O ports and make the CPU think they are part of RAM memory. This is known as memory-mapped I/O. Generally, memory-mapped devices are easier to program because they allow us to use the more flexible memory instructions instead of the rather inflexible and limited input/output instructions in the 8088 instruction set.

❏ NOTE: *The 8088 instruction set includes the IN and OUT instructions to read or write data to a port. BASIC includes the INP and OUT instructions to read or write data to ports in the same way, allowing us to experiment with different ports using simple BASIC routines and then incorporate them into our programs without having to resort to assembly-language programming.*

Family Differences in the Use of Ports

The uses of specific ports are determined by the hardware designers. Programs that make use of these ports need to be aware of the port numbers, as well as their use and meaning. Since the port assignments differ slightly among the PC family members, we have included a list of the standard ports, their numbers, and their uses in Figure 2-9. In many cases, the uses are common to the whole PC family. However, you will notice that the PCjr and AT have introduced a few changes to the port number assignments.

☛ Before using these port addresses, read the descriptions of the chips in Chapter 1. Chapter 7, which covers the use of the ports for sound generation, shows how the ports can be used for some direct hardware programming to control sound output.

Writing to certain ports can disrupt the operation of the computer, but reading a port may also have an adverse effect. Don't assume that simply reading a port will not interfere with the computer's operation, *or* that what is safe on one PC model is safe for the entire family. For example, the following program works perfectly well on most models of the PC, but locks up a PCjr.

```
10 FOR I = 50 TO 75
20   IF I = 64 THEN PRINT "What happens next?"
30   PRINT I, INP (I)
40 NEXT I
```

This program simply uses BASIC's INP command to read data from a port (INP stands for *IN from a Port*). It tries to read data from ports 50 through 75, a seemingly innocuous endeavor. However, this little program locks up the PCjr when it reaches port number 64, although it works quite smoothly on the other PCs. The reasons are buried in the details of hardware design, and to be honest, I don't know them. However, this sort of curiosity is interesting to know about.

HOW THE 8088 USES INTERRUPTS

Whenever a hardware device or a program needs the assistance of the CPU, it sends a signal or instruction called an *interrupt* to the microprocessor, identifying the particular task it wants performed. When the microprocessor receives the interrupt signal, it generally stops all other activities and activates a subroutine stored in memory, called an *interrupt handler,* that corresponds to that particular interrupt number. After the interrupt handler has performed its task, the computer's activities continue from where they were when the interrupt occurred.

JR

PC

XT

AT

Description	Range		
	PCjr	PC/XT	AT
DMA controller (8237)	n/a	000–00F	000–01F
Interrupt controller (8259)	020–027	020–021	020–03F
Timer (8253; 8254.2 in AT)	040–047	040–043	040–05F
PPI (8255)	060–067	060–063	n/a
Keyboard (8042)	n/a	n/a	060–06F
DMA page register (74LS612)	n/a	080–083	080–09F
NMI (non-maskable interrupt) mask register	0A0–0A7	0A	070–07F
Interrupt controller 2 (8259)	n/a	n/a	0A0–0BF
Sound generator (SN76496N)	0C0–0C7	n/a	n/a
DMA controller 2 (8237)	n/a	n/a	0C0–0DF
Clear/reset math coprocessor	n/a	n/a	0F0–0F1
Math coprocessor	n/a	n/a	0F8–0FF
Joystick (game controller)	200–207	200–20F	200–207
Expansion unit	n/a	210–217	n/a
Parallel printer (secondary)	n/a	n/a	278–27F
Serial port (primary)	2F8–2FF	3F8–3FF	3F8–3FF
Serial port (secondary)	n/a	2F8–2FF	2F8–2FF
Prototype card	n/a	300–31F	300–31F
Fixed disk	n/a	320–32F	1F0–1F8
Parallel printer (primary)	n/a	378–37F	378–37F
SDLC (secondary bisynchronous communications in AT only)	n/a	380–38F	380–38F
Bisynchronous communications (primary)	n/a	n/a	3A0–3AF
Monochrome adapter/printer	n/a	3B0–3BF	3B0–3BF
Color/graphics adapter	n/a	3D0–3DF	3D0–3DF
Diskette controller	0F0–0FF	3F0–3F7	3F0–3F7

Figure 2-9. The ports and port addresses used in the PCjr, the PC/XT, and the AT computers

There are three main categories of interrupts. First, there are interrupts generated by the computer's circuitry in response to some event, such as a key-press on the keyboard. These interrupts are managed by the interrupt controller chip (the 8259), which prioritizes them in order of importance before sending them on to the CPU to be acted on. Second, there are interrupts that are generated by the CPU as a by-product of some unusual program result, such as division by zero. And third, there are interrupts deliberately generated by programs as a way of invoking distant subroutines stored in either RAM or ROM. These interrupts, often called software interrupts, are usually part of the ROM-BIOS and DOS services. (☛ They are covered thoroughly in Chapters 8 through 18.) It is possible to change software interrupt-handling routines or even write new ones if our application requires it.

In addition to these interrupts, there is also one special type of interrupt, called the non-maskable interrupt (NMI), that is used to demand immediate attention from the CPU. It often signals an emergency, such as a drop in voltage or a memory error. When an NMI is sent, it is given top priority and the CPU acts on it before all other interrupts.

However an interrupt is generated, the originator of the interrupt doesn't need to know the memory address of the required interrupt handler; it only needs to know the number of the interrupt. The number points to a table stored in the lowest memory locations, which contains the segmented address of the interrupt-handling subroutine. The interrupt handler's address is called its *interrupt vector*, and the table is called the *interrupt vector table*. The vector table is normally supervised by the BIOS and DOS. (☛ We'll discuss this more in Chapter 3.) When we create new interrupt-handling subroutines, we either have them use an existing interrupt number and vector, or we assign new ones.

Interrupts automatically save the current code segment (CS) and instruction pointer (IP) values on the stack, so the computer can return to where it was working when the interrupt occurred. In addition, the interrupt process saves the flag register on the stack and clears the interrupt flag (IF), temporarily preventing further interrupts. Normally, an interrupt-handling subroutine turns interrupts back on as soon as possible, usually within the first few instructions. There is a special interrupt return instruction, IRET, which performs this function; it corresponds to the RET instruction used with subroutine calls. IRET also restores the flags, the CS, and the IP.

It is quite common to link assembly-language subroutines to programs or even to programming languages so that we can gain access to DOS and BIOS service routines or otherwise enhance a program's performance. For such interface routines, especially those that call DOS or BIOS services, it is necessary to be able to program in assembly language. But for most purposes, these interfaces will consist of simple subroutine calls and returns, or interrupt calls using the INT instruction. Only the most advanced assembly-language programming involves the creation of interrupt handlers and the use of the IRET instruction.

3

The ROM Software

I t takes software to make a computer go. And getting a computer going and keeping it going is much easier if some of that software is permanently built into the computer. That's what the ROM programs are all about. ROM stands for read-only memory—memory that is permanently recorded in the circuitry of the PC's ROM chips and that can't be changed, erased, or lost.

Our PCs come with a substantial amount of ROM that contains the programs and data needed to start and operate the computer and its peripheral devices. The advantage of having a computer's fundamental programs stored in ROM is that they are right there—built into the computer—and there is no need to load them into memory from disk the way that DOS must be loaded. Because they are permanent, the ROM programs are very often the foundation upon which other programs (including DOS) are built.

There are four elements to the ROM in IBM's PC family: the start-up programs, which do the work of getting the computer started; the ROM-BIOS—an acronym for Basic Input/Output System—which is a collection of machine-language routines that provide support services for the continuing operation of the computer; the ROM-BASIC, which provides the core of the BASIC programming language; and the ROM extensions, which are programs that are added to the main ROM when certain optional equipment is added to the computer. We'll be examining each of these four major elements throughout the rest of this chapter.

The highest memory block is set aside to hold the ROM programs, starting at segment paragraph hex F000. Different models of the PC family use different amounts of this 64K space depending upon how complex their needs are for ROM software. For example, the original PC model, with its relatively simple hardware, used only 40K of the 64K F block for the ROM programs, while both the PCjr and the AT, with their much more complex hardware, use the full 64K space.

THE START-UP ROM

The first job the ROM programs have is to supervise the start-up of the computer. Unlike other aspects of the ROM, the start-up routines have little to do with programming the PC family—but it is still worthwhile to understand what they do.

There are several tasks performed by the start-up routines. For example, they run a quick reliability test of the computer (and the ROM programs) to make sure everything is in working order; they initialize the chips and the standard equipment attached to the computer; they set up the interrupt vector table; they check to see what optional equipment is attached and, if a disk drive is attached, they often end by loading the operating system from disk.

The reliability test, part of a process known as the Power On Self Test (POST), is an important first step in making sure the computer is ready. All of the POST routines are quite brief except for the memory tests, which can be annoyingly lengthy when the computer contains a large amount of memory.

The initialization process is slightly more complex. One routine sets the default values for interrupt vectors. These default values either point to the standard interrupt handlers located inside the ROM-BIOS, or they point to do-nothing routines that our programs will later supply. Another initialization routine determines what equipment is attached to the computer, and then places a record of it at standard locations in low memory. (☛ We'll be discussing this equipment list in more detail later in the chapter.) How this information is acquired varies from model to model—for example, **PC** in the PC it is taken mostly from the settings of two banks of switches located on the computer's system board; **JR** in the PCjr, it is mostly determined by a logical inspection and test (in effect, the initialization program shouts to each possible option, "Are you there?" and listens for a response); **AT** and in the AT, the information is read out of a special nonvolatile memory area (which can be set by the diagnostic programs).

Whatever method is used, the status information is recorded and stored in the same way for every model so that our programs can monitor it. The initialization routines also check for new equipment and extensions to ROM. If they find any, they momentarily turn control over to the ROM extensions so that they can initialize themselves. The initialization routines then continue executing the remaining start-up routines (more on this later).

The final part of the start-up procedure, after the POST tests, the initialization process, and the incorporation of ROM extensions, is called *the boot-strap loader*. It's a short routine that is used to load a program from disk. In essence, the ROM boot loader attempts to read a record, called a boot record, from a disk, and if successful, passes control of the computer to the program stored in that record. The program in the disk's boot record has the job of loading the rest of the disk program. Usually, this program is a disk operating system such as DOS, but it could be a self-contained and self-loading program, such as Microsoft's Flight Simulator. If the ROM boot loader cannot read a disk's boot record, it simply activates the built-in ROM "cassette" BASIC. (For non-IBM members of the extended PC family, a non-boot error message is displayed instead.) As soon as either of these two processes occurs, the system start-up procedure is finished and the other programs are ready to take over.

❑ NOTE: *The ROM extensions can alter or prevent the booting process.* **JR** *As we will see toward the end of this chapter, this is most noticeable in some of the PCjr's software cartridges.*

THE ROM-BIOS

The ROM-BIOS is the part of ROM that is in active use all the time the computer is at work. The role of the ROM-BIOS is to provide the fundamental services that are needed for the operation of the computer. For the most part, the BIOS controls the computer's peripheral devices, such as the display screen, keyboard, and disk drives. When we use the term BIOS in its narrowest sense, we are referring to the device control programs—the programs that translate a simple command, such as read-something-from-the-disk, into all the steps needed to actually perform the command, including error detection and correction. In the broadest sense, the BIOS not only refers to the routines that are needed to control the PC's devices, but also to the routines that contain information or perform tasks that are fundamental to other aspects of the computer's operation, such as keeping track of the time of day.

Conceptually, the BIOS programs lie between our programs (including DOS) and the hardware. In effect, this means that the BIOS works in two directions in a two-sided process. One side receives requests from programs to perform the standard BIOS input/output services. These services are invoked by our programs with a combination of an interrupt number (which indicates the subject of the service request, such as printer services) and a service number (which indicates the specific service to be performed). The other side of the BIOS communicates with the computer's hardware devices (display screen, disk drives, etc.), using whatever detailed command codes each device requires. This side of the BIOS also handles any hardware interrupts that a device generates to get attention. For example, whenever we press a key, the keyboard generates an interrupt to let the BIOS know.

Of all the ROM software, the BIOS services are probably the most interesting and useful to programmers—as a matter of fact, we have devoted five chapters to the BIOS services in Chapters 8 through 13. Since we deal with them so thoroughly later on, we'll skip any specific discussion of what the BIOS services do and instead focus on how the BIOS as a whole keeps track of the computer's input and output processes.

Interrupt Vectors

The IBM PC family, like all computers based on the Intel 8086 family of microprocessors, is controlled largely through the use of interrupts, which can be generated by hardware or software. The BIOS service routines are no exception; each one is assigned an interrupt number that we must call when we want to use the service.

When an interrupt occurs, control of the computer is turned over to an interrupt-handling subroutine that is often stored in the system's ROM (a BIOS service routine is nothing more than an interrupt handler). The interrupt handler is called by loading its segmented address into the registers that control program flow: the CS (code segment) register and the IP (instruction pointer) register—together known as the CS:IP register pair. The segmented addresses used to locate interrupt handlers are called *interrupt vectors*.

The interrupt vectors are preset during the system start-up process to point to the interrupt handlers in ROM. They are stored in a table in RAM as a pair of words, with the relative-offset portion first, and the segment portion second (the 8088 stores them in backward order in memory; ☞ see page 27 for an explanation of the "back-words" storage format). The interrupt vectors can be changed to point to a new interrupt handler simply by locating the vector and changing its value.

As a general rule, the PC family's interrupts can be divided into seven categories: microprocessor, hardware, software, DOS, BASIC, address, and general use.

The microprocessor interrupts, often called logical interrupts, are designed into the microprocessor. Four of them (interrupts 0, 1, 3, and 4) are generated by the microprocessor itself, and another (interrupt 2, the non-maskable interrupt) is activated by a signal generated by one of the external devices.

The hardware interrupts are built into the PC hardware. Eight of these hardware interrupts are hard-wired into either the microprocessor or the main system board and cannot be changed. All hardware interrupts are supervised by the 8259A PIC chip. The reserved codes are 2, 8, 9, and 11 through 15.

The software interrupts incorporated into the PC design are part of the ROM-BIOS programs. The BIOS routines invoked by these interrupts cannot themselves be changed, but the vectors that point to the routines can be changed to point to different routines. The reserved codes are 5, 16 through 28, and 72.

The Part DOS Plays

After the ROM boot-strap loader turns control over to a disk's boot record, the boot record checks to see if DOS is stored on the disk by looking for two hidden program files named IBMBIO.COM and IBMDOS.COM. If it finds them, it loads them into memory along with the DOS command interpreter, COMMAND.COM. During this loading process, optional parts of DOS, such as installable device drivers, may also be loaded.

The **IBMBIO.COM file** contains extensions to the ROM-BIOS. These extensions may be changes or additions to the basic I/O operations and often include corrections to the existing ROM-BIOS, new routines for new equipment, or customized changes to the standard ROM-BIOS routines. Since they are part of disk software, the IBMBIO.COM routines provide a convenient way to modify the ROM-BIOS. All that is necessary, besides the new routine, is that the interrupt vectors for the previous routines be changed to point to the location in memory where the new routines are placed. Whenever any new devices are added to the computer, their support programs can be included in the IBMBIO.COM file or as installable device drivers, eliminating the need to replace ROM chips. ☛ See Appendix A for more on device drivers.

We can think of the ROM-BIOS routines as the lowest-level system software available to us, performing the most fundamental and yet primitive input and output operations. The IBMBIO.COM routines, being extensions of the ROM-BIOS, are essentially on the same low level, also providing basic functions. By comparison, the IBMDOS.COM routines are more sophisticated, and we can think of them as occupying the next level up, with our programming languages on top.

The **IBMDOS.COM file** contains the DOS service routines. The DOS services, like the BIOS services, can be called by our programs through a set of

---

The DOS interrupts are always available when DOS is in use. Many programs and programming languages use the services provided by DOS through the DOS interrupts to handle their basic operations, especially disk I/O. The reserved codes are 32 through 255 (32 through 96 are used; the others are set aside).

The BASIC interrupts are assigned by BASIC itself and are always available when BASIC is in use. The reserved codes are 128 through 240.

The address interrupts are part of the interrupt vector table and are used to store segmented addresses. There are no actual interrupts or interrupt-handling subroutines associated with these interrupts. Three of them are associated with three very important tables: the video initialization table, the disk base table, and the graphics characters table. These tables contain parameters that the ROM-BIOS uses in start-up procedures and for graphics character generation. The reserved codes are 29 through 31, 68, and 73 (**JR** 68 and 73 are used in the PCjr only).

interrupts whose vectors are placed in the interrupt vector table in low memory. One of the DOS interrupts, interrupt 33 (hex 21), is particularly important because when invoked, it gives us access to a rather large group of secondary routines, called DOS functions. The DOS functions provide us with more sophisticated and efficient control over the I/O operations than the BIOS routines do, especially with regard to disk file operations. All of the standard disk processes—formatting diskettes; reading and writing data; opening, closing, and deleting files; performing directory searches—are included in the DOS functions and provide the foundation for many of the higher-level DOS programs, such as FORMAT, COPY, and DIR. Our programs can use the DOS services when we need more control of I/O operations than our programming languages allow, and when we are reluctant to dig all the way down to the BIOS level. The DOS services are a very important part of this book and we have devoted five chapters to them, Chapters 14 through 18.

The COMMAND.COM file is the third and most important part of DOS, at least from a utilitarian standpoint. This file contains the routines that interpret what we type in through the keyboard when we are in the DOS command mode. By comparing our input to a table of command names, the COMMAND.COM program is able to differentiate between internal commands that are part of the COMMAND.COM file, such as RENAME or ERASE, and external commands such as the DOS utility programs (like DEBUG) or one of our own programs. It acts on our input by executing the required routines for internal commands or by searching for the requested programs on disk and loading them into memory. The whole subject of the COMMAND.COM file and how it works is intriguing and well worth investigating—as are the other DOS programs. I recommend you read the DOS Technical Reference manual or *Inside the IBM PC* for additional information.

The general-use interrupts are established by our programs for temporary use. The reserved codes are 96 through 103.

The interrupt vectors are stored at the lowest memory locations; the very first location in memory contains the vector for interrupt number 0, and so on. Since each vector is two words in length, we find a particular interrupt's location in memory by multiplying its interrupt number by 4. For example, the vector for interrupt 5, the print-screen service interrupt, would be at byte offset 20 ($5 \times 4 = 20$). You can examine the interrupt vectors by translating this decimal number into hex notation and using DEBUG (which only accepts hex values). For interrupt 5, location 20 translates into the hex address 14, and the following commands:

```
DEBUG
D 0000:0014 L 4
```

will show four bytes, in hex, like this:

```
54 FF 00 F0
```

Converted to a segmented address and allowing for "back-words" storage, we can see that the interrupt vector for the entry point in ROM of the print-screen service routine (interrupt 5) is F000:FF54. The same DEBUG instruction can be used to find any other interrupt vector just as easily.

Figure 3-1 is a listing of the main interrupts and their vector locations. These are the interrupts that programmers will probably find most useful. ☞ Details are available for most of these interrupts in Chapters 8 through 18. Interrupts that are not mentioned in this list are, for the most part, reserved for future development by IBM.

Changing Interrupt Vectors

The main programming interest in interrupt vectors is not to read them but to change them so that they point to a new interrupt-handling routine. To do this, we must write a routine that performs a different function than the standard ROM-BIOS or DOS interrupts perform, store the routine in RAM, and then assign a new address to an existing interrupt in the table.

A vector can be changed byte by byte on an assembly-language level, or by using a programming-language instruction like the POKE statement in BASIC. In some cases, there may be a danger of an interrupt occurring in the middle of a change to the vector. If you are not concerned about this, you may as well use the POKE method. Otherwise, there are two separate ways to change a vector while taking precautions against its being used while we're in the middle of changing it.

In the first method, we'll change the vector by hand and suspend interrupts while we're doing it, using the clear interrupt instruction (CLI). CLI suspends all interrupts except for the non-maskable interrupt (NMI). NMI is supposed to be used only to signal a truly urgent, the-machine's-on-fire type of situation, but unfortunately it has come to be used for some very ordinary situations as well, such as signaling keyboard action on the PCjr. As a consequence, while masking interrupts with CLI gives us reasonable insurance against being disrupted in the middle of changing an interrupt vector, it's not perfect.

I'll show you two examples of this first method—how to set an interrupt vector with interrupts suspended. The first example sets the vector with two MOV instructions, which move the two words of the vector into place:

```
XOR     AX,AX                           ; zero segment register
MOV     ES,AX                           ; zero segment register
CLI                                     ; suspend interrupts
MOV     WORD PTR ES:36,XX               ; move vector offset part
MOV     WORD PTR ES:38,YY               ; move vector segment part
STI                                     ; activate interrupts
```

Interrupt				Interrupt			
Dec	Hex	Address	Use	Dec	Hex	Address	Use
0	0	0000	Generated by CPU when division by zero is attempted	26	1A	0068	Invokes time and date services in BIOS
1	1	0004	Used to single-step through programs (as with DEBUG)	27	1B	006C	Interrupt generated on keyboard break under BIOS; a routine is invoked if we create it
2	2	0008	Non-maskable interrupt; in PCjr, NMI has some special uses	28	1C	0070	Interrupt generated at each clock tick; a routine is invoked if we create it
3	3	000C	Used to set break-points in programs (as with DEBUG)	29	1D	0074	Points to table of video control parameters
4	4	0010	Generated when arithmetic result overflows	30	1E	0078	Points to disk base table
5	5	0014	Invokes print-screen service routine in BIOS	31	1F	007C	Points to high video graphics characters
8	8	0020	Generated by hardware clock tick	32	20	0080	Invokes program-terminate service in DOS
9	9	0024	In most models, generated by keyboard action; simulated on PCjr for model compatibility	33	21	0084	Invokes all function-call services in DOS
13	D	0034	Generated during CRT vertical retrace, for video control	34	22	0088	If we create it, an interrupt routine is invoked at program end under DOS
14	E	0038	Signals diskette attention (e.g. to signal completion)	35	23	008C	If we create it, an interrupt routine is invoked on keyboard break under DOS
15	F	003C	Used in printer control	36	24	0090	If we create it, an interrupt routine is invoked at critical error under DOS
16	10	0040	Invokes video display services in BIOS	37	25	0094	Invokes absolute diskette read service in DOS
17	11	0044	Invokes equipment-list service in BIOS	38	26	0098	Invokes absolute diskette write service in DOS
18	12	0048	Invokes memory-size service in BIOS	39	27	009C	Ends program, but keeps it in memory under DOS
19	13	004C	Invokes diskette services in BIOS	68	44	0110	Points to low video graphics characters; only on PCjr
20	14	0050	Invokes communications services in BIOS	72	48	0120	Invokes program to translate PCjr keyboard into PC keyboard
21	15	0054	Invokes cassette tape services in BIOS	73	49	0124	Points to translation table for keyboard-supplement devices
22	16	0058	Invokes standard keyboard services in BIOS				
23	17	005C	Invokes printer services in BIOS				
24	18	0060	Activates ROM-BASIC language, or override for it				
25	19	0064	Invokes boot-strap start-up routine in BIOS				

Figure 3-1. The main interrupts used in the IBM personal computer family

While this technique is straightforward, it runs a small risk of an NMI coming between the two MOV instructions (admittedly a very small risk). The risk can be reduced by combining the two moves into a single repeated, or string, move instruction (MOVS). Using the string move instruction is much clumsier, because it requires a lot of register set-up. We'll use it, though, to give you an example of an alternate way of coding that yields the same result as the first example.

```
; first set up numerous registers for repeated move
XOR     DI,DI                              ; get a zero word
MOV     ES,DI                              ; set paragraph-to ( = 0)
MOV     DI,36                              ; set offset-to
MOV     SI,XXXX                            ; set offset-from
MOV     CX,2                               ; count of words
CLD                                        ; set forward direction
; now do move with interrupts suspended
CLI                                        ; suspend interrupts
REP     MOVSW                              ; repeated move of words
STI                                        ; reactivate interrupts
```

Unfortunately, there's an error in some revisions of the 8088 such that the MOVS instruction can be interrupted.

We've shown you two different ways to change an interrupt vector using the do-it-yourself method. The other method is to let DOS do it for you using DOS service number 37, which was designed for this purpose. There are two very important advantages to letting DOS set interrupts for us instead of doing it ourselves. One advantage is that DOS takes on the task of putting the vector into place in the safest possible way. The other advantage is more far-reaching. With the appearance of the 80286 processor chip in the AT model, the PC family is beginning to pass into realms where such familiar items as interrupt vectors and segment registers aren't what they used to be. Using a DOS service to set an interrupt vector instead of setting it ourselves is just one of the many ways that we can reduce the risk that our new programs will be incompatible with new machines or new operating-system environments.

So, here is an example of how to use DOS service 37 to set an interrupt vector:

```
MOV     DX,XX                              ; load vector offset part
MOV     DS,YY                              ; load vector segment part
MOV     AH,37                              ; request set-interrupt function
MOV     AL,9                               ; change interrupt number 9
INT     33                                 ; DOS function-call interrupt
```

This example shows, in the simplest possible way, how to use the DOS service. However, it glosses over an important and subtle difficulty: We have to load one of the addresses that we're passing to DOS into the DS (data segment) register—which effectively blocks normal access to our data through the DS register. Getting around that problem calls for some fancy footwork. Here is one way it can be done, using a real example taken from my own Norton Utilities programs:

```
PUSH    DS                         ; save current data segment
MOV     DX,OFFSET PGROUP:XXX       ; get vector offset
PUSH    CS                         ; move our own code segment...
POP     DS                         ; ...into the data segment
MOV     AH,37                      ; request set-interrupt function
MOV     AL,9                       ; change interrupt number 9
INT     33                         ; DOS function-call interrupt
POP     DS                         ; restore our original data segment
```

Key Low-Memory Addresses

Much of the operation of the PC is controlled by data that is stored in low-memory locations, particularly in the two adjacent 256-byte areas beginning at hex 400 and 500. Data is loaded into these areas from the BIOS during the start-up process. Although the control data is supposed to be the private reserve of the BIOS, our programs are allowed to inspect or even change it. Even if you do not intend to use the information in the BIOS control area, it is worth studying because it reveals a great deal about what makes the PC family tick.

To avoid confusion about these low-memory addresses, keep in mind that memory address 400 might also be expressed in segmented format as either 0040:0000 or 0000:0400. All three notations refer to exactly the same location.

The Control Information Area

Some of the memory locations in the hex 400 and 500 areas are particularly interesting. Most of them contain data that is vital to the operation of various BIOS and DOS service routines. In many instances, our programs can return the information stored in these locations by invoking a BIOS interrupt; in all cases, they can access the information directly. You can easily check out the values at these locations on your own computer, using either DEBUG or BASIC.

To use DEBUG, enter these commands:

```
DEBUG
D 0:XXXX L 1
```

In this example, XXXX represents the hex address you want to examine. The L 1 tells DEBUG to display one byte. To see two or more bytes, enter the number of bytes (in hex) you wish to see after the L instruction.

To display the data with BASIC, you can use the simple program that is shown below, making the necessary substitutions for *address.in.hex* and *number.of.bytes:*

```
10 DEF SEG = 0
20 FOR I = 0 TO number.of.bytes.in.decimal - 1
30   VALUE = PEEK(&Haddress.in.hex + I)
40   IF VALUE < 16 THEN PRINT "0";          ' needed for leading zero
50   PRINT HEX$ (VALUE);" ";
60 NEXT I
```

I have listed the most useful addresses on the next few pages. All addresses are given in hex.

410 (a 2-byte word). This word holds the equipment-list data that is reported by the equipment-list service, interrupt 17 (hex 11). The format of this word, shown in Figure 3-2, was established for the PC and XT; certain parts may appear in a different format in later models, including the PCjr.

412 (one byte). This byte is used only on the PCjr to count the number of errors detected in the infrared keyboard link. Other models use this byte only during initialization. An interesting byte, but it has no programming significance for us.

413 (a 2-byte word). This word contains the usable memory size in K. In the PCjr, it returns the amount of memory that remains after setting aside memory for the display. In other models, this word has a slightly different meaning: It represents the total memory size. Regardless of the model, the use of this word has the same purpose: It tells you how much memory there is to use. BIOS interrupt service 18 (hex 12) reports the value in this word.

417 (two bytes of keyboard status bits). These bytes are actively used to control the interpretation of keyboard actions by the ROM-BIOS routines. Changing these bytes actually changes the meaning of key strokes. You may freely change the first byte, at address 417, but it is not a good idea to change the second byte. (**JR** A third byte, unique to the PCjr, is located at 488). ☞ See pages 137 and 206 for the bit settings of these two bytes.

419 (one byte). This byte is set aside in order to control alternate keyboard input. It is intended for future use.

41A (a 2-byte word). This word points to the current head of the BIOS keyboard buffer at 41E, where the key actions are stored until used.

41C (a 2-byte word). This word points to the current tail of the buffer.

41E (32 bytes, used as sixteen 2-byte entries). The keyboard buffer is used to hold up to sixteen keyboard actions until they are read via the

Bit		Meaning
F E D C B A 9 8	7 6 5 4 3 2 1 0	
X X	. . . .	Number of printers installed
. . X	. . . .	1 if serial printer installed (PCjr only)
. . . X	. . . .	1 if game adapter installed
. . . . X X X .	. . . .	Number of RS-232 serial ports
. . . . X	. . . .	0 if DMA chip installed; DMA is standard in all models but PCjr
. . . .	X X	+1 = number of diskette drives: 00 = 1 drive; 01 = 2 drives; 10 = 3 drives; 11 = 4 drives (see bit 0)
. . . .	. . X X	Initial video mode: 01 = PCjr 40-column color; 10 = 80-column color, 11 = 80-column monochrome for other models; 00 = none of the above
. . . .	. . . . X X . .	System board RAM: 00 = 16K; 01 = 32K; 10 = 48K; 11 = 64K (not used on AT)
. . . .	. . . . . . X .	1 if math coprocessor installed (not used in PCjr)
. . . .	 X	1 if any diskette drives present (if so, see bits 7 and 6)

Figure 3-2. The coding of the equipment-list word at hex 410

BIOS services through interrupt 22 (hex 16). This is a circular queue buffer, which is why there are two pointers to indicate the head and tail (at 41A and 41C). It is not wise to mess with any of this data.

43E (one byte). This byte indicates if diskettes need to be recalibrated before seeking to a track. Bits 0 through 3 correspond to drives 0 through 3. If a bit is set to 0, recalibration is needed. Generally, you will find that a bit is set to 0 if there was any problem with the most recent use of a drive. For example, the recalibration bit will be 0 if you try to request a directory (DIR) on a drive with no diskette, and then type *A* in response to the display:

```
Not ready reading error B:
Abort, Retry, Ignore?
```

43F (one byte). This byte returns the diskette motor status. Bits 0 through 3 correspond to drives 0 through 3. If the bit is 1, the diskette motor is running.

440 (one byte). This byte holds the count down until the diskette motor is shut off. The count is set to 37 (roughly 2 seconds) at the beginning of each diskette operation. At each clock tick, the count is decremented. The diskette motor is shut off when the count reaches zero.

441 (one byte). This byte indicates the diskette status, with each bit representing a particular kind of error (☛ see Figure 3-3). A bit value of 1 signals that the error occurred; a value of 0 indicates no error occurred.

442 (seven bytes). These seven bytes hold diskette controller status information.

Beginning at hex 449 is a 30-byte area that is used for video control. The BIOS uses this area to keep track of critical video information. It is safe for programs to inspect any of this data, but in most cases, it is risky to modify it. Changing any of this data can interfere erratically with the computer's operation—my own experiments have produced some wonderfully bizarre results. The only bytes that appear to be both safe to change and useful are the cursor-location fields. (☛ For more on cursors, see address 450H and page 92.)

449 (one byte). A value of 0 through 10 or 13 through 16 in this byte specifies the current video mode (☛ see Figure 3-4). This is the same video-mode coding used in the BIOS video services. (☛ See Chapter 9 for more on these services, and page 73 for general information concerning video modes.)

Our BASIC programs can read this byte to learn the video mode with these instructions:

```
DEF SEG = 0                           ' set DS register to 0
VIDEO.MODE = PEEK(&H449)              ' look at location hex 449
```

☛ See page 78 for a special discussion on modes 4 and 5 in BASIC.

Bit 7 6 5 4 3 2 1 0	Meaning
X	Diskette timed out: failed to respond in time
. X	Seek to track failed
. . X	Diskette controller chip failed
. . . X	Cyclical redundancy check (CRC): error in data
. . . . X . . .	DMA diskette error
. . . . . X . .	Sector not found: diskette damaged or not formatted
. . . . . . X .	Address mark on diskette not found
. . . . X	Invalid diskette command requested

Figure 3-3. The coding of the diskette-status byte at hex 441

Code	Meaning	Code	Meaning
0	40-column text, no color (EGA: 64 colors)	9	Medium-resolution graphics, 16-color (not on standard Color/Graphics Adapter)
1	40-column text, 16-color (EGA: 64 colors)		
2	80-column text, no color (EGA: 64 colors)	10	High-resolution graphics, 4-color (not on standard Color/Graphics Adapter)
3	80-column text, 16-color (EGA: 64 colors)	13	Medium-resolution graphics, 16-color (not on standard Color/Graphics Adapter)
4	Medium-resolution graphics, 4-color		
5	Medium-resolution graphics, no color (4 shades of grey)	14	High-resolution graphics, 16-color (not on standard Color/Graphics Adapter)
6	High-resolution graphics, 2-color	15	Special high-resolution graphics, 4-color (not on standard Color/Graphics Adapter)
7	Monochrome adapter mode		
8	Low-resolution graphics, 16-color (not on standard Color/Graphics Adapter)	16	Special high-resolution graphics, 64-color (not on standard Color/Graphics Adapter)

Figure 3-4. The coding of the video-mode byte at hex 449

44A (a 2-byte word). This word holds the screen width in text columns. Column widths are stored in the hex equivalent of 20, 40, or 80 columns (video mode 8, low-resolution graphics, has a text width of 20).

44C (a 2-byte word). The screen regeneration length. This is the number of bytes used for the screen page, which varies by mode.

44E (a 2-byte word). The screen location offset. This is the starting offset address into video display memory of the current display page. In effect, this address indicates which visual page is in use by giving the offset to that page.

450 (eight 2-byte words). These words give the cursor locations for eight separate visual pages, beginning with page 0. The first byte of each word gives the column (0 through 19, 39, or 79) and the second byte gives the row (0 through 24). The location of the cursor can be controlled by modifying this information. For programming languages that do not provide built-in cursor control, this can be a handy way to control the cursor without creating an assembly-language interface to the BIOS routines.

When changing the data in this byte, note that the change does not go into effect immediately, but waits until the *next* screen output. To demonstrate this, start DEBUG, and enter this command:

```
F 0:450 L 2 8 8
```

The cursor jumps to row 8, column 8 after you press return. Needless to say, this isn't a good programming technique—but it's one you might find worth knowing about.

460 (a 2-byte word). These two bytes hold the size of the cursor based on the range of cursor scan lines. The first byte gives the ending scan line, the second byte the starting scan line. Unlike the cursor-location fields, changing these values will not automatically change the cursor.

462 (one byte). This byte holds the current display page number.

463 (a 2-byte word). This word stores the port address of the 6845 video controller chip. Normally, it is set to hex 3D4.

465 (one byte). This byte contains the current setting of the CRT mode register.

466 (one byte). This byte contains the color-palette mask bit setting. ☛ For more on palettes see page 76.

467 (five bytes). These bytes are used for cassette tape control.

46C (four bytes stored as two 2-byte words but treated as one 4-byte number). This area is used as a master clock count, which is incremented once for each clock tick. It is treated as if it began counting from 0 at midnight. When the count reaches the equivalent of 24 hours, it is reset to 0 and the byte at hex 470 is set. DOS or BASIC calculates the current time by calculating from this value and sets the time by putting the appropriate count in this field. This value is reported or set by BIOS interrupt 26 (hex 1A).

470 (one byte). This byte indicates that a clock roll-over has occurred. When the clock count passes midnight (and is reset to 0), this byte is set to 1, which means that the date should be incremented. The value is set by the clock-tick routine to indicate midnight has passed. It is reset to 0 whenever the clock is read using interrupt 26 (hex 1A). This automatic reset is based on the assumption that any program that reads the clock will increment the date when it reads this signal.

❏ NOTE: *This byte is set to 1 at midnight and is not incremented. There is no indication if two midnights pass before the clock is read.*

471 (one byte). This byte is used to indicate a break keyboard action within the BIOS. If bit 7 is 1, the break-key combination was pressed.

472 (a 2-byte word). This word is set to hex 1234 after the initial power-up memory check. When a warm boot is instigated from the keyboard (via Ctrl-Alt-Del), the memory check will be skipped if this location is already set to 1234.

474 (four bytes). This area is used only in the PCjr for special diskette control.

478 (eight bytes, in two 4-byte fields). These bytes are used only in the PCjr to control time-out signals for the parallel printer and the serial port (or serial printer).

480 (a 2-byte word). This word points to the physical start of the keyboard buffer area.

482 (a 2-byte word). This word points to the physical end of the keyboard buffer area.

485 (one byte). This byte holds the character that will be repeated if a typematic repeat-key action takes effect. It is unique to the PCjr.

486 (one byte). This byte is used in timing the initial delay before repeat-key action begins. It is unique to the PCjr.

487 (one byte). This byte is used to hold the current Fn function code. It is unique to the PCjr.

488 (one byte). This byte is a third keyboard status byte that only applies to the PCjr's keyboard. (The other two keyboard status bytes at locations hex 417 and 418 are used in all other models, including the PCjr.) ☛ The bit settings for this byte are listed on page 142.

500 (one byte). This byte is used by DOS and BASIC to control the print-screen operation. There are three possible hex values stored in this location:

00	Indicates OK status
01	Indicates a print-screen operation is currently in progress
FF	Indicates that an error occurred during a print-screen

504 (one byte). This byte is used by DOS when a single-diskette system, such as an XT or a PCjr, mimics a two-diskette system. The value indicates whether the one real drive is acting as drive A or drive B. These values are used:

00	Acting as drive A
01	Acting as drive B

510 (a 2-byte word). This area is used by BASIC to hold the default data segment (DS) value. This is BASIC's default data segment pointer.

BASIC allows us to set our own data segment value with the DEF SEG = *value* statement. (The offset into the segment is specified by the PEEK or POKE functions.) We can also reset the data segment to its default setting by using the DEF SEG statement without = *value*. Although BASIC does not give us a simple way to find the default value stored in this location, we can get it by using this little routine:

```
DEF SEG = 0
DATA.SEGMENT = PEEK(&H511) * 256 + PEEK(&H510)
```

❑ NOTE: *BASIC administers its own internal data based on the default data segment value. Attempting to change it is likely to sabotage BASIC's operation.*

512 (four bytes). This area is used by BASIC as an interrupt vector that points to BASIC's clock-tick interrupt service routine.

❑ NOTE: *In order to perform better, BASIC runs the system clock at four times the standard rate, so BASIC must replace the BIOS clock interrupt routine with its own. The standard BIOS interrupt routine is invoked by BASIC at the normal rate; that is, once for every four fast ticks.* ☛ *There's more about this on page 149.*

516 (four bytes). This area is used by BASIC as an interrupt vector that points to BASIC's break-key handling routine.

51A (four bytes). This area is used by BASIC as an interrupt vector that points to BASIC's diskette error handling routine.

The Intra-Application Communications Area

Although the BIOS control information comprises the largest and most important part of the 400-block area, the intra-application communications area, or ICA, is also located there. The ICA is a 16-byte reserved area from locations 4F0 through 4FF that is used to store data that can be shared by several different programs. It is particularly useful for programs that are executed as separate DOS programs but have to leave information for other parts of the program set. The ICA is not used extensively. Among the few programs that are known to use it are some versions of IBM's Asynchronous Communications, Lifetree's Volkswriter, and my TimeMark.

Since any number of programs may store data in the ICA, it may contain information from several programs. This may mean that some data will be overwritten. If your programs make use of the ICA, I recommend that you include a check-sum and also a signature so that you can identify that the data in the ICA is yours and that it has not been changed by another program.

❑ WARNING: *The ICA is definitely located in the 16 bytes from 4F0 through 4FF. A typographic error in some editions of the IBM Technical Reference manual places it at 500 through 5FF. This is incorrect.*

The ROM Version and Machine ID Markers

Since the BIOS programs are fixed in memory, they can't be easily changed when additions or corrections are needed. This means that ROM programs must be tested very carefully before they are frozen onto memory chips. Although there is a good chance for serious errors to exist in a system's ROM programs, IBM has a fine track record; so far, only small and relatively unimportant errors have been found in the PC family's ROM programs, and all of them have been corrected in the new machines.

The different versions of ROM software could present a small challenge to programmers who discover that the differences affect the operating characteristics of their programs. But an even greater challenge for programmers is that some family members (the PCjr and the AT in particular) use a slightly different set of ROM-BIOS routines than those that come with the standard IBM PC.

To ensure that our programs are working with the appropriate ROM programs and the right computer, IBM has supplied us with two identifying markers that are permanently available at the end of memory in the system ROM. One marker identifies the ROM release date, which can be used to identify the BIOS version, and the other gives the machine model. These markers are always present in IBM's own machines and we'll also find them supplied by the manufacturers of a few of the members of the extended PC family.

The ROM release date can be found in an 8-byte storage area from F000:FFF5 to F000:FFFC (two bytes before the machine ID byte). It consists of ASCII characters in the common American date format; for example, 06/01/83 stands for June 1, 1983. This release marker is a common feature of the IBM personal computers, but is only present in a few IBM compatibles. For example, the Compaq computers do not have it, but the Panasonic Senior Partner does.

The only use of dates in the release marker is to identify the different versions of ROM (☛ see Figure 3-5). I suggest that it be used only when you have found a problem that requires your programs to work differently with different ROM releases. (Programs will more likely need to identify the machine ID byte to respond to the unique features of different models.)

Release Marker	Machine
04/24/81	Original PC
10/19/81	Revised PC (some bugs fixed)
08/16/82	Original XT
10/27/82	Upgrade of PC to XT BIOS level
11/08/82	Original Portable PC
06/01/83	Original PCjr
01/10/84	Original AT

Figure 3-5. The release dates of the various versions of ROM

You can look at the release date with DEBUG, using the following commands:

```
DEBUG
D F000:FFF5 L 8
```

Or you can let your program look at the bytes using this technique:

```
10 DEF SEG = &HF000
20 FOR I = 0 TO 7
30   PRINT CHR$(PEEK(&HFFF5 + I));
40 NEXT
50 END
```

Here's an example of what you may encounter: I have three PCs and each came with a different ROM. One has the 04/24/81 version, another the 10/19/81 version, and the last the 10/27/82 version.

BIOS upgrades are available under some circumstances; for example, the PC expansion unit that brings a PC up to XT specifications comes with the 10/27/82 upgrade. Occasionally, the BIOS upgrade is available separately as well.

The machine ID is a byte located at F000:FFFE. Figure 3-6 lists the published ID values for five IBM PC models. We can probably expect this pattern to continue in future models.

Beware that there are some inconsistencies in the way machine IDs are assigned. FE was the value announced originally as the identifier for the XT and later for the Portable PC, yet many XTs actually have the PC signature FF. In general, we can't count on these signature assignments to be rock-solid; IBM has definitely waffled a bit about some of them, both in what it published the signatures as and in what they have actually been. I believe, though, that there is a simple rule that we can follow in interpreting the machine signatures. Where the differences between the models are significant enough to require that a program be able to unequivocally identify the machine, then the signatures are rock-solid and

| ID | | |
Dec	Hex	Machine
255	FF	PC (the original IBM personal computer)
254	FE	XT and Portable PC
253	FD	PCjr
252	FC	AT

Figure 3-6. The machine IDs for the five IBM PC models

	ID		
Dec	Hex	Machine	
45	2D	Compaq (PC-equivalent)	
154	9A	Compaq-Plus (XT-equivalent)	

Figure 3-7. Unofficial machine IDs for two
Compaq models

as advertised; cases in point: the PCjr and the AT, which each have their own special characteristics. But when the variations between machine models are minor, such as between the original PC, the standard PC, the PC-2 (which accepts 256K of memory on its system board), the XT, and the Portable PC, then signatures may vary. For all practical purposes, we can consider both the FF and the FE signatures as identifying one machine: the more-or-less standard PC.

It is possible that IBM-compatible computers can be identified in the same way, but I do not know of any reliable published information. My own programs identify two signatures for the first two Compaq computers, but you should not consider them official.

You can explore the machine ID byte with DEBUG, using the following commands:

```
DEBUG
D F000:FFFE L 1                           ' displays one byte at specified location
```

A program can inspect this byte using techniques such as this:

```
10 DEF SEG = &HF000                       ' defines segment F000 in DX register
20   IF PEEK(&HFFFE) = 253 THEN PRINT "I should be a Junior"
30   IF PEEK(&HFFFE) = 254 THEN PRINT "I should be an XT"
40   IF PEEK(&HFFFE) = 255 THEN PRINT "I should be a PC"
50   IF PEEK(&HFFFE) = 252 THEN PRINT "I should be an AT"
60 END
```

THE ROM-BASIC

Now we move on to the third element of ROM: the ROM-BASIC. The ROM-BASIC acts in two ways. First, it provides the core of the BASIC language, which includes most of the commands and the underlying foundation, such as memory management, that BASIC uses. The disk versions of BASIC, which we see in the program files BASIC.COM and BASICA.COM, are essentially supplements to the ROM-BASIC, and they rely on the ROM-BASIC to get much of their work done. The second role of the ROM-BASIC is to provide what IBM calls "cassette" BASIC—the BASIC that is activated when we start-up our computers without a disk.

Whenever we use any of the interpreted BASICs, such as cassette BASIC, the PCjr's cartridge BASIC, or either of the disk BASICs (BASIC or BASICA), the ROM-BASIC programs are also used—although there's nothing to make us aware of it. On the other hand, compiled BASIC programs don't make use of the ROM-BASIC.

This ROM-BASIC is unique to IBM's own PC family. None of the members of the extended PC family, such as the Compaq computers, has a ROM-BASIC; instead, the equivalent parts of BASIC are included in their disk-based BASIC programs.

THE ROM EXTENSIONS

The fourth element of the ROM has more to do with the PC's design than the actual contents of its memory. The PC was designed to allow for two kinds of extensions to the built-in software in ROM: one for permanent extensions to the ROM-BIOS software, and the other for extensions provided by removable software cartridges. Special areas of memory are set aside for each.

Permanent ROM-BIOS extensions are programs that operate like the built-in ROM-BIOS, but add features not supported by the basic ROM-BIOS. Usually, these are support programs for new peripheral devices. The best example of this kind of ROM extension is the ROM-BIOS support for the IBM fixed disk, which was introduced with the XT. Another is found in the Enhanced Graphics Adapter. Since the original ROM-BIOS could not anticipate providing support programs for future hardware, ROM extensions are obviously a necessary and helpful addition.

Two memory areas are to be used for the permanent ROM-BIOS extensions. One is the unused part of the F block of memory, which, unfortunately, can vary from model to model. On most models, the 24K area from segment paragraph F000 to F600 is available (the non-IBM hard-disk ROM-BIOS for one of my PCs plugs into paragraph F400). The other memory area for ROM extensions is the C block of memory, from segment paragraph C000 through CFFF. The IBM XT hard-disk ROM-BIOS plugs into this area, at segment paragraph C800, and the IBM Enhanced Graphics Adapter plugs in at paragraph C000. Although the permanent ROM extensions provided by IBM have predictable locations, there is always some potential for conflict between BIOS extensions provided by other manufacturers.

Normally, the permanent ROM extensions are semipermanently installed in a computer, either plugged in as part of an expansion board or plugged into an available ROM socket in the computer's system board.

Software cartridges, on the other hand, are intended to be freely plugged in and removed. Generally, cartridges are used in the same way as diskettes: to load temporary programs for a specific purpose. A large 128K area of memory, filling the entire D and E blocks of memory, is set aside for software cartridges to use.

Both kinds of ROM extensions are integrated into the rest of ROM during the start-up process. To find the ROM extensions, the standard ROM starts at the C000 block and examines every 2K block for the signature (hex 55 AA) that identifies the ROM extensions. When the identifying signatures are found, the start-up routine passes control temporarily to the ROM extension so that the extension can do whatever it needs to do to merge itself into the operation of the computer. At this point, the ROM extension can do anything it pleases, including seize complete control of the computer. Some software cartridges do exactly that. However, a more normal thing for an extension to do is to simply test any equipment that it supervises (for example, a hard-disk ROM-BIOS extension might fire up the hard disk and metaphorically shake hands through the low-memory data areas with the rest of the BIOS, so that each BIOS section knows who its working partners are). Once any initialization is done, a ROM extension customarily returns control to the main BIOS, which then finishes the business of starting up the computer.

The Software Cartridges

Since we can't paint a complete picture of ROM extensions without discussing software cartridges, we'll devote a short section to providing just the bare essentials about them. You'll find more detailed information in *Exploring the IBM PCjr* and in IBM's Technical Reference manual.

ROM software cartridges contain prerecorded programs, stored in ROM chips, which can be plugged into any PC model that will accommodate them (such as the PCjr). Each software cartridge can contain as little as 2K bytes or as much as 64K bytes, depending on the hardware design.

A cartridge can make itself appear in any one of six memory locations—the actual location it chooses is written into the cartridge program. In segment-paragraph notation, the six possible locations are D000, D800, E000, E800, F000, and F800. The four addresses in the D and E memory blocks are conventional cartridge locations. The two addresses in the F block are ROM-BIOS override addresses, which may allow a cartridge to temporarily replace the computer's built-in ROM-BIOS.

There is a standard cartridge header format, which the ROM-BIOS uses to identify cartridges in memory and determine their contents. The information stored in the header also indirectly identifies the type of cartridge that is plugged in and what it will be used for.

The Cartridge Header

Each cartridge begins with the standard ROM extension 2-byte signature, hex 55 AA, followed by a 1-byte length code. The length is given in cartridges and other ROM extensions in units of 512 bytes, or ½K. For example, an 8K game cartridge has a length code of 16, while a 32K BASIC language cartridge has a length code of 64.

Following the length code are three bytes that are set aside for a single cartridge initialization instruction. The three bytes allowed for this field are enough to contain any instruction of three bytes or less; normally they contain either a 1-byte FAR RETurn instruction or a 3-byte JMP instruction. The instruction here controls what initialization—if any—is done for the cartridge. With a BASIC program cartridge (a cartridge containing a program written in BASIC that must therefore be used with the BASIC language cartridge), these three bytes contain a special code: the standard FAR RETurn instruction (hex CB), followed by the *reversed* signature (hex AA 55). To avoid being confused with a BASIC program cartridge, any other type of cartridge must have something other than hex AA 55 in the last two bytes of this field.

Following the initialization field, beginning at the seventh byte of the cartridge, is a DOS table of contents that identifies any DOS command programs that may be on the cartridge. If there are such programs on the cartridge, they effectively become additions to the internal commands, such as DIR, COPY, and TIME at DOS's disposal. If there are no such programs, the cartridge should have an *empty* table of contents (explained in a moment), rather than *no* table of contents. The format of the DOS table of contents is a series of command-name entries, followed by a zero byte, which identifies the end of the table. An empty table of contents simply has the zero byte.

The command-name entries each consist of three fields: a 1-byte field recording the length of the name; a field containing the same number of bytes for the command name, in ASCII capital-letter characters; and a 3-byte jump-instruction field, which jumps to the program that carries out the command.

❏ WARNING: *Some IBM Technical Reference manuals incorrectly identify the last command-name field as a 2-byte offset word; it is in fact a 3-byte jump instruction.*

Following the cartridge header are the actual contents of the cartridge—usually machine-language programs. If the cartridge is a BASIC program cartridge, then the contents are a tokenized BASIC program, stored in the same format as that used for storing BASIC programs on disk. Keep in mind that the first byte of a tokenized BASIC program identifies it as either normal (hex FF) or protected (hex FE).

Offset	Contents	Description
0	55 AA	Signature
2	40	Length: hex 40 = 64* ½K = 32K
3	E9 1D 00	JMP 0023: jump to initialization code
6	05	Length (5) of following command name
7	"BASIC"	Command name, in ASCII
12	E9 91 01	JMP 0191: jump to start BASIC
15	06	Length (6) of following command name
16	"BASICA"	Command name, in ASCII
22	E9 91 01	JMP 0191: jump to start BASICA (same as start of BASIC)
25	00	End of table of contents

Figure 3-8. A specific example of a cartridge header, taken from the PCjr's BASIC language cartridge. Note that the table of internal DOS commands (DIR, TIME, etc.) that is stored inside the command interpreter, COMMAND.COM, is quite similar to this cartridge's DOS command table.

COMMENTS

The ROM program listings could fill volumes, and in fact do take up a fair amount of space in the IBM Technical Reference manual. Although IBM frowns on direct use of any of the information found in ROM listings, particularly the BIOS listings, it can be fun and very enlightening to browse through it on occasion. Since I have made every effort in this book to point out the ROM-BIOS routines that are safe to use, I also recommend that you read through what I have to say before venturing out on your own.

4

Video Basics

To many people, the video display is the computer. Programs are often judged by their display quality and visual design alone. In this chapter, we'll see what kinds of displays the IBM PC family uses and how they are produced. More importantly, we'll learn how to manipulate the video displays to get the effects we want.

THE DISPLAY ADAPTERS

To produce the video display, most members of the PC family (including the PC, the XT, and the AT) require a display adapter—a special circuit board that is normally plugged into one of the computer's expansion slots. Display adapters were designed into the PCjr, and models such as the Portable PC and the Compaq also come with display adapters, though, in their case, we can change the adapters.

The display adapter connects the computer to the display monitor through a chip called the CRT controller. The adapter also has a set of programmable I/O ports, a ROM character generator, and RAM memory to hold the display information.

There are several kinds of display adapters, but they are all modeled after the two adapters originally released by IBM for the PC: the Color/Graphics Adapter and the Monochrome Adapter. We'll mostly be discussing these two adapters, with additional remarks on others.

Video displays are produced by two fundamentally different modes, called *text mode* and *graphics mode* by IBM. Text mode displays only characters, though many of these characters are suitable for producing simple line drawings (☛ see Appendix C for more on characters). Graphics mode is mainly used to produce complex drawings but can produce text characters in a variety of shapes and sizes equally well.

The Color/Graphics Adapter can operate in both text and graphics modes to produce both drawings and characters in several formats and colors. It is designed to work with all kinds of displays, from standard TVs to high-resolution color monitors.

By contrast, the Monochrome Adapter can operate only in text mode, using a stored set of ASCII alphanumeric and graphics characters and displaying them in only one color. Designed for serious business applications, the Monochrome Adapter only works with the IBM Monochrome Monitor (or its equivalent), which is a special, high-resolution display monitor. (☛ See page 72 for more on monitors.) Many business and professional users prefer a monochrome display to a color/graphics display because it is easier to read. But in choosing monochrome, they sacrifice graphics and color, two valuable assets for any display.

To overcome these limitations, some hardware manufacturers have come up with variations of the IBM Monochrome Adapter, such as the popular Hercules display adapter, which successfully combines the graphics (but not the color) capabilities of the Color/Graphics Adapter with the higher-quality text display of the Monochrome Adapter, and adds unique features of its own. The resulting graphics quality is even better than the Color/Graphics Adapter can produce. The IBM Enhanced Graphics Adapter can create graphics on the monochrome screen in a similar way.

Roughly two-thirds of all PCs are equipped with the standard Monochrome Adapter and therefore have no graphics or color capability. While there are real advantages to using color and graphics, most PCs get along nicely without either. When you are planning computer applications, keep in mind that most computers and most PCs display text *only*.

The best way to understand the PC's display capabilities is to cover the features of the original Color/Graphics Adapter, noting where the Monochrome Adapter differs (mostly small details). We'll also point out where extensions to the Color/Graphics Adapter have been made in the Enhanced Graphics Adapter and in the PCjr.

Memory and the Display Adapters

The display memory is physically located with the other display circuitry on the adapter card. However, it is logically (to the CPU) a part of the computer's main memory address space. A full 128K of the memory address space is set aside for display use in the A and B memory blocks, at hex addresses A0000 through BFFFF, but the two original display adapters use only two small parts of this memory area. The Monochrome Adapter provides 4K of display memory located at hex paragraph address B000. The original Color/Graphics Adapter provides 16K of display memory located at address B800. The remaining space, particularly the 64K block from A000 up to B000, is set aside for advanced display use; for example, by the Enhanced Graphics Adapter.

The PCjr strays from the family tradition by using low address locations in main memory for its display memory. However, special circuitry in the PCjr closely mimics the conventional Color/Graphics Adapter. This circuitry, called the video gate array (VGA), makes it appear as though the PCjr's display memory is located at the Color/Graphics Adapter's B800 address. References to the B800 area are rerouted by the VGA's circuitry to whatever location is actually in use as display memory. The PCjr can use any part of the first 128K of RAM for video memory; the VGA keeps track of the actual location. For all practical programming purposes, the PCjr should be treated as a PC equipped with a Color/Graphics Adapter, which uses the display memory address beginning at B800.

Creating the Screen Image

The Monochrome and Color/Graphics Adapters store display information in *memory-mapped display,* so called because each address in the display memory corresponds to a specific location on the screen (☞ see Figure 4-1). The display circuitry repeatedly reads information from memory and places it on the screen. The information can be changed as fast as the computer can write new information from our programs into memory. The CRT controller is the link between the display memory and the display monitor, translating the stream of bits it receives from memory into bursts of light at particular locations on the screen.

These dots or dashes of light are generally called *pixels* and they are produced by an electron beam striking the phosphorescent surface of the CRT. The electron beam is produced by an electron gun that scans the screen line by line. As the gun moves across and down the screen in a fixed path called a raster scan, the CRT controller generates a video control signal that turns the beam on and off, matching the pattern of the bits in memory.

The video circuitry refreshes the screen 60 times a second making the changing images appear clear and steady. At the end of each screen refresh cycle, the electron beam must move from the bottom right corner to the top left corner of the screen to begin a new cycle. This movement

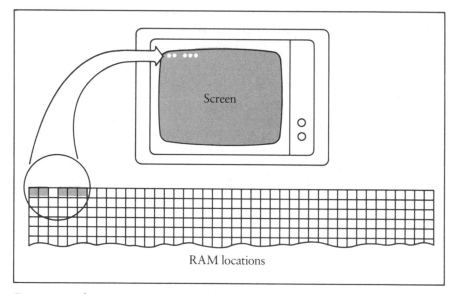

Figure 4-1. The memory-mapped display

is called the *vertical retrace*. During the retrace, the beam is blanked and information cannot be written to the screen.

The vertical retrace period (1.25 milliseconds) is important to the programmer for one main reason, which requires some explanation. The special dual-ported design of the display adapter's memory gives the CPU and the CRT controller equal access to the display memory. This allows the CPU and the CRT controller to access video memory at the same time. If the CPU happens to access a memory byte while the CRT controller is writing to the screen, a "snow" effect may briefly appear on the screen. However, if we instruct the CPU to access memory only during the vertical retrace, when the CRT controller is not accessing memory, then snow can be eliminated. For systems using the Color/Graphics Adapter, our programs can poll a status bit, called the *vertical sync signal,* in one of the adapter's I/O ports (location hex 3DA). This bit is set on at the beginning of a retrace and then set off at the end. During this 1.25-millisecond pause, we can have our programs write as much data as possible to the video display memory. At the end of the retrace, the CRT controller can write this data to the screen without snow. This technique is useful for any application that requires a rapid succession of clear images.

THE VIDEO DISPLAY FORMATS

Originally, there were eight video formats, or modes, defined for the IBM personal computers. Another seven or more have been added. The video modes define the display characteristics, including the amount of text that can be displayed, the resolution or detail of the graphics, and the display colors. The Color/Graphics Adapter accommodates several different format options in both text and graphics modes. The Monochrome Adapter offers only a single, one-color text format. Both the PCjr and the Enhanced Graphics Adaptor (EGA) support a variety of old and new formats.

Each of the fifteen modes we'll be discussing is identified by a number from 0 through 16 (☛ see Figure 4-2). Modes 0 through 3 are the text modes and modes 4 through 6 are the graphics modes for the Color/Graphics Adapter. Mode 7 is a monochrome text mode that can be used only with the IBM Monochrome Adapter (or its equivalent). Modes 8 through 10 were introduced with the PCjr (which also uses modes 0 through 6) and cannot be used with the standard IBM display adapters. Modes 13 through 16 apply to the EGA (which also uses modes 0 through 7).

Color may be used in any display mode except the one provided for the Monochrome Adapter (mode 7). Through the modes available with

Monitors

The type of display screen, or monitor, that might be used has an important effect on program design. Many monitors cannot produce color or graphics, and some produce such a poor quality image that we can only use the 40-column text display format. There are many kinds of monitor that can be used with the PC family of computers. The two major categories are the monochrome monitor and the color monitor, which can be broken down into four basic types.

Direct-drive monochrome monitors. These monitors are designed to display high-resolution text and character graphics, but no pixel graphics. The direct-drive monochrome monitors only work with the Monochrome Adapter. Graphics screens that will display on any other type of monitor will not show at all on the direct-drive monitor unless a special interface is used, such as the Hercules adapter card.

Monochrome composite monitors. These monitors are among the most widely used and least expensive monitors available. They are connected to the composite video output on the Color/Graphics Adapter and provide a fairly clear one-color image (usually green or amber). The Compaq portable and the IBM Portable PC use this type of monitor. A monochrome composite monitor can display graphics but not colors. Some monochrome monitors provide limited "color" support, with shades of intensity replacing the colors. However, most of them produce an illegible and sometimes invisible display when we give them a color signal. Don't confuse the composite monitor with the direct-drive monochrome monitor. The composite monochrome monitor uses the Color/Graphics Adapter, whereas the direct-drive monochrome monitor uses the Monochrome Adapter.

Composite color monitors and TV sets. Composite displays are produced by a single combined signal that travels through the composite video output on the Color/Graphics Adapter. The composite monitor produces color and graphics but has limitations: An 80-column display is often unreadable; only certain color combinations work well; and graphics resolution is low in quality, so graphics must be kept simple by using low-resolution graphics modes.

Although the standard television set (color or black-and-white) is technically a composite monitor, it usually produces an even lower-quality image than the dedicated composite monitor. Text displays must be in 40-column or even 20-column mode to ensure that the display is readable. TVs are connected to the composite video output of the Color/Graphics Adapter or its equivalent (in the case of the PCjr, there is a special TV output), but the composite signal must be converted by an RF adapter before going into the TV.

RGB color monitors. The RGB monitors are considered the best of both worlds. They combine the high-quality text display of the monochrome monitors with high-resolution graphics and color. RGB stands for red-green-blue and RGB monitors are so named because they use separate wires for each of the color signals (unlike the composite monitors, which use only one wire). These wires are connected to the RGB output of the Color/Graphics Adapter or its equivalent. A top-quality RGB monitor can produce the clearest, most legible images, second only to the IBM Monochrome Monitor. The image and color quality is usually much better than that available through any screen that connects to the composite video output.

Mode	Type	Dimensions	Colors	Adapter	Display
0	Text	40×25	16 (grey) EGA: 64 color	CGA, EGA, PCjr	Enhanced Color
1	Text	40×25	16 foreground, 8 background EGA: 64 color	CGA, EGA, PCjr	Enhanced Color
2	Text	80×25	16 (grey) EGA: 64 color	CGA, EGA, PCjr	Enhanced Color
3	Text	80×25	16 foreground, 8 background EGA: 64 color	CGA, EGA, PCjr	Enhanced Color
4	Graphics	320×200	4	CGA, EGA, PCjr	Enhanced Color
5	Graphics	320×200	4 (grey)	CGA, EGA, PCjr	Enhanced Color
6	Graphics	640×200	2	CGA, EGA, PCjr	Enhanced Color
7	Text	80×25	b/w	EGA, MA	Monochrome
8	Graphics	160×200	16	PCjr	Enhanced Color
9	Graphics	320×200	16	PCjr	Enhanced Color
10	Graphics	640×200	4	PCjr	Enhanced Color
11	Apparently internal to the EGA				
12	Apparently internal to the EGA				
13	Graphics	320×200	16	EGA	Enhanced Color
14	Graphics	640×200	16	EGA	Enhanced Color
15	Graphics	640×350	b/w	EGA	Monochrome
16	Graphics	640×350	16/64	EGA	Enhanced Color

Figure 4-2. The format characteristics of the fifteen video modes

the Color/Graphics Adapter, we can choose from two to sixteen color combinations, including a selection of grey tones, called color-suppressed modes. Although no color choices are available with the Monochrome Monitor, there are some character-display variations that are partially equivalent to color: bright and dim intensity, underlining, and reverse video. ☞ We'll discuss the use of color with text and graphics displays, as well as the Monochrome Adapter's answer to color, in the section entitled "The Use of Color" on page 75.

Display Resolution

Graphics images are built up from individual dots, called picture elements, or pixels. The display resolution is defined by the number of rows, or scan lines, from top to bottom and the number of pixels from left to right in each line. The number of rows a monitor can display is determined by the hardware and the video signals, which we have little or no control over; a standard PC display always has 25 text rows and 200 graphics rows. So to change the screen's resolution, we have to change the number of pixels on each line.

The PC graphics modes have three resolutions—low, medium, and high—with 160, 320, and 640 pixels on each line. **JR** Low resolution (160 × 200 pixels) was introduced with the PCjr and is not available with either the original Color/Graphics Adapter or the Enhanced Graphics Adapter. Since text characters can also be displayed in the graphics modes, the medium and high graphics resolutions each have an equivalent text size (☛ see Figure 4-3).

A narrow character that fits in an 80-column-by-25-line format uses 640 × 200 pixel resolution, and a broader character that fills a 40-column-by-25-line format uses a 320 × 200 pixel resolution. (The 80 × 25 character display of the Monochrome Adapter shows clearer text because its characters are built from a higher pixel resolution—720 × 350.)

You will notice that low-resolution graphics have their own unique 20-column text format, which has no equivalent in the standard text modes. **JR** Text width 20, along with the low-resolution mode, was introduced with the PCjr and neither format exists in the other adapters.

Video Mode Control

Video modes are controlled by the ROM-BIOS through interrupt 16 (hex 10), service 0. (☛ See Chapter 9.) BASIC gives us full control over the video modes through the SCREEN statement, but refers to them in its own way, using different mode numbers than the ROM-BIOS routines. We can also control some of the video modes through DOS. But at the command level, DOS insists on a text mode and there are no DOS commands that switch to any of the graphics modes, as we can see in Figure 4-4.

Resolution	Pixels	Characters
Low	160 × 200	20 × 25
Medium	320 × 200	40 × 25
High	640 × 200	80 × 25

Figure 4-3. The resolution of text characters drawn in graphics modes

Mode	BASIC Statement to Change Mode	DOS Statement to Change Mode
0	SCREEN 0,0 : WIDTH 40	MODE BW40
1	SCREEN 0,1 : WIDTH 40	MODE CO40
2	SCREEN 0,0 : WIDTH 80	MODE BW80
3	SCREEN 0,1 : WIDTH 80	MODE CO80
4	SCREEN 1,0 *or* SCREEN 4	n/a
5	SCREEN 1,1	n/a
6	SCREEN 2	n/a
7	n/a	MODE MONO
8	SCREEN 3	n/a
9	SCREEN 5	n/a
10	SCREEN 6	n/a

Figure 4-4. The BASIC and DOS commands used to change video modes

THE USE OF COLOR

There is a variety of colors available in every display mode except the mode provided for the Monochrome Adapter. You may have noticed that among the various modes there are substantial differences in the number of colors available. In this section, we will describe the color options for the video modes.

Colors for the PC's display screens are produced by combinations of four elements: three color components—red, green, and blue—plus an intensity, or brightness, component. Text and graphics modes use the same colors and intensity options but they combine them in different ways to produce their colored displays. The text modes, whose basic unit is a character composed of several pixels, use an entire byte to set the color, the intensity, and the blinking characteristics of the character and its background. The graphics modes, having a much smaller basic unit (the pixel), use only one to four bits to define the color and brightness because the pixel does not have blinking or background characteristics. ☛ We'll see how to set the attributes for text and graphics modes on page 79. First, a word about the colors themselves.

The color numbers (0 through 15) used by BASIC, and used in general to identify the PC colors, can be derived by interpreting the four color elements as the bits of a binary number. ☛ The colors and their bit codes are listed in Figure 4-5. When we use a sixteen-color mode, we get all the colors, from 0 through 15. When we use an eight-color mode, we get colors 0 through 7; that is, all the colors without bright intensity. With a four-color mode, we get a selection of four colors from the list of sixteen. This four-color selection is called a *palette*. In a two-color mode, we get colors 0 and 7—black and ordinary white.

So far we've described the basic 16-color palette of the standard PC, which is built of the three RGB colors and the intensity setting (I). We might call this basic color scheme IRGB. A 64-color palette has been added to the PC family, but is only available with the combination of the Enhanced Graphics Adapter and Enhanced Color Display—the EGA/ECD combination. This 64-color palette is built out of the standard three colors (red, green, and blue), but each color has two independent signals: a brighter one and a dimmer one. The notation for the 64-color palette is RrGgBb, where the capital letters stand for the dimmer colors. Note that we're not talking about two intensity levels but about two separate color signals, which allow for a total of four intensities of each of the three colors. For the reds, the four intensities would be Rr (most intense), R., .r, and .. (no red). All possible combinations of RrGgBb work out to 64 colors.

Intensity	Red	Green	Blue	Number	Description
0	0	0	0	0	Black
0	0	0	1	1	Blue
0	0	1	0	2	Green
0	0	1	1	3	Cyan (blue-green to civilians)
0	1	0	0	4	Red
0	1	0	1	5	Magenta
0	1	1	0	6	Brown (or dark yellow)
0	1	1	1	7	Light grey (or ordinary white)
1	0	0	0	8	Dark grey (black on many screens)
1	0	0	1	9	Light blue
1	0	1	0	10	Light green
1	0	1	1	11	Light cyan
1	1	0	0	12	Light red
1	1	0	1	13	Light magenta
1	1	1	0	14	Yellow (or light yellow)
1	1	1	1	15	Bright white

*Figure 4-5. The PC family's full color array,
with the four bit codes that specify them*

We won't be discussing the 64-color palette of the EGA/ECD combo in any detail because it's quite rare and specialized and doesn't really fit into the mainstream of the PC family. (If we really wanted to treat all the exotic, non-mainstream elements of the PC family, we would fill a wonderful book several times the size of this one.) Another even more specialized adapter and display combination, the IBM Professional Graphics Adapter and Display has a palette of 256 colors and remarkably high resolution; but it is even farther removed from the PC mainstream, so we won't be discussing it, either. Instead, we'll go back to a more detailed discussion of the standard color palettes.

There are several things to keep in mind when choosing colors. The four color elements (IRGB) all actively produce light. The more elements in use, the brighter the color will be, but also the more washed out it will seem. To the eye, the pure single colors (red, green, and blue) are more visually intense than either the mixed colors (cyan, magenta, and yellow) or the so-called "intense" (brightened) versions of the pure colors. Here are three other factors that should be considered when choosing colors:

■ Some color display screens do not respond to the intensity bit. This deficiency makes color 8 the same as color 0, color 9 the same as color 1, and so on.

■ When a composite monochrome display screen is used with a color/graphics adapter, colors other than black (0) and white (7) may produce illegible information.

■ Finally, programs that are run on a PC or XT with the IBM Monochrome Adapter must take into account the unusual way the monochrome display treats color (☞ see page 81).

In considering color, check the discussions in each of the remaining sections. There are important color-related items in each section.

Color-Suppressed Modes

In an effort to make the graphics modes compatible with a wide range of monitors, both color and monochrome, IBM included a few modes that do not produce color, called color-suppressed modes. There are three color-suppressed modes: modes 0, 2, and 5. In these modes, colors are converted into shades of grey, or whatever color the screen phosphor produces. There are four even shades in mode 5, and a variety of shades in modes 0 and 2. Color is suppressed in the display adapter's composite output but *not* in its RGB output. This inconsistency is the result of an unavoidable technical limitation.

❑ NOTE: *For each color-suppressed mode, there is a corresponding color mode, so modes 0 and 1 correspond to 40-column text, modes 2 and 3 to 80-column text, and modes 4 and 5 to medium-resolution graphics. The fact that modes 4 and 5 reverse the pattern of modes 0 and 1 and modes 2 and 3, where the color-suppressed mode comes first, has lead to a complication in BASIC. The burst parameter of the BASIC SCREEN statement controls color. The meaning of this parameter is reversed for modes 4 and 5, so that the statement SCREEN,1 activates color in the text modes (0, 1, 2, and 3) but suppresses color in the graphics modes (4 and 5). This inconsistency may have been a programming error at first, but it is now part of the official definition of the SCREEN statement. Figure 4-6 shows the proper SCREEN statement syntax for modes 0 through 5.*

Color in Text and Graphics Modes

We need to be aware of the differences in the use of color between text and graphics modes, particularly the apparent inconsistencies in the way text colors are handled. In text mode, we have completely independent control over the color of each character position: We can freely use the full sixteen-color palette in the foreground and the eight-color palette in the background. In graphics mode, we have complete control over the color of each pixel and over the color of any graphics drawing operations (as provided by BASIC, for example).

In theory, the graphics modes should give us richer use of color over the entire screen. However, when we write text in a graphics mode, we do not have control over the background color: It is always set to the

Mode	Color Suppressed	Color Active
0	SCREEN 0,0:WIDTH 40	
1		SCREEN 0,1
2	SCREEN 0,0:WIDTH 80	
3		SCREEN 0,1:WIDTH 80
4		SCREEN 1,0
5	SCREEN 1,1	

Figure 4-6. The color burst parameters of modes 0 through 5. Notice that modes 0 through 3 and modes 4 through 5 follow different patterns

universal background color that is in effect. (☞ See the discussion of palette value 0 under the four-color modes, page 83.) This means that even though the graphics modes provide more control of color in principle, they actually provide less control of color when we are displaying text. This is an inherent characteristic of the text-writing services in the graphics modes. (☞ See Chapter 9.)

Setting Color in Text Modes

In the text modes, each character position on the display screen is controlled by two adjacent bytes in memory (☞ see page 87 for more about the location of these bytes in memory). The first byte contains the ASCII code for the character that will be displayed. (☞ See Appendix C for a chart of characters.) The second byte controls how the character will appear, specifying its colors and so forth. This second byte is called the character attribute.

Before we go any further, we need to explain a couple of terms that may present some confusion. In IBM PC display terminology, the terms *color* and *attribute* are used interchangeably. Although there are precise technical meanings to these two terms, which are distinct but closely related, you'll often find the two terms used imprecisely to mean roughly the same thing. To avoid confusion, think of both words as slightly vague terms that refer both to the way things appear on the screen and to the data coding in memory that controls the character's appearance.

There are three components to the text character attribute: the foreground color (the color of the character itself), the background color (the color of the area not covered by the character), and the character blink component. The foreground color can be any of the sixteen colors in the full PC range. The background color can be one of only eight colors: color numbers 0 through 7 (the basic colors without bright intensity).

Each character position on the screen has its own attribute control, independent of all other screen characters. The eight bits in the attribute byte act independently to control one element of the display attribute. ☞ The bit settings are shown in Figure 4-7. The default attribute used by DOS and BASIC is hex 07, normal white (7) on black (0), without blinking.

Bit 7 6 5 4 3 2 1 0	Use
1	Blinking of foreground character
. 1	Red component of background color
. . 1	Green component of background color
. . . 1	Blue component of background color
. . . . 1 . . .	Intensity component of foreground color
. . . . . 1 . .	Red component of foreground color
. . . . . . 1 .	Green component of foreground color
. . . . 1	Blue component of foreground color

*Figure 4-7. The coding of the color
attribute byte*

With the PCjr, when we use text characters in a sixteen-color graphics mode (modes 8 or 9) we can use any one of the sixteen colors for the background color, but that one background color will apply to all text characters written in the graphics mode. Though this may seem rather limiting, it can actually be quite useful. For example, characters can be displayed on the screen, yet made invisible by setting the foreground color to match the background color. This is the ideal way to allow passwords or other confidential information to be invisibly entered on the screen. (There is also an invisible mode for the Monochrome Adapter; ☞ see page 81.)

Color quality varies with the monitor. For many color displays, the bright, high-intensity colors are clearly legible when displayed on a background of the same color but without the intensity. On the other hand, some color displays do not act on the intensity setting. With these displays, otherwise legible foreground and background combinations, such as yellow on brown, are simply not distinguishable.

Although the graphics modes can display text quite nicely, there are several obvious advantages to using the text modes for text displays. Perhaps the most important advantage of text-mode characters is that they can be displayed faster than graphics characters. This is due in part to the fact that text-mode characters are taken from a table of characters, while the graphics characters must be drawn bit-by-bit from memory. The text modes use less memory than the graphics modes, so they have extra memory available for display pages, allowing us to store several "pages" of text information directly in the video display memory and call them up one at a time in quick succession. There are also more special effects available for text-mode characters. For one thing, there is a wider choice of colors. And for another, text modes can blink characters, while graphics modes have no blinking capability at all.

Setting Attributes in the Monochrome Mode

The monochrome mode (mode 7) used by the IBM Monochrome Adapter has a limited selection of display variations that are the equivalent of color. The same general coding scheme is used to set the display attributes for monochrome characters as is used for text-mode characters in graphics modes 0 through 3.

The blinking and intensity bits are used in the monochrome mode. However, only four foreground and background "color" combinations produce distinct results:

- Normal white-on-black, produced by selecting white (foreground bits 111) on black (background bits 000), or hex 07.

- Underlined characters, produced by setting the attribute byte to hex 01, which selects blue (foreground bits 001) on black (background bits 000).

- Reverse video, or black (foreground bits 000) on white (background bits 111), produced with hex 70.

- Invisible characters, created using black (foreground bits 000) on black (background bits 000), or hex 00.

All other color combinations show the same as normal white-on-black, hex 07. Other color combinations that might seem logical, such as invisible white-on-white or a reverse video/underlined combination, do not exist in monochrome mode; only the four results mentioned exist. Note that the blinking and intensity attribute bits are independent of these four "color" combinations.

Setting Color in Graphics Modes

So far, we've seen how to set color (and the monochrome equivalent of color) in the text modes. Setting color in the graphics modes is quite different. In the graphics modes (modes 4 through 6, 8 through 10, and 13 through 16), each pixel on the screen has a color associated with it. The color is set the same way attributes are set in text mode, but there are important differences. First, graphics pixels cannot blink. Second, since each pixel is a discrete dot of color, there is no foreground and background—each pixel is simply one color or another. When text is written in graphics mode, one color is used for the pixels that make up the "background" and any of the colors can be used for the pixels that make up the characters.

❑ NOTE: *The use of graphics mode in BASIC gives us the impression that there is a background color for graphics. But this is simply a convenient convention that BASIC adopts: Any pixels that aren't explicitly set to some "foreground" color are given the "background" color. The ROM-BIOS video services (☛ Chapter 9) also make use of this background-color convention.*

For each graphics mode, there are predefined color choices, known as palettes. The standard palettes can be changed in the PCjr or the EGA, but not in the original Color/Graphics Adapter. Once the palette colors for any graphics mode are set, each pixel color can be selected from the available colors by setting the color value of the bits assigned to each pixel. In a two-color mode, there is one bit for each pixel and the pixel's color value is given as 0 or 1. In a four-color mode, there are two bits with the color values of 0 through 3. In a sixteen-color mode, there are four bits and color values of 0 through 15. The color values used to define a pixel are not necessarily the same as the numbers (0 through 15) used to identify the actual colors that appear on the screen.

In two-color mode 6, there is only one standard palette, shown in Figure 4-8. In four-color modes 4 and 5, there are two standard palettes: palette 0, shown in Figure 4-9, and palette 1, shown in Figure 4-10. Two things should be noted about these palettes. First, palette value 0 can be changed from black (color 0) to any color. Second, palette value 0 is the "background" color and palette value 3 is the "foreground" color when writing text characters. In four-color mode 10 there is one standard palette, which is the same as palette 1. In sixteen-color modes 8, 9, 13, and 14, there is one standard palette. This palette matches the palette values 0 through 15 to the actual color numbers, as you might expect. Remember, color modes 8 and 9 are only available with the PCjr, and 13 and 14 are only available with the EGA.

Bit	Value	Color
0 0	0	Black
0 1	1	White

Figure 4-8. The standard palette for the two-color graphics mode (mode 6)

Bit	Value	Color
0 0	0	Black (default; may be changed to any color)
0 1	1	Green
1 0	2	Red
1 1	3	Brown

Figure 4-9. Palette 0, one of two standard palettes for the four-color graphics modes (modes 4 and 5)

Bit	Value	Color
0 0	0	Black (default; may be changed to any color)
0 1	1	Cyan
1 0	2	Magenta
1 1	3	Normal white

Figure 4-10. Palette 1, one of two standard palettes for the four-color graphics modes (modes 4 and 5)

Remapping Palettes in the PCjr and EGA

Up to this point, we've been discussing the standard colors that are produced using the standard palettes. With the original Color/Graphics Adapter, the palette color assignments are fixed and cannot be changed. However, in the PCjr and in any display adapter, such as the EGA, designed to provide it, the palettes can have their colors remapped. By remapping a color, we merely reassign a color value so that a request for color 1 (blue) might actually display color 4 (red).

The mapping of any requested palette value into an actual color number is under the control of the palette currently in effect. The palettes can be changed in BASIC with the palette statements, or with the BIOS video services (☞ see page 181).

INSIDE THE DISPLAY MEMORY

Now we come to the inner workings of the video map. In this section, we'll see how the information in the display memory is related to the display screen.

We should be aware that for the video modes that have their display memory in the B block (color/graphics modes 0 through 6 and monochrome mode 7), we can have our programs safely tinker with the display memory. This is true even for the PCjr, which only *appears* to use the B block for modes 0 through 6. IBM didn't want our programs to directly touch the display memory at first, but since most worthwhile programs do, IBM is now resigned to it and fully intends to support it in all present and future display adapters. But IBM is drawing the line with these modes. For new enhanced modes, such as the PCjr's modes 8 through 10 and the EGA's modes 13 through 16, IBM is making the display memory as hands-off as possible. In the case of the EGA, the display memory is theoretically located in the A block but can't actually be found at that address by our programs. We'd be fools to try to break through this barrier.

The use and coding of the video display memory varies according to which of video modes 0 through 10 is being used. (Recall that modes 0 through 6 apply to the original IBM Color/Graphics Adapter and mode 7 to the IBM Monochrome Adapter. Modes 8 through 10 were introduced with the PCjr model, which also uses modes 0 through 6; these modes cannot be used with the standard IBM Color/Graphics Adapter or any of its equivalents. Modes 11 through 16 apply only to the EGA.)

In modes 0 through 6 and also 8, the display map occupies 16K bytes; in modes 9 and 10, the display map fills 32K. In the Monochrome Adapter's mode 7, it uses only 4K bytes. The text-mode displays of both the monochrome and graphics display adapters use less memory than do the graphics-mode displays because only two bytes are needed to store one character (☞ more about this on page 87). Consequently, an 80- by 25-character text display requires only 4,000 bytes. A graphics display, as we can see in Figure 4-11, may require anywhere from 16K bytes to 32K bytes, depending on the number of colors we use. In the two-color graphics modes, a pixel uses one bit. In the four- and sixteen-color modes, each pixel requires from two to four bits in order to store the larger color values. This means that a 320×200 sixteen-color bit-mapped display requires a full 32K (two pixels per byte).

Since a typical text display occupies 4,000 bytes (only 2,000 bytes in 40-column mode), there is some space left over in the Color/Graphics Adapter's 16K display memory. We can use this space for more text by dividing it into display pages.

Mode	Minimum Memory Used (K)	Starting Paragraph Address (hex)	Adapter
0	2	B800 (location varies on PCjr)	CGA
1	2	B800 (location varies on PCjr)	CGA
2	4	B800 (location varies on PCjr)	CGA
3	4	B800 (location varies on PCjr)	CGA
4	16	B800 (location varies on PCjr)	CGA
5	16	B800 (location varies on PCjr)	CGA
6	16	B800 (location varies on PCjr)	CGA
7	4	B000	MA
8	16	PCjr main memory (location varies)	n/a
9	32	PCjr main memory (location varies)	n/a
10	32	PCjr main memory (location varies)	n/a
13	32	A000	EGA
14	32	A000	EGA
15	64	A000	EGA
16	64	A000	EGA

Figure 4-11. Minimum amount of memory needed by each video mode and its starting location in memory

Display Pages in Text Modes

In text modes 0 through 3, less than 16K is actually used by the screen at any one time. Modes 0 and 1 use 2K, and modes 2 and 3 use 4K. For these modes, the 16K of available memory is divided into multiple screen images, called *pages*. At any given time, one page is actively displayed. Information can be written into the displayed page or any of the other pages. Using this technique we can build a screen on an invisible page while another page is being displayed, then switch to the new page when the appropriate time comes. Switching screen images this way makes them appear to regenerate instantaneously.

The display pages are numbered 0 through 7 in modes 0 and 1, or 0 through 3 in modes 2 and 3, with page 0 starting at the beginning of the 16K display memory area. Each page begins on an even K memory boundary. ☛ The display page offset addresses are shown in Figure 4-12. The EGA doesn't abide by these conventions; use the word at hex 44E to find the offset of the current video page.

We set the display page by changing the starting address used by the 6845 controller chip. Normally, we do this by using ROM-BIOS video service 5 through interrupt 16 (hex 10). (☛ See Chapter 9.)

Page	Modes 0 and 1 2K displacements	Modes 2 and 3 4K displacements
0	B800	B800
1	B880	B900
2	B900	BA00
3	B980	BB00
4	BA00	
5	BA80	
6	BB00	
7	BB80	(See text for note on EGA)

Figure 4-12. Offset addresses for display
pages in modes 0 through 3

In any of these modes, if the pages are not actively used (actually displayed on the screen), then the unused part of the display memory can conceivably be used for another purpose, although it is not normal (or advisable) to do so. Making any other use of this potentially free memory is just asking for trouble in the future.

Display Pages in Graphics Modes

For the PCjr, the EGA, and any other display adapter that has the memory to accommodate it, the page concept is just as readily available in the graphics modes as in the text modes. Obviously there is no reason not to have graphics pages if the memory is there to support them.

The main benefit of using multiple pages for either graphics or text is to be able to instantly switch from one display screen to another without taking the time to build the display information from scratch. In theory, multiple pages could be used in graphics mode to produce smooth and fine-grained animation effects, but there wouldn't be enough display pages to take the animation very far. However, the potential for using display pages in graphics mode is there with the newer display adapters.

Displaying Characters in Text and Graphics Modes

As we have learned, the text modes of the Monochrome and Color/ Graphics Adapters do not store a character image in display memory, but instead store only the ASCII values of the character and its display attributes. The character is drawn on the screen by a character generator that is part of the adapter. The Color/Graphics Adapter has a character generator that produces characters in an 8-by-8 pixel block format, while the

Monochrome Adapter's character generator uses a 9-by-14 pixel block format. The larger format is one of the factors that makes the Monochrome Adapter's display output easier to read.

The standard ASCII characters (CHR$(1) through CHR$(127)) represent only half of the ASCII characters that we can use in the text modes. We also have 128 graphics characters available through the same character generator (CHR$(128) through CHR$(255)). Over half of them can be used to make simple line drawings. ☞ A complete list of both the standard ASCII characters and the graphics characters provided by IBM is given in Appendix C.

The graphics modes can also display characters, but they are produced quite differently. The graphics modes can only store information bit-by-bit and characters are no exception: They must be drawn one bit at a time. The big advantage to a bit-mapped display as far as characters are concerned is that you can design your own characters. In the original IBM Color/Graphics Adapter, the table for the second 128 characters is located in RAM and can therefore be modified. Having modified the table, we can directly access and display a custom set of characters instead of the standard IBM set. With the PCjr, all 256 characters are in RAM, so all of them can be modified.

Mapping Characters in Text Modes

In text modes, the memory map begins with the top left corner of the screen, using two bytes per screen position. The memory bytes for succeeding characters immediately follow in the order we would read them—from left to right and from top to bottom.

Modes 0 and 1 are text modes with a screen format of 40 columns by 25 rows. Each row occupies $40 \times 2 = 80$ bytes. A screen occupies only 2K bytes in modes 0 and 1, which means the 16K memory can accommodate eight display pages. If the rows are numbered 0 through 24 and the columns numbered 0 through 39, then the offset to any screen character in the first display page is given by the BASIC formula:

```
CHARACTER.OFFSET = (ROW.NUMBER * 80) + (COLUMN.NUMBER * 2)
```

Since the attribute byte for any character is in the memory location next to the ASCII character value, we can locate it by simply adding 1 to the character offset.

Modes 2, 3, and 7 are also text modes with 80 columns in each row instead of 40. The byte layout is the same, but each row requires twice as many bytes, or $80 \times 2 = 160$ bytes. Consequently, the 80-by-25 screen format uses 4K bytes and the 16K memory can accommodate four display pages. The offset to any screen location in the first display page is given by the BASIC formula:

```
CHARACTER.OFFSET = (ROW.NUMBER * 160) + (COLUMN.NUMBER * 2)
```

When using the Color/Graphics Adapter, the beginning of each text display page traditionally starts at an even K boundary. Since each screen page in the text modes actually uses only 2,000 or 4,000 bytes, there are some unused bytes following each page: either 48 or 96 bytes depending on the size of the page. So, to locate any screen position on any page in text mode, use this general formula:

```
LOCATION = (SEGMENT.PARAGRAPH * 16) + (PAGE.NUMBER * PAGE.SIZE)
+ (ROW.NUMBER * ROW.WIDTH * 2) + (COLUMN.NUMBER * 2) + WHICH
```

where:

> LOCATION is the 20-bit address of the screen information.
>
> SEGMENT.PARAGRAPH is the location of the video display memory (for example, hex B000 or B800).
>
> PAGE.NUMBER is in the range 0 through 3 or 0 through 7.
>
> PAGE.SIZE is 2K or 4K.
>
> ROW.NUMBER is from 0 through 24.
>
> ROW.WIDTH is 40 or 80.
>
> COLUMN.NUMBER is from 0 through 39 or 0 through 79.
>
> WHICH is 0 for the display character or 1 for the display attribute.

Mapping Pixels in Graphics Modes

When we use a graphics mode, pixels are stored as a series of bits, with a one-to-one correlation between the bits in memory and the pixels on the screen. We generally use one of three schemes to map out the display memory in graphics modes.

The original Color/Graphics Adapter organizes the display into 200 lines, numbered 0 through 199. The number of pixels in each line varies with the mode we use. Modes 4, 5, and 9 are medium resolution, with 320 pixels in each line. Modes 6 and 10 are high resolution, with 640 in each line. Mode 8, which was introduced in the PCjr and is not available for use with the standard IBM Color/Graphics Adapter, is low resolution, with 160 pixels in each line. The pixel columns for low-, medium-, and high-resolution graphics modes are numbered 0 through 199, 319, or 639.

The storage for the rows is divided into "banks" of lines that occupy contiguous memory locations. For modes 4, 5, 6, and 8, there are two banks, the first bank holding the memory for the even-numbered lines 0, 2, 4... through 198, and the second holding the memory for the odd-numbered lines 1, 3, 5... through 199. Modes 9 and 10 have four banks, with similarly staggered lines:

1st bank	0, 4, 8, 12...196
2nd bank	1, 5, 9, 13...197
3rd bank	2, 6, 10, 14...198
4th bank	3, 7, 11, 15...199

These banks of lines are similar to text-mode display pages in two respects: The lines within each bank run one right after another without any gap in memory, and each bank begins on an even K boundary, leaving some unused bytes at the end of each bank. However, unlike the display pages, all banks of lines are actively used by the display screen. Each bank is 8K in size, so the offsets to the beginning of the banks are 0, 8K, 16K, and 24K.

As we can see in Figure 4-13, the amount of memory used to support each pixel varies by mode. Mode 6 uses one bit, which can select from two colors; modes 4, 5, and 10 use two bits, selecting from four colors; and modes 8 and 9 use four bits, selecting from sixteen colors.

Except for mode 10, which is treated specially, the bits needed for each pixel in each row are taken in consecutive order from memory. For example, in mode 6, which uses one bit per pixel, the eight bits in the first byte of the display memory control the first eight pixels on the screen.

Mode	Columns	Colors	Bits	Banks	Memory (K)
4	320	4	2	2	16
5	320	4	2	2	16
6	640	2	1	2	16
8	160	16	4	2	16
9	320	16	4	4	32
10	640	4	2	4	32

Figure 4-13. The formats and memory requirements for the graphics modes

The first (high-order) bit controls the first pixel, and so forth. In mode 4, with two bits per pixel, the eight bits of each byte control four pixels. In mode 8, with four bits per pixel, each byte controls two pixels. ☞ All three bit formats are shown in Figure 4-14.

In mode 10, bit-mapping is different (☞ see Figure 4-15). Like modes 4 and 5, mode 10 requires two bits for each pixel, but unlike modes 4 and 5, the pixel information is not stored adjacent within one byte. Instead, it is stored in corresponding bits from two adjacent bytes. The bit from the first byte is the higher-order bit. When it is combined with the corresponding bit in the second byte, the two bits produce a color number from 0 through 3.

In modes 4, 5, 6, and 8, each line of pixels uses 80 bytes; in modes 9 and 10, each line uses 160 bytes.

CONTROLLING THE VIDEO DISPLAY

In general, control of the display screen, like most other computer operations, can be done in four ways:

- By using the programming-language services (for example, BASIC's SCREEN statement).

- By using the DOS services (☞ see Chapters 16 and 17).

- By using the ROM-BIOS video services (☞ see Chapter 9).

- By direct manipulation of the hardware, via memory or ports.

The video services that are available through programming languages, DOS, and the ROM-BIOS automatically place screen output data

Bit 7 6 5 4 3 2 1 0	Pixel	Bit 7 6 5 4 3 2 1 0	Pixel
Mode 6		*Modes 4 and 5*	
X	1	X X	1
. X	2	. . X X	2
. . X	3	. . . . X X . .	3
. . . X	4	. . . . . . X X	4
. . . . X . . .	5		
. . . . . X . .	6	*Modes 8, 9, 13, and 14*	
. . . . . . X .	7	X X X X	1
. . . . X	8	. . . . X X X X	2

Figure 4-14. A bit map of the first pixels in three graphics formats

1st Byte 7 6 5 4 3 2 1 0	2nd Byte 7 6 5 4 3 2 1 0	Pixel
X	X	1
. X	. X	2
. . X	. . X	3
. . . X	. . . X	4
. . . . X . . .	. . . . X . . .	5
. . . . . X . .	. . . . . X . .	6
. . . . . . X .	. . . . . . X .	7
. . . . X	 X	8

*Figure 4-15. A bit map of the first pixels in
mode 10 graphics format*

in the display memory, each type of service offering varying levels of control. Seventeen ROM-BIOS services are particularly powerful, providing nearly all the services that are needed to generate display-screen output, control the cursor, and manipulate screen information. (☞ All sixteen services are fully described in Chapter 9). For maximum control over the video display, we also have the option of bypassing the software services and placing data directly in the display memory—when we feel we have good reason to.

Before opting for direct video output, you should know that it does interfere with windowing systems and more advanced multitasking operating environments. All the same, many important programs for the PC family generate direct video output—so many, in fact, that this has become a standard and accepted way of creating output. So, even though in the long run it's probably not wise to place video output directly on the screen, everyone seems to be doing it.

Basically, we can't mix programs that write directly into the display memory and windowing systems because two programs would be fighting over the control of the same memory and messing up each other's data. But because so many programs now generate direct video output, IBM's own multitasking windowing system, Topview, goes to great lengths to accommodate programs that write directly to the display memory. A system like Topview can make this accommodation simply by keeping a separate copy of the program's display memory; when the program is running, the copy is moved into the display buffer, and when the program is stopped, a fresh copy of the display buffer is made. This technique allows Topview to run programs that work with the display memory, but at an enormous cost: First, computing and memory overhead go

About the Cursor

A blinking cursor is a feature of the text modes that is used to indicate the active location on the display screen. The cursor is actually a group of scan lines that fill the entire width of the character box. The size of the character box varies with the display adapter; the Monochrome Adapter uses a 9-pixels-wide-by-14-scan-lines-high format, and the Color/Graphics Adapter uses an 8-pixels-by-8-scan-lines format. (The extra scan lines in the monochrome mode allow for a more detailed character drawing, as you'll see in Appendix C).

The default cursor format uses every scan line, but it may be changed to display any number of lines within its small range. For example, we can set the cursor to start and stop on any set of scan lines and even to wrap around from a lower scan line to a higher one. This allows us to make a one-part cursor located anywhere in the character box, or a two-part cursor located at the top and bottom of the character box. (☛ See page 174 for a discussion of the character box and the relationship of the scan lines to the characters.)

Since the blinking cursor used in text modes is a hardware-created feature, software has only limited control over it. We can change its format and we can change its location on the screen in a number of ways. To read or change the location of the cursor we can use some of the ROM-BIOS services (☛ see Chapter 9) or we can read or write directly to memory (☛ see the discussion of location hex 450 on page 55). Likewise, we can read and change the cursor format by using the ROM-BIOS services or we can read the format directly by inspecting memory (☛ see the discussion of location hex 460 on page 56). Most programming languages also offer these services.

If we ever want to bypass this hardware-controlled blinking cursor (and many of us do), we can use the reverse-video display attribute (hex 70) whenever the real cursor is located. This will produce a block cursor that doesn't blink. Another way to do this is to use the ASCII block characters, either CHR$(219) or CHR$(254).

So far, we've been talking about the text-mode cursor. In the graphics modes, there is no displayed cursor, but a logical cursor location is recorded that tells us the active screen location. As in the text modes, to find out the cursor's location, we can either use the ROM-BIOS services or read the location word (hex 450) directly.

To create a cursor in graphics modes, many programs, including BASIC, simulate the block cursor by using a distinctive background color at the cursor location or by using the ASCII block characters.

up; second, the program can't run in the background simultaneously with other programs; and third, the display information can't be "windowed"; that is, it can't be moved or adjusted in size.

Programmers are faced with a conflict here: Direct output to the screen has the benefit of speed and power, while using BIOS or higher-level services for screen output has the benefit of more flexibility for adapting to windowing systems, new display adapters, etc. The solution that I adopted for my own programs was to use both techniques, activating one or the other as needed.

Direct Hardware Control

Much of the information that we've provided in this chapter, particularly the information on the internal mapping of the display memory, is meant to help you write video information directly into the display memory. But remember, there is a risk in any kind of direct programming, and you'll find that it is both safer and easier to use the highest available means to control the video display. Lower means, particularly direct manipulation, can be very disruptive. There are only a few instances when direct control is safe and reliable. Wherever possible, I will point out these circumstances.

Monochrome Adapter I/O Ports

The Monochrome Adapter uses four I/O ports: the CRT control and status ports and the 6845 CRT controller registers.

The CRT control port (hex 3B8). We can set three of this port's eight bits: the high-resolution, video, and blink bits. The high-resolution bit must always be on to use the Monochrome Adapter. The video and blink settings turn the video display and the character blink on and off. Sending the value hex 29 to this port will set the three bits to their normal setting. (☛ See Figure 4-16.)

The CRT status port (hex 3BA). This port stores the state of the horizontal sync signal in bit 0 and the video bit stream to the display in bit 3. Although we can read these two bits, neither one is particularly useful. The other bits are not used.

Bit 7 6 5 4 3 2 1 0	Use
. . . . X	High-resolution mode: must be set to 1
. . . . . X X .	Not used
. . . . X . . .	0 = disable video signal; 1 = enable video signal
. . . X	Not used
. . X	0 = blinking function off; 1 = blinking function on
X X	Not used

Figure 4-16. The coding for the CRT control port

The 6845 CRT controller (start address hex 3B0). There are 19 programmable internal registers in the 6845. They specify such things as the timing of the vertical and horizontal sync signals, the number of display lines, and the number of characters per line. Only four registers are safe to use: registers (hex) 0A, 0B, 0E, and 0F. Registers 0A and 0B determine the lines on which the cursor starts and ends, and registers 0E and 0F determine the screen position of the cursor, with a value ranging from 0 to 1,999. Both functions are also available through interrupt 16 (hex 10) in the ROM-BIOS services. Don't mess around with the other values; they can be disruptive. (For example, you can damage a monochrome display if you program the 6845 video controller incorrectly.) If you want to know more about them, refer to the IBM PC Technical Reference manual.

Color/Graphics Adapter I/O Ports

In order to accommodate the graphics functions, the Color/Graphics Adapter has more I/O ports than the Monochrome Adapter. We will list the most important aspects of each of the seven ports.

The mode select register (hex 3D8). We set this byte to change from one display mode to another. (☞ See Figure 4-17.)

The color select register (hex 3D9). We set this byte to change the screen border colors for the text modes and the background and foreground colors for the graphics modes. (☞ See Figure 4-18.)

Bit 7 6 5 4 3 2 1 0	Use
. . . . X	0 = select 40 × 25 text mode; 1 = select 80 × 25 text mode
. . . . . . X .	0 = select text mode; 1 = select 320 × 200 graphics mode
. . . . . X . .	0 = select color mode; 1 = select b/w mode
. . . . X . . .	0 = disable video signal; 1 = enable video signal
. . . X	1 = 640 × 200 b/w graphics
. . X	0 = blinking function off; 1 = blinking function on
X X	Not used

Figure 4-17. The coding for the mode select register

Bit 7 6 5 4 3 2 1 0	Use
. . . . X	Selects blue foreground, background, or border
. . . . . . X .	Selects green foreground, background, or border
. . . . . X . .	Selects red foreground, background, or border
. . . . X . . .	Selects intensity setting
. . . X	Selects alternate, intensified palette
. . X	0 = palette 0; 1 = palette 1
X X	Not used

Figure 4-18. The coding for the color select register

The status register (hex 3DA). This register stores useful information for those of us who prefer a flicker/snow-free screen update. When bit 0 is set to 1, we can access the buffer memory without disturbing the display. When bit 3, the vertical sync, is set to 1, the raster is in vertical retrace and we can update the screen. This register also has two light-pen status signals. (☞ See Figure 4-19.)

The light-pen latch ports (hex 3DB and 3DC). Writing to either of these ports clears or sets a toggle switch that is connected to the 6845's light-pen input.

The 6845 video controller (start address hex 3D0). The controller functions the same way with the Color/Graphics Adapter as it does with the Monochrome Adapter.

Control of the video display is complicated, and has been made much more complicated by the steady stream of additions to the list of PC display features. Whatever you decide to do, it is a very good idea to test your understanding of any part of video control by experimenting with it before you incorporate it into your programming efforts.

Bit 7 6 5 4 3 2 1 0	Use
. . . . X	1 = memory access can occur without display interference
. . . . . . X .	1 = light-pen trigger set
. . . . . X . .	0 = light pen on; 1 = light pen off
. . . . X . . .	1 = raster is in vertical retrace
X X X X	Not used

Figure 4-19. The coding of the status register

COMPATIBILITY CONSIDERATIONS

For our programs to be compatible with all the IBM personal computer models, we need to keep several things in mind. First, a standard PC model cannot create graphics displays if it is equipped only with the Monochrome Adapter. In addition, graphics modes 8 through 10 cannot be used with the original or the enhanced version of the Color/Graphics Adapter; they are part of the PCjr color enhancements. Likewise, modes 13 through 16 belong to the EGA. These restrictions also apply to any re-mapping of the color palettes, as this capability is also linked to the PCjr and the EGA. It is also important to remember that the Monochrome Adapter for the PC and XT models treats the text-mode color attributes in a special way (☛ as discussed on page 79).

It's a good idea for a program to adapt its use of color, or the choice between the text and graphics mode, to accommodate either the IBM Monochrome Monitor or a composite monochrome monitor, which usually doesn't show color well. Keep in mind that composite mono-chrome monitors may often be used with PCs, especially when the primary work is with text—such as word processing or accounting. There are many PCs equipped this way and it is wise for our programs to ac-commodate them.

In order to accommodate these systems, our programs should find out the video mode and act accordingly. For programs that are already using an assembly-language interface to the BIOS, the preferred way to do this is to use BIOS video service 15 (☛ see Chapter 9). For other pro-grams, service 15 is a stumbling block. The problem can be circumvented by reading memory location 0000:0449, where the video mode is stored (☛ see page 54). We can read this location in BASIC like this:

```
DEF SEG = 0
VIDEO.MODE = PEEK (&H449)
```

Video mode 7 identifies the use of the IBM Monochrome Monitor. There is no automatic way to identify the use of a composite monochrome dis-play; however, if a knowledgeable user of such a display uses the DOS MODE command to suppress color, our programs can detect it in a video mode of 0 or 2.

When we wish to consider the working compatibility of our pro-grams with the IBM personal computers and the different kinds of dis-play screens, we can lay out several compatibility criteria to consider. These criteria are not completely consistent with each other, reflecting the internal inconsistency in the design of the IBM personal computer and the variety of display formats that can be used. Still, there are overall guidelines for compatibility, which we'll outline here.

First, text-only display output increases compatibility. There are many PCs equipped with Monochrome Adapters, which cannot show graphic output. If you are weighing a text-versus-graphics decision in the design of a program, there are two factors to consider, one for the use of a text-only display and one against. On the one hand, as many programs have dramatically demonstrated, it is possible to create very effective drawings using just standard IBM text characters. (See Appendix C for more information on the effective use of text characters for drawing.) On the other hand, it is more and more common for computers to include graphics capability. For example, both the PCjr and the IBM Portable PC, as well as the Compaq model, come with built-in graphics capability. So, in the future, text-only output will probably lose its importance and we'll be able to design graphics directly into our programs without worrying about compatibility.

Second, the less our programs depend on color, the wider the range of computers with which they will be compatible. This does not mean that we need to avoid color for compatibility; it simply means that for maximum compatibility, our programs should use color as an enhancement, not as an essential ingredient. If programs can get along without color, then they will be compatible with computers that use monochrome displays, including PCs with Monochrome Adapters, as well as Compaq and IBM Portable PC computers with their built-in monochrome displays.

In considering these guidelines in the light of the particulars of your own programs, you must weigh the advantage of broad compatibility against the convenience and simplicity of writing programs for a narrower range of displays. My own experience and judgment tell me that far too often programmers err by opting for a narrower range of displays, thereby gravely reducing the variety of computers their programs can be used on. Be forewarned.

5

Disk Basics

▬

M ost computer systems have some way to store information permanently, whether it is on cassette tapes, floppy disks, or hard disks. These storage devices come in various sizes and capacities but operate in basically the same way: They magnetically encode information on their surfaces in patterns determined by the device itself and by the software that controls the device.

When the PC family was introduced in 1981, it used one main type of storage device: the standard 5¼-inch floppy disk, which was double-density, single-sided, and soft-sectored, and stored only 160K bytes. Since then, IBM has increased the diskette's storage capacity and has added 10- and 20-megabyte hard disks to some of their PC systems. In the future, we can expect to see continued advances in disk technology by IBM and others, including higher-capacity hard disks and 3½-inch mini-diskettes.

Although the type of storage device is important, as programmers, it is the way stored information is laid out and managed that concerns us. In this chapter, we will focus on how information is organized and stored on floppy disks, since they are the most common storage medium for the PC family. Although we will primarily be discussing floppy disks, we will really be painting a portrait that represents all disk-type storage devices. The information provided in this chapter applies equally well to RAM disks—that is, the simulation of disk storage in memory—as it does to conventional diskettes, hard disks, disk cartridges, and mini-diskettes.

THE DISK'S PHYSICAL STRUCTURE

The disk drives and operating system of the computer establish the *capacity* of the disks used, but a disk's *structure* is essentially the same, regardless of the setup. Data is always recorded on the disk surface in a series of concentric circles, called *tracks*. Each track is further divided into segments, called *sectors*. (☛ See Figure 5-1.) The amount of data that can be stored on each side of a disk depends on the number of tracks (its density), the number of sectors, and the size of the sectors. Disk density may vary considerably from drive to drive: The standard double-density drives can record 40 tracks of data, while the new quad-density drives can record 80 tracks.

For the PC's standard 5¼-inch diskettes, the location of each track and the number of usable sides are set by the hardware characteristics of the disks and disk drives, and as such, they are fixed and unchangeable.

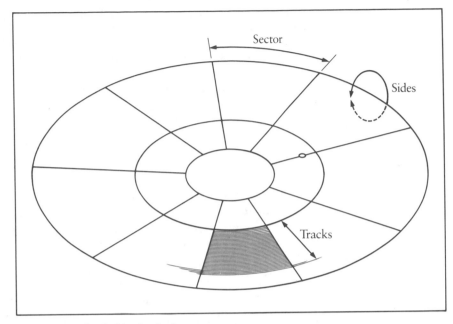

Figure 5-1. The disk's physical structure

However, the location, size, and number of the sectors within a track are under software control. This is why the PC's diskettes are known as soft-sectored. The characteristics of a diskette's sectors (their size, and the number per track) are set when each track is formatted. Disk formatting can be done either by the operating system or by the ROM-BIOS format service. In most of this chapter, we will discuss the DOS formats. However, we can easily create unusual formats and make them part of a workable copy-protection scheme by using the ROM-BIOS diskette services (☞ see service 5 on page 192).

The 5¼-inch diskettes supported by the standard PC BIOS may have sectors that are 128, 256, 512, or 1,024 bytes in size. DOS, from versions 1.00 through 3.1, has consistently used sectors of 512 bytes, and it is quite possible that this will continue. However, any program which depends upon or makes use of the 512-byte DOS sectors should allow for future changes in sector size, particularly for larger sectors.

A diskette, of course, has two sides, and the sectors and tracks can be placed on one or both sides. Hard-disk systems can have one or more disks (called platters) in them, so they may contain more than two sides. **XT** For example, the 10-megabyte hard disk introduced with the XT has two platters and it uses all four sides of those platters.

DOS DISK FORMATS

In the early versions of DOS used by IBM, a limited number of disk formats could be used, even though the disk drives themselves could read and write many formats. Beginning with DOS 2.00 and continuing with all subsequent versions, DOS has been equipped with only a few standard formatting options but allows virtually any physical disk format to be integrated. (The logical format, as we'll see, is more tightly constrained to a standard set by DOS.) This integration is possible because DOS provides us with the necessary tools to write an installable device driver—a machine-language routine that can configure our disk drive to read or write different formats, or allow us to hook up a non-IBM disk drive to our system (☞ see Appendix A for more on installable device drivers).

Because there are many potential disk formats, we cannot possibly consider all of them. We will examine seven common disk formats, including four regular 5¼-inch diskette formats, one special 5¼-inch diskette format, one 3½-inch mini-diskette format, and one hard-disk format. Together, these seven common formats should serve as examples to provide you with enough guidance to work with any disk type.

Standard DOS Formats

We'll begin with the four most common PC formats, those used as standard formats by IBM for 5¼-inch diskettes. The four formats are derived from the number of sides and the number of sectors on each track: single- or double-sided and eight or nine sectors (☞ see Figure 5-2).

The reason why there are four standard formats is quite simple: IBM has to make sure that all versions of DOS support all earlier PC models. The first PCs came equipped with single-sided diskette drives. Later, IBM introduced double-sided drives and discontinued using single-sided drives. Now, although relatively few PCs have single-sided drives, the single-sided formats are supported by all versions of DOS for compatibility with the early machines.

In the earliest releases of DOS, only eight 512-byte sectors were placed on each track, even though up to ten sectors of that size could be squeezed in successfully. Later, nine 512-byte sectors were accepted as safe and reliable, and the nine-sector format became the standard. Once again, the other formats were preserved to maintain compatibility.

The format expansions are tied to the history and development of DOS. The original DOS version 1.00 supported only what I call the S-8 format. The next release, 1.10, added D-8. Version 2.00 added the two nine-sector formats, S-9 and D-9. No new formats were added with DOS 2.10, but DOS 3.0 added the quad-density format that we'll discuss shortly.

Our Notation	Sides	Sectors	Tracks	Nominal Size (bytes)
S-8	1	8	40	160K
D-8	2	8	40	320K
S-9	1	9	40	180K
D-9	2	9	40	360K

Figure 5-2. The standard DOS formats

Although there are many formats, only two are in widespread use: S-8 and D-9. S-8 is the lowest common denominator, so it has traditionally been used for commercial programs, since the use of S-8 guarantees that a diskette can be read by any version of DOS. However, this practice is going out of style, especially in companies that sell large programs needing more disk space. The D-9 format is the highest-capacity format that most 5¼-inch drives can use, so that's the one most people use for their actual working diskettes. The other formats, D-8 and S-9, are not as common, but they are used occasionally.

Quad-Density Formats

You will notice that the one constant factor in the four standard formats is the number of tracks: All of them have 40. This is because the 5¼-inch diskette drives that we use most often with the PC family are designed to read and write 40 tracks of data. But some 5¼-inch diskette drives, and many 3½-inch drives, can record 80 tracks of data in the same space. This type of drive, and the diskettes used with it, is often referred to as quad-density. Of the many possible quad-density formats, we are going to discuss the two that are most common in the PC family. We'll call them QD-9 and QD-15. (☞ See Figure 5-3.)

The QD-9 format is very much like the D-9, except that it has 80 tracks of data instead of 40. Like the D-9 format, the QD-9 format has two sides, with nine sectors per track on each side.

Although IBM has avoided using the QD-9 format, it has been available with other equipment, such as Data General's DG-1 lap computer, a

Our Notation	Sides	Sectors	Tracks	Nominal Size (bytes)
QD-9	2	9	80	720K
QD-15	2	15	80	1,200K

Figure 5-3. The quad-density formats

cousin of the PC family. The DG-1 uses 3½-inch mini-diskettes rather than the standard 5¼-inch diskettes, but the logical structure of their formats is the same. Although the mini-diskette drives are quad-density, their disks can be formatted not only in the QD-9 format but also in the other four formats, S-8, S-9, D-8, and D-9. Quad-density drives can also be attached to regular PCs as nonstandard equipment, using a DOS device driver (☞ see Appendix A for more on device drivers). Many people believe that this format will become widely used, so it's of real interest to us.

The high-capacity QD-15 format used by the AT follows the same basic structure we've discussed: 80 tracks per side and standard 512-byte sectors. The special characteristic of QD-15 is that each side of every track holds fifteen sectors, instead of eight or nine. Fitting that many sectors onto a track is only possible because the AT uses special high-capacity diskettes, which have a different magnetic coating than ordinary diskettes. Only these special diskettes—which look the same as the regular 5¼-inch diskettes—and the special high-capacity diskette drives can accept the QD-15 format.

The Hard-Disk Format

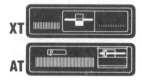

High-capacity hard-disk systems, such as the XT's 10-megabyte hard disk or the AT's 20-megabyte hard disk, present some special problems and opportunities.

There are two aspects to any disk: its physical format and its logical format. The physical format of a disk determines the sector size in bytes, the number of sectors per track (per cylinder for hard disks), the number of tracks (cylinders), and the number of sides. The logical format determines the way the information on the disk will be organized and where different types of information will be placed.

When we format a floppy disk with DOS or any other operating system, we set both the physical and the logical format of the diskette and we're unaware of any distinction between them. Unlike a diskette, the physical format of a hard disk is already established when it comes to us—it's set by the manufacturer.(☞ See Figure 5-4.) What is not present in the factory-set physical format is the logical structure of the disk, which we have to establish before the operating system can use it. This is done in two stages. First, we must divide the hard disk into logical *partitions* to house the data and programs for each operating system we use. (We can use several operating systems with our hard-disk system; ☞ see page 110.) Then we must define the organization of the partitions so that each individual operating system can locate the information within its partition. It is this process of "organizing the disk" that is usually called formatting.

Our Notation	Sides	Sectors	Cylinders	Nominal Size (megabytes)
XT	4	17	306 (See page 109)	10
AT	4	17	615	20

Figure 5-4. The physical formats of the XT and AT hard disks

THE DISK'S LOGICAL STRUCTURE

Regardless of what disk we use, DOS disks are all logically formatted in the same way: The disk's sides, tracks, and sectors are identified numerically using the same notation, and certain sectors are always reserved for special programs and indexes that DOS uses to manage disk operations. Before we find out how DOS organizes space on a disk, we need to briefly cover the conventional notation used by DOS and the BIOS to locate information.

As we have seen from earlier discussions, our 5¼-inch diskette formats have 40 tracks, numbered from 0 (the outside track) through 39 (the inside track, closest to the center). Other disk formats can have more tracks. For example, the tracks on quad-density diskettes are numbered 0 through 79, **XT** the XT's hard-disk cylinders are numbered 0 through 305, **AT** and the AT's hard-disk cylinders are numbered 0 through 614.

On a double-sided diskette, the two sides are numbered 0 and 1 (the two recording heads of a double-sided disk drive are also numbered 0 and 1). The one side of a single-sided diskette is referred to as side number 0. **XT** The XT's hard disk has four sides (and four recording heads) numbered 0 through 3.

The sectors on floppy disks are numbered 1 through 8 or 9. **XT** On the XT's **AT** and AT's hard disk, they are numbered 1 through 17. Note that sector numbers begin with 1, while track and side numbers begin with 0.

The BIOS locates the sectors on a disk by a three-dimensional coordinate composed of a track number (also referred to as the cylinder number), a side number (also called the head number), and a sector number. DOS, on the other hand, locates information by sector number, and numbers the sectors sequentially from outside to inside. (☞ See Figure 5-5.) The sequence begins with the first sector on the disk: sector 1 of side 0 and track 0, followed by the remaining sectors on the same side and track. For double-sided diskettes, the ninth sector of side 0 and track 0 is followed by the first sector of side 1 and track 0. The order proceeds through all sectors of one side and track location, then through the next side, at the same track location (so all sides at one track location come before the next track location).

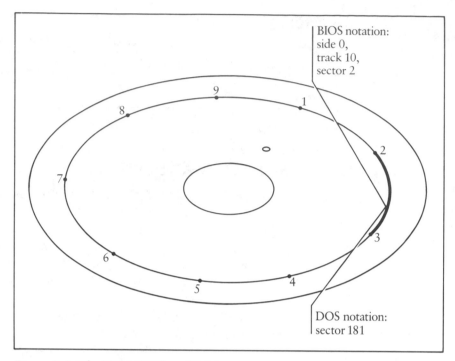

Figure 5-5. The ROM-BIOS and DOS sector
notation

We can refer to particular sectors either by their three-dimensional coordinates or by their sequential order. All ROM-BIOS operations use the three-dimensional coordinates to locate a sector. All DOS operations and tools such as DEBUG use the DOS sequential notation. ☞ See page 250 for how to convert DOS notation to ROM-BIOS notation and vice versa.

HOW DOS ORGANIZES THE DISK

As we've already seen, when we instruct DOS to format our diskettes, it divides each of the 40 tracks into either eight or nine 512-byte sectors. In terms of raw storage capacity, this amounts to 368,640 bytes of data space on our standard D-9 diskettes. But not all of that space can be used to store data; a certain amount is used to store system control information and indexes that DOS uses to find the location and relationship between individual sectors. So, in addition to dividing the disk into sectors, DOS performs several other operations when it formats our disks.

Diskette Space Allocation

The formatting process divides the sectors on a disk into four sections, for four different uses. The sections, in the order they are stored, are the boot record, the file allocation table (FAT), the directory, and the data space ☞ see Figure 5-7 overleaf). The size of each section varies between formats, but the structure and the order of the sections don't vary. Hard disks, such as the 10-megabyte hard disk on the XT, follow the same basic layout, though hard disks that can be partitioned present extra complications because the partition sizes directly affect the size of each section. ☞ See page 110 for a discussion of hard-disk partitions.

The boot record is always a single sector located at sector 1 of track 0, side 0. The boot record contains, among other things, a short program to start the process of loading the operating system from a diskette that has the operating system on it. All diskettes have the boot record on them even if they don't have the operating system. Aside from the start-up program, the exact contents of the boot record vary from format to format.

The file allocation table, or FAT, follows the boot record, usually starting at sector 2 of track 0, side 0. The FAT contains the official record of the disk's format and maps out the location of the sectors used by the disk files. DOS uses the FAT to keep a record of the data-space usage. Each entry in the table contains a specific code to indicate what space is being used, what space is available, and what space is unusable (due to defects on the disk). Because the FAT is used to control the entire usable data storage area of a disk, two identical copies of it are stored in case one is damaged. Both copies of the FAT may occupy as many sectors as needed: 2 or 4 on floppy disks, 14 on the QD-15 diskettes, up to 16 on the XT's hard disk, and up to 82 on the AT's hard disk. On all types of hard disk, the FAT size varies with the size of the partition.

| Format | Total Sectors | Overhead Sectors | | | | Data Sectors |
		Boot	FAT	Directory	Total	
S-8	320	1	2	4	7	323
D-8	640	1	2	7	10	630
S-9	360	1	4	4	9	351
D-9	720	1	4	7	12	708
QD-9	1,440	1	10	7	18	1,422
QD-15	2,400	1	14	14	29	2,371

Figure 5-6. The sector allotment of the standard floppy-disk formats

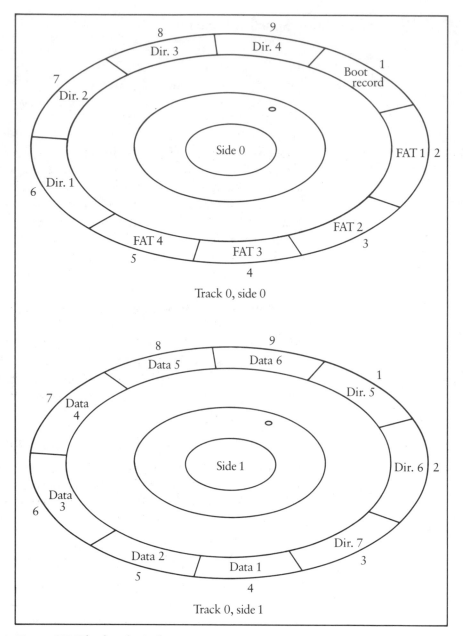

*Figure 5-7. The four logical sections
of a diskette*

The **file directory** is the next item on the disk. It is used as a table of contents, identifying each file on the disk with a directory entry that contains several pieces of information, including the file's name and size. One part of the entry is a number that points to the first group of sectors used by the file (this number is also the first entry for this file in the FAT). The size of the directory varies with the disk format. It occupies four sectors on single-sided diskettes and seven on double-sided diskettes. On hard disks, the directory, like the FAT, varies with the size of the partition.

The **data space,** which occupies the bulk of the diskette (from the directory through the last sector), is used to store data, while the other three sections are used to support the data space. Sectors in the data space are allocated to files on an as-needed basis, in units known as *clusters*. The size of a cluster varies by format. On single-sided diskettes, the clusters are one sector long and on double-sided diskettes, they are a pair of adjacent sectors. Diskettes with a higher capacity may have clusters containing several sectors. **AT** For example, the AT's 20-megabyte hard disk uses a cluster size of four sectors, **XT** and the XT's 10-megabyte hard disk uses up to eight sectors per cluster.

Hard-Disk Space Allocation

For hard-disk systems, the amount of space that DOS allocates to the FAT, directory, and data space varies depending upon the size of the partition given to DOS. The boot record occupies one sector regardless of the partition size, so we won't bother to mention it any further.

To get an idea of how DOS allocates space in a partition, we will examine three different partition sizes. Our example focuses on the XT's 10-megabyte hard disk, which has 512 bytes per sector, 17 sectors per cylinder per side, 4 sides (heads) per cylinder, and 306 cylinders per disk.

The table in Figure 5-8 shows the specific space allocations for three DOS partition sizes. 305 cylinders (an entire XT-disk—the first cylinder is used for partition data, and is therefore not available for the DOS partition), 100 cylinders, and 5 cylinders. In general, these figures can be interpolated to determine the space allocations for other partition sizes.

THE LOGICAL STRUCTURE IN DETAIL

Now it's time to delve a little more deeply into each of the four sections of a disk: the boot record, the directory, the data space, and the file allocation table.

Partitioning a Hard Disk

Every operating system has its own peculiar way of formatting and managing disk storage space, which is incompatible with other operating systems. Although DOS is, by far, the dominant operating system for the PC family, it is not the only one that is used and, in the years to come, it is quite possible that DOS may be superseded by new operating systems, such as XENIX.

Since different operating systems may need to use the same disk, a scheme has been worked out to partition or divide a hard disk into logical sections so that several operating systems can each have their share of it. A partition is actually a set of contiguous cylinders, the size of which is determined by the user and laid out by the operating system. A hard disk must be partitioned before an operating system can use it. After it is partitioned, the separate partitions must be formatted using the formatting procedures of the controlling operating systems. Normally, an operating system uses only one partition. However, occasionally some vendors will partition their hard disks into the equivalent of separate disk drives, with DOS using each partition. Fortunately, this is an exception rather than a rule.

The DOS program FDISK is used to create the partitions and to mark one of them as the DOS partition. We can specify whether we want the DOS partition to comprise all or only part of the disk. The operating system is able to adapt to whatever size disk partition it is assigned. If we do not expect to use another operating system, we might as well partition the entire disk for DOS.

We can change the size and number of partitions any time we want. However, changing the partition destroys any existing partition contents, so when adjusting the size or number of partitions, we should first off-load any data that needs to be saved, repartition the disk, and then reload the data.

Formatting the Partition

A hard disk has two levels of logical structure. On one level, we have the division of the disk into partitions, a phenomenon that is common to all operating systems. On another level, we have the specific format and location of the information that is stored in each partition, which is different for every operating system. Once a DOS partition has been established with FDISK, that partition must be formatted with the DOS FORMAT command to establish the logical structure that DOS needs to operate.

Just as a DOS disk has a boot record containing both a start-up program and some general information about the disk in its first sector (☞ see page 107 for details), the first sector of a partitionable disk has a master boot record containing both a master start-up program and a record of how the disk is partitioned. This partitioning information includes how many partitions there are (there is often only one), the size and location of each partition, the partition type, and which partition is active, as well as other information. The master start-up program is a short program that finds out which partition is active and then passes control to the start-up, or boot, program for that partition.

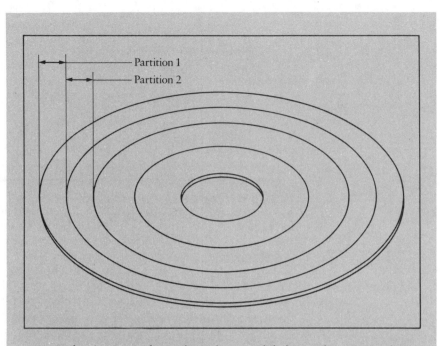

So far, these general remarks apply to any disk that can be partitioned to work with several operating systems. To illustrate the mechanics of partitioning, we will use the XT's 10-megabyte hard disk as an example.

The master boot record for the XT's hard disk contains a partition table with room for up to four partitions. Each partition is marked in the table to indicate whether or not it is the currently active partition, and has an ID byte to identify the operating system that governs it (hex 01 identifies DOS).

The location and size of the partition are stored in the table in the master boot record in two equivalent ways. The first way gives the starting and ending location of the partition using the cylinder (or track), head (or side), and sector numbers of the first and last sectors in the partition. The second way gives the sector number of the first sector in the partition relative to the first sector on the disk, followed by the total number of sectors in the partition.

Each partition occupies a contiguous set of cylinders that begins at the first sector of the first cylinder in the set and ends on the last sector of the last cylinder. One minor exception to this occurs in the partition that uses the very first cylinder on the disk. On this cylinder, the partition begins at the second sector because the first sector is occupied by the disk's master boot record.

| | Partition Size (cylinders) | | |
	305 (all)	100	5
FAT size (sectors)	8	5	1
Directory size (sectors)	32	16	4
Number of directory entries	512	256	64
Cluster size (sectors)	8	4	1
Number of clusters	2,587	1,699	333
Data space size (K)	10,348	3,372	166.5

Figure 5-8. The space allocation for three partitions in the XT's 10-megabyte hard disk

The Boot Record

The boot record consists primarily of a short machine-language program that starts the process of loading DOS into memory. To perform this task, the program first checks to see whether the disk is system-formatted (contains the IBMBIO.COM and IBMDOS.COM files) and then proceeds accordingly.

You can inspect the boot program by using the DOS DEBUG program, which combines the ability to read data from any sector on a disk and the ability to disassemble—or unassemble—machine language into assembly-language code. If you want to learn more about the boot program and you aren't intimidated by DEBUG's terse command format, try entering these commands:

```
DEBUG
L 0 0 0 1            ; load first sector
U 0 L 2              ; unassemble and list first and second bytes
U 2E                 ; unassemble and list all bytes from 2E on
```

These commands allow you to see the first instructions of the boot program located on the disk in drive A.

❑ NOTE: *The code that begins at byte 2E is the beginning of the boot program for the standard IBM PC only. For all models, the second byte of the first sector stores the location of the first byte of the boot code, so if you are not using a PC, when you enter the third command line, you should use the byte value shown in the JMP instruction produced by the second command line instead of the value 2E.*

For all disk formats except S-8 and D-8 you will find some key parameters in the boot record, beginning with the fourth byte (☞ see Figure 5-9). These parameters are part of the BIOS parameter block used by DOS to control any disk-type device. The rest of the boot program is located in the first three bytes (bytes 0, 1, and 2) and continues in the bytes following the BIOS parameter block. At the end of the boot records for DOS-2 versions and beyond, there is a 2-byte signature, hex 55 AA.

The Directory

Disk directories are used to hold most of the basic information about the files stored on the disk, including the file's name, its size, the starting FAT entry, the time and date it was created, and a few special file attributes (☞ see Figure 5-10). The only information that the directory does not contain is the exact location of the individual clusters that make up a file; these are stored in the file allocation table.

There is one directory entry for each file on the disk, including entries for the subdirectory files and for the disk's volume ID label. Each of the entries is 32 bytes long, so one sector in the directory can hold 16 entries. Single-sided diskettes with four directory sectors can hold 64 entries. Double-sided diskettes with seven sectors can hold 112 directory entries. Subdirectories are treated like files and there is no limit to the number of subdirectory entries they can hold. (☞ For more on subdirectories, see page 115.) Each 32-byte entry in the directory is divided into eight fields.

Offset	Length	Description
3	8 bytes	System ID (e.g. IBM 2.1)
11	1 word	Number of bytes per sector (e.g. 512, hex 0200)
13	1 byte	Number of sectors per cluster (e.g. 01 or 02)
14	1 word	Number of reserved sectors at beginning: 1 for diskettes
16	1 byte	Number of copies of FAT: 2 for diskettes
17	1 word	Number of root directory entries (e.g. 64 or 112)
19	1 word	Total number of sectors on disk (e.g. 720 for D-9)
21	1 byte	Format ID (e.g. F8, F9, or FC through FF; see page 123)
22	1 word	Number of sectors per FAT (e.g. 1 or 2)
24	1 word	Number of sectors per track (e.g. 8 or 9)
26	1 word	Number of sides (heads) (e.g. 1 or 2)
28	1 word	Number of special reserved sectors

Figure 5-9. The parameters in the boot record

Field	Offset	Description	Size (bytes)	Format
1	0	Filename	8	ASCII characters
2	8	Filename extension	3	ASCII characters
3	11	Attribute	1	Bit coded
4	12	Reserved	10	Unused; zeros
5	22	Time	2	Word, coded
6	24	Date	2	Word, coded
7	26	Starting cluster number	2	Word
8	28	File size	4	Integer

*Figure 5-10. The eight parts of a
directory entry*

The first eight bytes in the directory entry contain the filename, stored in ASCII format. If the filename is less than eight characters, it is filled out to the right with blanks (CHR$(32)). Letters should be upper-case, since lowercase letters will not be properly recognized. Normally, there should not be any blanks embedded in the filename, as in AA BB. Most DOS command programs, such as DEL or COPY, will not recognize filenames with embedded blanks. However, BASIC can work successfully with these filenames, and the DOS services (☞ see Chapters 16 and 17) usually can as well. This capability suggests some useful tricks, such as creating files that cannot be easily erased.

Three codes, used to indicate special situations, may appear in the first byte of the filename field. Completely unused directory entries have hex 00 in the first byte. This makes it possible for DOS to know when there are no further active directory entries, without searching to the end of a directory. This convention began with DOS 2.00 and also applies to later versions, but not to the earlier DOS-1 versions.

If the first byte of the filename field is hex E5, it normally indicates that the file has been erased. However, since the DOS-1 versions did not use the 00 (never-used) code, hex E5 in this field might indicate either that a file has been erased or that the entry has never been used.

When a file is erased, only two things on the disk are affected: The first byte of the filename is set to hex E5 and the file's space allocation chain in the FAT is wiped out (☞ we'll cover this in the section on the FAT). All other directory information about the file is retained, including the rest of its name, its size, and even its starting cluster number. The lost

Subdirectories

There are two types of directories: root directories and subdirectories. The contents and use of each type are essentially the same—both store the names and locations of files on the disk—but their characteristics are different. The root directory (we've just been calling it the directory) has a fixed size and is stored in a fixed location on the disk. A subdirectory is an addition to the root directory, has no fixed size, and can be stored anywhere on the disk. Any disk used with DOS 2.00 or later may use subdirectories.

A subdirectory is stored in the disk's data space, just like any other file. The field format and contents of a subdirectory are identical to those of the root directory, except that a subdirectory is not limited in size. Like an ordinary file, a subdirectory can grow without bounds as long as there is disk space available. Subdirectories can be created and used with any type of disk. However, since subdirectories take up precious data space, they are primarily intended for use with high-capacity hard disks; their use with diskettes is generally avoided.

Subdirectories are always attached to a parent directory, which can be either the root directory or another subdirectory, and can branch from several other levels of directories, forming a tree structure.

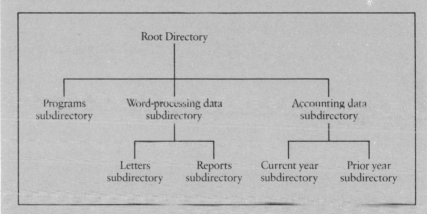

The parent directory has one entry for each of its subdirectories, which is like every other file entry, except that the attribute byte marks the entry as a subdirectory and the file-size field is set to zero. The actual size of the subdirectory is found by tracing its allocation chain through the FAT.

When subdirectories are created, two special entries are placed in them, with "." and ".." as filenames. These act like entries for further subdirectories, but "." actually refers to the present subdirectory itself and ".." refers to its parent directory. The starting cluster number in each of these directory entries gives the location of the subdirectory or its parent. When the starting cluster number is zero, it means that the parent of this directory is the root directory.

If a file is reduced in size, DOS can generally be counted on to release any unused space. However, in the case of subdirectories, clusters of space that are no longer used (because the directory entries that once occupied that space are now erased) will not be released until the entire subdirectory is destroyed.

information can be recovered, with suitably sophisticated methods, provided that the directory entry has not been reused for another file. Be forewarned that whenever a new directory entry is needed, DOS uses the first available entry, quickly recycling an erased file's old entries and making recovery impossible.

The third code that might be found in the filename byte is the period character, hex 2E, which is used to specify a subdirectory (☞ see page 115). If the second byte is also hex 2E, we know that we are looking at the parent directory entry of the current subdirectory, in which case the starting cluster field (field 7) contains the cluster number of the parent directory.

Field 2: The Filename Extension

Directly following the filename is the standard filename extension, stored in ASCII format. It is three bytes long and, like the filename, it is padded with blanks if it is less than the full three-character length. While a filename must have at least one ordinary character in it, the extension can be all blanks. Generally, the same rules apply to the filename extension as apply to the filename.

❑ NOTE: *When the directory contains a volume ID label entry, the filename and extension fields are treated as one combined field of eleven bytes. In this case, embedded blanks are permitted. Normally, lowercase letters are not used in labels, but they can be.*

Field 3: The File Attribute

The third field of the directory entry is one byte long, each bit of which is used to categorize the directory entry. The bits of the attribute byte are individually coded as bits 0 through 7, as shown in Figure 5-11.

Bit 7 6 5 4 3 2 1 0	Value Dec	Hex	Meaning
. . . . 1	1	1	Read-only
. . . . . . 1 .	2	2	Hidden
. . . . . 1 . .	4	4	System
. . . . 1 . . .	8	8	Volume label
. . . 1	16	10	Subdirectory
. . 1	32	20	Archive
. 1	64	40	Unused
1	128	80	Unused

Figure 5-11. The eight file-attribute bits

Bit 0, the low-order bit, marks a file as read-only. In this state, the file is protected from being changed or deleted by any DOS operation. We should point out that the DOS-1 versions ignore this attribute, so while it can provide a worthwhile protection of data, it is not foolproof.

Bits 1 and 2 mark files as either hidden or system files. Files marked as hidden or system or both cannot be seen by ordinary DOS operations, such as the DIR command. Our programs can gain access to such files by setting these attribute bits in the file control block, or FCB (☛ see page 288). The two DOS files IBMBIO.COM and IBMDOS.COM (which may also appear under the names IO.SYS and MSDOS.SYS) are both hidden and system files. There is no particular significance to the system attribute; it exists to perpetuate a feature of CP/M and has absolutely nothing to do with DOS.

Bit 3 marks a directory entry as a label, meaning that the entry holds the disk's volume ID label. A label entry is only properly recognized in the root directory, and it only uses a few of the eight fields available in the entry. The label itself is stored in the filename and extension fields, which are treated as one unified field for this purpose. The size and starting cluster fields are not used, but the date and time fields are.

Bit 4, the subdirectory attribute, is used to identify directory entries which, in turn, identify subdirectories. Since subdirectories are stored on disk like ordinary data files, they need a supporting directory entry. All the directory fields are used for these entries, except for the file-size field, which is zero. The actual size of a subdirectory is found simply by following its space allocation chain in the FAT.

Bit 5, the archive attribute, was created to assist in making backup copies of the many files that can be stored on a hard disk. This bit is off on all files that haven't changed since they were last backed up; the bit is normally on for all diskette files. The archive attribute serves no particularly useful purpose for diskettes.

Field 4: Reserved

This 10-byte area is set aside for possible future uses. All 10 bytes are normally set to hex 00.

Field 5: The Time

Field 5 contains a 2-byte value that marks the time that the file was created or last changed. It is used in conjunction with the date field and the two together can be treated as a single 4-byte unsigned integer. This 4-byte integer can be compared with those in other directory entries for greater-than, less-than, or equal values. The time, by itself, is treated as an unsigned word integer that is built out of the hour, minutes, and seconds using this formula:

$$\text{Time} = \text{Hour} \times 2048 + \text{Minutes} \times 32 + \text{Seconds} \div 2$$

The hour is based on a 24-hour clock, with a value ranging from 0 through 23. Since the 2-byte word used to store the time is one bit too short to store all the seconds, they are stored in units of 2 seconds from 0 through 29; a value of 5, for example, would represent 10 seconds. The time of 11:32:10 would be stored as the value 23557.

Field 6: The Date

Field 6 contains a 2-byte value that marks the date the file was created or last changed. It is used in conjunction with the time field and the two together can be treated as a single 4-byte unsigned integer that can be compared with those in other directory entries for greater-than, less-than, or equal values. The date, by itself, is treated as an unsigned word integer that is built out of the year, month, and day using this formula:

$$\text{Date} = (\text{Year} - 1980) \times 512 + \text{Month} \times 32 + \text{Day}$$

You will notice that this formula compresses the year by subtracting 1980 from it. Thus, the year 1984 will be calculated as a value of 4. Using this formula, a date such as December 12, 1984 will be stored by the formula as 2828:

$$(1984 - 1980) \times 512 + 12 \times 32 + 12 = 2828$$

Although this scheme allows for years up to 2108, the highest year supported by DOS is 2099.

Field 7: The Starting Cluster Number

The seventh field is a 2-byte value that gives the starting cluster number for the file's data space. It acts as the entry point into the file's space allocation chain in the FAT. For files with no space allocated and for volume-label entries, the starting cluster number is zero, rather than the hex FFF value used in the FAT to indicate the end-of-file.

Field 8: The File Size

The last field of a directory entry gives the size of the file in bytes. It is coded as a 4-byte unsigned integer, which allows file sizes to grow very large—much larger in fact than the capacity of our disks.

As far as DOS knows, the size indicated by this field is the true size of a file. However, sometimes this stored value may be larger than the actual file size. For example, some ASCII text files created by word processors mark the true end-of-file with the Ctrl-Z character (CHR$(26), hex 1A). For these files, the file-size attribute may report a larger number, such as the next multiple of 128 bytes. This is a common occurrence in most text-editor programs, which read and write data in large blocks rather than one byte at a time. It is important to point out that when DOS is reading a file for us, it reports the end of the file when it comes to either the end of the file size or the end of the FAT space allocation chain (denoted by hex FFF)—whichever comes first.

The Data Space

All data files and subdirectories (which act much like data files) are stored in the space that occupies the last and largest part of each disk.

Space is given to files on an as-needed basis, one cluster at a time. (Remember, a cluster is one or more consecutive sectors; the number of sectors per cluster is a fixed characteristic of each disk format.) As a file is being created, or when an existing file is extended, the file's allocated space grows. When more space is needed, a cluster is allocated to the file. In DOS versions 1 and 2, the first available cluster is always allocated to the file. Later versions of DOS select clusters by more complicated rules that we won't go into.

Under many circumstances, a file is stored in one contiguous block of space. However, a file may be broken into several noncontiguous blocks, especially when information is added to an existing file, or when a new file is stored in the space left by an erased file. It's not unusual for one file's data to be scattered throughout the disk.

This sort of file fragmentation slows access to the file's data to some degree. Also, it is much harder to "unerase" a file that we have unintentionally erased if it is fragmented, simply because we have to do a lot more searching for the individual sectors that make up the file's data space. But fragmentation has no other effect. In general, programs do not need to be concerned about where on a disk their data is stored. But if you want to know whether a file is fragmented, there are two simple ways to find out. You can use the /V option of the CHKDSK command to test for file fragmentation, or you can use a program such as the Norton Utilities to see a graphic map of the location of each file on your disk.

If your diskette files are fragmented, you can clean them up by copying them to a newly formatted, empty diskette. Naturally, the file can become fragmented again if there is a lot of update activity on the disk. On a hard disk, you can do little to eliminate fragmentation. Don't worry too much about it. We've mentioned it so that you'll understand it, but in practice, a fragmented file is harmless.

Whether you ever look at your fragmented files or not, it will help if you understand how DOS uses the file allocation table (FAT) to allocate disk space, and how the FAT forms a space allocation chain to connect all of the clusters that make up a file.

The File Allocation Table

The file allocation table holds a record that shows how the disk space is utilized. We will make a distinction between how the FAT is organized, which is relatively simple and straightforward, and how it is stored on disk, which is more convoluted.

As we've mentioned, standard disk formats store two copies of the FAT, although there can be more than two copies, or even only one copy. Each copy of the FAT occupies one sector on eight-sector diskettes and two sectors on nine-sector diskettes. With the high-capacity diskette format that we called QD-15, the FAT uses seven sectors.

For most disk formats, DOS writes two copies of the FAT just in case one of them is damaged or unreadable. The CHKDSK program, which tests for most errors that can occur in the FAT and directory, does not even notice if the two FATs are different.

There are two FAT formats: a 12-bit format and a 16-bit format. The 12-bit FAT format is the more common and the more complicated of the two. The 16-bit FAT is used only with disks that exceed the capacity of a 12-bit FAT, such as the AT's 20-megabyte hard disk. We'll discuss the standard 12-bit FAT first, and then explain how the 16-bit FAT differs.

The FAT is organized as a table of up to 4,086 numbers ranging from 0 through 4,095 (hex 0 through FFF), with an entry for each cluster in the data space. The number in each entry indicates the status and use of the cluster that corresponds to the FAT entry. Notice that the range of numbers kept in the FAT table is defined so that it does not exceed three hex digits. This is a key element in how the 12-bit FAT is stored, as we will see shortly.

If the FAT entry is 0, it indicates that the cluster is free and available for use. If the FAT entry is 4,087 (hex FF7) and this FAT entry is not part of any space allocation chain, then the cluster is marked as unusable due to a formatting error; this is also called bad-track marking.

❑ NOTE: *It's worth pausing here to note that there is nothing unusual or alarming about having "bad tracks" marked on a disk, particularly a hard disk. In fact, it is quite common for a hard disk to have a few bad patches on it. For example, the hard disk in the AT that I used to write this book has three small bad-track areas. The disk formatting procedure notices bad tracks and marks them as such in the FAT, as we've just discussed. Later, the bad-track marking tells DOS that these areas should be bypassed. Bad tracks are also common on floppy disks; with a floppy, unlike a hard disk, we have the option of throwing it away and only using perfect disks.*

The clusters are numbered sequentially from 2 to a number that is one greater than the total number of clusters on the disk (☞ see Figure 5-12). A 12-bit FAT entry containing any number between 2 and 4,080 (hex 02 and FF0) indicates that the corresponding cluster is used by a file. A FAT value of 4,095 (hex FFF) indicates that the corresponding cluster contains the last part of the file's data. The values 4,088 through 4,094 (hex FF8 through FFE) may be similarly used, but in my experience, they aren't.

With all of this in mind, we can see that the FAT entries form a *space allocation chain;* the file's directory entry contains the starting cluster number (☞ see page 118) and the FAT entries indicate further clusters used by the file and the end of the file (☞ see Figure 5-13). When a file is erased, all the FAT entries for its space allocation chain are marked as available (set to 0); but the actual file data in the data space is not changed and most of the information in the file's directory entry is maintained.

Although the FAT is organized as a fairly simple table of numeric values, it is stored in a rather convoluted form in order to make the table as compact as possible. To do this, it makes use of some tricks of the 8088's data format, specifically "back-words" storage. For the FAT, simplicity is sacrificed for efficiency.

The range of cluster numbers is defined so that FAT entries are 4,095 (hex FFF) or less. This makes it possible to store each 3-hex-digit entry in 12 bits, or 1½ bytes. The FAT entries are organized in pairs, where each pair

Format	Sectors	Sectors per Cluster	Clusters	Cluster-Number Range
S-8	313	1	313	2 to 314
D-8	630	2	315	2 to 316
S-9	351	1	351	2 to 352
D-9	708	2	354	2 to 355
QD-9	1,422	2	711	2 to 712
QD-15	2,371	1	2,371	2 to 2,372

Figure 5-12. The number of clusters for different DOS formats

		Value		
	FAT Entry	Dec	Hex	Meaning
	0	253	FD	Disk is double-sided, double density, 9 sectors/track
	1	4,094	FFE	Entry unused; *not* available
From directory entry; →	2	3	3	File's next cluster is cluster 3
beginning of file's space allocation chain	3	5	5	File's next cluster is cluster 5
	4	4,087	FF7	Cluster is unusable; bad track
	5	6	6	File's next cluster is cluster 6
	6	4,095	FFF	Last cluster in file, and end of this file's space allocation chain
	7	0	0	Entry unused; available

Figure 5-13. The space allocation chain for one file in the file allocation table

occupies three bytes (0 and 1 occupy the first three bytes, 2 and 3 the next three bytes, and so forth). The three bytes decode by the following pattern: If a pair of FAT entries is hex 123 and 456, then the three bytes containing them would be, in hex, 23 61 45. Reversing the pattern, if the three bytes are AB CD EF, then the two FAT values are DAB and EFC. As we see in Figure 5-12, in formats S-8, S-9, D-8, QD-9 and QD-15, the last cluster number is even and is consequently paired with a dummy entry in the FAT.

This pattern seems curious when we work it out in our terms, but it is quick and efficient when done with machine-language instructions. Given any cluster number, we can find the FAT value by multiplying the cluster number by 3, dividing by 2, and then using the whole number of the result as a displacement into the FAT. By grabbing a word at that address, we have the three hex digits of the FAT entry, plus one extraneous hex digit, which can be removed by any one of several quick machine-language instructions. If the cluster number is even, we discard the high-order digit; if odd, the low-order digit. The value derived from all of this is the next cluster number in the file, unless it's FFF, which indicates the last cluster in the file.

This complex scheme was originally designed for 8-sector diskette formats. It is not quite so ideal when used for other formats, including the 9-sector formats, where the FAT becomes slightly larger than one sector. Overall, though, it is a very tight and efficient plan.

The details we've covered so far are for 12-bit FATs, which can accommodate up to 4,080 clusters. If a disk format has more clusters than that, then we need the 16-bit FAT.

A 16-bit FAT works just the same as a 12-bit one, except it's simpler. The entries in a 16-bit FAT are obviously four bits larger, which allows for a wider range of cluster numbers. Since sixteen bits are exactly two bytes, or one word, a 16-bit FAT doesn't need the convoluted storage arrangement used with a 12-bit FAT. Instead, a 16-bit FAT is a straightforward table of word values, one stored right after another.

The special values for a 16-bit FAT (for such things as bad-track marking) are a logical extension of those used for 12-bit FATs; they just have a high-order hex F added on. For example, the end-of-file value is hex FFFF (instead of FFF) and the bad-cluster value is hex FFF7 (instead of FF7).

As we have said, the actual data clusters are numbered from 2, while each FAT begins with entries 0 and 1. These first two FAT entries, in both 12- and 16-bit formats, are not used to indicate the status of the clusters; instead, they are set aside, so that the very first byte of the FAT can be used as an ID byte, indicating the format of the disk; see Figure 5-14. However, you should not assume that these IDs uniquely identify formats: They don't necessarily. If we considered every disk format in use, we'd find quite a few duplications. Beware.

Our programs can learn the format of a disk by reading and inspecting the FAT ID byte. However, the official way of finding out the format is to use DOS function 27 (hex 1B). ☛ For more information about this function, see page 282.

Special Notes on the FAT

Normally, our programs do not look at or change a disk's FAT; the FAT is left completely under the supervision of DOS. The only exceptions are programs that perform space allocation functions not supported by DOS; for example, programs that recover erased files, such as the Un-Erase program in my Norton Utilities program set.

Format	ID Byte
D-8	FF
S-8	FE
D-9	FD
S-9	FC
QD-9	F9
QD-15	F9
Fixed disk	F8

Figure 5-14. The ID byte values of common disk formats

It is important to note that a FAT can be logically damaged; for example, an allocation chain can be circular, referring back to a previous link in the chain; or two chains can converge on one cluster; or a cluster can be orphaned, meaning that it is marked as in use even though it is not part of any valid allocation chain. Also, an end-of-file marker (hex FFF or FFFF) may be missing. The DOS programs CHKDSK and RECOVER are designed to detect and repair most of these problems, as well as can reasonably be done.

☞ For special notes on the interaction of the space allocation chain in the FAT and DOS's record of a file's size, see page 118.

COMMENTS

Although this chapter has included detailed information for the direct use of the disk itself, including the boot record, the FAT, and the directories, it is not a good idea to use it directly unless you have a compelling reason. In fact, except where completely unavoidable, as in a copy-protection program, it is unwise to incorporate any knowledge of the disk format into your programs. On the whole, the best thing to do is to consider the standard hierarchy of operations and use the highest level of services that can satisfy your needs:

- First choice: Language services (the facilities provided by your programming language, such as BASIC's OPEN and CLOSE statements).

- Second choice: DOS services (described in Chapters 16 and 17).

- Third choice: ROM-BIOS disk services (described in Chapter 10).

- Last choice: Direct control (for example, direct programming of the floppy-disk controller (FDC) through commands issued via ports).

Most disk operations for the PC family can be accomplished quite nicely with the services that your programming language provides. However, there are two obvious circumstances that may call for more exotic methods. One, which we've already mentioned, is when your programming involves the control of a disk on the same level as the control that DOS exercises. This would be called for if you were writing a program similar to DOS's CHKDSK, or to my Norton Utilities. The other circumstance involves copy protection. All copy-protection schemes, in one way or another, involve some variety of unconventional diskette I/O. This usually leads to the use of the ROM-BIOS services, but it may lead to the extreme measure of directly programming the floppy-disk controller.

Copy Protection

There is a variety of commercially available copy-protection schemes, including a quite unsophisticated one that is part of my software set, Access Tools for the IBM/PC. However, you may want to devise your own scheme.

There are dozens of ways to approach copy protection. Perhaps the most common methods involve reformatting the sectors in certain tracks on the disk by using the ROM-BIOS format routines. Since DOS cannot read sectors that do not conform to its specific formats, the DOS COPY program is unable to copy a disk that has an occasional odd sector size interspersed with normal sectors. Naturally, this DOS limitation has inspired a number of companies to produce copy programs that can read and copy sectors of any size, so it is not a particularly effective method of copy protection.

On a more advanced level, there are two special things that are worth noting about copy protection. First, some of the most exotic and unbreakable protection schemes have been based on the discovery of undocumented abilities hidden in the floppy-disk controller (FDC). Second, some protection schemes are intentionally or unintentionally dependent upon the particular characteristics of different diskette drives. Or they may be dependent upon the details of the software control of the drive, which can differ within the PC family. For example, the PCjr drive control software works in a very different way from that of the PC and XT. The AT's software is also different. So a copy-protected program may function on one model of computer but fail to function on another model, even though the copy protection has not been tampered with. If you use a copy-protection scheme, you should keep this in mind.

There is no particular additional guidance that I can give you here, except to remind you that variety and ingenuity are the keys to successful copy protection.

6

Keyboard Basics

Tis chapter is mainly about the standard IBM PC keyboard, although we have scattered a few comments about the slightly different PCjr and AT keyboards throughout the text. We avoid a thorough discussion of the specialty models of the IBM PC, such as the 3270 PC, the AT, and the PCjr, as well as some non-IBM members of the extended PC family, because they have keyboards that do not exactly match the standard PC keyboard. In most cases, these nonstandard keyboards are either enhanced or scaled-down versions of the PC standard. For example, IBM moved a few keys around on the AT and added one new key and some fancier hardware, but fortunately they didn't change the operating characteristics much. The PCjr has fewer keys than the standard PC keyboard, yet it, too, manages a convincing simulation of the standard keyboard. Fortunately, this practice of matching or simulating the regular PC keyboard seems to be standard among the extended PC family members, making the slight differences between them of little concern to programmers.

The first part of this chapter explains how the keyboard interacts with the computer on a hardware and software level. In the second part, we'll see how the ROM-BIOS treats keyboard information and makes it available to our programs. ☛ If you plan to play around with keyboard control, I urge you to consider the recommendations on page 139 first, and not apply the information in this chapter to your programs unless there is a particular reason to do so. One example of an appropriate use for the information here is to create a program that modifies the operation of the keyboard, such as the popular and highly regarded ProKey keyboard-enhancer program. ☛ If you have any such application in mind, take a look at the ROM-BIOS keyboard services in Chapter 11.

THE KEYBOARD OPERATION

The PC keyboard contains the 8048 keyboard controller, which performs a variety of jobs, all of which help cut down on system overhead. The main duty of the 8048 is to watch the keys and report to the ROM-BIOS whenever a key has been pressed or released. If any key remains pressed for longer than a half second, the 8048 sends out a repeat action at specific intervals. The 8048 controller also has limited diagnostic and error-checking capabilities, and has a buffer that can store 20 key actions should the main computer be unable to accept them (this rarely happens). **AT** The AT model uses a different keyboard-controller chip, the 8042, but it performs essentially the same functions as the 8048.

Keyboard-Enhancer Programs

Thanks to the flexible software design of the PC, it's possible to create programs that manipulate the keyboard. There are many programs of this type available, but the best known and most popular is probably ProKey.

Keyboard-enhancer programs monitor the data that comes in from the keyboard and change it in any way we want. Typically, these programs are fed instructions, called keyboard macros, that tell them what keystrokes to look for and what changes to make. The change might involve suppressing a keystroke (acting as if it never happened), replacing one keystroke with another, or replacing one keystroke with a long series of keystrokes. The most common use of keyboard macros is to abbreviate phrases we commonly type; for example, we might instruct ProKey to convert a key combination, such as Alt-S, into the salutation we use in our correspondence, such as *Sincerely yours*. We can also use keyboard macros to abbreviate program commands so that a three- or four-keystroke command can be condensed to a single keystroke.

Keyboard enhancers work by combining the powers of two special facilities—one that's part of DOS and one that's part of the PC's ROM-BIOS. The DOS facility allows the enhancer program to remain resident in the computer's memory, quietly monitoring the operation of the computer while the ordinary control of the computer is turned over to a conventional program, such as a word processor. The ROM-BIOS facility makes it possible for programs to divert the stream of keyboard information so that it can be inspected and changed before it is passed on to a program. A program like ProKey uses the DOS "resident program" facility to stay active in memory while other programs are run; then it uses the ROM-BIOS keyboard-monitoring facility to preview keyboard data and change it as needed.

Every time we press or release one of the keys on the PC keyboard, the keyboard circuits generate a 1-byte number, called a scan code, that uniquely identifies the keystroke. The keyboard produces a different scan code for each key press and key release. Whenever we press a key, the scan-code byte contains a number ranging from 1 through 83 (on a standard PC keyboard). When we release the same key, the keyboard generates a scan code 128 (hex 80) higher than the key-press scan code, by setting bit 7 of the scan-code byte to 1. For example, when we press the letter Z, the keyboard generates a scan code of 44; when we release it, the keyboard generates a scan code of 172 (44 + 128). ☞ The keyboard diagram in Figure 6-1 shows the standard keyboard keys and their associated scan codes.

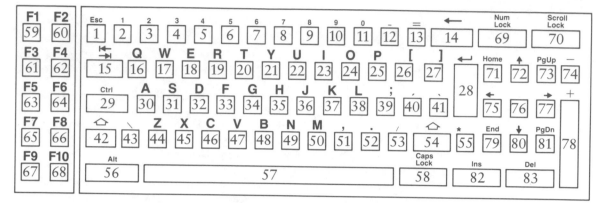

*Figure 6-1. The standard PC keyboard
layout and scan codes*

As we type, the keyboard doesn't know the meaning of the keystrokes; it merely reports the actions that take place. It is the job of the
ROM-BIOS keyboard routines to translate the key actions into meaningful
information that programs can use. As we will see, the keyboard communicates with the ROM-BIOS by way of ports and interrupts.

Communicating with the ROM-BIOS

Each time any key on the PC keyboard is either pressed or released,
the action is reported to the PC's ROM-BIOS as an interrupt 9, the keyboard-action interrupt. The interrupt 9 calls an interrupt-handling subroutine, which responds by reading port 96 (hex 60) to find out which
key action took place. The awaiting scan code is then returned to the
BIOS where the keyboard service routines translate it into a 2-byte code.
The low-order byte of this code usually contains the ASCII value of the
key, and the high-order byte usually contains the keyboard scan code.
Special keys, such as the function keys and the numeric keypad keys,
have a zero in the low-order byte with the keyboard scan code in the
high-order byte (☛ more about this later, on page 134).

The BIOS routines then place the translated codes in a queue, which
is kept in low memory in location 0000:041E. The codes are stored here
until they are requested by a program, such as DOS or BASIC, that expects to read keyboard input.

Translating the Scan Codes

The scan-code translation job is moderately complicated because the
IBM keyboard has several shift options that can change the meaning of a
key press. If we press the Shift key and a *c* we get a capital *C;* if we press

the Ctrl key and a *c* we generate the Ctrl-C or "break" signal. These are both examples of different shift states. We can change the shift state while we type by pressing the Shift key, the Alt key, or the Ctrl key. When one of these keys is pressed and not released, the ROM-BIOS recognizes that all subsequent key actions will be influenced by that shift state.

The Shift and Toggle Keys

In addition to the normal Shift key, the Ctrl key, and the Alt key, there are two toggle keys that also affect the keyboard's shifting mechanism: the Caps Lock key and the Num Lock key. When Caps Lock is activated, it reverses the meaning of the Shift key for the alphabet keys, but not for the rest of the keys. The Num Lock key switches between numbers and cursor-control functions on the numeric keypad.

The shift-key or toggle-key status information is kept by the ROM-BIOS in low-memory locations (hex 417 and 418), where we can use or change it. When we press a shift key or a toggle key, the ROM-BIOS sets a specific bit in one of these two bytes. As soon as the ROM-BIOS receives the release scan code of a shift key, it switches the status bit back to its original shift state.

Whenever the ROM-BIOS receives a scan code for an ordinary keystroke, such as the letter *z* or a right arrow key, it first checks the shift state, then translates the key into the appropriate 2-byte code. (☞ We'll discuss the status bytes in more detail on page 136.)

The Combination Keys

While the ROM-BIOS routine is translating scan codes, it constantly checks for certain shift-key combinations; specifically, the Ctrl-Alt-Del, Shift-PrtSc, Ctrl-Num Lock, and Ctrl-Break combinations. These four command-like key actions cause the ROM-BIOS to act immediately and perform a specific task, rather than buffering the characters.

Ctrl-Alt-Del causes the computer to reboot, or reload the command program. Ctrl-Alt-Del is probably used more often than any other key combination. It works dependably as long as the keyboard interrupt service is working. If the interrupt service is not working, there are two possible reasons: Either the keyboard interrupt vector (in memory locations hex 36 through 39) has been changed or a clear interrupt instruction (CLI), which disables interrupts, has been performed without an accompanying start interrupt instruction (STI). In either of these cases, the only recourse you have is to turn the power off, wait a few seconds, and then turn it on again; the power-on program resets all interrupt vectors and services.

□ NOTE: *Some programs may leave the interrupts disabled by mistake. This is not possible on the PCjr since the keyboard interrupt is a non-maskable interrupt (NMI).*

Shift-PrtSc writes the screen contents to the standard printer device. The operation is done on a primitive BIOS level through interrupt 5. To redirect the printer output to different devices (which is not a normal thing to do), you must change the PrtSc interrupt vector to point to a new subroutine. The GRAPHICS.COM routine in DOS 2.00 and subsequent versions circumvents the PrtSc operation by first checking the video mode that is in effect. If it turns out to be a graphics mode, a routine takes over and sends the screen output, pixel-by-pixel, to an IBM-compatible graphics printer (if it's attached). Otherwise, the conventional print-screen operation is called and the information is sent out character-by-character.

Ctrl-Num Lock suspends operation of the program until another keystroke occurs.

Ctrl-Break causes the computer to issue a "break" signal by generating an interrupt 27. If our programs have established a new interrupt 27 handler, they can intercept the break interrupt and act on it (or ignore it) according to the requirements of the program. If our programs don't change the interrupt routine, DOS will use its default routine, and shut down the program.

These are the only key combinations that are specially meaningful to the ROM-BIOS. When an invalid combination is reported from the keyboard, the ROM-BIOS simply ignores it and moves on to work on the next sensible key action.

There are two more things about the PC keyboard that we need to discuss before passing on to the details of keyboard coding: repeat key action and duplicated keys.

Repeat Key Action

The PC keyboard features automatic repeat key action, a process called *typematic* by IBM. The circuitry inside the PC keyboard watches how long each key is pressed, and if a key is held down more than half a second, it automatically generates repeat key actions ten times per second. The typematic action is reported as successive key-press scan codes, without the intervening key-release codes. This makes it possible for a clever interrupt 9 handler to distinguish between actual key presses and typematic action. However, the ROM-BIOS does not always distinguish between the two. The ROM-BIOS keyboard-handling routine treats each automatic repeat key action as though the key had actually been pressed, and interprets the key accordingly. For example, if we press and hold the

A key long enough for the keyboard to begin generating successive key-press signals, then the ROM-BIOS will create a series of *A*s to be passed on to whatever program is reading keyboard data. On the other hand, if we press and hold a shift key—as we often do—the ROM-BIOS will recognize the first shift-press signal and put us in the shifted state. But it will ignore the subsequent shift-press signals generated by the auto-repeat mechanism until it gets a shift-release signal. All this boils down to the simple fact that the ROM-BIOS treats repeat key actions in a sensible way, acting on them or ignoring them as needed.

Duplicated Keys

Another thing that we should be aware of is that there are duplicate keys on the keyboard. There are, for example, two asterisks: one on the upper row, above the 8 key, and one on the right, on the PrtSc key. There are also duplicate periods, pluses, minuses, and digits (0 through 9), and two seemingly identical Shift keys.

The ROM-BIOS, quite sensibly, translates these duplicate keys into the same character codes; for example, either asterisk key gets us the asterisk character, CHR$(42). The ROM-BIOS also lets our programs tell the difference between them, in case it matters. The duplicated character keys retain their scan codes in the high-order byte; our programs need only check the scan code in this byte to see which key was pressed. As for the two Shift keys, each one sets a different bit in the shift-status byte (location hex 417). If we want our programs to know which Shift key was pressed, we need to look at the appropriate bit value. (☛ See the discussion of location hex 417 on pages 52 and 136.)

Generally, it is best for programs to ignore the distinction between duplicate keys, although some of the most sophisticated programs make use of this information for special purposes. Notable among them are Microsoft's Flight Simulator and Ashton-Tate's Framework.

Entering ASCII Codes Directly

We should mention that the PC keyboard, in conjunction with the ROM-BIOS, provides us with an alternate way to enter nearly any ASCII character code. This is done by holding down the Alt key and then entering the decimal ASCII character code from the numeric keypad on the right side of the keyboard. This method allows any of the ASCII codes to be entered, from CHR$(1) through CHR$(255). The only ASCII code that can't be keyed in directly is CHR$(0), because it is reserved to signal non-ASCII characters, such as cursor-control and function keys. ☛ In the next section we'll discuss this in more detail.

KEYBOARD DATA FORMAT

Once a keyboard action has been translated, it is stored as a pair of bytes in the ROM-BIOS buffer. We call the low-order byte the *main byte* and the high-order byte the *auxiliary byte*.

The ASCII Keys

When the main byte is an ASCII character value from CHR$(1) to CHR$(255), we know either that one of the standard keyboard characters was pressed, or that an extended ASCII character was entered using the Alt-number method mentioned above. (☛ See Appendix C for the complete ASCII character set.) For these ASCII characters, the auxiliary byte contains the keyboard scan code of the pressed key. Under ordinary circumstances, this scan code has no use (the BASIC INKEY$ function does not report the auxiliary byte). However, the auxiliary byte can be used to distinguish between duplicate keyboard characters with different scan codes. When ASCII characters have been entered "artificially" by the Alt-number method, the scan code in the auxiliary byte is zero.

The Special Keys

When the main byte is zero (CHR$(0)), it means that a special key is being reported. The special keys include function keys, shifted function keys, cursor-control keys such as Home and End, and many of the Ctrl and Alt key combinations. When any of these keys are pressed by themselves or in combination with other keys, the auxiliary byte contains a single value that represents the key press. This makes it possible for us to define our own special key codes, without interfering with the extended ASCII characters (CHR$(128) through CHR$(255)). All of the 97 special key values are arranged in Figure 6-2 in a rough mixture of logical and numerical order.

Auxiliary-Byte Value (dec)	Keys Pressed	Auxiliary-Byte Value (dec)	Keys Pressed	Auxiliary-Byte Value (dec)	Keys Pressed
59	F1	110	Alt-F7	44	Alt-Z
60	F2	111	Alt-F8	45	Alt-X
61	F3	112	Alt-F9	46	Alt-C
62	F4	113	Alt-F10	47	Alt-V
63	F5			48	Alt-B
64	F6	120	Alt-1	49	Alt-N
65	F7	121	Alt-2	50	Alt-M
66	F8	122	Alt-3		
67	F9	123	Alt-4	3	Would-be null
68	F10	124	Alt-5		character
		125	Alt-6		CHR$(0)
84	Shift-F1	126	Alt-7		
85	Shift-F2	127	Alt-8		
86	Shift-F3	128	Alt-9	15	Reverse Tab
87	Shift-F4	129	Alt-0		(Shift-Tab)
88	Shift-F5	130	Alt-Hyphen		
89	Shift-F6	131	Alt- =	71	Home
90	Shift-F7			72	Up arrow
91	Shift-F8	16	Alt-Q	73	PgUp
92	Shift-F9	17	Alt-W		
93	Shift-F10	18	Alt-E	75	Left arrow
		19	Alt-R		
94	Ctrl-F1	20	Alt-T	77	Right arrow
95	Ctrl-F2	21	Alt-Y		
96	Ctrl-F3	22	Alt-U	79	End
97	Ctrl-F4	23	Alt-I	80	Down arrow
98	Ctrl-F5	24	Alt-O	81	PgDn
99	Ctrl-F6	25	Alt-P	82	Insert
100	Ctrl-F7			83	Delete
101	Ctrl-F8	30	Alt-A		
102	Ctrl-F9	32	Alt-S	114	Echo
103	Ctrl-F10	32	Alt-D		(Ctrl-PrtSc)
		33	Alt-F	115	Ctrl-Left arrow
104	Alt-F1	34	Alt-G	116	Ctrl-Right
105	Alt-F2	35	Alt-H		arrow
106	Alt-F3	36	Alt-J	117	Ctrl-End
107	Alt-F4	37	Alt-K	118	Ctrl-PgDn
108	Alt-F5	38	Alt-L	119	Ctrl-Home
109	Alt-F6			132	Ctrl-PgUp

Figure 6-2. The auxiliary byte value of the 97 special keys on the standard IBM PC keyboard. The main byte value is always 0.

The codes for the complete set of characters and special keys are generated by the ROM-BIOS, but different programming languages vary in the way they handle the codes. BASIC, for example, takes a mixed approach to the special keys. When we use ordinary input statements, BASIC hands over the regular ASCII characters to the BIOS and filters out any special keys. Some of these keys can be acted on with the ON KEY statement, but we can use the BASIC INKEY$ function to get directly to the ROM-BIOS coding for keyboard characters and find out immediately what special key was pressed. If the INKEY$ function returns a 1-byte string, it is reporting an ordinary or extended ASCII keyboard character. If INKEY$ returns a 2-byte string, the first byte in the string is the ROM-BIOS's main byte and will always be CHR$(0); the second byte is the auxiliary byte and will indicate which special key was pressed.

KEYBOARD CONTROL

The keyboard operation and keyboard data collection that is supervised by the ROM-BIOS makes use of a data area in low memory, from hex 417 through 43D, hex 471 and 472, hex 480 to 483, and for the PCjr only, hex 412 and 485 through 488. Our programs can make use of these locations to check the keyboard status or to modify the keyboard operation. Now we'll discuss the locations that are useful for our programs to read and the locations that are safe to change.

The Status Bytes

We'll begin with the two standard keyboard status bytes, at locations hex 417 (shown in Figure 6-3) and 418 (shown in Figure 6-4). These status bytes are coded with individually meaningful bits that indicate which shift keys and toggle keys are active. All the standard models of the PC family have these two bytes. **JR** Currently, the only individual difference between the models is bit 2 of byte 2. This bit, called the click bit, is unique to the PCjr. The other aspects of the bit format are common to all standard PC models.

The Insert State

The ROM-BIOS keeps track of the insert state in bit 7 of byte 1. Every program that I know of ignores this bit and keeps its own record of whether the insert state is on or off, so although it is possible, it is not a standard practice to use the ROM-BIOS insert-status bit in our programs.

Bit 7 6 5 4 3 2 1 0	Meaning
X	Insert state: 1 = active; 0 = inactive
. X	Caps Lock: 1 = active; 0 = inactive
. . X	Num Lock: 1 = active; 0 = inactive
. . . X	Scroll Lock: 1 = active; 0 = inactive
. . . . X . . .	Alt shift: 1 = active (Alt depressed); 0 = inactive
. . . . . X . .	Ctrl shift: 1 = active (Ctrl depressed); 0 = inactive
. . . . . . X .	Normal shift: 1 = active (left Shift depressed); 0 = inactive
. . . . X	Normal shift: 1 = active (right Shift depressed); 0 = inactive

*Figure 6-3. The coding of the first keyboard
status byte, at location hex 417*

The Caps-Lock State

Many programmers force the Caps-Lock state to be active by setting bit 6 of byte 1 on. This can confuse or irritate some program users,
so I don't recommend it. However, it works reliably and there is plenty of
precedent for using this trick.

The Keyboard-Hold State

The keyboard-hold state is an interesting feature of the PC although
it has no practical relationship to our programs. As we mentioned before,
one of the special key combinations that the keyboard BIOS monitors is

Bit 7 6 5 4 3 2 1 0	Meaning
X	1 = Ins depressed
. X	1 = Caps Lock depressed
. . X	1 = Num Lock depressed
. . . X	1 = Scroll Lock depressed
. . . . X . . .	1 = hold state active (Ctrl-Num Lock)
. . . . . X . .	1 = PCjr keyboard click active
. . . . . . 0 .	Not used
. . . . 0	Not used

*Figure 6-4. The coding of the second
keyboard status byte, at location hex 418*

Ctrl-Num Lock. When the BIOS detects the Ctrl-Num Lock combination, it goes into a state known as keyboard hold by setting bit 3 in status byte 1. During keyboard hold, the BIOS program waits until a printable key is pressed; it doesn't return control of the computer to whatever program is running until this happens. This feature is used to suspend the operation of the computer.

During keyboard hold, all interrupts are handled normally. For example, if the disk drive generated an interrupt (signaling the completion of a disk operation), the disk interrupt handler would receive the interrupt and process it normally. But, when the interrupt handler finished working, it would pass control back to whatever was happening when the interrupt took place—which would be that endless do-nothing loop inside the keyboard BIOS. So, during the keyboard hold, the computer can respond to external interrupts but programs are normally completely suspended. The keyboard BIOS continues to handle interrupts that signal key actions, and when it detects a normal keystroke (for example, the Spacebar or a function key, but not just a shift key), it ends the keyboard hold, finally returning control to whatever program was running and letting it continue.

The keyboard-hold state is of no practical use to us in programming, except that it provides a standard way for users of our programs to suspend the program's operation.

Be aware that the keyboard-hold state is not "bullet-proof." It is possible for a program to continue working through the keyboard hold by acting on an external interrupt, such as the clock-tick interrupt. If a program really wanted to avoid being put on hold, it could set up an interrupt handler that would work through the hold state, or it could simply turn the hold state off whenever it was turned on.

The Toggle-Key State

Notice that bits 4 through 7 in each byte refer to the same keys. In the first byte, the bits show the current state of the toggle keys; in the second byte, they show whether the corresponding toggle key is depressed.

You may read the status of any of these bits to your heart's content, but few, if any, are likely to be useful to your programs. With the partial exception of controlling the Caps-Lock state, I don't think it's wise to change any of the shift-state bits (bits 4 through 6 of byte 1). And it is potentially very disruptive to change any of the key-is-pressed bits (bits 0 through 3 of byte 1; bits 4 through 7 of byte 2).

| Interrupt | | Origin of Interrupt | Use |
Dec	Hex		
9	9	Keyboard	Signals keyboard action
22	16	ROM-BIOS	Invokes standard BIOS keyboard services (see Chapter 11)
27	1B	ROM-BIOS	Generates an interrupt when break-key combination is pressed under BIOS control; a routine is invoked if we create it
35	23	DOS	If we create it, an interrupt routine is invoked when break-key combination is pressed under DOS control

Figure 6-5. The interrupts related to keyboard action

COMMENTS

If you wish to gain a deeper understanding of the PC's keyboard operation, study the ROM-BIOS program listing in the IBM Technical Reference manual. When you do this, be careful to avoid making a simple mistake that is common when anyone first sets out to study the ROM-BIOS, particularly the interrupts used by the ROM-BIOS. The ROM-BIOS provides two different interrupts for the keyboard: one that responds to keyboard interrupts (interrupt 9) and collects keyboard data into the low memory buffer, and one that responds to an interrupt requesting keyboard services (interrupt 22, hex 16) and passes data from the low memory buffer to DOS and our programs. It is very easy to confuse the operation of these two interrupts, and it is just as easy to further confuse them with the break-key interrupts, 27 and 35 (hex 1B and 23). The table in Figure 6-5 lists the keyboard interrupts.

A general theme running throughout this book advises you not to play fast and loose, but to play by the rules. This means, again, to write programs that are general to the IBM PC family rather than tied to the quirks of any one model, and to write programs that use official means, such as the ROM-BIOS services to manipulate data, instead of direct hardware programming. These rules apply to keyboard programming as much as they do to any other type of programming.

HOW THE PCjr IS DIFFERENT

The PCjr is designed to mimic, as closely as possible, the operation of the original 83-key PC. But as we can see in Figure 6-6, the Junior's native keyboard has only 62 keys, which means that it does not exactly match the PC keyboard. Resolving this problem has resulted in some clever keyboard fakery.

The PCjr has 61 keys in common with the PC, plus one new key, the Fn (function) key. Each of the 22 missing keys is mimicked in one way or another by various key combinations on the PCjr keyboard. However, it's not quite as easy as it sounds because the PCjr equivalents of PC keyboard actions are not particularly straightforward (☞ see Figure 6-7).

The PCjr also has five special key combinations that are unique to it and have no equivalent in the PC. These are listed in Figure 6-8. The fifth one, Shift-Fn-Esc, is rarely mentioned in the Junior's documentation.

PCjr Keyboard Operation

The PC keyboard stages of operation that we outlined on page 128 are followed closely by the PCjr. However, since the Junior's keyboard is different, an entirely new (but familiar) layer of operations has been added up front.

Each PCjr key action, like the PC key actions, causes an interrupt, but it's a special one: interrupt 2, the non-maskable interrupt (NMI). This in turn calls interrupt hex 48, which translates the 62-key scan codes into their corresponding 83-key scan codes. The interrupt hex 48 routine also generates an interrupt 9 (simulating a PC keyboard interrupt) and everything follows from there, as close to the PC standard as is possible, with the ROM-BIOS translating the PC action codes into their end meanings.

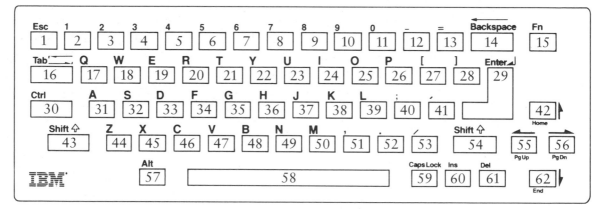

Figure 6-6. The IBM PCjr keyboard layout and scan codes

PC Key	PCjr Equivalent
F1 through F10	Fn key, followed by 1 through 0
|	Alt-[
\	Alt-/
~	Alt-]
`	Alt-'
PrtSc	Fn-P
* (on PrtSc key)	Alt-. (not the same as Shift-8 asterisk)
Ctrl-PrtSc (echo)	Fn-E
Num Lock	Alt-Fn-N
Ctrl-Num Lock (pause)	Fn-Q
Scroll Lock	Fn-S
Break	Fn-B
Home	Fn-Up arrow
Ctrl-Home	Ctrl-Fn-Up arrow
PgUp	Fn-Left arrow
Ctrl-PgUp	Ctrl-Fn-Up arrow
5 (on numeric keypad)	No replacement
End	Fn-Down arrow
Ctrl-End	Ctrl Fn-Down arrow
PgDn	Fn-Right arrow
Ctrl-PgDn	Ctrl-Fn-Right arrow
- (on numeric keypad)	Fn-Hyphen
+ (on numeric keypad)	Fn- =

*Figure 6-7. The PCjr key equivalents
of the 22 missing PC keys*

Key Combination	Use
Ctrl-Alt-Left arrow	Shifts display screen left
Ctrl-Alt-Right arrow	Shifts display screen right
Ctrl-Alt-Caps Lock	Turns keyboard clicking on and off
Ctrl-Alt-Ins	Invokes diagnostics programs
Shift-Fn-Esc	Makes digit keys act as function keys

*Figure 6-8. Special key combinations
unique to the PCjr*

Bit 7 6 5 4 3 2 1 0	Meaning
X	Function flag
. X	Signals break-key action (Fn-B)
. . X	Function pending: Fn depressed
. . . X	Function lock: makes numeric keys function keys
. . . . X . . .	Controls typematic repeat-key action: 0 = enable; 1 = disable
. . . . . X . .	Controls full- or half-speed repeat-key action: 0 = half speed, 1 = full speed
. . . . . . X .	Controls longer delay before starting repeat action: 0 = enable, 1 = disable
. . . . X	Signals that repeat key is due to be generated

Figure 6-9. The coding of the PCjr keyboard status byte at location hex 488

The reason why all this up-front processing is necessary is because the Junior's keyboard has no 8048 microprocessor to help it out. The PC keyboard is smart enough to be able to store several key actions, which makes it practical to temporarily mask off the keyboard-action interrupt whenever other parts of the computer need attention. The PCjr doesn't have this ability, so its keyboard-action interrupt is more urgent and supersedes all other interrupts.

One of the biggest differences between the Junior and its more powerful relatives is that the ROM-BIOS manages the operation of both the keyboard and the disk drive. A conflict arises because the ROM-BIOS favors the disk drive, since the disks have no direct memory access. Consequently, if the disk drive is in operation, the entire system is masked and keyboard input can't take place (asynchronous communications through the serial port can't take place, either).

The PCjr Keyboard Status Byte

The PCjr has a third keyboard status byte in addition to the two standard status bytes mentioned earlier. It is located at memory address hex 488. This byte is peculiar to the operation of the PCjr's 62-key keyboard.

The meaning of the individual bits in the status byte are shown in Figure 6-9. Generally, you will gain nothing by reading or changing these bits, but you should know that we can suppress the typematic (the repeat-key operation) by setting bit 3 to 1. Additionally, we can double the time-repeat or begin-repeating mechanisms by setting bits 2 and 1 to 1. If you want to experiment and suppress key repetition on a PCjr, you can insert your DOS utilities disk and try entering these commands (this will only work on a PCjr):

```
DEBUG
F 0:488 L 1 08
```

PCjr Programming Recommendations

The Junior keyboard is designed to emulate a full PC keyboard, and it is clearly intended to be replaced or augmented by other keyboard-like devices, such as a mouse or a full keyboard. This design makes it particularly shortsighted to integrate the peculiarities of the PCjr keyboard into our programs.

However, for one exception, I would recommend that your programs take the peculiarities of the Junior keyboard into account: when you are selecting which special keys to use in a program. Many programs created for the original PC had their key use (especially function-key use) fine-tuned to the full PC keyboard. With the emergence of the PCjr keyboard, it is wise to rethink key selection because the two keyboards are so different. You might decide to choose the best use for either the Junior or the PC, to compromise between the two, or to adjust the program's operation to the machine it is working on. (☛ See page 60 for how to find the machine ID.) The choice you make depends on the scope and the potential market of your program.

HOW THE AT IS DIFFERENT

The AT's keyboard also differs from the standard PC keyboard. In contrast with the PCjr keyboard, the differences in the AT keyboard that are visible to the user and to our programs are very slight. However, as far as the hardware and BIOS are concerned, the AT keyboard is similar to the PCjr keyboard in that it does not actually function like the PC keyboard, but rather is made to simulate it. Since the internal differences in the AT keyboard are essentially invisible to our programs, we won't need to cover them in much detail.

The AT keyboard layout is almost the same as that of the original PC keyboard, with a few keys repositioned and one key added. The repositioning of some of the keys doesn't call for any changes in the way we program for keyboard use or in our selection of keys to use, but it is worth noting that one key that is used very heavily for program control, the Esc key, has been moved to an entirely new location, from the top left area to the top right area—a real nuisance for anyone who has to use both the PC and the AT keyboards.

The one new key on the AT keyboard is the Sys Req key. This key has no use *within* the operation of any program. Instead, it was created to activate switching between programming system tasks when the AT is working in a multitasking mode and using the special capabilities of the AT's 286 microprocessor. This is a hands-off key for our PC programs.

The hardware link between the AT and the AT keyboard is two-way, so that the keyboard can send information to the AT and the AT can send commands back to the keyboard, including commands to set the keyboard indicator lights. It would be very foolish of us to fiddle with these keyboard-control commands.

It is worth noting that French, German, Spanish, Italian, and British variations on the American-oriented AT keyboard were introduced at the same time as the AT itself.

Second-guessing IBM's future moves is a very risky business, but it is my opinion that the AT keyboard layout (and its international variations) will become and remain the new standard for all future PC-family products introduced by IBM. Whether or not this happens isn't of much importance to us here, though, because from a programming point of view, the AT keyboard is not truly different from the PC keyboard (unlike the PCjr keyboard, which does have some truly practical differences).

7

Sound Generation

A ll standard members of the PC family are able to create simple sounds using the computer's programmable timer chip (the 8253-5) and the computer's built-in speaker. **JR** The PCjr also has extended sound capabilities that include a special sound-generating chip, additional sound sources, and additional sound outputs. Since these features are unique to the PCjr, we'll save a brief discussion of them for the last part of the chapter and devote the first part to the sound features that are universal to the PC family.

To understand how to make sounds on our computers, we need to know some of the basic principles of sound, which we'll outline here.

THE PHYSICS OF SOUND

Sounds are simply regular pulses or vibrations in air pressure. Sound is produced when air particles are set into motion by a vibrating source. When the vibrating source pushes out, it compresses the air particles around it. As it pulls in, the pressure release pulls the particles apart. A vibration composed of both the pressing and the pulling actions causes air particles to bump into each other. This motion begins a chain reaction that carries the vibration through the air away from the original source. Such a motion is called a sound wave.

The speaker in the IBM PCs is made to vibrate by the electrical impulses sent to it by the computer. Since computers normally deal with binary numbers, the voltages they produce are either high or low. Every transition from one voltage state to another either pushes the speaker cone out or relaxes it. A sound is produced when the voltage to the speaker goes from low to high to low again, causing the speaker to move out, then in. This single vibration, consisting of a pulse out and a pulse in, is called a cycle and is measured in hertz (a hertz is simply one cycle per second). Through the PC speaker, a single cycle of sound is heard as a click. A continuous sound is produced when a number of cycles per second are sent to the speaker. As the cycles per second increase, the clicks blend together and become a tone of a certain frequency. For example, if we pulse the speaker in and out 261.63 times a second (that is, at a rate of 261.63 hertz), we hear the musical note known as middle C.

The average person can hear sounds ranging from 20 to 20,000 hertz. The IBM PC can generate sounds through its speaker at frequencies that could theoretically range from about 18 to over a million hertz, far beyond the range of human hearing. To give this frequency range some perspective, compare it to an average human voice, which has a range of only 125 to 1,000 hertz.

Note	Frequency	Note	Frequency	Note	Frequency	Note	Frequency
C_0	16.35	C_2	65.41	C_4	261.63	C_6	1046.50
$C_{\#0}$	17.32	$C_{\#2}$	69.30	$C_{\#4}$	277.18	$C_{\#6}$	1108.73
D_0	18.35	D_2	73.42	D_4	293.66	D_6	1174.66
$D_{\#0}$	19.45	$D_{\#2}$	77.78	$D_{\#4}$	311.13	$D_{\#6}$	1244.51
E_0	20.60	E_2	82.41	E_4	329.63	E_6	1328.51
F_0	21.83	F_2	87.31	F_4	349.23	F_6	1396.91
$F_{\#0}$	23.12	$F_{\#2}$	92.50	$F_{\#4}$	369.99	$F_{\#6}$	1479.98
G_0	24.50	G_2	98.00	G_4	392.00	G_6	1567.98
$G_{\#0}$	25.96	$G_{\#2}$	103.83	$G_{\#4}$	415.30	$G_{\#6}$	1661.22
A_0	27.50	A_2	110.00	A_4	440.00	A_6	1760.00
$A_{\#0}$	29.14	$A_{\#2}$	116.54	$A_{\#4}$	466.16	$A_{\#6}$	1864.66
B_0	30.87	B_2	123.47	B_4	493.88	B_6	1975.53
C_1	32.70	C_3	130.81	C_5	523.25	C_7	2093.00
$C_{\#1}$	34.65	$C_{\#3}$	138.59	$C_{\#5}$	554.37	$C_{\#7}$	2217.46
D_1	36.71	D_3	146.83	D_5	587.33	D_7	2349.32
$D_{\#1}$	38.89	$D_{\#3}$	155.56	$D_{\#5}$	622.25	$D_{\#7}$	2489.02
E_1	41.20	E_3	164.81	E_5	659.26	E_7	2637.02
F_1	43.65	F_3	174.61	F_5	698.46	F_7	2793.83
$F_{\#1}$	46.25	$F_{\#3}$	185.00	$F_{\#5}$	739.99	$F_{\#7}$	2959.96
G_1	49.00	G_3	196.00	G_5	783.99	G_7	3135.96
$G_{\#1}$	51.91	$G_{\#3}$	207.65	$G_{\#5}$	830.61	$G_{\#7}$	3322.44
A_1	55.00	A_3	220.00	A_5	880.00	A_7	3520.00
$A_{\#1}$	58.27	$A_{\#3}$	233.08	$A_{\#5}$	932.33	$A_{\#7}$	3729.31
B_1	61.74	B_3	246.94	B_5	987.77	B_7	3951.07
						C_8	4186.01

Note: Equal Tempered Chromatic Scale; A4 = 440
American Standard pitch—adopted by the American Standards Association in 1936

Figure 7-1. Eight octaves of musical note frequencies

The speaker that comes with the standard IBM personal computers has no volume control and is not really intended for accurate sound reproduction. As a result, different frequencies will produce different effects; some may sound louder than others and some may have a more accurate pitch. This fluctuation is a by-product of the speaker design, and is not something we can control.

HOW THE COMPUTER PRODUCES SOUND

We can generate sounds through the speaker in two ways, using one or both of two different sound sources. One method is to write a program that turns the speaker on and off by manipulating two speaker bits in the programmable peripheral interface chip (the PPI). When using this method, our program controls the timing of the pulse and the resulting sound frequency. The other method is to use the PC's built-in programmable timer chip (the 8253-5) to pulse the speaker at a precise frequency. Using the timer chip is a more popular method for two reasons: Because the speaker pulses are controlled by the timer chip instead of a program, the CPU is free to devote its time to the other demands of the computer system; and the timer chip is not dependent on the working speed of the CPU (which is faster for the AT and slower for the PCjr).

Both the program method and the timer method can be used together or separately to create a variety of simple and complex sounds. We'll explain timer-chip sound control and direct speaker control more thoroughly in the next few pages, and then move on to describe some of the enhancements the PCjr has brought to the PC family.

Timer-Chip Sound Control

The 8253-5 programmable timer is the heart of the standard PC models' sound-making abilities—but it is also the heart of the system's real time clock. Although we'll be concentrating mainly on its use as a sound generator, the 8253-5 is called a timer chip because its primary function is to keep time—in much the same way as a metronome keeps time for a musician.

Here is how it works. The 8253 gets a signal from the computer's main clock (the 8284A) that oscillates at a frequency of 1,193,180 times a second, or 1.193 megahertz (MHz). The timer is programmed to produce a clock interrupt (interrupt 8) once every 65,536 main clock cycles, or about 18.2 times a second. This clock interrupt is usually called a clock tick. The ROM-BIOS keeps track of the clock ticks, calculates the time of day by incrementing its clock counter at each tick, and also issues its own interrupt, called a clock-tick interrupt (interrupt 28).

The ROM-BIOS clock-tick interrupt is often used by programs to keep time, although some programs bypass this interrupt and work directly with the timer chip. For example, BASIC uses the timer chip directly to count the duration of a sound, which is measured in clock ticks. However, since the standard rate of 18.2 ticks per second is often not fast enough to provide the precision that some kinds of music demand, BASIC reprograms the timer to tick four times faster, which causes interrupt 8 (the clock tick) to occur 72.8 times per second instead of 18.2. When BASIC counts against the quadruple rate, it is able to more accurately reproduce the proper tempo of a piece of music.

❑ NOTE: *BASIC quadruples the clock rate during the execution of the PLAY command. It avoids interfering with the BIOS clock-tick interrupt number 28, which is vital to many other system functions, by resetting the vector for interrupt 8 to point to a routine that then signals the ROM-BIOS on every fourth tick. On the fourth tick, the interrupt handler momentarily turns control over to the BIOS, enabling it to increment its counter and issue an interrupt 28 on schedule, after which it returns control to BASIC.*

Programming the Timer Chip

Creating sounds with the timer chip involves two basic steps: First, we must program the timer to generate a frequency, then we must direct the output of the timer to the speaker. These two steps can be performed separately. A sound is emitted when both steps have been performed, and the sound stops when either of the two steps is ended.

The timer can be programmed to produce pulses at whatever frequency we want, but since it does not keep track of how long the sound continues, the sound will continue forever unless it is turned off. Therefore, our programs must choose when to end a sound through some sort of timing instruction.

We program the timer to generate sounds in the same way BASIC programs it to generate clock ticks: by giving it a number. On command, the timer counts the system clock pulses (which are oscillating at 1.193 MHz) until the total matches our number. Then it outputs a pulse (instead of an interrupt) and begins counting again from zero. In effect, the timer "divides" our number into the clock frequency to produce an output frequency. The result is that the timer sends out a series of pulses that produce a sound of a certain frequency when we turn on the speaker.

Our controlling count and the resulting frequency are in a reciprocal relationship, as shown by these formulas:

$$\text{Count} = 1{,}193{,}180 \div \text{Frequency}$$
$$\text{Frequency} = 1{,}193{,}180 \div \text{Count}$$

From these formulas, we see that a low-frequency (low-pitched) sound is produced by a high count and that a high-frequency (high-pitched) sound is produced by a low count. A count of 100 would produce a high pitch of roughly 11,931 cycles per second, and a count of 10,000 would produce a low pitch of about 119 cycles per second.

We can produce just about any frequency, within the limitations of 16-bit arithmetic. The lowest frequency is 18.2 hertz (with a divisor of 65,535, hex FFFF) and the highest is 1.193 megahertz (with a divisor of 1).

BASIC holds this to a practical range of 37 to 32,767 hertz. The program below demonstrates that the actual frequency range of the internal speaker is even less than BASIC provides.

Once we have calculated the count that we need for the frequency we want, we send it to the 8253 timer registers. This is done with three port outputs. The first port output notifies the timer that the count is coming by sending the value 182 (hex B6) to port 67 (hex 43). The next two outputs send the low- and high-order bytes of the count, a 16-bit unsigned word, to port 66 (hex 42)—the low-order byte followed by the high-order byte. This BASIC program illustrates the process:

```
10 COUNT = 1193280! / 3000      ' 3000 is our frequency
20 LO.COUNT =COUNT MOD 256      ' calculate low-order byte value
30 HI.COUNT = COUNT / 256       ' calculate high-order byte value
40 OUT 67, 182                  ' get timer ready
50 OUT 66, LO.COUNT             ' load low-order byte
60 OUT 66, HI.COUNT             ' load high-order byte
```

Activating the Speaker

After we have programmed the timer, we still need to activate the speaker circuitry in order to use the signal that the timer is generating. As with most other parts of the PC, the speaker is manipulated by sending certain values to a specific port, a process that is illustrated in Figure 7-2. The speaker is supervised by the programmable peripheral interface (PPI) chip and uses port 97 (hex 61). Only two of the port's eight bits are used by the speaker: the low-order bits numbered 0 and 1. The other bits are used for other purposes, so it is important that we don't disturb them while working with the speaker.

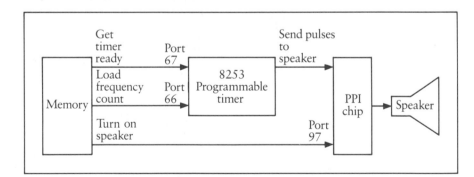

Figure 7-2. How sound frequencies are generated through the 8253 timer and speaker

The lowest bit, bit 0, controls a timer signal used to drive the speaker. The second bit, bit 1, controls the pulsing of the speaker. Both bits must be turned on (set to 1) to make the speaker respond to the timer. We can turn them on without disturbing the non-speaker bits with an operation like this:

```
70 OLD.PORT = INP (97)              ' assign value of port 97 to old.port
80 NEW.PORT = (OLD.PORT OR &H03)    ' set bits 0 and 1 to on
90 OUT 97, NEW.PORT                 ' turn speaker on
```

Direct Speaker Control

The timer controls the speaker by sending periodic signals that pulse the speaker in and out. We can do the same thing a different way: with a program that sends in or out signals directly to the speaker. We do this by setting bit 0 of port 97 (hex 61) to zero to turn the speaker on, and then alternately setting bit 1 on and off, which pulses the speaker. When we use this method, the timing of the program determines the frequency of the sound—the faster the program executes, the higher the pitch. This BASIC program demonstrates how it's done (the example assumes that port 97 (hex 61) has a value of 76):

```
10 X = INP (97) AND &HFC    ' change port value, turn off last 2 bits
20 OUT 97, X                ' pull speaker in
30 OUT 97, X + 2            ' push speaker out
40 GOTO 20
```

The two actions in lines 20 and 30 pulse the speaker in and out. Each one is a half-cycle, and the two together produce one complete sound cycle.

This example runs as fast as BASIC can process it, producing as high a note as possible. If we needed more range in our application, we would probably use a faster language and insert deliberate delays equal to half the frequency cycle time between each complete cycle (half the cycle time, because each ON or OFF operation is a half cycle). Whatever language we use, we have to include a duration count to end the sound. To produce different sounds at a particular frequency, such as clicking or buzzing sounds, we just vary the delays between pulses.

Despite all these wonderful possibilities, generating sounds through the speaker by direct program action is not a good way to make sounds. It has three big disadvantages over the use of the timer:

- A program requires the constant attention of the CPU, so the computer has a hard time getting any other work done.

- The frequency is at the mercy of the speed of the computer; that is, the same program would make a lower or higher sound on a slower or faster model.

■ The clock-tick interrupts interfere with the smoothness of the sound, making a warble. The only way to avoid this is to suspend the clock tick by disabling the interrupts—and that disrupts the computer's sense of time.

As far as I know, there is only one advantage to making sounds using the direct method over the timer method: With the proper control over the program delays, it is possible to make a rich polyphonic sound. Be forewarned, though, that this requires some very clever and tedious programming and, all in all, it may not be worth the trouble.

SPEAKER VOLUME AND SOUND QUALITY

There is no volume control of any kind in the computer's internal speaker. However, the computer's speaker—like all speakers—varies in how well it responds to different frequencies, and some frequencies may sound louder than others. In the case of a crude speaker like that found on most PCs, the loudness of the sound varies widely with the frequency. You can use the following program to test this—it may help you choose the best sound pitch for your purpose:

```
10 PLAY "MF"                                    ' plays each sound separately
20 FREQUENCY = 37
30 WHILE FREQUENCY < 32000                      ' use all frequencies to 32000 Hz
40   PRINT USING "##,###"; FREQUENCY            ' display frequency
50   SOUND FREQUENCY, 5                          ' produce sound with duration of 5
60   FREQUENCY = FREQUENCY * 1.1                 ' increment frequency by 1/10
70 WEND
```

You should also be aware that the speakers in the various PC models may not sound alike, partly because the materials of each system housing resonate differently as speaker enclosures. For example, the timbre of the PCjr is quite different from that of the Portable PC and from the PC and XT models. Be prepared for these variations in sound.

SOUND AND THE PCjr

The PCjr has the standard programmable timer chip and a built-in speaker, just like the rest of the family, but it also has other sources of sounds and other outputs for the sound signals.

The best-known source of sound in the Junior is the TI SN76496A sound-generator chip, an addition that is great for special effects in games and educational applications. But the Junior also has two lesser-known sound sources: the cassette tape input and the audio line (line B30) of the I/O channel connector. The selection among these four sound

Bit 5	Bit 6	Value	Sound Source
0	0	0	8253 timer (standard IBM sound source)
0	1	1	Cassette tape interface
1	0	2	I/O channel
1	1	3	TI sound chip

Figure 7-3. The settings for the four PCjr sound sources for bits 5 and 6 of port 97 in the 8255.

sources is controlled by the 8255 programmable peripheral interface, or the PPI (☞ see page 11). Our programs can control what source is used by setting bits 5 and 6 in the 8255, which is done through port 97 (hex 61). (☞ See Figure 7-3.)

The cassette tape and I/O channel sound sources can be hooked up to a stereo amplifier to produce better sound quality than the internal speaker, but since they are not widely used, we will not consider them any further in this chapter. Instead, we'll briefly focus our attention on the TI sound chip.

The TI Sound Chip

The TI sound chip has four separate sound generators, or voices. Three of these voices are completely independent, and generate pure tones (as does the timer chip). The fourth voice is a "noise" source that generates irregular noise sounds in a variety of ways. All four voices have an independent volume control, providing an evenly graduated set of 15 volume levels, plus a zero volume (off). Each of the three pure voices has an independently selected frequency. The noise voice has three pre-selected frequencies and a fourth option, which borrows the frequency of the third pure voice. We'll cover each of the sound elements separately, then explain how they are used together to program the TI sound chip.

The Tone Generators

Each of the three tone generators, or voices, is controlled by a 10-bit number that our programs send to the TI sound chip. The TI sound chip follows the same philosophy to create frequencies as the programmable timer: The fast system clock is divided by a count and the quotient determines the frequency. However, the details are different. For the timer, the frequency count is a 16-bit number divided into the 1.193 megahertz bus clock frequency. For the TI sound chip, the count is a 10-bit number divided into $\frac{1}{32}$ of the system clock frequency (3.579 MHz), which turns out to be 111,860 Hz.

The only limitation of the 10-bit controlling number is that it reduces the number of frequencies we can choose from by a factor of 32. For example, if we use a count of 100, the TI sound chip produces a frequency of 1118.6 Hz, and the next divisor, 101, gives us 1107.5 Hz; we can't get any of the frequencies in between. By contrast, the timer chip would give us 32 frequencies in that same range. In practice, this limitation is only a problem for the most musically demanding sounds, such as three-part chords—they may sound off-key.

Attenuation

Each voice in the TI sound chip has an independent sound-level control, which is calculated in terms of decibels of attenuation, or softening. There are four bits used to control the volume. These bits, labeled A0 through A3, can be set independently or added together to produce sixteen volume levels, as shown in Figure 7-4. When a bit is set on, the sound is attenuated (reduced) by a specific amount: either 2, 4, 8, or 16 decibels. When all four bits are set on, the sound is turned completely off. When all four bits are set off, the sound is at its fullest volume. Although the sound levels can be calculated, it is easier to choose the sound we want by experimentation.

The Noise Generator

There are two modes for the noise operation, besides the four frequency selections. One, called periodic noise, produces a steady sound; the other, called white noise, produces a hissing sound. These two modes are controlled by a bit known as the FB bit. When FB is 0, the periodic noise is generated; when FB is 1, the white noise is produced.

A A A A 0 1 2 3				Value	Attenuation (decibels)
.	.	.	1	1	2
.	.	1	.	2	4
.	1	.	.	4	8
1	.	.	.	8	16
1	1	1	1	32	Volume off

Figure 7-4. The attenuation bit settings

NF0	NF1	Noise Frequency
0	0	$1{,}193{,}180 \div 512 = 2{,}330$
0	1	$1{,}193{,}180 \div 1024 = 1{,}165$
1	0	$1{,}193{,}180 \div 2048 = 583$
1	1	Borrowed from Voice 3

Figure 7-5. Noise-generator frequencies produced by NF0 and NF1 bit combinations

Two bits, known as NF0 and NF1, control the frequency at which the noise generator works. Three of the four possible combinations of NF0 and NF1 set an independent noise frequency based on the timer. The fourth combination borrows the frequency from the third of the three pure voices made by the tone generators. Figure 7-5 shows the possible noise bit values and their associated frequencies.

Controlling the Sound Chip

We program the TI sound chip by passing to it 3-bit register addresses (which select voice frequencies, attenuation control, and noise voice control), 10-bit frequency divisors, 4-bit attenuation settings, a 2-bit noise frequency selection, and a 1-bit noise type selection—all through port 192 (hex C0). Not a tidy set to shoehorn into an 8-bit port!

The TI sound chip has eight registers that control what it does. Three bits, known as R0 through R2, select the registers and identify the parameter that's being set. The register values are shown in Figure 7-6.

R0	R1	R2	Parameter
0	0	0	Voice 1 frequency control number (10 bits)
0	0	1	Voice 1 attenuation (4 bits)
0	1	0	Voice 2 frequency control number (10 bits)
0	1	1	Voice 2 attenuation (4 bits)
1	0	0	Voice 3 frequency control number (10 bits)
1	0	1	Voice 3 attenuation (4 bits)
1	1	0	Noise voice control (4 bits; 3 used)
1	1	1	Noise voice attenuation (4 bits)

Figure 7-6. The parameter indentification bits

All programming of the TI sound chip is done by writing out to port 192 (hex C0). Don't read this port: If you do, you will lock up the machine. This byte contains the ID bit (identifying it as the command byte), three register bits (R0 through R2), and some data bits. The command byte may be used to load the frequency, attenuation, or noise control bits, along with the register bits. The data bit formats will vary depending on their purpose. In the case of the pure voice frequency counts, this first byte is followed by a second byte that contains an ID bit, along with the six remaining frequency bits that couldn't fit into the first byte. By deliberate design, the TI sound chip will accept the second byte over and over again, without the first command byte preceding each one. This allows for quick frequency changes without the program overhead that would be necessary to load both bytes. Figures 7-7 through 7-10 show the bit formats for the various byte settings.

❑ NOTE: *Before you attempt to program the TI chip, you should be aware of an irritating difference in the design approaches of Texas Instruments and Intel. They don't use the same bit order notation. As a result, in the PCjr Technical Reference manual, you will find the sound-chip bits referred to in the opposite order from the notation usually used in the manual (and used by us in this book). For example, what would otherwise be referred to as bit 7 of a byte, you find called bit 0 MSB (for most significant bit). If you use the reference manual, follow the MSB/LSB notation and ignore the bit numbering—and then grumble about the inconsiderate switch of notation.*

It should be pretty obvious from this overview that programming the TI sound chip is annoyingly complex. Whenever I've tried it, I've been reduced to counting bits on my fingers and toes. A further drawback is that programs using the sound chip can only be fully utilized on the PCjr and will not make music on the other members of the PC family—definitely something to keep in mind before you go through all the trouble of learning to program the sound chip!

Sound Output in the PCjr

There are two sound destinations for the PCjr's sound signals: the internal speaker, and the external paths. The external paths are three of the sockets on the back of the PCjr: the A-audio output (which is usually connected to a hi-fi system), the D-direct driving output (which can be connected to an RGB monitor, where the sound signal is usually ignored), and the T-television output (which can be connected to a TV set through an RF modulator).

7	6	5	4	3	2	1	0	Use
1	.	.	.	.	.	.	.	Identifies first byte (command byte)
.	R0	R1	R2	.	.	.	.	Register number in TI chip (0, 2, or 4)
.	.	.	.	F6	F7	F8	F9	4 of 10 bits in frequency count

Figure 7-7. The bit setting for the first byte of
a frequency count

7	6	5	4	3	2	1	0	Use
0	.	.	.	.	.	.	.	Identifies second byte (completing count)
.	X	.	.	.	.	.	.	Unused, ignored; we can set to 0 or 1
.	.	F0	F1	F2	F3	F4	F5	6 of 10 bits in frequency count

Figure 7-8. The bit setting for the second
byte of a frequency count

7	6	5	4	3	2	1	0	Use
1	.	.	.	.	.	.	.	Identifies first byte (command byte)
.	R0	R1	R2	.	.	.	.	Register number in TI chip (1, 3, 5, or 7)
.	.	.	.	A0	A1	A2	A3	4 attenuation bits

Figure 7-9. The coding of the attenuation
bits in the first byte of a frequency count

7	6	5	4	3	2	1	0	Use
1	.	.	.	.	.	.	.	Identifies first byte (command byte)
.	1	1	0	.	.	.	.	Register number in TI chip (6)
.	.	.	.	X	.	.	.	Unused, ignored; we can set to 0 or 1
.	.	.	.	.	FB	.	.	1 for white noise, 0 for periodic
.	.	.	.	.	.	NF0	NF1	2 noise frequency control bits

Figure 7-10. The coding of the noise control
bits in the first byte of a frequency count

The PCjr's internal speaker, like all other PC internal speakers, can only get its sound signals from the timer. The external paths get their sound from any of the four sources that generate sound. It's important to note that the sounds made by the TI sound chip cannot be directed to the computer's internal speaker. This is because the internal speaker is driven in a way that is completely incompatible with the rich capabilities of the TI sound chip—a shame, but that's the way it is.

If you study the PCjr Technical Reference manual for material related to this, you may notice that bit 4 of port 97 can be used to control the internal speaker. Setting this bit to 1 will disable the speaker, but don't do it! For one thing, there are other ways to control the speaker, as we have seen in the previous section. But more importantly, this bit has a radically different use in the other PC models: When this bit is set, the use of memory is disabled, which shuts down the computer quite thoroughly.

8

ROM-BIOS Basics

159

One secret of successful programming for the PC family lies in the effective use of the software that is built right into the machine: the ROM-BIOS services. Conceptually, the ROM-BIOS services are sandwiched between the hardware and the high-level languages (including the operating system). They work directly with the computer's hardware and peripheral devices, performing some of the system's most fundamental tasks, such as reading and writing individual bytes of data to the display screen or disk. Programming-language services and DOS services are often built from these basic functions and enhanced to make a particular process more efficient. We can enhance our programs in the same way by plugging them directly into the ROM-BIOS, thereby gaining access to an extremely powerful set of tools and using our computers in the way that IBM intended them to be used.

That last point is worth emphasizing. IBM has gone to considerable lengths to create a clean and well-defined method for directing the operation of the computer through the ROM-BIOS services. As each new PC model is designed, IBM (and any other computer maker who is faithfully extending the PC family) makes sure its ROM-BIOS services are thoroughly compatible with those of the other members of the family. As long as we control our computers through the ROM-BIOS, whether directly or indirectly, we are safe from any compatibility problems. If we bypass the ROM-BIOS and program directly to the hardware, we are not only asking for trouble, but we are also severely limiting the range and viability of our programs.

In the next five chapters, we will discuss the BIOS service routines. Fortunately, the routines fall naturally into groups that are derived from the hardware devices they support, so the video services, disk services, and keyboard services can all be reviewed separately. But before we take a closer look at the individual services, we need to find out how we can incorporate them into our programs. This chapter sets the stage by explaining what goes into writing an interface routine, the bridge between our programming language and the ROM-BIOS services. First, a word on how the ROM-BIOS operates.

THE BIOS PHILOSOPHY

All ROM-BIOS services are invoked by interrupts. The interrupt instructions point to a particular location in the interrupt vector table in low memory that contains an interrupt vector: the address of the service routine stored in ROM. This design makes it possible for any program to request a service without knowing the specific memory location of the ROM-BIOS service routine. It also allows the services to be moved around, expanded, or adapted without affecting the programs that use the services. Although IBM has tried to maintain the absolute memory location of some parts of the ROM-BIOS, we would be foolish to use these addresses since there is always a chance they may be changed in the future. The standard, preferred, and most reliable way to invoke a ROM-BIOS service is to use its interrupt rather than its absolute location.

The ROM-BIOS services could be supervised by one master interrupt, but instead they are divided into subject categories, each category having its own controlling interrupt. The primary benefit of this design is that it allows each interrupt handler to be replaced with a minimum amount of disruption. For example, if a hardware manufacturer created a radically different video display, printer, or anything else that required a completely new BIOS program to operate it, the manufacturer could provide us with a new BIOS program along with the hardware. The new BIOS program might be stored in RAM rather than ROM and it would replace just that one part of IBM's ROM-BIOS that was used with the old hardware. By making the ROM-BIOS modular, IBM has made it easier to improve and extend the capabilities of our computers.

THE ROM-BIOS SERVICES INTERRUPTS

There are twelve ROM-BIOS interrupts in all, falling into five groups: Six of the twelve interrupts serve specific peripheral devices; two report on the computer's equipment; one works with the time/date clock; one performs the print-screen operation; and finally, two interrupts wrench the computer into another state altogether, activating ROM-BASIC and the system start-up routine. As we'll see, most of the interrupts are tied to a group of subservices that actually do the work. For example, the video services interrupt 16 (hex 10) has seventeen subservices that do everything from setting the video mode to changing the size of the cursor. We call a subservice by invoking its governing interrupt and specifying the subservice number in register AH. ☛ This process is explained in the example at the end of this chapter.

BIOS-SERVICE OPERATING CHARACTERISTICS

The ROM-BIOS services use some common calling conventions that provide consistency in the use of registers, flags, the stack, and memory. We'll outline the characteristics of these operating conventions, beginning with the segment registers.

Interrupt		Use
Dec	Hex	

Peripheral Devices Services

16	10	Video-display services (see Chapter 9)
19	13	Diskette services (see Chapter 10)
20	14	Communications services (see Chapter 12)
21	15	Cassette-tape services (see Chapter 12)
22	16	Standard keyboard services (see Chapter 11)
23	17	Printer services (see Chapter 12)

Equipment Status Services

17	11	Equipment-list service (see Chapter 12)
18	12	Memory-size service (see Chapter 12)

Time/Date Service

26	1A	Time and date services (see Chapter 12)

Print-Screen Service

5	5	Print-screen service (see Chapter 12)

Special Services

24	18	Activate ROM-BASIC language (see Chapter 12)
25	19	Activate bootstrap start-up routine (see Chapter 12)

Figure 8-1. The twelve ROM-BIOS services

The code segment register (CS) is automatically reserved, loaded, and restored as part of the interrupt process. Consequently, we don't have to worry about our program's CS. The DS and ES registers are preserved by the ROM-BIOS service routines, except in the few cases where they are explicitly used. The stack segment register (SS) is left unchanged, and the ROM-BIOS services depend upon us to provide a working stack. (Everything depends upon a working stack!)

The stack requirements of the ROM-BIOS services are not spelled out and they can vary considerably, particularly since some services invoke other services. (One of the flaws of the IBM personal computers, and all computers based on the Intel 8088, is the very fuzzy specification of stack usage and stack boundaries.) Generally, most programs ought to be working with a much larger stack than the ROM-BIOS services need.

In connection with the segment registers, the program counter (PC or IP) is preserved by the same mechanism that preserves the code segment. In effect, the stack pointer (SP) is preserved because all the ROM-BIOS services leave the stack clean, POPping off anything that was PUSHed on during the service-routine execution.

As usual, the general-purpose registers, AX through DX, are considered fair game. The standard rule is not to expect any contents of these registers to be maintained when you pass control to another routine, and that applies to the ROM-BIOS services as well. If you closely inspect the coding of the services in the IBM Technical Reference manual, you will find that one or more registers are left undisturbed in one service or another, but you would be foolish to try to take advantage of this. As a general rule, when a simple result is returned from a subroutine, it is left in the AX register; this applies to both the ROM-BIOS and to all programming languages. We'll see how often this really happens when we cover the ROM-BIOS services in detail.

The index registers (SI and DI) may be changed, just like the AX through DX registers.

The various flags in the flag register are routinely changed as a by-product of the instruction steps in the ROM-BIOS routines. You should not expect any of them to be preserved. In a few instances, the carry flag (CF) or the zero flag (ZF) are used to signal the overall success or failure of a requested operation.

The details that we have been poring over are important but rather tedious, and there is little reason for you to pay much attention to them. If your programs follow the general interface rules given in the next section, and if they follow the specific requirements of your programming language (☛ covered in Chapters 19 and 20), you may not need to be concerned with them at all.

❑ NOTE: *If you set out to use the ROM-BIOS services in your programs, you'll naturally be concerned about the possible conflicts between the services and the operating conventions that your language follows. Put your mind at ease. You will find that you do not have to take any extraordinary precautions to protect your programming language from the ROM-BIOS, or vice versa.*

CREATING AN ASSEMBLY-LANGUAGE INTERFACE

In order to make direct use of the ROM-BIOS services from our programs, we need to create an assembly-language interface routine to link our programming language to the ROM-BIOS. When we say "interface routine," we are referring to conventional program-development subroutines—subroutines that are assembled into object modules (.OBJ files) and then linked into working programs (.EXE or .COM files in DOS). ☛ For more on this subject, see Chapter 19.

Working with assembly language can seem a fearsome task if you are not already comfortable with it. While there are plenty of good reasons to be intimidated by assembly language—after all, it is the most difficult and demanding kind of programming—it's really not that difficult to create an assembly-language interface routine. As I have often related, when I first needed to create an interface routine for the Norton Utility programs that I was writing in Pascal, I had absolutely no prior experience with either the IBM Assembler or the 8088 machine and assembly language. Even though I started out cold, I had my first working and tested interface done in 45 minutes flat. I mention this not to brag, but to emphasize that it's just not as hard as many people think.

To create your own interfaces, you will need to have an assembler that is compatible with the DOS standards for object files. The one I use is the IBM Macro Assembler, but there are others available. Do not, however, plan to use the justly famous "cheap assembler" CHASM, by David Whitman. CHASM and some other assemblers are set up to produce only complete assembly-language programs rather than modules that can be linked to other programs, such as the interface routines that we are interested in. All the examples we give here are for the IBM Macro Assembler.

❑ NOTE: *BASIC can work with machine-language subroutines put directly into memory. In interpreted BASIC they are CALLed and in compiled BASIC they are CALLed absolute. Preparing the sort of assembler subroutine that will work with BASIC can be done as easily with DEBUG's A-assemble command as it can with an ordinary assembler.*

The Basic Form of an Interface Routine

The exact form an interface routine must take varies with its eventual use. An assembly-language interface is a handshaker between our programming language and a ROM-BIOS service, so it has to be tailored to meet the needs of both ends. *It matters* which programming language is being used; *it matters* which ROM-BIOS service is being invoked; and *it matters* whether any data is being passed in one direction or the other.

However, the general outline of an assembly-language interface is basically the same, no matter what we are doing.

One of the best ways to understand how an assembly-language interface is coded is to view it as five nested parts, which are outlined here:

Level 1: General assembler overhead
Level 2: Subroutine assembler overhead
Level 3: Entry code
Level 4: Get parameter data from caller
Level 5: Invoke ROM-BIOS service
Level 4: Pass back results to caller
Level 3: Exit code
Level 2: Finishing up subroutine assembler overhead
Level 1: Finishing up general assembler overhead

In this outline, levels 1 and 2 are needed to tell the assembler what's going on, but they don't produce any working instructions. Levels 3 through 5 produce the actual machine-language instructions.

We'll dig our way down through each of these levels to show you the rules and explain what's going on. Don't forget that the specific requirements of an interface routine change for different circumstances. We'll point out the few design elements that are universal to all routines.

Level 1: General Assembler Overhead

Here is an outline of a typical level-1 section of an interface routine, with the lines numbered for reference:

```
1-1    INTERFACE SEGMENT 'CODE'
1-2              ASSUME   CS:INTERFACE
       ; levels 2 through 5 appear here
1-3    INTERFACE ENDS
1 4              END
```

In line 1-1, INTERFACE is an arbitrary name we have given this assembly routine; SEGMENT is essential and is used to define an assembly routine; CODE is a category that may vary by language (we'll see another example shortly).

Line 1-2 is not always needed, and assembler experts will recognize it as a piece of illegal fakery. Quite simply, the ASSUME instruction allows us to do some if-then type programming without getting into trouble; we'll make use of it in later chapters.

Line 1-3 ends the segment started in line 1-1, and line 1-4 ends the whole assembly routine.

The format conventions we have shown here are taken from IBM/Microsoft Pascal (☞ which we'll cover in Chapter 20). For an example of something different, C needs these two lines in place of line 1-1:

```
PGROUP     GROUP     PROG
           INTERFACE SEGMENT   BYTE PUBLIC 'PROG'
```

Level 2: Subroutine Assembler Overhead

Next, let's look at an outline of a typical level 2, the assembler overhead for a subroutine (called a *procedure* in assembler parlance). Here is some typical level-2 coding:

```
2-1                PUBLIC   MEMSIZE
2-2    MEMSIZE     PROC     FAR
       ; levels 3 through 5 appear here
2-3    MEMSIZE     ENDP
```

Line 2-1 instructs the assembler to make the name of our procedure, MEMSIZE, public information, which means that the link program can then connect it to its users.

Lines 2-2 and 2-3 bracket our procedure, which has arbitrarily been named MEMSIZE. PROC and ENDP are mandatory and surround any procedure, with PROC defining the beginning of the procedure and ENDP signaling the end of it. FAR tells the assembler that the procedure is located outside of the current segment. We could have used either FAR or NEAR in this position. If we had used NEAR, it would have indicated the procedure was located inside the current segment instead of outside. FAR calls are the most common, but some languages do (C) or can (Pascal) use NEAR calls. Except for FAR or NEAR, what you see here is universal for all languages and all purposes.

Level 3: Entry Code

Level 3 begins the actual working instructions. It takes care of the housekeeping overhead that is needed for a subroutine to work cooperatively with the language that called it. Here is an example:

```
3-1    PUSH    BP
3-2    MOV     BP,SP
       ; levels 4 and 5 appear here
3-3    POP     BP
3-4    RET     0
```

Lines 3-1 and 3-2 are used to gain access to and preserve any parameters that the caller has passed. These will appear one way or another on the stack. The base pointer register (BP) is used universally to keep track of the entry-point location on the stack. Our calling program will have its own BP, which we preserve in line 3-1 by PUSHing it onto the stack and restore in line 3-3 by POPping it off.

In line 3-2, we get our own stack frame reference by grabbing the current stack pointer (SP) and moving it to the BP. From that point on, no matter what gets pushed onto the stack, we'll have kept track of where our caller's parameters are on the stack. If we needed to preserve any other registers for our caller, they would be PUSHed to the stack immediately following line 3-2, and POPped, in reverse order, just before line 3-3. Normally this would not be necessary.

Line 3-4 is used to pass control back to our caller; the assembler translates our terse RET into a NEAR or FAR return, depending upon whether our PROC was declared NEAR or FAR. The 0 in line 3-4 is cleanup work that we usually have to do to remove any caller's parameters from the stack. If there were no parameters or if the conventions of the programming language have the caller clean parameters off the stack, as C does (☞ see pages 381–382), then this value will be zero. If there were parameters and the programming language doesn't clean up the stack, we have to know how big to make this value so as to remove every parameter. The value must be increased by 2 for every 1- or 2-byte parameter (byte, word, or offset address), and by 4 for each 4-byte parameter (segmented address) that was passed to the procedure. As long as we can identify the nature of our parameters (they are sure to be one of these four types), we'll be OK.

Level 4: Get Parameter Data from Caller

Level 4 deals with the parameters by passing them from the caller to the ROM-BIOS, and with the results by passing them from the ROM-BIOS to the caller. The caller's parameters are on the stack, either in the form of data or addresses (☞ see Chapter 20 for help with this). The registers, mostly AX through DX, are used for ROM-BIOS input and output. The trick here—and it can be tricky—is to use the correct stack offsets to find the parameters. We'll sneak up on this problem in stages.

First, we get to the parameters on the stack by addressing relative to the BP frame reference that we snatched earlier. Here's a typical layout:

Location	Contents
BP	Caller's saved BP
BP + 2	Return address, offset and segment
BP + 6	One parameter
BP + 8	Another parameter
BP + 10	Yet another parameter

The return address at BP+2 is four bytes for a FAR procedure, as we've shown it, but only two bytes for a NEAR procedure. If yours is a NEAR procedure, all the subsequent offsets should be 2 less than shown here. Most languages PUSH their parameters onto the stack in the order they are written. This means that the *last* parameter is the one closest to the top of the stack, at BP+6. However, Lattice/Microsoft C uses the reverse order, so that the closest parameter is the *first* one written in the calling program.

Parameters normally take up two or four bytes on the stack, though two bytes is the most common. Our example here has the locations BP+6, +8, and +10 two bytes apart. If any of these parameters were four bytes in size, we would adjust the subsequent references accordingly.

If *data* was placed on the stack, then we can get it immediately by addressing it like this: [BP+6]. If an *address* was placed on the stack, two steps are needed: First, get the address, and second, get the data. Here is a level-4 example showing both data ([BP+6]) and address ([BP+8]) retrieval:

```
4-1   MOV    AX,[BP+6]              ; value of parameter1
4-2   MOV    BX,[BP+8]              ; address of parameter2
4-3   MOV    DX,[BX]               ; value of parameter2
      ; level 5 appears here
4-4   MOV    BX,[BP+8]              ; address of parameter2 (again)
4-5   MOV    [BX],DX               ; pass back new value
```

All of these MOV instructions move data from the second operand to the first operand. Line 4-1 grabs data right off the stack and slaps it into the AX register. Lines 4-2 and 4-3 get data via an address on the stack; line 4-2 first gets the address (parking it in BX), and then line 4-3 uses that address to get to the actual data, which is moved into DX. Lines 4-4 and 4-5 reverse this process; line 4-4 gets the address again, and then line 4-5 moves the contents of DX into that memory location.

❑ NOTE: *A crucial bit of assembler notation is demonstrated here: BX refers to what's in BX, and [BX] refers to a memory location whose* address *is in BX.*

While I don't claim that sorting out these references is a snap, if you think it through carefully, it works out right.

Level 5: Invoke ROM-BIOS Service

Level 5 is our final step: It simply invokes the ROM-BIOS service. Typically, this step involves two simple instructions, like this:

```
5-1   MOV    AH,15                 ; function 15
5-2   INT    16                    ; call BIOS routine
```

Line 5-1 selects the interrupt subservice. Typically, there are several subservices numbered from 0 on up. They are always selected with a code in the AH register.

Line 5-2 generates the interrupt that requests the service; in this example, it's interrupt 16 (hex 10), the video-services interrupt.

This five-step process outlines the basic principles of nearly all aspects of an assembly-language interface. In the following chapters, we'll see how this design is used in specific examples.

9

ROM-BIOS
Video Services

I n this chapter, we will discuss each of the video or screen-control services provided by the ROM-BIOS. We have devoted most of the chapter to detailed descriptions of each video service. Beginning on page 185, we have included some programming hints and an assembly-language routine that makes use of some of the video services. ☛ For a more general discussion of video-display characteristics in the PC family, see Chapter 4. For information on the low-memory locations used by the ROM-BIOS for video status information, turn to page 54.

ACCESSING THE BIOS VIDEO SERVICES

The ROM-BIOS video services are all requested by generating interrupt 16 (hex 10). There are sixteen principle services and one AT service available under this interrupt (☛ see Figure 9-1). Like all other ROM-BIOS services, the video services are numbered from 0 and are selected by placing the service number in the AH register. The services often need additional parameters from the caller, which are placed in BX, CX, or DX, depending on the specifications of the service routine. We'll cover the purpose and placement of the parameters under each service description.

| Service | | Description |
Dec	Hex	
0	0	Set video mode
1	1	Set cursor size
2	2	Set cursor position
3	3	Read cursor position
4	4	Read light-pen position
5	5	Set active display page
6	6	Scroll window up
7	7	Scroll window down
8	8	Read character and attribute
9	9	Write character and attribute
10	A	Write character
11	B	Set color palette
12	C	Write pixel dot
13	D	Read pixel dot
14	E	Write character as TTY
15	F	Get current video mode
19	13	Write character string

Figure 9-1. The seventeen video services

Service 0: Set Video Mode

Service 0 is used to select from the fifteen video modes shown in Figure 9-2. ☞ For details of the video modes, see page 71.

You may recall from our discussion in Chapter 4 that modes 0 through 6 apply to the standard Color/Graphics Adapter; mode 7 applies to the Monochrome Adapter; modes 8 through 10 were introduced with the PCjr; and modes 13 through 16 were added for the Enhanced Graphics Adapter, which also supports all other modes except 8, 9 and 10.

Something else you may want to keep in mind if you are working with the black-and-white or color-suppressed modes (modes 0, 2, and 5) is that they only suppress color on the composite output and not on the RGB output of a display adapter.

Mode	Type	Size	Colors	Adapter	Display
0	Text	40 × 25	16 (grey) EGA: 64 color	CGA, EGA, PCjr	Enhanced Color
1	Text	40 × 25	16 foreground, 8 background EGA: 64 color	CGA, EGA, PCjr	Enhanced Color
2	Text	80 × 25	16 (grey) EGA: 64 color	CGA, EGA, PCjr	Enhanced Color
3	Text	80 × 25	16 foreground, 8 background EGA: 64 color	CGA, EGA, PCjr	Enhanced Color
4	Graphics	320 × 200	4	CGA, EGA, PCjr	Enhanced Color
5	Graphics	320 × 200	4 (grey)	CGA, EGA, PCjr	Enhanced Color
6	Graphics	640 × 200	2	CGA, EGA, PCjr	Enhanced Color
7	Text	80 × 25	b/w	EGA, MA	Monochrome
8	Graphics	160 × 200	16	PCjr	Enhanced Color
9	Graphics	320 × 200	16	PCjr	Enhanced Color
10	Graphics	640 × 200	4	PCjr	Enhanced Color
11	Apparently internal to the EGA				
12	Apparently internal to the EGA				
13	Graphics	320 × 200	16	EGA	Enhanced Color
14	Graphics	640 × 200	16	EGA	Enhanced Color
15	Graphics	640 × 350	b/w	EGA	Monochrome
16	Graphics	640 × 350	16/64	EGA	Enhanced Color

Figure 9-2. The video-mode settings for service 0

Normally, the ROM-BIOS clears the screen memory buffer when the mode is set, even if it is set to the same mode again and again. In fact, setting the same mode repeatedly can be an easy and effective way to clear the screen. However, it is not an ideal clear-screen operation for the Compaq PC-compatibles, as they show a noticeable delay when this technique is used.

☞ See Chapter 4, page 71 for more on video modes. See page 54, memory location hex 449, for more on how a record of the mode is stored in memory. See service 15 (hex F) to find out how to read the current video mode.

Service 1: Set Cursor Size

Service 1 controls the form and size of the blinking cursor that appears in the text modes. The standard IBM cursor normally appears as one or two blinking scan lines at the bottom of a character display position. We can change the default cursor size by redefining the number of lines that are displayed.

The Color/Graphics Adapter can display a cursor that has eight scan lines, numbered from 0 at the top to 7 at the bottom. The Monochrome Adapter and the EGA can display a cursor that has fourteen scan lines, also numbered from the top, from 0 through 13. We set the cursor size by specifying the starting and ending scan lines. (These are the same as the start and stop parameters of BASIC's LOCATE statement.) The start line number is loaded into the CH register and the stop line number into the CL register. The default cursor setting is CH = 6, CL = 7 for the Color/Graphics Adapter, and CH = 11, CL = 12 for the Monochrome Adapter.

If the start line is less than the stop line, a normal one-part cursor appears. If the start line is greater than the stop line, the cursor will wrap around and produce a two-part cursor.

You will notice that the valid line numbers occupy only four of the bits (bits 0 through 3) placed in these registers. If bit 5 of CH is set on with a value of 32 (hex 20), the cursor will disappear. When a graphics mode is set, bit 5 is automatically set on to keep the cursor mechanism from interfering with the graphics display. This is one of two techniques that we can use to remove the cursor in the text modes. The other technique is to actually move it off the screen, say to row 26, column 1. Since there is no true cursor in the graphics modes, any cursor that we see is simulated with the solid-block character, CHR$(223), or with a change of background attributes.

Service Number	Parameters
AH = 1	CH = starting scan line of cursor
	CL = ending scan line of cursor

Figure 9-3. The registers used to set the
cursor size using service 1

Service Number	Parameters
AH = 2	DH = row number
	DL = column number
	BH = page number (set to 0 in graphics modes)

Figure 9-4. The registers used to set the
cursor position using service 2

☛ For more on cursors, see page 92. See service 3 for the reverse operation: Read cursor position.

Service 2: Set Cursor Position

Service 2 sets the position of the cursor using row and column coordinates. In text modes, there can be multiple display pages, each one having an independently recorded cursor position. Even though the graphics modes do not have a visible cursor, they keep track of the logical cursor position in the same way as the text modes. This logical cursor position is used to supervise character I/O.

The cursor position is specified by placing a row number in register DH, a column number in DL, and a page number in BH. The numbering for the rows and columns begins with coordinates 0,0 in the top left corner. The graphics modes also use the character row and column coordinates to identify the cursor location, rather than the pixel coordinates. The page number is the conventional display page number used by BASIC: pages 0 through 7 in 40-column modes and pages 0 through 3 in 80-column modes. The page number must be set to 0 in the graphics modes.

☛ See Figure 9-4 for a summary of register settings. See page 85 for more on display pages. See page 86 for more on text display formats. See service 3 for the reverse operation: Read cursor position.

Service 3: Read Cursor Position

Service 3 is the opposite of services 1 and 2. When we specify the page number in BH, the ROM-BIOS reports the cursor size by returning

Service Number	Parameters
AH = 3	BH = page number (set to 0 in graphics modes)
	DH = row number
	DL = column number
	CH = starting scan line of cursor
	CL = ending scan line of cursor

Figure 9-5. The registers used to read the cursor position using service 3

Service Number	Parameters
AH = 4	DH = character row number
	DL = character column number
	CH = pixel line number (0 through 199)
	CX = pixel line number for new EGA graphics modes
	BX = pixel column number

Figure 9-6. The registers used to read the light-pen position using service 4

the starting scan line in CH and the ending scan line in CL. It reports the cursor position by returning the row in DH and the column in DL. As with service 2, the page must be specified as 0 in the graphics modes.

☞ See Figure 9-5 for a summary of register settings. See page 85 for more on display pages. See page 86 for more on text display formats.

Service 4: Read Light-Pen Position

Service 4 reports the light-pen status, specifically whether or not it has been triggered, and where it is on the screen if it has been triggered.

Register AH is set to indicate triggering: If AH is 1, the light pen has been triggered; if AH is 0, it has not been triggered. The light pen's pixel location on the screen is sensed by the hardware, and the ROM-BIOS reports it to us translated into two forms: the character position (row in DH, column in DL), and the pixel location (raster line in CH, column/dot in BX). Since the pixel column location can be larger than 255, it is reported in a full-word register. All other values are handled as bytes.

Service 5: Set Active Display Page

Service 5 sets the active display page for text modes 0 through 3. We specify the page number in register AL. In the 40-column modes, we may

Service Number	Parameters
AH = 5	AL = new display page number (0–3 for modes 2 and 3, 0–7 for modes 0 and 1)

Figure 9-7. The registers used to set the
active display page using service 5

choose from pages 0 through 7, and in the 80-column modes, from pages 0 through 3. Page 0 is used by default. Page 0 is located at the beginning of display memory, with each subsequent page following either 2K bytes (in 40-column modes) or 4K bytes (in 80-column modes) behind. The higher page numbers are in higher memory locations.

☛ See page 85 for more on display pages.

Service 6: Scroll Window Up

Service 6 and companion service 7 are used to define a rectangular text-window area on the screen and to scroll its contents up or down one or more lines. To accomplish the scrolling effect, blank lines are inserted at the bottom of the window area with service 6 (at the top with service 7) and the top lines of the window (the bottom lines with service 7) are scrolled off and disappear.

The number of lines to be scrolled is specified in AL. If AL is 0, the entire window is blanked (the same thing would happen if we scrolled more lines than the window size allowed). The location or size of the window is specified in the CX and DX registers: CH is the top row, and DH is the bottom row; CL is the left column, and DL is the right column. The display attribute for the new blank lines inserted by the two services is taken from BH. Figure 9-8 shows a summary of the register settings for both services 6 and 7:

Service Number	Parameters
AH = 6	AL = number of lines to scroll
	CH = row number of upper left corner
	CL = column number of upper left corner
	DH = row number of lower right corner
	DL = column number of lower right corner
	BH = display attribute for blank lines

Figure 9-8. The registers used to set the win-
dow size for scrolling using services 6 and 7

Window scrolling is normally a two-stage process: When a new line is ready to be written in the window, service 6 (or service 7) is used to scroll the current window contents. Then the new information is written to the new line using the cursor-positioning and character-writing services. The following example demonstrates this window action.

```
DEBUG                    ; invoke DEBUG from DOS utilities
A                        ; ask to assemble instructions
INT 10                   ; create interrupt hex 10 instruction
[Return]                 ; finish assembling
R AX                     ; ask to see and change contents of AX
0603                     ; specify service 6 (scroll up), using 3-line window
R CX                     ; ask to see and change contents of CX
050A                     ; specify top left corner: row 5, column 10
R DX                     ; ask to see and change contents of DX
1020                     ; specify bottom right corner: row 16, column 32
D 0 L 180                ; fill screen with nonsense
G = 100 102              ; execute INT 10, then stop
```

☛ See Chapter 8 for more on assembly-language routines. See the IBM DOS reference manual for more on DEBUG.

Service 7: Scroll Window Down

Service 7 is, as we've already mentioned, the mirror image of service 6. The primary difference between the two services is the scrolling action. In service 7, the new blank lines appear at the top of the window and the old lines disappear at the bottom. The opposite scrolling action takes place in service 6. ☛ See the description under service 6 for the parameter settings.

Service 8: Read Character and Attribute

Service 8 is used to read characters "off the screen," that is, directly out of the display memory. This service is unusually spiffy because it works in both text and graphics modes.

In graphics modes, the same character drawing tables that are used to write characters are also used to recognize them by a pattern matching operation. Even if we create our own character set in graphics mode, this service will be able to recognize them. In text mode, of course, the ASCII character codes are directly available in the display memory.

Service Number	Parameters
AH = 8	BH = active display page number (not needed in graphics modes)
	AL = ASCII character read from cursor location
	AH = attribute of text character

Figure 9-9. The registers used to read a text character and attribute using service 8

Service 8 returns the ASCII character code of the character read from the screen in AL. In graphics mode, if the character does not match any standard ASCII code, it is reported as hex 00. In the text modes, the service also returns the text color attributes in AH. The text-mode display page number must be specified in BH. The display-page setting is not needed in the graphics modes.

☞ See page 79 for more on text characters and attribute bytes. See page 86 for more on text- and graphics-mode characters. See Appendix C for more on ASCII characters.

Service 9: Write Character and Attribute

Service 9 writes one or more copies of a single character and its color attribute. The character is specified in AL, and the text-mode attribute or graphics-mode color is specified in BL. The number of times the character is to be written (one or more times) is placed in CX.

For the text modes, the display page number must be specified in BH; it need not be given for the graphics modes.

The character and its color attributes are written as many times as requested, starting at the current cursor location. Although the cursor is not moved, duplicate characters are written at subsequent screen locations. In text mode, the duplicated characters will successfully wrap around from line to line, which increases the usefulness of this service. In graphics mode, the characters will not wrap around.

Service 9 is quite useful both for writing individual characters and for replicating a character. The repeat operation is most often used to rapidly lay out blanks or other repeated characters, such as the horizontal lines that are part of box drawings (☞ see Appendix C). When you wish to make a single copy of the character, be sure to set the count in CX to 1. If it's set to 0, the number of repetitions will run away.

Service 9 has an advantage over the similar service 14, in that we can control the color attributes. However, its one disadvantage is that the cursor is not automatically advanced.

Service Number	Parameters
AH = 9	AL = ASCII character to write to screen
	BL = character attribute to write to screen
	BH = active display page number (not needed in graphics modes)
	CX = number of times to write character and attribute

Figure 9-10. The registers used to write a
text character and attribute using service 9

In graphics mode, the color specified in BL is the foreground color—the color of the pixels that make up the character drawing. If bit 7 is 1 (with the value of 128 or hex 80), then the color bits in BL are combined with the current pixel color bits with an exclusive-or (XOR) operation. This is a convenient way to ensure that the resulting color is different from what was there before—a near-guarantee of legibility. If bit 7 of BL is 0, then the color in BL simply replaces the existing pixel colors. The same feature also applies to the character and pixel writing services, services 10 and 12.

☛ See page 79 for more on display attributes in text modes. See page 81 for more on color attributes in graphics modes.

Service 10 (hex A): Write Character

Service 10 is the same as service 9 (write character and attribute to cursor location) with one exception: Service 9 allows us to change the existing screen color attribute in text mode while service 10 does not.

Service Number	Parameters
AH = 10	AL = ASCII character to write to screen
	BL = color attribute for graphics modes
	BH = active display page number
	CX = number of times to write character

Figure 9-11. The registers used to write a
character using service 10

However, in the graphics mode, the color still needs to be specified in BL, making the description of this service as only a character-writing service partly incorrect. The same graphics color rules apply as with services 9 and 12: The color can be used directly, or XORed with the existing color. (☞ See service 9 for an explanation.)

☞ See page 79 for more on display attributes in text modes. See page 81 for more on color attributes in graphics modes.

Service 11 (hex B): Set Color Palette

Service 11 is used to select one of the two medium-resolution graphics palettes. To use this service, we load BH with the palette color ID and BL with a color value. (☞ See page 82 for more on color palettes.)

One variation of this service applies to the text modes; all others apply only to the graphics modes. In the text modes, if BH is 0, then BL specifies the color of the border around the text area—a color selected from the full 16-color palette. In any graphics mode, if BH is 0, then BL specifies the default color of the background and of the border area as well. The border area is merged with any part of the working screen area that is set to the background color. The BL value can be selected from the full 16-color palette.

On the other hand, if BH is 1, then BL selects the palette being used. For the Color/Graphics Adapter, this applies only to mode 4 (medium-resolution, four-color graphics). For more advanced display adapters, including the PCjr's, it can apply to other modes as well. In this discussion, we will cover just the standard four-color palettes that are provided by

Service Number	Parameters
AH = 11	BH = palette color ID (0 or 1 in 320 × 200 graphics)
	BL = color or palette value to be used with color ID

Figure 9-12. The registers used to set the color palette using service 11

mode 4: palettes 0 and 1. The palette number is selected with BL. Palette 0 has these four colors:

> 0: Current background color
> 1: Green (2)
> 2: Red (4)
> 3: Brown (6)

Palette 1 has these four colors:

> 0: Current background color
> 1: Cyan (3)
> 2: Magenta (5)
> 3: White (7)

Service 12 (hex C): Write Pixel Dot

Service 12 writes an individual pixel. Since the cursor position used in services 9, 10, and 14 applies only to characters, this service requires a raster line and column/pixel specification. As usual, the locations are numbered from 0,0 starting at the top left corner of the screen.

The row (raster) number is specified in DX. The column number is specified in CX. The color is given in AL, with the option of direct color or XORed color (☞ see service 9 for an explanation).

☞ See page 88 for more on pixels in graphics modes.

Service 13 (hex D): Read Pixel Dot

Service 13 is the reverse of service 12: It reads the pixel contents rather than writing them. A pixel has only a single color attribute, which is exactly the information that is returned through service 13. (The read-character service 8 returns both a color and an ASCII character code.) The row is specified in DL, not DX (☞ see the note in service 12), and the column in CX. The pixel color code is returned in AL. All high-order bits are set to 0, as you would expect.

Service Number	Parameters
AH = 12	AL = pixel color code (0–15)
	DX = row number of pixel
	CX = column number of pixel

Figure 9-13. The registers used to write a pixel using service 12

Service Number	Parameters
AH = 13	AL = pixel color code (0–15)
	DX = row number of pixel
	CX = column number of pixel

Figure 9-14. The registers used to read a pixel using service 13

Service 14 (hex E): Write Character as TTY

Service 14 is the workhorse service of conventional character output. It writes individual characters to the screen in what is known as teletype (TTY) mode. This makes the screen act as the simplest and crudest form of printer—exactly what is needed for routine text output. As such, it has no regard for such niceties as color, blinking characters, or control over the cursor location.

When this service is used, the character is written at the current cursor location and the cursor is advanced one position, wrapping to new lines or scrolling the screen as needed. The character to be written is specified in AL.

In text mode, the current screen attributes are maintained from one character to the next. In graphics mode, the foreground color must be specified each time in the BL register.

There are four characters that service 14 reacts to according to their ASCII meaning: CHR$(7)—beep, CHR$(8)—backspace, CHR$(10)—line feed, and CHR$(13)—carriage return. All other characters are simply displayed normally.

The primary advantage of this service over service 9 is that the cursor is automatically moved; the advantage of service 9 is that we can control the color attribute. Now, if we could only combine the two....

Service Number	Parameters
AH = 14	AL = ASCII character to write
	BL = foreground color of character (in graphics modes only)
	BH = active display page (not needed in graphics modes)

Figure 9-15. The registers used to write a character as TTY using service 14

Service Number	Parameters
AH = 15	AL = current display mode
	AH = number of characters per line
	BH = active display page (0 in graphics modes)

Figure 9-16. The registers used to read the video mode using service 15

Service 15 (hex F): Get Current Video Mode

Service 15 returns the current video mode and two other useful pieces of information: the screen width in characters (80, 40, or 20) and the display page number.

The video mode, as explained under service 0, is returned in AL. The screen width is returned in AH in number of characters per line (low-resolution graphics mode will be correctly reported as 20 characters wide). The display page will be returned in BH. Figure 9-16 summarizes the register settings.

☞ See page 72 for more on video modes. See page 54, memory location hex 449, for more on how a record of the mode is kept.

Service 19 (hex 13): Write Character String

AT

Service 19, available only with the AT, allows us to write a string of characters to the display screen. Through the four subservices that make up this service, we can specify the character attributes individually or as a group. We can also move the cursor to the end of the string or leave it in place, depending on which subservice we choose.

The subservice number is placed in AL; the pointer to the string in ES:BP; the length of the string in CX; the starting position where the string is to be written in DX; and the display page number in BH.

Subservices 0 and 1 write a string of characters to the screen using the attribute specified in register BL. With subservice 0, the cursor is not moved from the location specified in register DX; with subservice 1, the cursor is moved to the location following the last character in the string.

Subservices 2 and 3 write a string of characters and attributes to the screen, writing first the character and then the attribute. With subservice 2, the cursor is not moved from the location specified in register DX; with subservice 3, the cursor is moved to the location following the last character in the string.

COMMENTS AND EXAMPLE

In cruising through the ROM-BIOS video services, we've shown how they work individually. With that information in mind, the next question usually is: Given a choice between using the ROM-BIOS services directly or using higher-level services such as the DOS services or the services built into your programming language, which is best? The general advice that we always give is to use the highest-level services that will accomplish what you want to do. In this case, there is no specific reason for you to avoid using the ROM-BIOS video services—you can't do any great harm by using them. But in the next chapter on the diskette services, we'll argue the case the other way, advising you to avoid using the ROM-BIOS diskette services since there is more risk associated with them.

The video capabilities of the PC models are remarkable, and the ROM-BIOS services give us the full use of them. The DOS services, as you'll see in Chapters 14 through 18, are rather weak and provide only the simplest sort of character services. Likewise, many programming languages (for example, Pascal and C) only provide a dressed-up version of the DOS services and nothing more. So, if you need to use the PC's fancy screen capabilities and if you aren't using a language such as BASIC that provides the services you need, you should be using the ROM-BIOS services. Getting control of the display screen is one of the very best reasons for using the ROM-BIOS services.

Using the ROM-BIOS services directly usually calls for an assembly-language interface, so we'll give you an example of how one can be set up. For our example, we'll set up a module in a format that would be called by Pascal. We'll make the module switch to mode 1 (40-column text in color) and set the background color to blue.

Here is our assembly module (☞see Chapter 8, page 164, for general notes on the format):

```
MODULE      SEGMENT  'CODE'
            PUBLIC   BLUE40
BLUE40      PROC     FAR
            PUSH     BP            ; save old base pointer
            MOV      BP,SP         ; establish our base pointer
; set video mode
            MOV      AH,0          ; service 0: set mode
            MOV      AL,1          ; mode 1: 40-column text, in color
            INT      16            ; request video service
```

```
        ; set background color
                        MOV     AH,11           ; service 11: set color
                        MOV     BH,0            ; set background
                        MOV     BL,1            ; use color 1 = blue
                        INT     16              ; request video service
                        POP     BP              ; restore old base pointer
                        RET     0               ; return to caller
        BLUE40          ENDP
        MODULE          ENDS
                        END
```

10

ROM-BIOS
Diskette and Fixed Disk Services

W e're now going to cover the disk services provided by the ROM-BIOS. ☞ To understand the logical structure of the contents of a disk, see Chapter 5, particularly pages 106 through 124. For information about the higher-level disk services provided by DOS, see Chapters 15 through 18.

Generally speaking, disk operations are best left to disk operating systems. If you decide to use any of the ROM-BIOS disk services, I recommend that you read the section entitled "Comments and Examples" on page 199 of this chapter.

THE STANDARD ROM-BIOS DISK SERVICES

Since a disk drive can do only a few simple things, there are only six standard BIOS disk services common to all PC models. **AT** The AT, having introduced a more complicated disk drive, has added several new services to the ROM-BIOS. We will discuss these additions separately, beginning on page 194.

All ROM-BIOS disk services are invoked with interrupt 19 (hex 13) and selected by loading the service number into the AH register. The six standard services, shown in Figure 10-1, are numbered from 0 through 5, as is customary.

The disk services operate under the supervision of the disk base table, which is a set of over a dozen disk control parameters stored in ROM that specify such things as the sector size, the step-rate time, and the head-settle time. For most programmers, the disk base table is an invisible part of the disk services. However, occasionally some of its parameters may need to be changed for special purposes. For this reason we included a brief description of it toward the end of this chapter (☞ see page 196).

Service	Description
0	Reset disk system
1	Get disk status
2	Read disk sectors
3	Write disk sectors
4	Verify disk sectors
5	Format disk track

Figure 10-1. The six standard disk services provided by the ROM-BIOS

❑ *While the ROM-BIOS diskette services for the PCjr are identical to those for the other IBM personal computer models, the performance of the PCjr's diskette drives is radically different. This is primarily because the Junior's diskette controller does not use direct memory addressing (DMA), which allows data to be transferred directly between diskette and memory. Instead, the ROM-BIOS software does the transfer work, which ties up the computing power of the PCjr during diskette operations, making the timing and performance of the diskette services distinctly different from that of the other models. Among other things, this means that some copy-protection schemes designed on the other models will not operate successfully on the Junior.*

Service 0: Reset Disk System

Service 0 is used to reset the disk controller and drive. This service does not affect the disk itself. Instead, a reset through service 0 forces the ROM-BIOS disk support routines to start from scratch for the next disk operation by recalibrating the disk drive's read/write head—an operation that positions the head on a certain track. In our programs this reset service is normally used after an error in any other drive operation.

Service 1: Get Disk Status

Service 1 reports the disk status in the eight bits of register AH. The status is preserved after each disk operation including the read, write, verify, and format operations described below. By preserving the disk status, it is possible for an error-handling or error-reporting routine to be completely independent of the routines that operate the disk. This can be very useful. Under the right circumstances, we can rely on DOS or our programming language to drive the disk (a wise choice; ☞ see "Comments and Examples" on page 199), and at the same time have our program find out and report the intimate details of what went wrong. ☞ See Figure 10-2 for details of the status byte.

Service 2: Read Disk Sectors

Service 2 reads one or more disk sectors into memory. If we want to read more than one sector, every sector must be on the same track and on the same side. This is largely because the ROM-BIOS doesn't know how many sectors there might be on a track, so it can't know when to switch from one side or track to another. Usually, this service is used

Value (hex)	Meaning	Value (hex)	Meaning
1	bad command	A	bad sector flag (F)
2	address mark not found	10	bad CRC or ECC
3	write attempted on write-protected disk (D)	11	ECC corrected data error (F)
		20	Controller failed
4	sector not found	40	seek failed
5	reset failed (F)	80	time out
6	diskette removed (D)	AA	drive not ready (F)
7	bad parameter table (F)	BB	undefined error (F)
8	DMA overrun (D)	CC	write fault (F)
9	DMA across 64 K boundary	EO	status error (F)
			(F) = for fixed disk only
			(D) = for diskette only

Figure 10-2. The value of the disk status byte returned to register AH by service 1

for reading either individual sectors or one side of an entire trackful of sectors for bulk operations such as DISKCOPY in DOS. Various registers are used for control information in a read operation. ☞ They are summarized in Figure 10-3 on page 192.

DL contains the drive number.

DH contains the disk side or read/write head number.

CH contains the track number. For diskettes, the track number normally has a value from 0 through 39 (hex 00 through 27) but it can be higher, and is higher for some copy-protection schemes. Many diskette drives work successfully with up to 42 tracks.

CL contains the sector number. For diskettes, the sector number normally ranges from 1 through 8 or 9, although sector numbers greater than 9 are sometimes used for copy-protection schemes. Note that sectors are numbered from 1, unlike drives, tracks, or heads (sides).

AL contains the number of sectors to be read. For diskettes, this is normally either 1, 8, or 9. We are warned by IBM not to request 0 sectors.

ES:BX contains the buffer location. The location of the memory area where the data will be placed is provided by a segmented address given in this register pair. The ES:BX register pair is normally used for all segmented addresses in the ROM-BIOS services.

The data area should be big enough to accommodate as much as is read; keep in mind that while normal DOS sectors are 512 bytes, sectors can be as large as 1,024 bytes (☞ see the format service that follows). When this service reads more than one sector, it lays the sectors out in memory one right after another.

CF contains the error status of the operation. The result of the operation is actually reported through a combination of the carry flag (CF) and the AH register. If CF is 0, it means there was no error and AH will also be 0, in which case the number of sectors read will be returned in AL. If CF is 1, it means there was an error and AH will contain the status bits detailed under service 1, the status service.

When using service 2 with a diskette drive, or any other active diskette service, remember that the diskette drive motor takes some time to reach a working speed and that none of these services waits for it to happen. Although my own experience with the ROM-BIOS diskette services suggests that this is rarely a problem, IBM recommends that any program using these services try three times before assuming an error is real and that it use the reset service between tries. The logic of the suggested operation is as follows, partly expressed in BASIC:

```
10 ERROR.COUNT = 0
20 WHILE ERROR.COUNT < 3
30   ' do read/write/verify/format operation
40   ' error checking here: if no error goto 90
50     ERROR.COUNT = ERROR.COUNT + 1
60   ' do reset operation
70 WEND
80   ' act on error
90   ' carry on after success
```

☞ Be sure to see the section on page 197 for the effect of the disk base table on the reset operation.

Service 3: Write Disk Sectors

Service 3 writes one or more sectors to a disk—the reverse of service 2. All the registers, details, and comments given for service 2 apply to service 3. (☞ Also see Figure 10-3.) The disk sectors must be formatted before they can be written to.

Service 4: Verify Disk Sectors

Service 4 "verifies" the contents of one or more disk sectors. This operation is not what many people think it is: No comparison is made between the data on the disk and the data in memory. The verification performed by this service simply checks that the sectors can be found and read and that the cyclical redundancy check (CRC) is correct. The CRC

Parameters	Status Results
DL = drive number	If CF = 0, then no error and AH = 0
DH = side or head number	If CF = 1, then error and AH contains service 1 status bits
CH = track number	
CL = sector number	
AL = number of sectors to be read	
ES:BX = address of buffer	

Figure 10-3. The registers used for control information by the read, write, verify, and format services

acts as a sophisticated parity check for the data in each sector and will detect most errors, such as lost or scrambled bits, very reliably.

We most often use the verify service to check the results of a write operation after using service 3, but we can verify any part of a disk at any time. However, many people regard verification as an unnecessary operation because the disk drives are so reliable and because ordinary error reporting works so well. DOS doesn't even verify a write operation unless we ask it to with the VERIFY ON command.

The verify service operates just like the read and write services and uses the same registers. The only difference between them is that the verify operation does not use any memory area and therefore does not use the register pair ES:BX.

Service 5: Format Diskette Track

Service 5 formats one track. The format service operates very much like the read and write services except that the sector number held in register CL is not used. All other parameters shown in Figure 10-3 are passed and returned in the registers.

Since formatting is done one full track at a time, we cannot format individual sectors. However, we can specify individual characteristics for each sector on a track.

Every sector on a track has four descriptive bytes associated with it that are located in the data area pointed to by the register pair ES:BX. They become the address marks that are later used to identify individual sectors during the read, write, and verify operations. These four address

N	Sector Size (bytes)	Sector Size (K)
0	128	⅛
1	256	¼
2	512	½
3	1,024	1

Figure 10-4. The four standard sizes of the N size code

bytes are referred to as C for cylinder (which is a more general term for track), H for head (or disk side), R for record (or sector number), and N for number of bytes per sector (also called the size code). There should be a 4-byte field for every sector specified in AL.

When a sector is being read or written, the ROM-BIOS searches the disk track for the sector's ID, the essential part of which is R, the record or sector number. The cylinder and head parameters are not actually needed in this address mark since the read/write head is seeked mechanically to the proper track and the side is selected electronically, but they are recorded and tested as a safety check.

The size code (N) can take on any one of the four standard values shown in Figure 10-4. The normal setting is code 2—512 bytes.

Sectors are written on the disk in the order specified by the address bytes and need not be written sequentially. In fact, the order of the sectors can be rearranged (interleaved), either for better performance or to create timing differences for copy-protection purposes. The XT's fixed disk has its sectors interleaved so that consecutive sectors are physically located six sectors apart. DOS diskettes have their sectors recorded in sequential order; 1, 2, 3, etc.

For a conventional nine-sector DOS diskette, the format addressing for track 0, side 1 would be like this:

```
C H R N     C H R N     C H R N     ...      C H R N
0 1 1 2     0 1 2 2     0 1 3 2     ...      0 1 9 2
```

When a diskette track is formatted, the diskette drive pays attention to the diskette's index hole and uses it as a starting marker to format the track. The index hole is ignored in all other operations (read, write, or verify), and tracks are simply searched for by their address marks.

Note that nothing in this format service specifies the initial data value that is written into each formatted sector. That is controlled by the disk base table (☞ see page 196).

Using Service 5 for Copy-Protection

Tracks can be formatted in all sorts of screwy ways, but most operating systems can only read certain formats. Consequently, most copy-protection schemes are based on an unconventional format that prevents an operating system from successfully reading and copying data. We can choose from several different copy-protection methods:

- We can rearrange the order of the sectors, which alters the access time in a way that the copy-protection scheme can detect.

- We can squeeze more sectors onto a track (ten is about the outside limit for 512-byte sectors).

- We can simply leave out a sector number.

- We can add a sector with an oddball number (for example, we can make R = 22).

- We can specify one or more sectors to be an unconventional size.

- We can record the wrong C and H values.

Any of these techniques can be used either for copy protection or for changing the operating characteristics of the diskette. Depending on what options are used, a conventionally formatted diskette may have its unusual characteristics completely hidden from DOS in such a way that a copy-protection mechanism is transparent to ordinary detection.

THE AT DISKETTE AND FIXED-DISK SERVICES

The AT uses disk drives that are different enough from the drives used in the other models that several new BIOS diskette services were added. They are designed to support the high-capacity diskettes and the variety of fixed disks that the AT can use. We'll outline the new services here, but we won't go into any great detail for the same reason we have passed lightly over many other model-dependent features: Our main concern in this book is to explore the general principles and programming practices that apply to the entire PC family, not to the peculiarities of one model or another.

Service 8: Get Current Drive Parameters

Service 8 returns disk-drive parameters. DL reports the number of disk drives (from 0 to 2); DH reports the maximum head-side number; CH returns the maximum cylinder/track number; and CL returns the highest sector number.

Service 9: Initialize Fixed-Disk Parameter Tables

Service 9 is used to set the disk base tables for two hard-disk drives. The interrupt vectors for interrupts 65 (hex 41) and 70 (hex 46) are used to provide the table addresses. This service would be used only to install a "foreign" disk drive.

Service 10 and 11 (hex A and B): Read and Write Long

Service 10 reads, and service 11 writes, "long" sectors on 20-megabyte fixed disks. A long sector includes an ECC (error correction code), a 4-byte error code that provides high-level error checking and error correction of the sector's data.

Service 12 (hex C): Seek to Cylinder

Service 12 performs a seek operation that positions the disk read/ write heads over a particular cylinder on the hard disk. Register DL provides the drive ID, DH the head number, and CH the cylinder number.

Service 13 (hex D): Alternate Disk Reset

Service 13 performs an alternate drive-reset operation for the fixed-disk drives. The drive is specified in register DL. This service operates the same way as diskette service 0.

Service 16 (hex 10): Test for Drive Ready

Service 16 tests to see if the fixed-disk drive is ready. The drive is specified in register DL and the status is returned in register AH.

Service 17 (hex 11): Recalibrate Drive

Service 17 recalibrates individual fixed-disk drives. The drive is specified in register DL and the status is returned in register AH.

Service 20 (hex 14): Controller Diagnostics

Service 20 invokes an internal diagnostic routine in the AT's disk controller. The status of the controller is returned in register AH.

Service 21 (hex 15): Get Disk Type

Service 21 is used to inquire about the type of disk drive installed. Given the drive ID in register DL, it returns in register AH one of four disk-type indicators: If AH is 0, it means there is no drive present; if AH is 1, it indicates the presence of a diskette drive that cannot sense when the disk has been changed (typical of most disk drives); if AH is 2, it indicates the presence of a diskette drive that can sense a change of disks (drives like the AT's high-capacity diskette drives); finally, if AH is 3, it means that a fixed-disk drive is installed. When the drive type is 3, the register pair CX:DX acts as a 4-byte integer that gives the total number of disk sectors on the drive.

Service 22 (hex 16): Change of Disk Status

Service 22 is used to inquire about a change of disks for drives that can sense when a disk has been changed, like the AT's high-capacity drives. Register AH is set to 0 to indicate no disk change and to 6 to indicate a change of disk. Register DL returns the number of the drive that had a disk change.

The change-of-disk sensing in services 21 and 22 is very useful to programs that need to know if a disk has been changed. For certain critical disk operations, such as reading a file allocation table (FAT), it helps to know if the disk has been changed or not. If it has been changed, then any disk data held in memory may have to be discarded and reread. When a disk drive can't report a diskette change, the program usually has to assume that it might have been changed and react accordingly, at a cost to program efficiency. If we are designing programs that control a disk drive, it is clearly useful and more efficient for them to be able to check this sort of information.

Service 23 (hex 17): Set Disk Type

Service 23 is used to set the diskette and drive combination for the AT. If AL is 0, there is no drive; if AL is 1, it indicates a regular diskette in a regular drive; if AL is 3, it indicates a high-capacity diskette in a high-capacity drive. This service is used with the format service (service 5) to set the disk type to be formatted.

THE DISK BASE TABLE

The overall operation of the diskette drive is controlled by a set of parameters called the disk base table. Although a default version of the disk base table is stored in ROM at the now-standard address of F000:EFC7, we can create a new table. The new table can be put into effect by placing it in ordinary memory and then changing the disk base table interrupt vector to point to it. The vector for interrupt 30 (hex 1E) is reserved to point to the new table. Every release of DOS since the very first 1.00 version has created its own disk base table rather than using the one in the ROM.

Offset	Use
0	Specify byte 1: step-rate time, head-unload time
1	Specify byte 2: head-load time, DMA mode
2	Wait time until motor turned off
3	Bytes per sector: $0 = 128$; $1 = 256$; $2 = 512$; $3 = 1,024$
4	Last sector number
5	Gap length between sectors for read/write operations
6	Data length when sector length not specified
7	Gap length between sectors for formatting operations
8	Data value stored in formatted sectors
9	Head-settle time
A	Motor start-up time

*Figure 10-5. The use of the eleven bytes in
the disk base table*

The disk base table is composed of the eleven bytes shown in Figure
10-5. We'll go over them byte by byte and compare the values used by
DOS 2.10 with the default tables in the original version of the PC. Most of
the information stored in the disk base table is of little use to us unless we
plan to write a new disk base table to override the one used by DOS.

Bytes 0 and 1 are referred to as the specify bytes. They are part of
the command strings sent to the floppy-disk controller (FDC), which is
also known as the NEC (Nippon Electric Company) controller. The first
four bits of the first byte are the step-rate time, or SRT, which is the time
the ROM-BIOS allows for the diskette drive to move from track to track.
The default value is 8 milliseconds for each track. DOS 2.10 reduces this to
6 milliseconds, which speeds up the drive performance. There is also a
mode setting for DMA in the first byte because the PCjr does not have
DMA for disk data transfer. As a result, the DMA mode bit is not set in the
PCjr's default disk base table. Oddly enough, in the disk base set up by
DOS 2.10, this bit is set to indicate that DMA is present. (It's a mystery to
me why this doesn't cause any problems on the Junior.)

Byte 2, at offset 2, specifies how long the diskette motor is to be left
running after each operation. The motor is left on in case the diskette is
needed again. The value is in units of clock ticks (roughly 18 ticks per
second). All versions of the table have this set to 37 (hex 25)—meaning
that the motor stays on for roughly 2 seconds.

Byte 3, at offset 3, gives the sector length code—the same N code that is used in the format operation (☞ see page 193 under service 5). This is normally set to 2, representing the customary sector length of 512 bytes. In any read, write, or verify operation, the length code in the disk base must be set to the proper value, especially when working with sectors of unconventional length.

Byte 4, at offset 4, gives the record number of the last sector on the track. This value is 8 in the ROM's default table and 9 in DOS 2.10's table.

Byte 5, at offset 5, specifies the gap size between sectors, which is used when reading or writing data. In effect, it tells the ROM-BIOS how long to wait before looking for the next sector's address marking, so it can avoid looking at nonsense on the diskette. In each standard disk base, the gap size is set to 42 (hex 2A).

Byte 6, at offset 6, is called the data transfer length (DTL) and is set to 255 (hex FF). This byte sets the maximum data length when the sector length is not specified.

Byte 7, at offset 7, sets the size of the gap between sectors when a track is formatted. Naturally, it is bigger than the search gap at offset 5. The normal value for this is 80 (hex 50).

Byte 8, at offset 8, provides the data value that will be stored in each byte of the sectors when a track is formatted. The standard value is hex F6, the division symbol. We can change it to anything we want, if we can think of a good reason to do so.

Byte 9, at offset 9, sets the head-settle time, which is how long the system waits for vibration to end after seeking to a new track. The default time for the head to settle is 25 (hex 19) milliseconds, but DOS 2.10 reduces it to 15 (hex F) milliseconds.

Byte 10, the final byte of the disk base at offset hex A, sets the amount of time allowed for the diskette-drive motor to get up to speed and is measured in ⅛ seconds. The default value is 4, or ½ second; DOS 2.10 changes this to 2, or ¼ second.

It's fun to tinker with the disk base values; there are enough of them to give us an opportunity for all sorts of excitement and mischief. The following program illustrates how to change the data value stored in a sector when it is formatted. We'll change it from hex F6 to hex AA just to show how it's done:

```
10 DEF SEG
20 OFFSET = PEEK(120+0)+256*PEEK(120+1)        ' disk base vector's offset
30 SEGMENT = PEEK(120+2)+256*PEEK(120+3)       ' disk base vector's segment
40 DEF SEG = SEGMENT
```

```
50   ' if the segment is in high memory then it's in ROM and can't be changed
60   IF SEGMENT >= &HF000 THEN PRINT "ROM disk base in use."
70   FORMAT.DATA = PEEK(OFFSET+8)          ' get old data
80   PRINT "Format sets data to " HEX$(FORMAT.DATA)
90   POKE OFFSET+8, &HAA                   ' change data value to hex AA
```

COMMENTS AND EXAMPLES

In the last chapter, where we covered the video ROM-BIOS services for the display screen, I was able to recommend that you make direct use of the ROM-BIOS services whenever you wished. But in the case of the diskette ROM-BIOS services, things are different.

For the diskette operations that a program would normally want performed, the manipulation and supervision of diskettes should be left to DOS and performed either through the conventional file services of a programming language or through the DOS services (☞ see Chapters 14 through 18). There are many reasons for this. The main reason is that it is far easier to let DOS do the work. The DOS facilities take care of almost every basic diskette function from interpreting the diskette format to redirecting data with the ASSIGN (drive) command. Most of the time it just isn't necessary to go any deeper into the system software. However, there are times when we want to work with the diskette contents in an absolute and precise way, usually for copy protection. This is when we should use the ROM-BIOS services.

For our example, we'll use Pascal to write a couple of subroutines that will read and write absolute diskette sectors. We start by defining how we want the interface to look from the Pascal side, which the following program will illustrate. If you are not familiar with Pascal and don't want to decipher this routine, you can pass over it and still get full benefit from studying the assembly-language interface example that follows it.

```
PROGRAM DISKETTE_INTERFACE;
{this defines our segment read/write area: }
  TYPE
    SEGMENT_TYPE = ARRAY [0..511] OF BYTE;
  VAR
    SEGMENT_DATA : SEGMENT_TYPE;
{this defines the assembly read/write routines: }
  FUNCTION  SEGREAD (
              VAR   S : SEGMENT_TYPE;      {data area}
                    D : INTEGER;           {drive number}
                    C : INTEGER;           {track number}
                    H : INTEGER;           {head number}
                    R : INTEGER )          {segment number}
              :   BYTE;                     {status code returned as a byte}
```

```
      EXTERNAL;
FUNCTION  SEGWRITE (
                VAR   S : SEGMENT_TYPE;     {data area}
                      D : INTEGER;          {drive number}
                      C : INTEGER;          {track number}
                      H : INTEGER;          {head number}
                      R : INTEGER )         {segment number}
             :  BYTE;                       {status code returned as a byte}
      EXTERNAL;
{this short program reads the disk boot record segment: }
   BEGIN
     IF SEGREAD ( SEGMENT_DATA, 0, 0, 0, 1 )  = 0
       THEN                                 {no error}
         ELSE ;                             {error}
   END.
```

With these two routines prepared, the stage is set and we can go on to the assembly-language interface routine. ☛ The form of the interface routine should be familiar to anyone who has read the general remarks in Chapter 8 on page 164 or studied the example in Chapter 9 on page 185.

In each of these examples, we're trying to show a variety of new things. Here we have two separate assembly-language routines combined into one. In this case, the two routines are identical except for their names and the ROM-BIOS service code that they use. You'll also notice that the methods used to take the parameters off the stack use addressing references of the form [BP] + x. In the case of this interface, the first parameter on the stack is an offset address, while the others are actual values (drive number, etc.). Even though the first parameter is an address and not a value, we handle it the same way because we are interested in the address itself, not the value stored at that address. Once we have the address, we simply hand it over to the ROM-BIOS service.

This is our segment read/write interface to Pascal. There are two nearly identical procedures for reading and writing disk data.

```
INTERFACE SEGMENT 'CODE'
          PUBLIC   SEGREAD
          PUBLIC   SEGWRITE
; this is the read service:
SEGREAD   PROC     FAR
          PUSH     BP
          MOV      BP,SP
          PUSH     DS              ; move DS...
          POP      ES              ; ...to ES
          MOV      BX,[BP+14]      ; get data offset
          MOV      DL,[BP+12]      ; get drive number
          MOV      CH,[BP+10]      ; get track number
```

```
                 MOV      DH,[BP+08]          ; get side number
                 MOV      CL,[BP+06]          ; get sector number
                 MOV      AL,1                ; ask for 1 sector
                 MOV      AH,2                ; ask for read service
                 INT      19                  ; request diskette service
                 MOV      AL,AH               ; put status where expected
                 POP      BP
                 RET      10                  ; 10 is size of parameters on stack
SEGREAD  ENDP
; this is the write service (only service number differs)
SEGWRITE PROC    FAR
                 PUSH     BP
                 MOV      BP,SP
                 PUSH     DS                  ; move DS...
                 POP      ES                  ;... to ES
                 MOV      BX,[BP+14]          ; get data offset
                 MOV      DL,[BP+12]          ; get drive number
                 MOV      CH,[BP+10]          ; get track number
                 MOV      DH,[BP+08]          ; get side number
                 MOV      CL,[BP+06]          ; get sector number
                 MOV      AL,1                ; ask for 1 sector
                 MOV      AH,3                ; ask for write service
                 INT      19                  ; request diskette service
                 MOV      AL,AH               ; put status where expected
                 POP      BP
                 RET      10                  ; 10 is size of parameters on stack
SEGWRITE ENDP
INTERFACE ENDS
                 END
```

11

ROM-BIOS
Keyboard Services

Although the ROM-BIOS services for the keyboard are not as numerous or as complicated as those for the display screen (Chapter 9) and for the diskette drive (Chapter 10), the ROM-BIOS keyboard services are important enough to warrant our covering them in their own chapter. All other ROM-BIOS services are gathered together in Chapter 12.

ACCESSING THE KEYBOARD SERVICES

The keyboard services are invoked with interrupt 22 (hex 16). There are three services, numbered 0 through 2. As with all other ROM-BIOS services, the keyboard services are selected in register AH.

Service 0: Read Next Keyboard Character

Service 0 reports the next keyboard input character. If a character is ready in the ROM-BIOS keyboard buffer, it is reported immediately. If not, the service waits until one is ready. As described on page 134, each keyboard character is reported as a pair of bytes, which we call the main and auxiliary bytes. The main byte, returned in AL, is either 0 for special characters (such as the function keys) or else an ASCII code for ordinary ASCII characters. The auxiliary byte, returned in AH, is either the character ID for special characters or the standard PC-keyboard scan code for ASCII characters.

If no character is waiting in the keyboard buffer when service 0 is called, the service waits until there is one, which essentially freezes the program. The service we'll discuss next allows a program to test for keyboard input without the risk of suspending program execution.

Contrary to what some versions of the IBM Technical Reference manual suggest, services 0 and 1 apply to both ordinary ASCII characters and special characters, such as function keys.

Service	Description
0	Read next keyboard character
1	Report whether character ready
2	Get shift status

Figure 11-1. The three ROM-BIOS keyboard services

Service 1: Report Whether Character Ready

Service 1 reports whether a keyboard input character is ready. This is a sneak-preview or look-ahead operation: Even though the character is reported, it remains in the keyboard input buffer of the ROM-BIOS until it is removed by service 0. The zero flag (ZF) is used as the signal: 1 indicates no input is ready; 0 indicates a character is ready. Take care to not be confused by the apparent reversal of the flag numbers—1 means no and 0 means yes, in this instance. When there is a character (ZF = 0), it is reported in AL and AH, just as it is with service 0.

This service is particularly useful for two commonly performed program operations. One is test-and-go, where a program checks for keyboard action but needs to continue running if there is none. Usually, this is done to allow an ongoing process to be interrupted by a keystroke. The other common operation is clearing the keyboard buffer. Generally, it's nice for programs to allow users to type ahead, entering commands in advance, however, in some operations (for example, at safety-check points, such as "OK to end?") this can be unwise. In these circumstances, our programs need to be able to flush the keyboard buffer, clearing it of any input. The keyboard buffer is flushed by using services 0 and 1, as this program outline demonstrates:

```
10  ' call service 1, to test whether the character is ready
20  WHILE ZF = 0
30  ' call service 0, to remove character
40  ' call service 1, to test for another character
50  WEND
```

Contrary to what some technical reference manuals suggest, services 0 and 1 apply to both ordinary ASCII characters and special characters, such as function keys.

Service 2: Get Shift Status

Service 2 reports the shift status in register AL. The shift status is taken bit by bit from the first keyboard status byte, which is kept at memory location hex 417. ☞ Figure 11-2 on the next page describes the settings of each bit. (☞ See pages 137 and 142 for information about the other keyboard status bytes, at hex 418 and hex 488.)

Generally, service 2 and the status bit information are not particularly useful. If you are planning to do some fancy keyboard programming, however, they can come in handy. You'll frequently see them used in programs that do unconventional things, such as differentiating between the left and right Shift keys.

Bit 7 6 5 4 3 2 1 0	Meaning
X	Insert state: 1 = active
. X	Caps Lock: 1 = active
. . X	Num Lock: 1 = active
. . . X	Scroll Lock: 1 = active
. . . . X . . .	Alt shift: 1 — active (Alt depressed)
. . . . . X . .	Ctrl shift: 1 = active (Ctrl depressed)
. . . . . . X .	Normal shift: 1 = active (left Shift depressed)
. . . . X	Normal shift: 1 = active (right Shift depressed)

Figure 11-2. The keyboard status bits returned to register AL using keyboard service 2

COMMENTS AND EXAMPLE

If you are in a position to choose between the keyboard services of your programming language or the ROM-BIOS keyboard services, I feel that you could safely and wisely use either one. While in some cases there are arguments against using the ROM-BIOS services directly, as with the diskette services, those arguments do not apply as strongly to the keyboard services. However, as always, I recommend that you fully examine the potential of the DOS services before resorting to the BIOS services; you may find all you need there, and the DOS services are more long-lived in the ever-changing environments of personal computers.

Most programming languages depend on the DOS services for their keyboard operations, a factor that has some distinct advantages. The primary advantage is that the DOS services allow the use of the standard DOS editing operations on string input (input that is not acted on until the Return key is pressed). Provided that you do not need input control of your own, it can save you a great deal of programming effort (and user education) to let DOS handle the string input, either directly through the DOS services or indirectly through your language's services. But if you need full control of the keyboard input, you'll probably end up using the ROM-BIOS routines in the long run. Either way, the choice is yours.

For our assembly-language example of the use of keyboard services, we'll get a little fancier than we have in previous examples and show you a complete buffer flusher. This routine will perform the action outlined under keyboard service 1, the report-whether-character-ready service.

Among the new things this buffer-flusher routine will illustrate is the use of labels and branching. When we discussed the generalities of assembly-language interface routines in Chapter 8, we mentioned that an ASSUME CS statement is necessary in some circumstances, and you will see one in action here.

When we use ASSUME CS here, we are actually misinforming the assembler about the contents of the CS register, since CS will not necessarily be pointing to where we say it is. This little act of deception is completely harmless, as long as all the branching instructions (such as JNZ in our example) are short jumps. This is because a short jump takes place relative to the current program location, which is indicated by the combination CS:IP. To perform a short jump, the assembler generates an address relative to IP, not to CS, and therefore doesn't really need to know anything about CS. In effect, what we are doing is telling the assembler to ASSUME something about the CS register only because the assembler is too thick-headed to realize that it doesn't need to know it. Here is our example:

```
; KBCLEAR, a routine to clear the keyboard buffer
INTERFACE SEGMENT 'CODE'
          PUBLIC  KBCLEAR
          ASSUME  CS:INTERFACE
KBCLEAR   PROC    FAR
          PUSH    BP
          MOV     BP,SP
          MOV     AH,1                    ; first test for data
          INT     22
WHILE:
          JNZ     SHORT RETURN            ; while ZF = 0
          MOV     AH,0                    ; discard data
          INT     22
          MOV     AH,1                    ; repeated test for data
          INT     22
          JMP     SHORT WHILE             ; wend
RETURN:                                   ; return to caller
          POP     BP
          RET
KBCLEAR   ENDP
INTERFACE ENDS
          END
```

12

Miscellaneous Services

I n this chapter, we'll be covering all the ROM-BIOS services that are either not important enough or not complex enough to be treated in their own chapters: RS-232 serial communications services, cassette tape services, AT extensions, and printer services. We'll also cover some services that are odd enough to be considered miscellaneous, even in a chapter of miscellany.

RS-232 SERIAL COMMUNICATIONS SERVICES

This section discusses the RS-232 asynchronous serial communications port services in the ROM-BIOS. Before we begin describing the ROM-BIOS services in detail, there are a few important things to know about the serial communications port, particularly in the terminology department. We assume you have a basic understanding of data communications, but if you discover that you don't understand the following information, turn to one of the many specialty books on communications for some background information.

Many words are used to describe the RS-232 data path in and out of the computer. One of the most common is *port*. However, this use of the word port is completely different from our previous use of the word. Throughout most of this book, we have used *port* to refer to the addressable paths used by the 8088 microprocessor to talk to other parts of the computer *within the confines of the computer's circuitry*. All references to port numbers, the BASIC statements INP and OUT, and the assembly-language operations IN and OUT refer to these addressable ports. The RS-232 asynchronous serial communications port differs because it is a general-purpose I/O path, which can be used to interconnect many kinds of information-processing equipment *outside the computer*. Typically, the serial ports in the PC are used primarily for telecommunications (meaning a telephone connection through a modem) and also to send data to a serial-type printer.

The serial communications services are invoked with interrupt 20 (hex 14). There are four services common to all IBM models. They're numbered 0 through 3 and selected through register AH. (☛ See Figure 12-1.)

The original design of the IBM personal computers allowed up to seven serial ports to be added, although it is rare for a computer to use more than one or two. No matter how many serial ports there are, the serial port number is specified in the DX register. A single serial port adapter is indicated by a zero in DX.

Service	Description
0	Initialize serial port parameters
1	Send out one character
2	Receive one character
3	Get serial port status

Figure 12-1. The four RS-232 serial port services available through interrupt 20 (hex 14)

Service 0: Initialize Serial Port Parameters

Service 0 sets the various RS-232 parameters and initializes the serial port. It sets four parameters: the baud rate, the parity, the number of stop bits, and the character size (also called the word length). The parameters are combined into one 8-bit code, which is placed in the AL register in the order shown in Figure 12-2. The bit settings for each code are shown in Figure 12-3. When the service is finished, the communication status is reported in AX, just as it is for service 3 (☞ see service 3 for the details).

❑ NOTE: *Though it is painfully slow, 300 baud used to be the most commonly used baud rate for personal computers using modems. A rate of 1,200 baud is now the most common, particularly for serious applications that require faster transmission, though we're likely to see a shift toward 2,400 baud.* **JR** *The PCjr has a maximum baud rate of 4,800. If we try to set it to 9,600 baud, it will still transmit at only 4,800 baud.*

Bit 7 6 5 4 3 2 1 0	Use
X X X	Baud-rate code
. . . X X . . .	Parity code
. . . . . X . .	Stop-bit code
. . . . . . X X	Character-size code

Figure 12-2. The bit order of the serial port parameters returned in register AL by service 0

BAUD RATE		
Bit 7 6 5	Value	Bits per Second
0 0 0	0	110
0 0 1	1	150
0 1 0	2	300
0 1 1	3	600
1 0 0	4	1,200
1 0 1	5	2,400
1 1 0	6	4,800
1 1 1	7	9,600

STOP BITS		
Bit 2	Value	Meaning
0	0	One
1	1	Two

PARITY		
Bit 4 3	Value	Meaning
0 0	0	None
0 1	1	Odd parity
1 0	2	None
1 1	3	Even parity

CHARACTER SIZE		
Bit 1 0	Value	Meaning
0 0	0	Not used
0 1	1	Not used
1 0	2	7-bit*
1 1	3	8-bit

*There are only 128 standard ASCII characters, so they can be transmitted as 7-bit characters, rather than the more conventional 8-bit byte.

Figure 12-3. The bit settings for the four serial port parameters

Service 1: Send Out One Character

Service 1 transmits one character out the serial port. The character is placed in AL and AH is used to report the results. If AH is 0, then the service was successful. If not, bit 7 of AH reports an error and the other bits of AH report the type of error. These bits are outlined in the discussion of service 3, the status service.

There is one anomaly in the error report supplied through this service: Since bit 7 reports that an error has occurred, it is not available to indicate a time-out error (as the details in service 3 would suggest). Consequently, when this service, or service 2, reports an error, the simplest and most reliable way to check the nature of the error is to use the complete status report given by service 3, rather than relying upon the less-complete status code returned with the error through services 1 and 2.

Service 2: Receive One Character

Service 2 receives one character from the communications line specified in DX and returns it in the AL register. The service waits for a character or any signal that indicates the completion of the service, such as a time-out. AH reports the success or failure of the service in bit 7, as explained in the discussion of service 1. Again, consider the advice under service 1 for error handling and see service 3 for the error codes.

Service 3: Get Serial Port Status

Service 3 returns the complete serial port status in the AX register. Each of the 16 bits individually reports a possible problem. The status bits are divided into two groups: AH reports the line status (which is also reported when errors occur with services 1 and 2) and AL reports the modem status, when applicable. Figure 12-4 contains the bit codings of the status bits. You will notice that some codes report errors, while others simply report a condition.

❏ NOTE: *There is one special thing worth noting about the time-out error (AH, bit 7). The earliest version of the ROM-BIOS for the original PC had a programming error that caused a serial-port time-out to be reported as a transfer-shift-register-empty/break-detect-error combination (bits 01010000 rather than 10000000). This has been corrected on all subsequent versions of the ROM-BIOS, but it has caused many communications programs to treat these error codes skeptically. You may wish to keep this in mind. ☛ See page 59 for details on identifying the ROM-BIOS version dates and machine ID codes.*

Bit 7 6 5 4 3 2 1 0	Meaning (when set to 1)	Bit 7 6 5 4 3 2 1 0	Meaning (when set to 1)
AH Register (line status)		*AL Register (modem status)*	
1	Time out error	1	Received line signal detect
. 1	Transfer shift register empty	. 1	Ring indicator
. . 1	Transfer holding register empty	. . 1	Data-set-ready
. . . 1	Break-detect error	. . . 1	Clear-to-send
. . . . 1 . . .	Framing error	. . . . 1 . . .	Delta receive line signal detect
. . . . . 1 . .	Parity error	. . . . . 1 . .	Trailing-edge ring detector
. . . . . . 1 .	Overrun error	. . . . . . 1 .	Delta data-set-ready
. . . . 1	Data ready	 1	Delta clear-to-send

Figure 12-4. The bit coding for the status bytes returned in register AX by service 3

CASSETTE TAPE SERVICES

The cassette tape services are used when working with the cassette tape connection, which is a part of some PC models, such as the original PC and the PCjr, but is not part of the XT, the Portable PC, the AT, the 3270-PC, and some other PC family members. So the cassette port is largely an orphaned feature—something that was created with the original PC on the assumption that there might be some demand for it. There wasn't, and it has remained almost totally unused.

The intended purpose of the cassette port was to allow data and programs, particularly BASIC programs, to be recorded on standard audio cassette tapes, as is done with many inexpensive diskless home computers. I have never encountered a PC program on tape for sale. In fact, about the only use of the cassette port that I am aware of is the homespun and jerry-rigged use of this port as a poor-man's serial port. Nevertheless, IBM does support the use of the cassette port, both through the ROM-BIOS services discussed here and through BASIC, which gives us the ability to read and write either data or BASIC programs on tape.

Keep in mind that any use of the cassette tape port brings with it certain inherent problems. First of all, not all PC models have this port. Secondly, few PCs are equipped with the proper cable connections necessary to work with a cassette tape recorder. And third, the use of a cassette tape recorder involves considerably more manual intervention than you might expect. For example, rewinding a tape cannot be done under program control.

The cassette services are invoked with interrupt 21 (hex 15). There are four services, numbered 0 through 3. As always, the service is specified in register AH. (☛ See Figure 12-5.)

Service	Description
0	Turn on cassette motor
1	Turn off cassette motor
2	Read data blocks
3	Write data blocks

Figure 12-5. The four ROM-BIOS cassette services invoked through interrupt 21 (hex 15)

Service 0: Turn On Cassette Motor

Service 0 turns on the cassette motor, which is not an automatic operation of the ROM-BIOS services as it is with the diskette services. Any program using this service should be prepared for a slight delay while waiting for the motor to start.

Service 1: Turn Off Cassette Motor

Service 1 turns off the cassette motor, also not an automatic operation of the ROM-BIOS services as it is with the diskette services.

Service 2: Read Data Blocks

Service 2 reads one or more cassette data blocks. Cassette data is transferred in standard-sized 256-byte blocks, just as diskette data normally uses a standard 512-byte sector. The number of bytes to be read is placed in the CX register. Although data is placed on tape in 256-byte blocks, any number of bytes can be read or written. Consequently, the number of bytes placed in the CX register need not be a multiple of 256. The register pair ES:BX is used as a pointer to the memory area where the data is to be placed.

After the service is completed, DX contains the actual number of bytes read, ES:BX points to the byte immediately after the last byte transferred, and the carry flag (CF) is set to 0 or 1 to report the success or failure of the operation. On failure, AH is set to report the nature of the error using the code shown in Figure 12-6.

Service 3: Write Data Blocks

Service 3 writes one or more cassette data blocks of 256 bytes each (☞ see service 2). As with service 2, the CX register gives the count of bytes requested and ES:BX points to the data area in memory. If the amount of data being written is not a multiple of 256 bytes, the last data block is padded out to full size.

Code	Meaning
1	Cyclical redundancy check (CRC) error
2	Lost data transitions: bit signals scrambled
3	No data found on tape

Figure 12-6. The error code in register AH if CF reports a failure to read the data blocks; returned by service 2

After the service is completed, CX should be decremented to zero and ES:BX should point just past the last memory byte that was written.

Curiously, there are no error signals provided for this service, essentially because a cassette tape recorder is not able to inform our computer of any difficulties. This forces the ROM-BIOS to write data in blind faith that all is well. Needless to say, it would be a good idea to read back any data written, just to check it.

EXTENDED SERVICES FOR THE AT

Several new BIOS services, listed below, were introduced with the AT to support the AT's extended memory and some of its more advanced features. They are called through interrupt 21 (hex 15) just like the cassette I/O services, with the service number (ranging from hex 80 through 91) placed in the AH register. We will not go into detail about these services in this chapter, ☛ but suggest you see Chapter 13 and the BIOS listing in the AT Technical Reference manual for more information.

Service (hex)	Description
80	Device open
81	Device close
82	Program termination
83	Event wait
84	Joystick support
85	SysReq-key press
86	Wait
87	Move block
88	Get extended memory size
89	Switch to virtual memory (*CAUTION:* See BIOS listing before use)
90	Device busy loop
91	Set flag and complete interrupt

Figure 12-7. The twelve extended services for the AT available through interrupt 21 (hex 15)

PRINTER SERVICES

The ROM-BIOS printer services support printer output. In the standard PC world, these services apply strictly to the parallel printer adapter. On some PC models, however, printer output can be automatically re-routed to a serial port. The PCjr's ROM-BIOS provides this feature.

The ROM-BIOS printer services are invoked with interrupt 23 (hex 17). There are three services, numbered 0 through 2, requested through the AH register. (☞ See Figure 12-8.) The general PC-family design allows more than one printer to be installed, so a printer number should be specified in register DX for all these services. Printer number 0 is automatically used by the print-screen service (☞ see page 218).

Service 0: Send One Byte to Printer

Service 0 sends one byte to the printer, placing the byte that is to be printed in AL. When the service is completed, AH is then set to report the printer status (☞ see service 2), which can be used to determine the success or failure of the operation. ☞ See the special notes on printer time-out under service 2.

Service 1: Initialize Printer

Service 1 initializes the printer. To do this, the service simply sends two control codes (hex 08 and 0C) to the printer control port (normally port 762, hex 2FA). As with the other two services, the printer status is reported in AH.

Service 2: Get Printer Status

Service 2 reports the printer status in the AH register. The individual bit codes are shown in Figure 12-9.

Service	Description
0	Send one byte to printer
1	Initialize printer
2	Get printer status

Figure 12-8. The three ROM-BIOS printer services invoked through interrupt 23 (hex 17)

Bit 7 6 5 4 3 2 1 0	Meaning (when set to 1)
1	Printer *not* busy (0 = busy)
. 1	Acknowledgment from printer
. . 1	Out-of-paper signal
. . . 1	Printer selected
. . . . 1 . . .	I/O error
. . . . . 1 . .	Not used
. . . . . . 1 .	Not used
. . . . 1	Time-out

*Figure 12-9. The printer status bits reported
in the AH register by services 0, 1 and 2*

The printer time-out has caused some difficulty in the IBM personal computers. Any I/O driver needs to set a time limit for a response from the device being controlled. Ideally, this time limit should not be excessively long, so that an unresponsive device can be reported in a timely manner. Unfortunately, there is a normal printer operation that can take a surprisingly long time: a page eject (or a skip to the top of the next page from near the top of the current page). The time allowed varies from version to version of the ROM-BIOS. Treat a time-out signal with care.

OTHER SERVICES

We now come to the grab bag of all other ROM-BIOS services: some services that IBM intended for us to use and some—most notably a service that sends a carriage-return/line-feed character combination to the

Interrupt		Description
Dec	Hex	
5	5	Print-screen service routine
17	11	Equipment-list service
18	12	Memory-size service
24	18	Activates ROM-BASIC language
25	19	Activates bootstrap start-up routine
26	1A	Time-of-day services

*Figure 12-10. Six miscellaneous ROM-BIOS
services supported by IBM, and their
associated interrupts*

display screen—that IBM didn't intend for us to use (I don't recommend it either). In this section, we'll cover the six interrupts shown in Figure 12-10, one by one.

Interrupt 5: Print-Screen Service

Interrupt 5 activates the print-screen service. It is used by the keyboard support routines in response to the Shift-PrtSc combination. Any other program that wishes to perform a print-screen operation may safely and conveniently do so by generating interrupt 5. The print-screen subroutine was specifically made to be interrupt-driven so that we could incorporate the service into our own programs.

The print-screen service will maintain the current cursor position on the screen and successfully print any printable characters from the screen in either the text or graphics mode. It makes use of the standard video services (those that waltz the cursor around the screen and read characters from the screen buffer), and also makes use of the standard printer services.

This service directs all of its output to printer number 0, the default printer. There are no input or output registers for this service. However, a status code is available at low-memory location hex 500 (☛ see page 57). If the byte at that location has a value of 255 (hex FF), then a previous print-screen operation was not completed successfully. A value of 0 indicates there was no error and the print-screen operation is ready to go. A value of 1 indicates that a print-screen is currently in progress; any request for a second one will be ignored.

Interrupt 17 (hex 11): Equipment-List Service

Interrupt 17 returns a basic report of the equipment installed in the computer. It is exactly the same as the information stored at low-memory location hex 410 (☛ see Chapter 3, page 52). The report is coded as shown in Figure 12-11, in the bits of a 16-bit word, which is placed in register AX. ☛ See interrupt 18 for a complementary service.

The equipment information is gathered on an accurate-as-possible basis and may not be exactly correct. Different methods are used for acquiring the information in the various models.

The equipment list is assembled only once at power-up time and is then left in memory. This means that we can change the equipment list

Bit F E D C B A 9 8	7 6 5 4 3 2 1 0	Meaning
X X	. . . .	Number of printers installed
. . X	. . . .	Serial printer: 1 = installed (PCjr only; not PC or XT)
. . . X	. . . .	Game adapter: 1 = installed (always true for PCjr)
. . . . X X X .	. . . .	Number of RS-232 serial ports
. . . . X	. . . .	DMA chip: 0 = installed (1 = not installed in ordinary PCjrs)
. . . .	X X	+1 = number of diskette drives: 0 = 1 drive (see bit 0)
. . . .	. . X X	Initial video mode: 10 = 80-column color, 11 = monochrome (PC or XT); 01 = 40-column (PCjr); 00 = none of the above
. . . .	. . . . X X . .	System board RAM: 11 = 64K (normal for all models)
. . . .	. . . . . . X .	1 if math co-processor installed
. . . .	 X	1 if any diskettes (if so, see bits 7 and 6)

*Figure 12-11. The bit coding for the
equipment list reported in register AX
and invoked by interrupt 17 (hex 11)*

under software control. For example, we could take some equipment off-line so that it is not used. However, modifying the equipment list is risky business—don't bet on its success. ☛ See interrupt 25, page 221, for comments on how to tamper with the equipment list and get reliable results.

The format of the equipment list was defined for the original PC model. As a result, some parts of the list are curiously mismatched to other models. Bit 13 (the serial-printer bit) is unused and undefined for all IBM models before the PCjr. **JR** On the Junior, this bit is set whenever the power-up routines in the ROM-BIOS find no parallel-printer option installed and find anything reasonable plugged into the serial port.

Interrupt 18 (hex 12): Memory-Size Service

Interrupt 18 invokes the service that reports the available memory size in kilobytes. It is exactly the same as the information stored at low-memory location hex 413 (☛ see page 52). The value is reported in AX. ☛ See interrupt 17 for a complementary service.

In the standard models of the PC, this value is taken from the setting of the physical switches inside the system unit. These switches are supposed to reflect the actual memory installed, although under some circumstances they are set to less memory than is actually present.

In the PCjr, the memory size is determined by software exploration during power up. The Junior adjusts the reported memory size by 16K to set aside memory for the display screen. When a program uses video modes 9 and 10, the display screen uses 32K, which reduces the usable memory. However, this is not reflected in the ROM-BIOS record of available memory reported by this interrupt service. The use of video modes 9 and 10 is a transitory phenomenon that only takes place within the operation of a program, and is not an ongoing state. So, there is very little reason for the ROM-BIOS to change its record of memory size when these modes are used.

Interrupt 24 (hex 18): BASIC Loader Service

Interrupt 24 is normally used to activate ROM-BASIC. It is made available as an interrupt service primarily to allow the default BASIC to be overridden. **JR** This is the technique used by the PCjr to load the BASIC cartridge as the default power-on BASIC instead of loading the computer's built-in ROM "cassette" BASIC.

Any program that wishes to do so may activate BASIC (or whatever has replaced it) by generating interrupt 24. This can be done to intentionally bring up BASIC, or, alternatively, to abruptly dead-end a program. ☛ However, see the next interrupt, number 25, for a better way to dead-end a program.

Interrupt 25 (hex 19): Bootstrap Loader Service

Interrupt 25 activates the standard bootstrap routine for the computer, which produces a similar result to powering on and nearly the same net result as the Ctrl-Alt-Del key combination. However, this bootstrap interrupt bypasses both the lengthy memory check of the power-on routines and the reset operations of Ctrl-Alt-Del.

There are two uses that I know of for this interrupt service. One is to immediately shut down, or dead-end, the operation of the computer. This can be done by a program when it encounters a situation that it finds intolerable, such as an apparent violation of copy protection. Many copy-protected programs end a program in exactly this way when they detect some hanky-panky.

The other use for this operation is to reboot the computer without going through the reset and restart operations, which would, for example, recalculate the memory size and equipment list reported by interrupts 17 and 18. This interrupt is particularly useful for any program that modifies either of these two items. The reasoning is simple: If we wish to change the equipment list or the memory size (for example, to set aside some memory for a RAM-disk), we cannot reliably count on all programs—including DOS—to check the actual memory or equipment specifications each time they are used. But a program could set aside some memory, change the memory specification, and then use this interrupt to reboot the system. When that is done and DOS is activated, DOS would take its own record of the available memory from the value set by our program. Neither DOS nor any civilized DOS program would be aware of, or interfere with, the memory area that was set aside.

To give you a brief example, here's a fragment of assembler code that will change the BIOS's record of the memory size and then use interrupt 25 to reboot the computer:

```
MOV     AX,40H                  ; get BIOS data segment of hex 40...
MOV     ES,AX                   ; ...into ES segment register
MOV     WORD PTR ES:19,256      ; set memory to 256K
INT     25                      ; reboot system
```

Interrupt 26 (hex 1A): Time-of-Day Services

Interrupt 26 provides the time-of-day services. Unlike any of the other interrupts covered in this section, but like all other ROM-BIOS services, more than a single service can be activated by this interrupt. The two normal services, numbered 0 and 1, are specified, as usual, in register AH. (☛ See Figure 12-12.)

The ROM-BIOS maintains a time-of-day clock that is based on a count of system-clock ticks since midnight. The system clock "ticks" by generating interrupt 8 at specific intervals. On each clock tick, the ROM-BIOS interrupt-8 service routine increments the clock count by 1. When

Service	Description	Register Settings
0	Read current clock count	CX = high-order part of clock count
		DX = low-order part of clock count
		AL = 0 if timer has not passed 24-hour period
		AL < > 0 if timer is counting new day
1	Set current clock count	CX = high-order part of clock count
		DX = low-order part of clock count

Figure 12-12. The two ROM-BIOS time-of-day services invoked by interrupt 26, and their register settings

the clock count passes 24 hours' worth of ticks, the count is reset to 0 and a record is made of the fact that midnight has been passed. This record is not in the form of a count, so there is no way to detect if two midnights have passed.

The clock ticks at a rate that is almost exactly 1,193,180 ÷ 64K, or roughly 18.2 times a second. The count is kept as a 4-byte integer at low-memory location hex 46C. The midnight count value, used to compare against the rising clock count, is 1,573,040 (hex 1800B0); when the clock hits the midnight count value, the byte at location 470 is incremented (see page 56), and the timer is reset. When DOS needs to know the time, it reads the clock count through the time-of-day service and calculates the time from this raw count. If it sees that the timer has been reset, it also increments the date.

We can calculate the current time of day from the clock count using these BASIC formulas:

```
HOUR = CLOCK \ 65543 (hex 10007)
REMAINDER = CLOCK MOD 65543
MINUTES = REMAINDER \ 1092 (hex 444)
REMAINDER = REMAINDER MOD 1092
SECONDS = REMAINDER \ 18.21                   ' for precision; otherwise use 18
REMAINDER = REMAINDER MOD 18.21
HUNDREDTHS = CINT( REMAINDER * 100 )
```

In reverse, we can calculate a nearly correct clock count from the time, by this formula:

```
COUNT = (HOUR * 65543.33) + (MINUTES * 1092.38)
+ (SECONDS * 18.21) + (HUNDREDTHS * .182)
```

AT As we will see shortly, the BIOS enhancements that come with the AT include time-of-day and date services that perform some of these tasks automatically.

Service 0: Read Current Clock Count

Service 0 returns the current clock count in two registers: the high-order portion in CX and the low-order portion in DX. AL is 0 if midnight has not passed since the last clock value was read or set, and AL is 1 if midnight has passed. The midnight signal is always reset when the clock is read. It is the responsibility of any program using this service to use the midnight signal to keep track of date changes. DOS programs normally should not use this service directly. If they do, they must undertake the tedious chore of calculating and setting a new date.

❑ NOTE: *I think it curious that version 2.00 of DOS did not consistently update the date on the midnight signal. The next version of DOS, 2.10, and all other versions of DOS, do.*

Service 1: Set Current Clock Count

Service 1 sets the clock count in location hex 46C.

The AT Time-of-Day Services

Services 2 through 7, also invoked through interrupt 26, were introduced in the AT version of the BIOS. Services 2, 3, 4 and 5 read and set the real time clock, providing both time-of-day and date information, and services 6 and 7 set an alarm to interrupt up to 24 hours from the present time. ☛ For more information on these services, see page 239 or the BIOS listing in the AT Technical Reference manual.

13

ROM-BIOS
Service Summary

T his chapter presents a summary of the ROM-BIOS service routines discussed in Chapters 8 through 12 to provide you with a quick reference guide. Once you understand the ROM-BIOS services, these tables should provide you with all the programming information you need.

SHORT SUMMARY

In this section, we briefly list all the ROM-BIOS services, so that they can be seen together, at a glance.

Subject	Interrupt Dec	Hex	Service (hex)	Description	Model Specific
Print screen	5	5	n/a	Send screen contents to printer	
Video	16	10	0	Set video mode	
Video	16	10	1	Set cursor size	
Video	16	10	2	Set cursor position	
Video	16	10	3	Read cursor position	
Video	16	10	4	Read light-pen position	
Video	16	10	5	Set active display page	
Video	16	10	5(AL:128)	Get display page registers	
Video	16	10	5(AL:129)	Set CPU display page register	
Video	16	10	5(AL:130)	Set CRT display page register	
Video	16	10	5(AL:131)	Set both display page registers	
Video	16	10	6	Scroll window up	
Video	16	10	7	Scroll window down	
Video	16	10	8	Read character and attribute	
Video	16	10	9	Write character and attribute	
Video	16	10	A	Write character	
Video	16	10	B	Set color palette	
Video	16	10	C	Write pixel dot	
Video	16	10	D	Read pixel dot	
Video	16	10	E	Write character as TTY	
Video	16	10	F	Get current video mode	
Video	16	10	10(AL:0)	Set one palette register	**JR**
Video	16	10	10(AL:1)	Set border register	**JR**
Video	16	10	10(AL:2)	Set all palette registers	**JR**
Video	16	10	13	Write character string	**AT**

(continued)

Figure 13-1. A short summary of the ROM-BIOS services

Subject	Interrupt Dec	Hex	Service (hex)	Description	Model Specific
Equipment	17	11	n/a	Get list of peripheral equipment	
Memory	18	12	n/a	Get usable memory size (in K-bytes)	
Disk	19	13	0	Reset disk system	
Disk	19	13	1	Get disk status	
Disk	19	13	2	Read disk sectors	
Disk	19	13	3	Write disk sectors	
Disk	19	13	4	Verify disk sectors	
Disk	19	13	5	Format disk track	
Disk	19	13	8	Get current drive parameters	AT
Disk	19	13	9	Initialize fixed-disk parameter tables	AT
Disk	19	13	A	Read long	AT
Disk	19	13	B	Write long	AT
Disk	19	13	C	Seek to cylinder	AT
Disk	19	13	D	Alternate disk reset	AT
Disk	19	13	10	Test for drive ready	AT
Disk	19	13	11	Recalibrate drive	AT
Disk	19	13	14	Controller diagnostics	AT
Disk	19	13	15	Get disk type	AT
Disk	19	13	16	Change of disk status	AT
Disk	19	13	17	Set disk type	AT
Serial port	20	14	0	Initialize serial port parameters	
Serial port	20	14	1	Send out one character	
Serial port	20	14	2	Receive one character	
Serial port	20	14	3	Get serial port status	
Cassette	21	15	0	Turn on cassette motor	
Cassette	21	15	1	Turn off cassette motor	
Cassette	21	15	2	Read data blocks	
Cassette	21	15	3	Write data blocks	
Devices	21	15	80	Device open	AT
Devices	21	15	81	Device close	AT
Devices	21	15	82	Device program termination	AT
Devices	21	15	83	Event wait	AT
Joystick	21	15	84	Joystick support	AT
System Request	21	15	85	Sys Req key press	AT
Devices	21	15	86	Wait	AT
Devices	21	15	87	Move block	AT

*Figure 13-1. A short summary of the
ROM-BIOS services (continued)*

Subject	Interrupt Dec	Hex	Service (hex)	Description	Model Specific
Memory	21	15	88	Get extended memory size	AT
Memory	21	15	89	Switch to virtual memory	AT
Devices	21	15	90	Device busy loop	AT
Devices	21	15	91	Set flag and complete interrupt	AT
Keyboard	22	16	0	Read next keyboard character	
Keyboard	22	16	1	Report whether character ready	
Keyboard	22	16	2	Get shift status	
Keyboard	22	16	3(AL:0)	Reset typematic	JR
Keyboard	22	16	3(AL:1)	Increase initial delay	JR
Keyboard	22	16	3(AL:2)	Increase continuing delay	JR
Keyboard	22	16	3(AL:3)	Increase both delays	JR
Keyboard	22	16	3(AL:4)	Turn off typematic	JR
Keyboard	22	16	4(AL:0)	Click off	JR
Keyboard	22	16	4(AL:1)	Click on	JR
Printer	23	17	0	Send one byte to printer	
Printer	23	17	1	Initialize printer	
Printer	23	17	2	Get printer status	
BASIC	24	18	n/a	Switch control to BASIC	
Bootstrap	25	19	n/a	Reboot computer	
Time	26	1A	0	Read current clock count	
Time	26	1A	1	Set current clock count	
Time	26	1A	2	Read real time clock	AT
Time	26	1A	3	Set real time clock	AT
Time	26	1A	4	Read date from real time clock	AT
Time	26	1A	5	Set date in real time clock	AT
Time	26	1A	6	Set alarm	AT
Time	26	1A	7	Reset alarm	AT

Figure 13-1. A short summary of the ROM-BIOS services (continued)

LONG SUMMARY

In this section, we expand the previous summary table to show the register usage for input and output parameters. The previous section is best used to quickly find *which* service you need; this section is best used to quickly find *how* to use each service.

Service	Interrupt (hex)	Register Input	Register Output	Description
Print screen	05	AH = 05	n/a	Send screen contents to printer. Status and result byte at low-memory address hex 500 (0050:0000)

Video Services

Service	Interrupt (hex)	Register Input	Register Output	Description
Set video mode	10	AH = 00 AL = video mode	none	Video modes in AL: 00: 40 × 25 text, 16 grey 01: 40 × 25 text, 16/8 color 02: 80 × 25 text, 16 grey 03: 80 × 25 text, 16/8 color 04: 320 × 200 graphics, 4 color 05: 320 × 200 graphics, 4 grey 06: 640 × 200 graphics, b/w 07: 80 × 25 text, b/w 08: 160 × 200 graphics, 16 color 09: 320 × 200 graphics, 16 color 0A: 640 × 200 graphics, 4 color
Set cursor size	10	AH = 01 CH = starting scan line CL = ending scan line	none	Color/Graphics Adapter uses lines 0–7 Monochrome Adapter uses lines 0–13
Set cursor position	10	AH = 02 BH = display page number DH = row DL = column	none	
Read cursor position	10	AH = 03 BH = display page number	CH = starting scan line CL = ending scan line DH = row DL = column	
Read light-pen position	10	AH = 04	AH = pen trigger signal BX = pixel column CH = pixel row DH = character row DL = character column	
Set active display page	10	AH = 05 AL = page number		

(continued)

Figure 13-2. A complete summary of the ROM-BIOS services

Service	Interrupt (hex)	Register Input	Register Output	Description
Video Services (continued)				
Get display page register	10	AH = 05 AL = 80	BH = CRT page register BL = CPU page register	**JR**
Set CPU display page register	10	AH = 05 AL = 81 BL = CPU page register	BH − CRT page register BL = CPU page register	**JR**
Set CRT display page register	10	AH = 05 AL = 82 BH = CRT page register	BH = CRT page register BL = CPU page register	**JR**
Set both display page registers	10	AH = 05 AL = 83 BH = CRT page register BL = CPU page register	BH = CRT page register BL = CPU page register	**JR**
Scroll window up	10	AH = 06 AL = lines to scroll up BH = filler attribute CH = upper row CL = left column DH = lower row DL = right column	none	
Scroll window down	10	AH = 07 AL = lines to scroll down BH = filler attribute CH = upper row CL = left column DH = lower row DL = right column	none	
Read character and attribute	10	AH = 08 BH = display page number	AH = attribute AL = character	
Write character and attribute	10	AH = 09 AL = character BH = page number BL = attribute CX = number of characters to repeat	none	
Write character	10	AH = 0A AL = character BH = page number BL = color in graphics mode CX = count of characters	none	
Set color palette	10	AH = 0B BH = palette color ID BL = color to be used with palette ID	none	

*Figure 13-2. A complete summary of the
ROM-BIOS services (continued)*

Service	Interrupt (hex)	Register Input	Output	Description
Video Services (continued)				
Write pixel dot	10	AH = 0C AL = color CX = pixel column DL = pixel row	none	
Read pixel dot	10	AH = 0D CX = pixel column DL = pixel row	AL = color read	
Write character as TTY	10	AH = 0E AL = character BH = page number BL = color for graphics mode	none	
Get current video mode	10	AH = 0F	AH = width in characters AL = video mode BH = page number	
JR Set one palette register	10	AH = 10 AL = 00 BH = palette value BL = palette register	none	
JR Set border register	10	AH = 10 AL = 01 BH = border color	none	
JR Set all palette registers	10	AH = 10 AL = 02 ES:DX = pointer to palette values	none	
AT Write string; don't move cursor	10	AH = 13 AL = 00 BL = attribute BH = display page number DX = starting cursor position CX = length of string ES:BP = pointer to start of string	none	
AT Write string; move cursor after string	10	AH = 13 AL = 01 BL = attribute BH = display page number DX = starting cursor position CX = length of string ES:BP = pointer to start of string	none	

Figure 13-2. A complete summary of the
ROM-BIOS services (continued)

Service	Interrupt (hex)	Register Input	Register Output	Description

Video Services (continued)

Service	Interrupt (hex)	Input	Output	Description
AT Write string of alternating characters, attributes; don't move cursor	10	AH = 13 AL = 02 BH = display page number DX = starting cursor position CX = length of string ES:BP = pointer to start of string	none	
AT Write string of alternating characters, attributes; move cursor	10	AH = 13 AL = 03 BH = display page number DX = starting cursor position CX = length of string ES:BP = pointer to start of string	none	

Equipment-List Service

Service	Interrupt (hex)	Input	Output	Description
Get list of peripheral attached equipment	11	none	AX = equipment list, bit-coded	Bit settings in AX: 00 = diskette drive 01 = math coprocessor 02, 03 = system board RAM in 16K blocks 04, 05 = initial video mode: 00 = unused; 01 = 40 × 25 color; 10 = 80 × 25 color; 11 = 80 × 25 b/w 06, 07 = number of diskette drives − 1 08 = DMA present? 00 = yes; 01 = no 09, 10, 11 = number of RS-232 cards in system 12 = game I/O attached (not used on AT) 13 = serial printer attached (Jr. only) 14, 15 = number of printers attached

Memory Service

Service	Interrupt (hex)	Input	Output	Description
Get usable memory size (in K-bytes)	12	none	AX = memory size	

Figure 13-2. A complete summary of the ROM-BIOS services (continued)

Service	Interrupt (hex)	Register Input	Register Output	Description
Disk Services				
Reset disk system	13	AH = 00	none	
Get disk status	13	AH = 01	AH = status code (hex) Status values: AH = A: bad sector flag (F) AH = AA: drive not ready (F) AH = BB: undefined error (F) AH = CC: write fault (F) AH = EO: status error (F) AH = 1: bad command AH = 2: address mark not found AH = 3: write attempted on write-protected disk (D) AH = 4: sector not found AH = 5: reset failed (F)	AH = 6: diskette removed (D) AH = 7: bad parameter table (F) AH = 8: DMA overrun (D) AH = 9: DMA across 64K boundary AH = A: bad sector flag (F) AH = 10: bad CRC or ECC AH = 11: ECC corrected data error (F) AH = 20: Controller failed AH = 40: seek failed AH = 80: time out (F) = fixed disk only (D) = for diskette only
Read disk sectors	13	AH = 02 AL = number of sectors CH = track number CL = sector number DH = head number DL = drive number ES:BX = pointer to buffer	CF = success/failure flag AH = status code AL = number of sectors read	Status codes in AH: see diskette service 01
Write disk sectors	13	AH = 03 AL = number of sectors CH = track number CL = sector number DH = head number DL = drive number ES:BX = pointer to buffer	CF = success/failure flag AH = status code AL = number of sectors written	Status codes in AH: see disk service 01
Verify disk sectors	13	AH = 04 AL = number of sectors CH = track number CL = sector number DH = head number DL = drive number	CF = success/failure flag AH = status code AL = number of sectors verified	Status codes in AH: see disk service 01

Figure 13-2. A complete summary of the ROM-BIOS services (continued)

Service	Interrupt (hex)	Register Input	Register Output	Description
Disk Services (continued)				
Format disk track	13	AH = 05 AL = number of sectors CH = track number CL = sector number DH = head number DL = drive number ES:BX = pointer to list of 4-byte address fields: Byte 1 = track Byte 2 = head Byte 3 = sector Byte 4 = bytes/sector: 00 = 128 01 = 256 10 = 512 11 = 1024	CF = success/failure signal AH = status code	Status codes in AH: see disk service 01
AT Get current drive parameters	13	AH = 08	DL = number of drives DH = max. number of sides CL = max. number of sectors CH = max. number of tracks CF = success/failure flag AH = status code	Status codes in AH: see diskette service 01
AT Initialize two fixed-disk base tables	13	AH = 09	CF = success/failure flag AH = status code	Interrupt 41 points to table for drive 0 Interrupt 46 points to table for drive 1 Status codes in AH: see diskette service 01
AT Read long	13	AH = 0A DL = drive ID DH = head number CH = cylinder number CL = sector number ES:BX = pointer to buffer	CF = success/failure flag AH = status code	Status codes in AH: see diskette service 01
AT Write long	13	AH = 0B DL = drive ID DH = head number CH = cylinder number CL = sector number ES:BX = pointer to buffer	CF = success/failure flag AH = status code	Status codes in AH: see diskette service 01
AT Seek to cylinder	13	AH = 0C DL = drive ID DH = head number CH = cylinder number	CF = success/failure flag AH = status code	Status codes in AH: see diskette service 01
AT Alternate disk reset	13	AH = 0D DL = drive ID	CF = success/failure flag AH = status code	Status codes in AH: see diskette service 01
AT Test for drive ready	13	AH = 10 DL = drive ID	CF = success/failure flag AH = status code	Status codes in AH: see diskette service 01

Figure 13-2. A complete summary of the ROM-BIOS services (continued)

Service	Interrupt (hex)	Register Input	Register Output	Description
Diskette Services (continued)				
AT Recalibrate drive	13	AH = 11 DL = drive ID	CF = success/failure flag AH = status code	Status codes in AH: see diskette service 01
AT Controller diagnostics	13	AH = 14	CF = success/failure flag AH = status code (see service)	Status codes in AH: see diskette service 01
AT Get disk type	13	AH = 15 DL = drive ID	AH = disk type CX, DX = number of 512-byte sectors when AH = 3	Disk types: AH = 0: disk not there AH = 1: diskette, no change detection present AH = 2: diskette, change detection present AH = 3: fixed disk
AT Change of disk status	13	AH = 16	DL = drive that had disk change AH = disk change status: 00 = no disk change 06 = disk changed	
AT Set disk type	13	AH = 17 AL = disk type		Disk type set in AL: AL = 00: no disk AL = 01: regular diskette in regular drive AL = 03: high-capacity (1.2-megabyte) diskette in high-capacity drive
Serial Port Services				
Initialize serial port parameters	14	AL = serial port parameters AH = 00 DX = serial port number	AX = serial port status	Serial port parameter bit settings: 00, 01 = word length 10 = 7 bits; 11 = 8 bits 02 = stop bits: 0 = 1; 1 = 2 03, 04 = parity: 00, 10 = none; 01 = odd; 11 = even 05, 06, 07 = baud rate; 000 = 110; 001 = 150; 010 = 300; 011 = 600; 100 = 1,200; 101 = 2,400; 110 = 4,800; 111 = 9,600 (4,800 on PCjr)

Figure 13-2. A complete summary of the ROM-BIOS services (continued)

Service	Interrupt (hex)	Register Input	Register Output	Description
Serial Port Services (continued)				
Send out one character	14	AH = 01 AL = character DX = serial port number	AH = success/failure status code	Status bit settings: see serial port service 03
Receive one character	14	AH = 02 DX = serial port number	AH = success/failure status code AL = character	Status bit settings: see serial port service 03
Get serial port status	14	AH = 03 DX = serial port number	AX = status code	Status code bit settings: AH bit settings: 00 = data ready; 01 = overrun error; 02 = parity error; 03 = framing error; 04 = break detected; 05 = transmission buffer register empty; 06 = transmission shift register empty; 07 = time out AL bit settings: 00 = delta clear-to-send 01 = delta data-set-ready; 02 = trailing edge ring detected; 03 = change, receive line signal detected; 04 = clear-to-send; 05 = data-set-ready; 06 = ring detected; 07 = receive line signal detected
Cassette Tape Services				
Turn on cassette motor	15	AH = 00	none	
Turn off cassette motor	15	AH = 01	none	
Read data blocks	15	AH = 02 CX = count of bytes ES:BX = pointer to data area	CF = error signal DX = count of bytes read ES:BX = pointer past last byte read	IF CF = 1: AH = 1: CRC error AH = 2: Lost transition AH = 3: No date on tape
Write data blocks	15	AH = 03 CX = count of bytes to write ES:BX = pointer to data area	ES:BX = pointer past last byte written CX = 0	

*Figure 13-2. A complete summary of the
ROM-BIOS services (continued)*

Service	Interrupt (hex)	Register		Description
		Input	Output	
Extended Services for the AT				
AT Device open	15	AH = 80 BX = device ID CX = process type	none	
AT Device close	15	AH = 81 BX = device ID CX = process type	none	
AT Device program terminate	15	AH = 82 BX = device ID	none	
AT Event wait	15	AH = 83 AL = subservice: 0 = set interval; 1 = cancel ES:BX = pointer to wait bit in caller's memory CX, DX = number of microseconds to wait	none	
AT Joystick support	15	AH = 84 DX = 0 get current switch settings	AL = switch settings	
AT Joystick support	15	AH = 84 DX = 1 read inputs	AX = A(x) value BX = A(y) value CX = B(x) value DX = B(y) value	
AT System Request key press	15	AH = 85 AL = 00 press AL = 01 break	none	
AT Wait	15	AH = 86 CX, DX = number of microseconds to wait before return	none	
AT Move block	15	AH = 87 CX = number of words to move ES:SI = pointer to descriptor table	none	

Figure 13-2. A complete summary of the ROM-BIOS services (continued)

Service	Interrupt (hex)	Register Input	Register Output	Description

Extended Services for the AT (continued)

Service	Interrupt (hex)	Input	Output	Description
AT Get extended memory size	15	AH = 88	AX = number of 1K memory blocks above address 1024K	
AT Switch to virtual mode	15	AH = 89 ES:SI = address of GDT (Global Descriptor Table) BH = offset to level 1 interrupt descriptor table BL = offset to level 2 interrupt descriptor table	none	Caution: See BIOS listing before use
AT Device busy loop	15	AH = 90 AL = type code	none	See BIOS listing
AT Set flag and complete interrupt	15	AH = 91 AL = type code	none	See BIOS listing

Keyboard Services

Service	Interrupt (hex)	Input	Output	Description
Read next keyboard character	16	AH = 00	AH = scan code (auxiliary byte) AL = character code (main byte)	
Report whether character ready	16	AH = 01	ZF = 0 if code available AH = scan code (auxiliary byte) AL = character code (main byte)	
Get shift status	16	AH = 02	AL = shift status bits	Shift status bits: Bit 0 = 1: right Shift depressed Bit 1 = 1: left Shift depressed Bit 2 = 1: Ctrl depressed Bit 3 = 1: Alt depressed Bit 4 = 1: Scroll Lock active Bit 5 = 1: Num Lock active Bit 6 = 1: Caps Lock active Bit 7 = 1: Insert state active
JR Reset typematic	16	AH = 03 AL = 00	none	
JR Increase initial delay	16	AH = 03 AL = 01	none	
JR Increase continuing delay	16	AH = 03 AL = 02	none	

Figure 13-2. A complete summary of the
ROM-BIOS services (continued)

Service	Interrupt (hex)	Register Input	Register Output	Description

Keyboard Services (continued)

Service	Interrupt (hex)	Input	Output	Description
JR Increase both delays	16	AH = 03 AL = 03	none	
JR Turn off typematic	16	AH = 03 AL = 04	none	
JR Click off	16	AH = 04 AL = 00	none	
JR Click on	16	AH = 04 AL = 01	none	

Printer Services

Service	Interrupt (hex)	Input	Output	Description
Send one byte to printer	17	AH = 00 AL = character DX = printer number	AH = success/failure status code	Status bit settings: 0 = time out 1 = unused 2 = unused 3 = 1: I/O error 4 = 1: selected 5 = 1: out of paper 6 = 1: acknowledge 7 = 1: not busy
Initialize printer	17	AH = 01 DX = printer number	AH = status code	Status code bit settings: see printer service 00
Get printer status	17	AH = 02 DX = printer number	AH = status code	Status code bit settings: see printer service 00

Miscellaneous Services

Service	Interrupt (hex)	Input	Output	Description
Switch control to BASIC	18	none	n/a	No return, so no possible output
Reboot computer	19	none	n/a	No return, so no possible output

Time-of-Day Services

Service	Interrupt (hex)	Input	Output	Description
Read the current clock count	1A	AH = 00	AL = midnight signal CX = tick count, high portion DX = tick count, low portion	
Set current clock count	1A	AH = 01 CX = tick count, high portion DX = tick count, low portion	none	

*Figure 13-2. A complete summary of the
ROM-BIOS services (continued)*

Service	Interrupt (hex)	Register Input	Register Output	Description

Time-of-Day Services (continued)

Service	Interrupt (hex)	Input	Output	Description
AT Read real time clock	1A	AH = 02	CH = hours (in BCD) CL = minutes (in BCD) DH = seconds (in BCD) CF = 1 if clock not operating	
Set real time clock	1A	AH = 03 CH = hours CL = minutes DH = seconds DL = 1 if daylight saving time; 0 if standard time		Input values in BCD
Read date from real time clock	1A	AH = 04	DL = day (in BCD) DH = month (in BCD) CL = year (in BCD) CH = century (19 or 20) (in BCD) CF = 1 if clock not operating	
Set date in real time clock	1A	AH = 05 DL = day DH = month CL = year CH = century (19 or 20)		Input values in BCD
Set alarm	1A	AH = 06 CH = hours CL = minutes DH = seconds	CF = 1 if clock not operating, or alarm already set.	Place address for alarm routine in interrupt 4A location Input values in BCD
Reset alarm	1A	AH = 07		

Figure 13-2. A complete summary of the
ROM-BIOS services (continued)

14

DOS Basics

Chapters 15 through 18 are going to focus on the program support services provided by DOS. The last chapter in the series, Chapter 18, is a summary of the technical details of each service. In this chapter, we will introduce some of the main concerns a programmer often faces when working with the DOS services.

We use the term *DOS services* to define the entire set of operations that DOS provides for our programs, but you will not find this term used in the DOS manual. In DOS's own terminology, these services are divided into two categories: DOS interrupts and DOS function calls. As far as I know, this separation was not based on any design decision, but rather emerged from a desire to achieve a reasonable degree of compatibility with DOS's predecessor, the CP/M operating system.

DOS interrupts are invoked by individual interrupt codes with the INT instruction. DOS function calls, on the other hand, are invoked in much the same way as the ROM-BIOS services: through one umbrella interrupt, interrupt 33 (hex 21). As with the ROM-BIOS services, the individual functions are selected through the AH register.

From the standpoint of both programming and design, the function-call mechanism is actually more efficient than a group of individual interrupts. Its main benefit is that it allows an unlimited number of new services to be added, since every service is called through a single interrupt. All the services introduced with the DOS-2 versions are additions to the function calls and not to the interrupts. Most of the services that were introduced with DOS-3 versions are also function calls, although there is one new interrupt.

THE PROS AND CONS OF USING THE DOS SERVICES

The question of whether or not to use the DOS services arises naturally during the design and development of sophisticated programs. My general advice, echoed throughout this book, is for you to use the highest available services that will accomplish what you need. This means that, whenever possible, you should use the built-in services of your programming language first, resorting only when necessary to the direct use of the DOS services or the ROM-BIOS services, and resorting only in extreme circumstances to direct programming of the computer's hardware.

In practical terms, either a program can be written entirely within the confines of the programming language's facilities or nearly all of its I/O work must be done outside of the programming language, at a lower level. When a lower level of programming is needed, I feel that, with very few exceptions, the DOS services are best suited for disk operations. When working with the keyboard or other I/O devices, either the DOS routines or the ROM-BIOS routines will be adequate, depending on the application. But for low-level video-display programming, the situation is more complex. Satisfactory screen output almost always seems to call for the ROM-BIOS services and direct-hardware programming, even though in some cases it may be best to leave it in the hands of DOS. We'll see why in a moment.

DOS: A Disk-Service Cornucopia

When we inspect the full range of tools and services that are placed in our hands by programming languages, by DOS, by the ROM-BIOS, and by the computer's hardware, it becomes quite clear that the richest concentration of disk-oriented services exists at the DOS level. This almost goes without saying since DOS, as a disk operating system, is inherently strongest in its support of disk operations.

As detailed in Chapters 16 and 17, the majority of services that DOS will perform for us are directly connected to the manipulation of disk files. Even some of the nominally program-controlled services, such as loading and executing another program (function 75 (hex 4B)), involve disk file operations. From this perspective, DOS is not so much a disk operating system as it is a system of disk services designed for use by our programs. When we are developing programs for the IBM personal computer family, it is a good idea to approach DOS from exactly this point of view: Think of DOS as a cornucopia of disk operations placed at our service.

DOS and Video: A Difficult Match

It has become a PC programming convention for most sophisticated programs to perform their screen output at a low level. Often, all display output is done at the very lowest level, with output placed directly into the display's memory area. Other operations, such as cursor movement, are usually done at the next highest level through the ROM-BIOS services.

In the beginning, this was necessary because DOS did not provide adequate video services. But starting with version 2.00, it became possible to perform most of the needed screen work through the DOS services enhanced with the ANSI driver program, also known as ANSI.SYS (☛ see Appendix A for more details). This program uses a set of commands that, when translated, will perform just about anything the screen is capable of doing. However, the ANSI driver services can be somewhat clumsy to work with because they not only require that our programs run under a

DOS-2 version but also that DOS be configured to include the ANSI driver. My experience is that many novice computer users are thoroughly confused by the procedures necessary to incorporate the ANSI driver, and this factor alone argues strongly against using any DOS facility that requires this driver.

If faced only with this factor, we could easily conclude that we should avoid using the DOS video services altogether, but it's not quite that simple. Many of the more sophisticated operating-system environments that are appearing, particularly windowing systems, expect the programs running under them to use officially available operating-system services and not work directly with the hardware. With these environments in mind, there is a strong argument to be made for the strict use of the DOS services whenever possible.

In trying to decide what is wisest to do, a great deal depends on the probable lifetime of your programs and the range of machines they might be used on. For a PC-specific game program with an expected life of a few months (common for games) you have little reason to worry about these things. The situation is completely different for a generalized business or professional application, which should be usable for many years and in many environments. Make your choice and place your bets.

DOS VERSION DIFFERENCES

DOS version 3.10 represents the sixth official release of DOS. Even though there have been both improvements and bug-fixes in every release, the driving force behind each release has been hardware, and a hardware change has usually involved a disk-drive change.

Version	Date	Hardware Change
1.00	8/04/81	Original PC model (single-sided drive)
1.10	5/07/82	Double-sided diskette drive
2.00	3/08/83	XT model (hard-disk drive)
2.10	10/20/83	PCjr and Portable PC models (half-high drives)
3.00	8/14/84	AT model (high-capacity diskette drive)
3.10	3/07/85	Networking (network disk drive)

Figure 14-1. The six DOS releases and the associated changes to hardware

In all but versions 2.10 and 3.10, changes to DOS involved significant modifications to disk support (including new disk-storage formats). The main change to 2.10 was a relatively minor one, but disk-related: The diskette control head settle time was adjusted to allow for differences in the performance of the half-high drives used in the PCjr and Portable PC. Version 2.10 also corrected a few of the known bugs in 2.00. Version 3.10 incorporated networking functions that were designed for version 3.00, but were not ready when 3.00 was released. Here is a simple summary of the main differences between versions:

Version 1.00 supported the single-sided, eight-sector diskette format. All the basic DOS services were included in this release.

Version 1.10 added support for double-sided diskettes. The DOS services remained the same.

Version 2.00 added support for nine-sector diskettes (both single- and double-sided) and for the fixed hard disk. The DOS services were enhanced extensively in this version (☛ see Chapter 17). Cartridge support was also added in 2.00, although this was not known until the release of the PCjr.

Version 2.10 added neither new disk formats nor new DOS services; it did, however, adjust its disk operation timing to benefit the PCjr and the Portable.

Version 3.00 added the high-capacity diskette and additional hard-disk formats. It also laid the groundwork for network disks.

Version 3.10 added network disks, which include a file-sharing capability.

❏ NOTE: *Each version of DOS is upwardly compatible with prior versions, except in some very detailed respects (these sorts of details always seem to be unavoidable).*

With each release of DOS, there has been a question among software developers about which version of DOS to target, because use of the larger diskette formats and the extended DOS services precludes the use of earlier DOS versions. This has been a messy situation and has led to some difficult decisions for program developers in the past. DOS-2 versions have been the usual choice for quite some time. Sales of all PC models have been accelerating, so the number of people using DOS-1 versions is becoming an increasingly smaller proportion of the PC community. This makes it relatively painless for us to target our programs on DOS-2 versions and take full advantage of the DOS-2 extended services. Even with the appearance of DOS-3 versions, DOS-2 remains the best choice for the time being—but who can say for how long?

DISK FORMAT CONSIDERATIONS

Besides deciding which DOS services or which version of DOS our programs should use, we also need to consider which diskette format we will use to deliver our programs. The convention has been for PC programs to be delivered on diskettes with the single-sided eight-sector format, since this format is the lowest common denominator of all DOS formats and can be used by any DOS version. Although the universal nature of the single-sided eight-sector format is useful, there is not much reason for it anymore. For one thing, single-sided drives are now all but extinct on PCs, the double-sided formats having taken their place long ago. And for another, any programs that require DOS-2 can use the nine-sector format; in fact, that is the format that DOS 2.00 and 2.10 themselves use. To accommodate the last of the DOS-1 owners, you may want to use the double-sided eight-sector format, but you should be able to use the double-sided nine-sector format without guilt or regret.

A program can, in an imperfect way, detect which version of DOS it is running under, using DOS function call 48 (hex 30). Unless you can be sure of your audience, you should include this safeguard in your programs and always check to make sure the correct DOS version is installed. ☛ See Chapter 17 for more details.

COMMENTS

In general, technical information about DOS is scarce; there are a great many details that IBM and Microsoft seem to keep the world in the dark about. Unfortunately, there is not much you and I can do about this dearth of information, except try to pass on what we've discovered and point out the gaps wherever they occur. We will attempt to do that in the following chapters.

❑ NOTE: *The official source of information about the DOS services is the DOS Technical Reference manual, which was introduced with version 2.10. For the previous versions of DOS, the equivalent information is found in the main DOS manual.*

15

DOS Interrupts

I n this chapter we'll be covering the DOS services that are invoked with their own individual interrupts. (☞ See Chapters 16 and 17 for information about the DOS function calls, which are selected by a function number under one umbrella interrupt.) There are nine interrupt services in all, which are listed below in Figure 15-1. Five of them, interrupts 32, 37 through 39, and 47 (hex 20, 25 through 27, and 2F), are true DOS interrupt services, each one having a specifically defined task associated with it. The other interrupts have more general uses. Perhaps the most important one is interrupt 33 (hex 21), which is used to invoke DOS function calls (☞ discussed in Chapters 16 and 17). The three remaining interrupts, 34 through 36 (hex 22 through 24), are used to hold segmented addresses. Our programs set these addresses (preferably using DOS function call 37) to point to special routines. Then, when the appropriate circumstances arise, DOS invokes the routines located at these addresses through these three address interrupts (☞ see page 255).

❏ NOTE: *Official IBM DOS doctrine disapproves of programmers using the DOS interrupt services. Consequently, IBM supplies alternate function calls through interrupt 33 (hex 21). Since there is always the possibility that new releases of DOS will not support the use of these "disapproved" interrupt services, it is wise to avoid using them and to rely mostly on the DOS function calls for special services.*

Interrupt		
Dec	Hex	Description
32	20	Program terminate: come to normal ending
33	21	Function-call umbrella interrupt
34	22	Terminate address
35	23	Break address
36	24	Critical error-handler address
37	25	Absolute disk read
38	26	Absolute disk write
39	27	Terminate-but-stay-resident
47	2F	Print spool control (DOS-3 versions only)

Figure 15-1. The nine DOS interrupt services

THE FIVE MAIN DOS INTERRUPTS

Of the nine DOS interrupts, five are true interrupts, meaning that they have built-in interrupt-handling programs associated with them, each of which performs a particular task.

Interrupt 32 (hex 20): Program Terminate

Interrupt 32 is used to exit from a program and pass control back to DOS. It is identical to DOS function call 0 (☞ see page 271). These services can be used interchangeably with any version of DOS to end a program.

Interrupt 32 does not automatically close files when it terminates a program, so you should always use DOS function 16 or 62 to close all changed files before exiting. If a file that has been changed is not formally closed, its new length will not be recorded in the file directory.

A program can set three operational addresses through DOS interrupts 34, 35, and 36, as we will see shortly. As part of the clean-up operations performed by DOS for interrupt 32, these addresses are reset to the values they had before the program was executed. Resetting these addresses is essential if the program that invoked interrupt 32 was executed as the "child" of another program. It serves to protect the "parent" program from using routines intended for the "child." (☞ See DOS function 75 (hex 4B) in Chapter 17.)

❏ NOTE: *When DOS executes a program, it constructs a program segment prefix (PSP) at a zero offset address in the code segment pointed to by the CS register. The PSP contains control information that, among other things, tells DOS where to go when a program is terminated. (☞ We discuss the PSP in detail at the end of this chapter.) DOS depends on the CS register to point to the PSP when the interrupt 32 terminate service is invoked. If the CS register has been changed, it will interfere with the operation of this service.*

❏ WARNING: *If control is passed to a subroutine by a FAR call, the CS register will be changed. Such subroutines should not use interrupt 32 to end program operation.*

Interrupts 37 and 38 (hex 25 and 26): Absolute Disk Read and Write

Interrupt 37 and its companion, interrupt 38, are used to read and write specific disk sectors. They are the only DOS services that ignore the logical structure of a disk and work only with individual sectors, paying no attention to the files, file directory, or FAT. All other DOS services work within the context of a disk's logical structure.

Interrupts 37 and 38 are similar to the corresponding ROM-BIOS disk services, except that the sectors are located by a different numbering method. With the ROM-BIOS services, the sectors are selected by their three-dimensional coordinate locations (track/cylinder, side/head, and sector), whereas with interrupts 37 and 38, the sectors are selected by their sequential sector numbers. (☛ DOS's sector-numbering system is discussed on page 105.)

The BASIC formula that converts the three-dimensional coordinates used by the ROM-BIOS to the sequential sector numbers used by DOS is as follows:

```
DOS.SECTOR.NUMBER = (BIOS.SECTOR - 1) + BIOS.SIDE
* SECTORS.PER.TRACK + BIOS.TRACK * SECTORS.PER.TRACK
* SIDES.PER.DISK
```

And here are the formulas for converting sequential sector numbers to three-dimensional coordinates:

```
BIOS.SECTOR = 1 + DOS.SECTOR.NUMBER MOD SECTORS.PER.TRACK
BIOS.SIDE = (DOS.SECTOR.NUMBER / SECTORS.PER.TRACK)
MOD SIDES.PER.DISK
BIOS.TRACK = DOS.SECTOR.NUMBER / (SECTORS.PER.TRACK
* SIDES.PER.DISK)
```

❏ NOTE: *For double-sided nine-sector diskettes, the PC's most common disk format, the value of SECTORS.PER.TRACK is 9 and the value of SIDES.PER.DISK is 2. Also note that sides and tracks are numbered differently in the ROM-BIOS numbering system: The sides and tracks are numbered from 0, but the sectors are numbered from 1.*

To select a block of sectors, the necessary parameters are all loaded into separate registers. The number of sectors is specified in the CX register, the starting sector number is specified in DX, and the memory address for data transfer is specified in DS:BX. The disk drive is selected by placing a number in the AL register: Drive A is 0 and drive B is 1.

Although the ROM-BIOS services work with true physical drives, the DOS services work with logical drives. DOS assumes that every computer has at least two logical drives. If there is no physical drive B, DOS will simulate it by using the one physical drive as either A or B, whichever one is needed. We can then remap these logical drives using DOS's ASSIGN command.

The results of interrupt services 37 and 38 are reported in a combination of the carry flag (CF) and the AL and AH registers. If there is no error, CF is 0. If there is an error (CF=1), AL and AH contain the error

| Error Code | | Meaning |
Dec	Hex	
12	0C	General, nonspecific error
11	0B	Read error
10	0A	Write error
8	08	Sector not found
7	07	Unknown media: disk format not recognized
6	06	Seek error: move to requested track failed
4	04	CRC (cyclical redundancy check) error: parity error
2	02	Drive not ready (e.g. no disk, or door open)
1	01	Unknown unit: invalid drive number
0	00	Write-protect error: attempt to write on protected diskette

Figure 15-2. The error-code values and meanings returned to the AL register following an error in a disk read or write through DOS interrupts 37 or 38

codes in two separate and somewhat redundant groups. The AL codes in Figure 15-2 are DOS's own and are based on those used with the critical-error handler through interrupt 36 (☛ see page 257), while the AH codes in Figure 15-3 are based on the error codes reported by the ROM-BIOS (☛ see page 190).

| Error Code | | Meaning |
Dec	Hex	
128	80	Time out: drive did not respond
64	40	Bad seek: move to requested track failed
32	20	Controller failed: diskette controller malfunction
16	10	Bad CRC: read found invalid parity check of data
8	08	DMA (direct memory access) failure
4	04	Bad sector: requested sector not on diskette
3	03	Write-protect error: attempt to write on protected diskette
2	02	Bad address mark: sector ID marking invalid or not found
0	00	Other errors

Figure 15-3. The error-code values and meanings returned to the AH register following an error in a disk read or write through DOS interrupts 37 or 38

Normally, interrupt handlers and other service routines leave the stack clean when they exit, returning it to its original size and contents. DOS interrupts 37 and 38 deliberately do not clean up the stack. Instead, they finish and return to the program with one word left on the stack. This word holds the contents of the flag register, showing how the flags were set when the program invoked the service. This is purportedly done to preserve the program's flag status before the service was used, since interrupts 37 and 38 use the flags for their return codes. I think this is a silly precaution, since any program that needs to preserve the flags can do what programs normally do when they need something saved: PUSH them onto the stack themselves. Any program that uses interrupts 37 and 38 should POP the two extra flag status bytes off the stack after this service returns. They can either be placed in the flag register with a POPF command (which should be done after testing CF for an error) or be discarded by using the POP command to move them to some extraneous location, such as the DX register.

Interrupt 39 (hex 27): Terminate-but-Stay-Resident

Interrupt 39 invokes one of the most interesting of all the services provided by DOS. In fact, it's so interesting and important that we have used it in the assembly-language example at the end of the chapter.

Like interrupt 32, interrupt 39 ends a program, but it does not erase it from memory. Instead, it leaves a specified portion of the program in memory (the program *stays resident*), and DOS's record of the first usable part of memory is changed to the paragraph address immediately following the resident program. The information that is made resident using interrupt 39 becomes an extension of DOS and will not be overwritten by other programs. In keeping with IBM's consistent effort to move away from using DOS interrupts, a DOS function call, function 49 (hex 31), also performs this service (☞ see page 302).

Interrupt 39 (or its function-call equivalent) is used by a number of sophisticated programs that act as loadable enhancements to DOS. One of the best-known of these programs is ProKey, a keyboard enhancer. Programs typically use this service to establish a new interrupt-handling routine meant to stay in effect indefinitely. Most often, these interrupt-handling routines replace existing interrupt handlers in order to change or extend their operation. But the resident item is not limited to interrupt handlers and program instructions; it could just as easily be data. For example, the same programming technique could be used to load status information into a common area that various programs would share, allowing them to communicate indirectly with each other.

Normally, a program that uses this technique will want to leave only part of itself resident, discarding, for example, the initialization code. So the program must have the portion that will stay resident at the beginning and must specify in the DX register the offset within the code segment of the first byte beyond the resident portion. (☞ See the program example on page 267.)

Anything left resident by this service normally remains resident as long as DOS is also resident. It is not unusual for several different programs to leave part of themselves resident. Since programs that use this technique are usually sophisticated and complicated, it is also not unusual for them to interfere with each other. To operate such a group of resident programs successfully, they must sometimes be loaded in a particular order and the order may have to be discovered experimentally (an unfair trick to play on an unsuspecting user). If you write a program using this technique, you should take great care to ensure that it is civilized in its behavior.

As with interrupt 32, the ordinary terminate service, DOS resets the address vectors for interrupts 34 through 36 (hex 22 through 24) when it performs this terminate-but-stay-resident service. This means that this service cannot be used to create resident interrupt handlers for the address interrupts. Although this may seem to be a limitation, it is actually fairly reasonable; the address interrupts are not meant to be used globally; they are only meant to be used by individual programs (☞ see the DOS address interrupts section that follows for further discussion).

❏ NOTE: *When an EXE-type program is link edited, it may be marked to be loaded into the highest available memory location rather than the lowest, as is conventional. Such programs cannot use interrupt 39, since it is designed only for low-memory residency.* ☞ *See page 342 for more on link editing and EXE-type programs.*

Interrupt 47 (hex 2F): Multiplex Interrupt

❏ NOTE: *Most of the material in this chapter applies to all versions of DOS; however, interrupt 47 is only available with DOS version 3.00 and later versions.*

A new DOS interrupt, interrupt 47 (hex 2F), was introduced with DOS version 3.00. This interrupt sets up a common interface between two processes.

Although this interrupt is in theory by no means limited to the print spooler, the only documented DOS use of it is for the print spooler. Therefore, the rest of this description will use the print spooler as an example.

Six separate functions make up the print spooler control services that are available through interrupt 47. These functions, coded 0 through 5, are invoked by first placing a function code in register AL and then issuing interrupt 47 (hex 2F).

❑ NOTE: *Before any of these functions are used, the multiplex number must be loaded into the AH register. The multiplex number for the printer spooler is 1; multiplex numbers 0 and 2–127 are reserved for DOS.*

Function code 0 reports whether or not the print spooler is installed. The return code is passed back in register AL. A value of 255 (hex FF) indicates that the print spooler is installed and can presumably be used. A value of 0 indicates that the spooler is not currently installed, but that it *can* be installed; a value of 1 indicates that the spooler is not installed and *cannot* be installed.

These last two return codes may seem rather curious until we examine them closely. A returned value of 0 seems to be a message from the print spooler that says, "I'm not here." We might respond, "If you're not there, how are you replying?" The answer is that a reply of 0 happens automatically when there is no interrupt handler installed to deal with our request. A returned value of 1 seems to say, "I'm here, but you can't use me." Strange as it may seem, that's exactly what is going on. A return code of 1 means we're not allowed to install the print spooler because interrupt 47 is being used for some other purpose by some other interrupt handler. This is a fascinating bit of business to contemplate.

Function code 1 is used to submit a file to the print spooler for printing. To tell the spooler what is to be printed, we set the register pair DS:DX to point to a 5-byte area called a *submit packet*. The first byte of the submit packet is a level code (which I know nothing about). The remaining four bytes of the submit packet are the segmented address of an ASCIIZ string (☛ see page 298) that defines the path name of the file to be printed. The path name must be a single file. The global filename characters * and ? are not allowed.

When a file is submitted using this function, it is added to the end of the queue, or list, of files to be printed. The files are printed in turn and are dropped from the queue when they've been printed.

Function code 2 cancels individual files that are queued for printing. The register pair DS:DX points to the ASCIIZ string that defines which file is to be removed from the queue. In this case, the global filename characters * and ? may be used. Note that DS:DX in function 2, unlike in function 1, points directly to the filename string, rather than pointing to a submit packet that points to the string.

Function code 3 cancels all files queued for printing. For both functions 2 and 3, if the file currently being printed is canceled, DOS stops printing the file and prints a short message to that effect.

Function code 4 gives programs access to the print queue so they can inspect it. The queue is frozen when this function is requested, so that we don't have to worry about the list changing while we inspect it. Issuing any other interrupt 47 function call will unfreeze the queue. Function 4 returns a pointer in the register pair DS:SI that points to a list of the filenames queued for printing. The entries in the list are strings with a fixed length of 64 bytes. The end of the list is indicated by an entry that begins with a zero byte.

The queue freeze imposed by function 4 doesn't need to halt the printing operation because it isn't necessary. But, it will suspend the removal from the queue of a file that is finished printing.

Function code 5 is essentially a null function that does nothing but unfreeze the queue of filenames frozen by function 4. (The other four functions can do this, too.)

THE THREE DOS ADDRESS INTERRUPTS

DOS uses three interrupts, 34 through 36 (hex 22 through 24), to handle three exceptional circumstances: the end of a program; a "break" keyboard action (Ctrl-Break or Ctrl-C on the standard PC keyboard; Fn-B on the PCjr), and any "critical error" (usually a disk error of some kind). Our programs can affect the action taken in each of these three circumstances by changing the corresponding interrupt vector to point to any operation we choose. This is why we call these interrupts the *address interrupts.*

DOS maintains a default address setting for each of these interrupts, which is preserved at the beginning of a program's operation and restored after the program is finished. This allows our programs to freely change these vectors according to their needs without disturbing the operation of subsequent programs or the operation of DOS itself.

It is also possible for our programs to change the preserved default settings, which would then make a semipermanent change in DOS's operation. The default settings are saved in the program's program segment prefix (☞ see page 260). Modifying the value in the PSP automatically changes the default setting that is restored when the program ends.

It's a normal and accepted practice for a program to change the interrupt addresses during its own operation; it's not normal for a program to change the default setting that will be in effect after the program ends.

Interrupt 34 (hex 22): Terminate Address

The address associated with interrupt 34 specifies where control of the computer will be passed when the program ends. This address is also copied into the program's PSP.

Normally, this service is used to pass control back to DOS's command interpreter, COMMAND.COM, when a program ends. Although the other two interrupt vectors covered in this section may be freely changed by our programs to point to new routines, this vector is not used that way. How it is used is best explained through an example.

A program—let's call it Prog1—may request that DOS set up and run another program—which we'll call Prog2. When Prog2 ends, DOS returns control to wherever interrupt 34's vector indicates. Consequently, if the default setting of this interrupt is in effect, it returns control to DOS and not back to Prog1. This may be what Prog1 wants, but if Prog1 wishes to continue operation after Prog2 is finished, Prog1 must change this terminate-address interrupt vector to point to a location within Prog1, *before* it runs Prog2. Later, Prog1 must reset this interrupt vector so that Prog1 can end normally and pass control back to DOS.

Unlike the other address interrupts, this interrupt is never actually generated. Instead, the interrupt vector is used as a place to store a segmented address. Interrupts 29 through 31, 68, and 73 (hex 1D through 1F, 44, and 49) are similarly used to store addresses (☞ see page 46).

This is exotic stuff. Don't mess with it if you don't understand it. If you are qualified to use this feature, then you probably understand it better than I can explain it.

Interrupt 35 (hex 23): Break Address

The address associated with interrupt 35 points to the interrupt-handling routine that will be invoked whenever DOS responds to a break-key action. The break key is generated on a standard PC keyboard by Ctrl-Break, and on any keyboard by Ctrl-C (a fact that is not widely advertised).

DOS is a bit quirky about when it will respond to a break-key action. In standard operation, DOS only acts on a break during certain keyboard and screen functions. However, the BREAK ON command allows DOS versions 2.00 and higher to act on a break at any opportunity.

DOS's default response to the break interrupt is to terminate the program or batch command file that is being executed. If our programs set up their own break interrupt handler, they can have DOS take any action they wish, no matter how extensive or complex. Through this interrupt, our programs can invoke any DOS services and they need not return control to DOS (though they should, to avoid stack growth).

The two most common actions are to completely ignore the break-key action or to use it as a signal to break out of a repeated operation.

Several DOS programs illustrate this second use. For example, the rudimentary Edlin text-editing program uses the break key to signal the end of the I (insert lines) subcommand. If you want a program to ignore the break key, use an interrupt handler that returns control to the active program. When using the break key to signal the end of a repeated operation, the interrupt handler should set a data signal switch, which the normal part of the program will inspect and act on, and then return control.

There are two ways an interrupt handler for this interrupt can return control. The normal method, for any interrupt handler, is to use the IRET (interrupt return) instruction. There is another method peculiar to this interrupt that gives the interrupt handler the option of telling DOS either to carry on or to end the program (the same way the default DOS interrupt handler terminates programs on a break-key action). To use this method, the interrupt handler sets the CF (carry flag) and ends with a FAR RET instruction; if CF is 1, it signals that DOS is to abort the program and if CF is 0, it signals that the program is to continue.

◻ NOTE: *Programs can simulate a break-key action by generating this interrupt.*

Interrupt 36 (hex 24): Critical-Error Handler Address

The address associated with interrupt 36 points to the interrupt-handling routine that is invoked whenever DOS detects a "critical error"—an emergency situation that prevents it continuing. Typically, the critical error is a disk error but other errors are also reported, as we'll see.

When an error handler is invoked, several sources of information about the error itself, and about the state of things before the error occurred, are available. These sources include the register pair BP:SI, the stack, the AH register, and the DI register. We will cover them one-by-one because the whole business is quite complicated.

If we are operating under DOS version 2.00 or higher, the register pair BP:SI is set to point to a device header control block. Our error handler can inspect this control block to learn more about the device (disk drive, printer, etc.) that experienced the error. (See the DOS Technical Reference manual for more about the device header.)

The stack contains the complete register set of the program that issued the DOS function call that ended in the critical error. This information may be quite useful to an error handler that is intimately integrated with the active program. Assuming that our error handler is going to

BP Offset	Stack Contents
0	BP that we pushed
2	IP:CS of DOS service invoking this handler
6	Flags of DOS service invoking this handler
8	AX of program invoking DOS service
10	BX of program invoking DOS service
12	CX of program invoking DOS service
14	DX of program invoking DOS service
16	SI of program invoking DOS service
18	DI of program invoking DOS service
20	BP of program invoking DOS service
22	DS of program invoking DOS service
24	ES of program invoking DOS service
26	IP:CS of program invoking DOS service
30	Flags of program invoking DOS service

*Figure 15-4. The stack contents of a
program that issued the DOS function call
that ended in a critical error*

gain access to the stack by traditional means, we can locate the stack
with an offset address from the BP using these two instructions:

```
PUSH    BP
MOV     BP,SP
```

which first saves the old BP (base pointer) and then sets the BP equal to
the SP (stack pointer). ☛ For more discussion about these instructions,
see page 166 (the section entitled "Level 3: Entry Code"). Having done
this, we'll find the stack contents shown in Figure 15-4.

The nature of a critical error is signaled primarily through a combination of the high-order bit of the AH register and the low-order byte of
the DI register (a curious choice, for sure). If the high-order bit of AH is 0
(AH<128), then the error is related to a disk operation; but if the same bit
is 1 (AH>127), then the error may be something other than a disk error, as
we shall see shortly. When the error is a disk device error (AH<128),
register AL gives the drive ID number (0 is drive A, 1 is B, etc.). Bits 0
through 2 of AH indicate further information about the error, as shown
in Figure 15-5.

Bit 2 1 0	Value	Meaning
. . 0	0	Read error
. . 1	1	Write error
0 0 .	0	Error involved DOS system files
0 1 .	1	Error involved FAT
1 0 .	2	Error involved directory
1 1 .	3	Error involved data area of disk

Figure 15-5. The bit values and associated errors returned in bits 0 through 2 of the AH register after interrupt 36 is invoked

If AH is greater than 127, then the error is not necessarily a disk error, though it may be. One disk error that is normally reported when AH is greater than 127 is an error in the disk's FAT. For DOS-1 versions, this is always the case. For versions 2.00 and higher, the error-handler program should inspect the device header control block (pointed to by BP:SI). If the returned value indicates that the device is a disk, then you'll know the error is a FAT error. Besides this one exception, AH>127 indicates a garden-variety error for a non-disk device and we have to rely on the basic error

Error Code Dec	Hex	Meaning
12	0C	General, nonspecific error
11	0B	Read error
10	0A	Write error
9	09	Printer out of paper
8	08	Sector not found
7	07	Unknown media: disk format not recognized
6	06	Seek error: move to requested track failed
5	05	Bad request structure length
4	04	CRC error
3	03	Unknown command requested
2	02	Drive not ready (e.g. no disk, or door open)
1	01	Unknown unit: invalid drive number
0	00	Write-protect error: attempt to write on protected diskette

Figure 15-6. The error code values returned in register DI after interrupt 36 is invoked

AL	DOS Action
0	Ignore the error and press onward
1	Retry the operation (we may have fixed the problem)
2	Kill the program (DOS issues interrupt 35 (hex 23), in effect generating a break-key action)

Figure 15-7. The values that can be loaded into the AL register to tell DOS what to do following an error-handler routine

codes relayed in the low-order byte of DI to define the exact problem (the high-order byte should be ignored). The DI error-code values shown in Figure 15-6 are essentially the same as those reported in AL for interrupts 37 and 38 (hex 25 and 26).

Depending on the circumstances, an error handler may need to use some of the DOS function-call services to report what's going on to the program's user. The simple keyboard and display services, function numbers 0 through 12 (hex 0 through C), may be used, but the services with higher function numbers, which mostly involve disk and other device operations, should not be used. Using the higher-numbered services while in the middle of an error handler for a previous operation will make a muddle of things that DOS is unlikely to recover from.

Normally, an error-handler routine will return to DOS after it has done whatever it chooses to do. DOS can then take three courses of action: It can ignore the error, try the operation again, or terminate the program. We tell DOS which course we want it to take by loading one of the values shown in Figure 15-7 into the AL register.

❑ NOTE: *Since the set-up process required before generating this interrupt is rather complex, it is not appropriate for our programs to simulate a critical error by generating an interrupt 36.*

THE PROGRAM SEGMENT PREFIX (PSP)

When DOS loads a program, it first sets aside a section of memory for the program called the program segment, or code segment. Then it constructs a control block called the program segment prefix, or PSP, in the first 256 (hex 00 through FF) bytes. Usually, the program is loaded directly after the PSP at the hex 100 offset.

The PSP contains a hodgepodge of information that DOS uses to help run the program. It is part of every DOS program, regardless of the language the program is written in. However, for programming purposes, the information stored in the PSP is more relevant to programs written in assembly language than programs written in high-level languages. This is because with high-level languages, the language is normally in charge of the program's working environment, memory usage, and file control— all the things that the PSP is concerned with. Therefore, we are normally only interested in and able to make good use of the PSP if our program is assembly-language based (although any program that can find out the setting of the CS register can use it to gain access to the PSP; ☞ more on this on page 266).

Before we describe the different elements of the PSP, we need to look at the relationship between the PSP and the program it supports.

The PSP is always located at offset 0 within the code segment. Even though the program location is typically located directly after the PSP at offset hex 100, its location may vary depending on the program command format we use. Regardless of its location, as soon as the program receives control, certain registers are set to point to the PSP. For a simple .COM-format program, all the segment registers are set to point to the beginning of the PSP and the program begins at offset hex 100. For a more complex .EXE-format program, which uses the DOS LINK operation, only the DS and ES registers are set to point to the PSP. The LINK program passes the settings for the CS, IP, SS, and SP registers and consequently may set the program's starting location in CS:IP to a location other than offset hex 100.

Wherever the program is located, the essential relationship between the program and its PSP remains the same. The important point is that at the beginning of a program's execution, we have access to the PSP through one of the segment registers. This means that even if the segment registers are changed in the course of a program's execution, a pointer to the PSP can be captured in the program's early stages, allowing us to maintain access to the PSP throughout the program's execution.

The best way to explain how the PSP and the program work together is to jump right into the PSP's internal structure. We will reveal the purpose and potential use of each element as we explain it.

The Internal Structure of the PSP

As you will soon discover, the PSP contains a rather confusing mixture of items. (☞ See Figure 15-8.) The background and history of DOS pull it in different directions—backward to the earlier CP/M system and forward to UNIX-type operating environments. As a result, the PSP contains elements that serve different purposes and are oriented to different programming methods. Don't be confused by any of this—it's just the

Field	Dec	Offset Hex	Length	Description
1	0	0	2	INT 32 instruction
2	2	2	2	Size of memory (in paragraphs)
3	4	4	1	Reserved; normally 0
4	5	5	5	Call to DOS function dispatcher
5	A	10	4	Terminate vector
6	E	14	4	Break vector
7	12	18	4	Error vector
8	16	22	22	Used by DOS
9	2C	44	2	Environment strings pointer
10	2E	46	34	DOS work area
11	50	80	3	INT 33, RETF instructions
12	53	83	2	Reserved
13	55	85	7	Reserved, or FCB #1 extension
14	5C	92	9	FCB #1
15	65	101	7	FCB #2 extension
16	6C	108	20	FCB #2
17	80	128	1	Parameter length
18	81	129	127	Parameters
19	80	128	128	Disk transfer area (DTA)

Figure 15-8. The parts of the program segment prefix (PSP)

nature of a critter like the PSP, which has such a diverse history behind it. We'll discuss the elements in the order they may appear.

Field 1 contains hex bytes CD 20, the interrupt 32 (hex 20) instruction. As we saw in the discussion of interrupt 32 in this chapter, this interrupt is just one of several standard ways for a program to end itself. This instruction is placed at the beginning of the PSP (at offset 0), so that a program can end itself simply by jumping to this location when the CS points to the PSP. As you might guess, this is not the most sensible thing for a program to do—it's always best to go through the appropriate interrupt or function call. I would guess that this odd-seeming scheme was designed as a safety note. If a linked program has an unresolved external reference, it will end up as a call to offset 0, which means it will go to this instruction and terminate the program.

Field 2 tells how much memory is available by listing the segment-paragraph address of the end of DOS memory. Multiplying this number by 16 gives the total bytes that DOS considers usable. The DOS command CHKDSK reports the same amount. Keep in mind that the amount of memory reported in this field may not be the actual physical size of memory; for example, many RAM disks use the memory in high locations and reset DOS's record of where usable memory ends. Any program that needs to make use of all available memory should use this memory indicator to find out how much memory it can use, instead of the similar BIOS interrupt service 18.

The conventional DOS working environment dedicates all available memory to each separately running program. In windowing or multitasking environments, where individual programs must share memory with other programs, a program can take what it needs and return the rest through the use of DOS function 74 (hex 4A), the SETBLOCK function. This function satisfies the DOS conventions for memory usage, but it may not work ideally with some windowing systems; such systems can use field 4 as another indicator of available memory.

Field 4 is more than it seems. Superficially, it is a long call to the DOS function dispatcher, which could be (but really shouldn't be) used to invoke DOS functions. But what this field is really good for is to indirectly determine whether our programs have less than 64K to work in. As a call, this instruction contains the address of the DOS function dispatcher routine; as a long call, it contains the address in segmented format. By a process too bizarre and complicated to explain, the segmented address is set so that it serves two purposes: Not only does it point to the DOS function dispatcher, but the offset part also indicates how much of the code segment we can use (up to hex FFF0, 16 bytes short of 64K). The offset part of the address, the part we are interested in, is located at offset 6 within the PSP, following the instruction's op-code at offset 5.

The upshot of this is that if DOS has less than 64K to give our programs, we can use this field to learn how many bytes are available—a technique that should work with most or all windowing and multitasking systems. If DOS can give us more than 64K, we can learn how much more by looking at field 2, the paragraph address limit. However, as we said earlier, this field may not give us an accurate answer in some windowing or multitasking environments.

Fields 5, 6, and 7 contain the default segmented addresses for the three address interrupts that we discussed earlier in this chapter. The default addresses are preserved at the beginning of a program's operation and restored when the program ends. You may recall that this allows our programs to use different service vectors while the program is running without disturbing the operation of subsequent programs or of DOS itself. If we do not provide new vectors, DOS uses the default setting stored in the PSP to point to the default service routine. If we tamper with the addresses stored in these fields, we can change the default values (and their associated service routines) that are restored when the program ends, thereby making a semipermanent change in DOS's operation. Under normal circumstances, there is no good reason for us to change or even to read these settings.

Field 9 contains a segment address that points to the environment strings supported by DOS 2.00 and later versions. The environment begins at offset 0 from this address.

☐ NOTE: *To avoid confusion about terminology, we use the word "environment" in this context to refer to the set of strings (defined in a moment) that DOS uses to communicate certain kinds of information between programs. Elsewhere in this book we've used the word "environment" to loosely refer to the operating conventions under which a program works.*

This DOS environment is a collection of ASCIIZ strings—that is, strings of ASCII characters with CHR$(0) marking their ends—that can define various kinds of information. The end of each environment setting is marked by a zero-length string (CHR$(0)) where we would expect to find the first byte of the next string. If an environment setting begins with CHR$(0), then there are no strings in it.

By convention, each individual environment string is in the form NAME = *value*, where NAME is capitalized and of any reasonable length and *value* can be just about anything. DOS sets an environment for the command processor, which is then passed to every program it invokes. Normally, this environment will contain at least the name COMSPEC (used by DOS to find the COMMAND.COM file on disk), and may also contain such names as PATH or SWITCHAR. The DOS command SET can be used to add, change, or delete strings in the environment.

Field 11 contains two instructions that will invoke a DOS function (interrupt 33, hex 21) and return to the caller (RETF or FAR return). This is another kludge that allows us to invoke DOS functions semi-indirectly. To use this feature, we set up everything necessary to invoke a DOS function (selecting the function in AH, etc.) and then, instead of bravely performing an interrupt 33 (a 2-byte instruction), we do a far call to offset hex 50 in the PSP (a 5-byte instruction).

You might expect that this feature is another flash from the past, a bit of CP/M compatibility, but actually it was introduced with DOS 2.00 and will not work with previous versions of DOS. So we can take this as an indication that this approach to invoking DOS services, as clumsy as it appears, looks to the future, not the past.

Fields 13, 14, 15, and 16 support old-fashioned file processing, using file control blocks, or FCBs. FCBs may be used for file I/O with any version of DOS, but their use is discouraged with DOS 2.00 and later versions, where more modern file I/O is available through the use of file handles. ☛ See page 288 for more on file control blocks, and page 298 for more on file handles.

This area of the PSP was set up as it is to make life easier for programs that receive one or two filenames as parameters. The basic idea, and a nice one I think, is to let DOS construct the necessary FCBs out of the first two program parameters (the parameters given on the command line, following the program name). If a program needs either or both FCBs, it can open and use them without having to decode the command parameters and construct the FCBs itself.

If you use this feature of the PSP, there are some complications that you should be aware of. First, the two FCBs overlap where they are placed. If your program needs only the first, fine; but if it needs the second one as well, one or both of them should be moved elsewhere before they are used. Also, you should be aware that these FCBs can involve FCB extensions, a fact that is overlooked in most DOS documentation for the PSP. I have called attention to the fact by documenting the location of the implied FCB extensions in Figure 15-8.

Keep in mind that the use of FCBs is considered somewhat obsolete, but if you want to use them, this information should help.

Fields 17 and 18 give our programs access to the parameters entered on the command line. Field 17 gives the entire length of the parameter string (which could be as short as 0 or as long as 127), and field 18 gives the contents.

Here are some peculiarities about the string that is passed: It does not contain the name of the program that was invoked. Instead, it begins with the character that immediately follows the program name, which is usually a blank. Separators, such as blanks or commas, are not stripped out or compressed. If we use the command line, we have to be prepared to scan through it, recognizing standard separators. Starting with DOS 2.00, the command line is tampered with in a particular way: Any redirection parameters (such as <INPUT or >OUTPUT) are extracted by DOS and the parameter line is reconstructed as if these items were not there. As a result of these two operations on the command string, a program cannot find out if its standard I/O is being redirected, nor can it find out its own name.

❑ NOTE: *Fields 17 and 18 overlap with field 19 in the PSP, so get your parameters while you can—the next field could wipe them out.*

Field 19 is the DOS default disk transfer area (DTA). It is a default buffer area of 128 bytes starting at PSP offset hex 80 and is established just in case we use a DOS service that calls for a DTA and haven't yet set up our own buffer area. ☛ See Chapters 16 and 17 for descriptions of the services that use or manipulate the DTA.

In considering the PSP as a whole, note that DOS makes use of several areas in the first 85 bytes of the 256-byte PSP (fields 1 through 12, offsets hex 0 through 54). If we want to tamper with any of the PSP, we should restrict ourselves to fields 13 through 19 (offsets hex 55 through FF). The program example that follows illustrates how the first part of the PSP can be left intact while the second part is reclaimed and used by a resident program.

AN EXAMPLE

For this chapter's interface example, we will create a program that uses the terminate-but-stay-resident DOS interrupt. Most of our assembly-language examples are set up as interfaces between a high-level language and ROM-BIOS or DOS service routines. This example is quite different: It is a stand-alone assembly-language program that uses interrupt 27B to leave part of itself resident.

Any program, and most especially terminate-but-stay-resident programs, must perform certain initialization functions when they are first loaded. In a terminate-but-stay-resident program, where compact size is highly desirable, a quick way to trip excess bytes is simply to discard this one-time initialization code before becoming resident; in other words, we want to keep all of the code except the initialization code.

DOS has just the function we need to perform this fat-trimming operation. Interrupt 27 hex terminates a program; as part of the interrupt call, we can stipulate (in the DX register) the first memory location of our program that is to be released. We can use this feature to release the memory taken by the initialization code, while keeping the rest of the program resident: we simply specify the first byte of the initialization code as the first memory location to be released.

```
                    ;Illustrates interrupt 39 (hex 27): terminate-but-stay-resident
          PROGRAM SEGMENT PUBLIC
                    ASSUME  CS:PROGRAM,  DS:PROGRAM
                    ORG  100h           ;Reserve room for program segment
                                         prefix
          TBSR    PROC
                    JMP  INITIALIZE   ;Start by skipping to initialization
                                       code
          START_RESIDENT:
           ;
           ;here would appear whatever we wanted to leave resident
           ;
          END_RESIDENT:
           ;
          INITIALIZE:                   ;the initialization code would follow
                                         here
           ;
           ;here's the one-shot initialization code
           ;
           ;and now we terminate, keeping all code resident up to
            ''INITIALIZE'' LEA DX, INITIALIZE
           ;First available location after resident code INT 27H
          TBSR    ENDP
          PROGRAM ENDS
          END     TBSR
```

Universal DOS Functions

I n this chapter, we are going to discuss the functions that are universal to all versions of DOS. In DOS terminology, the old (or universal) services covered in this chapter are called the "traditional functions." The new services, introduced with DOS 2.00 and covered in Chapter 17, are called the "extended functions."

SUMMARY OF THE UNIVERSAL FUNCTIONS

All of the DOS function calls are invoked by interrupt 33 (hex 21). Individual functions are selected by placing the function number in the AH register.

The traditional DOS function calls are organized into the logical groups shown in Figure 16-1. In an effort to make this figure as clear as possible, I have organized and described these function calls in a slightly different manner than the DOS Technical Reference manual. Figure 16-2 lists the individual function calls.

Before we get into the details of these functions, I should warn you that some aspects of the design and organization of a few of these functions, particularly numbers 1 through 12, are screwball—to put it mildly. They are this way for historical reasons. Many of the details of DOS, and especially the details of the DOS function calls, were designed to closely mimic the services provided by CP/M. This was an important and deliberate choice, made to make it much easier for 8-bit CP/M software to be converted to the 16-bit IBM PC and DOS. Although the creation of DOS provided a timely opportunity to break with and clean up the mistakes of the past, the opportunity was not taken (unfortunate, but wise, in my opinion). The clean (or cleaner) redesign of the DOS services was really started during the development of version 2.00 and realized in the extended functions (☛ see Chapter 17).

Function		
Dec	Hex	Group
0	00	Non-device function
1–12	01–0C	Character device I/O
13–36	0D–24	File management
37–38	25–26	More non-device functions
39–41	27–29, 2E	More file management
42–46	2A–2D	More non-device functions

Figure 16-1. The logical groups of traditional DOS function calls

| Function | | | Function | | |
Dec	Hex	Description	Dec	Hex	Description
0	0	Terminate: end program	24	18	Used internally by DOS
1	1	Keyboard input with echo	25	19	Report current drive
2	2	Display output	26	1A	Set disk transfer area
3	3	Serial input	27	1B	Get FAT information, current drive
4	4	Serial output	28	1C	Get FAT information, any drive
5	5	Printer output	29	1D	Used internally by DOS
6	6	Direct keyboard/display I/O	30	1E	Used internally by DOS
7	7	Direct keyboard input without echo	31	1F	Used internally by DOS
8	8	Keyboard input without echo	32	20	Used internally by DOS
9	9	Display string	33	21	Read file random
10	A	Buffered keyboard input	34	22	Write file random
11	B	Check keyboard input status	35	23	Get file size
12	C	Clear keyboard and do function	36	24	Set random record
13	D	Reset disk	37	25	Set interrupt vector
14	E	Select current drive	38	26	Create program segment
15	F	Open file	39	27	Read file records random
16	10	Close file	40	28	Write file records random
17	11	Search for first matching file	41	29	Parse filename
18	12	Search for next matching file	42	2A	Get date
19	13	Delete file	43	2B	Set date
20	14	Read sequential file record	44	2C	Get time
21	15	Write sequential file record	45	2D	Set time
22	16	Create file	46	2E	Set disk write verification
23	17	Rename file			

*Figure 16-2. The traditional DOS function
calls invoked by interrupt 33 and selected in
the AH register*

On the pages that follow we will detail the 46 original DOS function calls, universally used in all versions of DOS.

Function 0: Terminate

DOS function 0 is used to end a program and pass control back to DOS. It is functionally identical to DOS interrupt 32 (hex 20) discussed on page 249. Either service can be used interchangeably to exit a program.

DOS versions 2.00 and higher provide an enhanced terminate service through function 76 (hex 4C), which leaves a return code (an error code) in register AL when a program ends. Batch-processing files can act on the return codes using the DOS subcommand ERRORLEVEL. Use function 76 instead of function 0 if you wish to record any errors that occur when a program ends (☞ see page 317).

Like DOS interrupt 32, this function does not close files automatically when the program ends. To ensure that the proper length of a changed file is recorded in the file directory, use the close-file functions 16 or 62 before calling this function. Also, it is up to the program to make sure the PSP address is in the CS register before exiting. (As you may recall from our discussion in Chapter 15, the PSP contains the terminate address that tells DOS where to go when a program is terminated.)

Function 1: Keyboard Input with Echo

Function 1 waits for character input from the standard input device and returns it in the AL register when available. It should be compared with the other keyboard function calls, particularly functions 6, 7, and 8.

Here is how function 1 works: Key actions that result in an ASCII character are returned as one byte in AL and immediately reported by this service. The 97 special key actions that result in something other than an ASCII character (☞ see page 134) generate two bytes, which are passed to us through two consecutive calls to this service.

The standard way to use this service is to test for a 0 in AL. If AL is not 0, we have an ASCII character. If AL is 0, we have a special character (which should be recorded), and this function should be repeated immediately to get the pseudo-scan code that represents the special key action (☞ see page 135 for a list of the actions, codes, and their meanings). As with all the DOS keyboard input services, the scan code for ASCII characters is not available, even though the ROM-BIOS services make it available in what we call the auxiliary byte (☞ see page 134).

The various DOS keyboard service functions are distinguished primarily by three criteria: whether they wait for input, or report no input when none is available; whether they echo input onto the display screen; and whether the standard break-key operation is active for that service. (Recall that standard DOS operation calls for DOS to act on a break-key action—Ctrl-Break or Ctrl-C—only during a limited number of operations. However, beginning with version 2.00, DOS introduced the BREAK ON command, which gives DOS authority to act on the break key under any circumstances.) Function 1 performs all three of these operations: It waits for input, echoes input to the screen, and if it detects a break-key operation, it executes interrupt 35, the break address interrupt.

❏ NOTE: *For DOS versions 2.00 and higher, this "keyboard" service is actually connected to the DOS standard input device. This is the keyboard by default, but it can be redirected to other input devices.*

☛ If you wish to avoid waiting when input is not ready, but wish to use this service, see function 11, which also reports whether or not input is ready. See functions 8 and 12 for variations on this service.

Function 2: Display Output

Function 2 writes a single ASCII character to the display screen (or, for DOS 2.00 and later, to the standard output device, which can be redirected from the display screen). The character written is placed in DL.

In general, this service acts on the ASCII control characters, such as backspace or carriage return. In the case of the backspace character, the display screen cursor is moved backward one column. Contrary to the information given in the DOS Technical Reference manual (and in all DOS manuals since the very first), a blank character (hex 20) is *not* written after the cursor is moved, which would effectively erase any previous character. Instead, any information that has been backspaced over remains intact.

Function 3: Serial Input

Function 3 inputs one character into AL from the standard auxiliary device, which is normally known as AUX: or COM1:. By the magic of the DOS MODE command, we can change the setting to receive input from other devices, such as COM2:. Normally, the source of this input is the first RS-232 serial port.

❏ NOTE: *This service waits for input. It does not report status information about the many miseries that a serial port can suffer. If you want to know the status of the serial port, use the ROM-BIOS serial services (☛ see page 210).*

Function 4: Serial Output

Function 4 outputs one character from register DL to the standard auxiliary device. ☛ See the remarks under function 3.

Function 5: Printer Output

Function 5 outputs one byte from DL to the standard printer device, which is normally known as PRN: or LPT1: (but, with the DOS MODE command, can be other devices). In the absence of any DOS redirection, the standard printer is always the first parallel adapter, even if a serial port is used for printer output.

Function 6: Direct Keyboard/Display I/O

Function 6 is a complex and screwball service that combines the operations of keyboard input and display output into one untidy package. As with everything else in DOS 2.00 and later, the I/O is not connected to the keyboard and display, but rather to the standard input and output devices (which default to the keyboard and display).

Here is how this service works: The AL register is used for input and the DL register for output. If DL is 255 (hex FF), then AL is ready to accept an input character. The zero flag (ZF) signals whether input is ready. If ZF is 1, no input is ready; if ZF is 0, an input byte is placed in AL. If DL is not 255, then it is assumed to contain a legitimate output character, which, on request, is sent out to the standard output device through DL.

Function 6 does not wait for keyboard input, it does not echo input to the display screen, and the break-key operation is not active. (☞ See function 1 for an explanation.)

☞ Compare this service with functions 1, 7, and 8. See function 12 for a variation of this service.

Function 7: Direct Keyboard Input Without Echo

Function 7 waits for character input from the standard input device and returns it in the AL register when available. It does not echo input to the display screen and it does not use the break-key operation.

Function 7 works the same way as function 1: ASCII character key actions are returned as single bytes in AL and are immediately reported by this service. The 97 special key actions that result in something other than an ASCII character (☞ see page 134) generate two bytes, which are passed to us through two consecutive calls to this service.

The standard way to use this service is to test for a 0 in AL. If AL is not 0, we have an ASCII character. If AL is 0, we have a special character. This character should be recorded and then the function should be repeated at once to get the pseudo-scan code that represents the special key action (☞ see page 135 for a list of the actions, the codes, and their meanings). As with all the DOS keyboard input services, the scan code for ASCII characters is not available, even though the ROM-BIOS services make it available in what we call the auxiliary byte (☞ see page 134).

☞ Compare this service with functions 1, 6, and 8. If you want to use this service but avoid waiting when input is not ready, see function 11, which reports whether or not input is ready. See function 12 for a variation of this service.

Function 8: Keyboard Input Without Echo

Function 8 waits for input, does not echo, and breaks on a break-key action. It is identical to function 1, except it does not echo the input to the display screen (or standard output device).

☛ See the discussion under function 1 for a description of this function. Compare this service with functions 1, 6, and 7. If you want to use this service but avoid waiting when input is not ready, see function 11, which reports whether or not input is ready. See function 12 for a variation of this service.

Function 9: Display String

Function 9 sends a string of characters to the display screen or to the standard output device (which defaults to the display screen). The register pair DS:DX provides the address of the string. A $ character, CHR$(36), is used to mark the end of the string.

❏ NOTE: *For bad historical reasons, this function is referred to as "print string" in the DOS literature. We would be better off thinking of it as "display string," as it is called here.*

While this service can be tremendously more convenient than the byte-by-byte display services (functions 2 and 6), it is flawed by the use of a real, displayable character, $, as its string delimiter. This is not a recent mistake; it's another by-product of CP/M compatibility. Unless you know there is absolutely no possibility of ever outputting a dollar sign, you should avoid this service.

Incidentally, the extended DOS functions (☛ see Chapter 17) use CHR$(0) as a string delimiter. This practice follows the convention set by the UNIX operating system and the C programming language.

Function 10 (hex A): Buffered Keyboard Input

Function 10 is a wonderful service that puts the power of the DOS editing keys to work in our programs. The service gets a complete string of input, which is presented to our programs whole, rather than character by character. Assuming that the input is actually from live keyboard action and is not redirected elsewhere, the full use of the DOS editing keys is available to the person who is typing the input string. When the Return key is pressed (or a carriage return, CHR$(13), is encountered in the input file), the input operation is complete and the entire string is presented to our program.

There are many advantages to using this service, particularly when our programs need complete, coherent strings of keyboard input, rather than byte-by-byte input. The two foremost benefits are that we are spared the effort of writing detailed input-handling code, and our programs' users are given a familiar set of input editing tools: the DOS editing conventions.

To use this service, we must provide DOS with an input buffer area, where the input string will be built. The register pair DS:DX points to this buffer. We inform DOS of the working size of the buffer in the buffer's first byte; this is the number of bytes that DOS can use for input. The second byte of the buffer is used for DOS to report the actual number of bytes that were input. DOS places the input string, which consists entirely of ASCII characters, beginning at the third byte in the buffer. The end of the input string is signaled by the carriage-return character, CHR$(13). The carriage return is placed in the buffer so there must be room for it, but it is not included in the character count that DOS returns to us in the second byte.

By these rules, the longest buffer we can give DOS is 255 working bytes, and the longest string that DOS can return to us is one less than the working length. Since the first two bytes of the buffer are used for status information, the actual working size of the buffer is two bytes less than the buffer's overall size. This may explain some of the mysteries of the input conventions in both DOS and BASIC.

If input continues beyond what DOS can place in the buffer (which is one byte short of its working length), then DOS will discard any further input, beeping all the while, until a carriage return is encountered.

You can test some elements of this function by counting the input that the DOS command interpreter will accept. Simple experiments will reveal that the command interpreter uses a working buffer size of 128 bytes (the total length is 130 bytes). DOS will complain about any input other than a carriage return beyond the 127th byte.

☛ See function 12 for a variation of this service.

Function 11 (hex B): Check Keyboard Input Status

Function 11 reports whether input is ready from the keyboard (or standard input device). An input-ready signal is reported when AL is set to 255 (hex FF). But if no input is ready, AL is set to 0.

The standard break-key operation is active for this service (☛ see the discussion under function 1 for an explanation).

Function 12 (hex C): Clear Keyboard and Do Function

Function 12 clears the keyboard buffer in RAM and then invokes one of five DOS services: function 1, 6, 7, 8, or A. The AL register is used to select which of these functions will be performed after the keyboard buffer is flushed. With the keyboard buffer clear of extraneous characters, this function forces the system to wait for new input before it acts on the invoked function.

Note that since function 6 is supported, the follow-up service need not be keyboard input: It may be display output.

Function 13 (hex D): Reset Disk

Function 13 resets the disk and flushes all file buffers. It doesn't automatically close files when the program ends. To ensure that the proper length of a changed file is recorded in the file directory, use the close-file functions 16 or 62 before calling this function.

Contrary to what earlier DOS manuals indicate, this service doesn't change the default drive back to A (or make any other such change), not even with the versions of DOS that make this claim.

Function 14 (hex E): Select Current Drive

Function 14 selects the current default drive and reports the number of drives installed. The drive is selected in DL, with 0 indicating drive A, 1 drive B, and so on. The number of drives is reported in AL. Once DOS knows the number of drives installed, any number can be used for the default drive number, from 0 to one less than the total number reported.

There are a few things to keep in mind when using this service. First, there are never any gaps in the drive IDs used by DOS; they are consecutively numbered. Second, if there is only one physical disk drive, DOS will simulate a second drive, drive number 1 (drive B). And third, the drive ID letter is found by adding the drive number to the character A, CHR$(65). In the unusual case that there are more than 26 drives, some rather peculiar drive "letters" can result.

Function 25 (hex 19) reports the current drive number, and functions 14 and 25 can be combined to learn the number of drives without disturbing the current default drive setting. This is done in assembly language like this:

```
MOV     AH,25                    ; report current drive
INT     33                       ; function call
MOV     DL,AL                    ; copy current drive number
MOV     AH,14                    ; set current drive
INT     33                       ; function call
```

At this point, AL will contain the number of drives, without any change to the current drive. To convert the number to the highest drive letter, we can add this instruction:

```
ADD    AL,'A'-1
```

Function 15 (hex F): Open File

Function 15 opens a file in the traditional DOS manner, by using a file control block (FCB). The FCB is a group of 128 logical records within a file. It contains a set of information supplied by our program about the open file that DOS uses to locate the file and the file's data (☞ see page 288 for FCB details). Our programs point to the FCB using the register pair DS:DX. DOS will attempt to open the file given the specifications in the FCB. The result is reported with AL set to 255 (hex FF) for failure to open the file and AL set to 0 for success. Remember, a file must exist in order to be opened (☞ see function 22 for a create-file service). Normally, this function would be used when opening an input file and function 22 would be used when opening an output file.

On a successful open, several fields in the FCB are set by DOS. If we specify the default drive through function 14, DOS will fill in the actual drive used. (This is done with an unconventional drive ID number. In this case, drive A is indicated by 1, rather than 0 as in most drive operations.) DOS also fills in the file's date and time, and sets the current block to 0.

Something unusual happens with the FCB record-size field, which indicates the record size we wish to use in reading and writing the file. Normally, we supply this field after the file is opened. However, on opening the file, DOS will set this field to a default record size of 128 (hex 80) bytes. We can either use this record size or change it, depending on our application. Many text-editing programs use the 128-byte record-size for efficient I/O operations. Ironically, DOS's editor, Edlin, does not. ☞ See page 291 for more on the record-size field.

Function 16 (hex 10): Close File

Function 16 closes a file when given a pointer to the FCB in the register pair DS:DX. If the operation is successful, AL is set to 0; if the operation fails, AL is set to 255 (hex FF).

A file must be closed after any operation to update the file directory. DOS makes an intelligent attempt to detect that we are closing the same file on the same disk that we opened by comparing the drive specifier in the file directory with that in the open FCB. This offers some protection against the scrambling of diskette information that can occur when a user changes diskettes and writes to the new disk before the old file has been closed.

Function 17 (hex 11): Search for First Matching File

Function 17 begins the operation of searching for multiple files that match a file specification. The register pair DS:DX points to the FCB containing the filename to be searched for. The intended use of this service is to handle filenames that include the global characters ? and *. This service begins the process and the next service, function 18, continues the search for subsequent files.

AL signals failure (255, hex FF) or success (0). If a matching filename is found, a new FCB is created at the current disk transfer address (DTA), and the filename is entered into the FCB's filename field.

If the FCB has an FCB extension (☞ see page 289), then we can name the attributes of the file that we wish to search for. There is a particular logic that is followed for this attribute search. If we specify any combination of the hidden, system, or directory attribute bits, the search will match normal files and also any files with those attributes. If we specify the volume-label attribute, this function will only search for a directory entry with that attribute. With DOS versions prior to 2.00, neither the directory nor the volume-label attributes can be used in the file search operation. The archive and read-only attributes cannot be used as search criteria in any DOS release.

This is a good service to use, even when we do not intend for our programs to operate on more than one file. Even if the first matching file is the only one that will be worked on, by using this service before opening a file, we give our programs the flexibility to accept global filenames.

Function 18 (hex 12): Search for Next Matching File

Function 18 finds the next of a series of files, following the set-up preparation performed by function 17. ☞ See function 17 for details of the set-up operation and return codes.

Function 19 (hex 13): Delete File

Function 19 deletes files that match the FCB pointed to by the register pair DS:DX. AL is 0 if the operation is a success and all matching file directory entries have been deleted. AL is 255 (hex FF) if the operation is a failure, meaning that there were no matching directory entries.

☞ See page 288 for details on the FCB.

Function 20 (hex 14): Read Sequential File Record

Function 20 is used to read the next sequential record in a file. Before calling this function, we must use the DS:DX pair to point to the file's FCB. The sequential record number is taken from the values in the current block and current record fields of the FCB. Then the file is read, and on a successful or partially successful operation, the data is placed in the current disk transfer area (☞ see function 26).

DOS increments the FCB record address fields after each read to expedite the sequential read of the file. We can change the address fields ourselves if we want to skip around in the file, but this is not wise in sequential files; it is best to use the random I/O functions, 33 and 34, if we need random access to a file's records. (☞ See page 291 for a discussion of the curious difference in the accounting methods of sequential and random record numbers.)

AL is used to report the results of the read. Complete success is signaled when AL is 0; if AL is 1, it signals an end-of-file, indicating that no data was read; if AL is 2, it signals that data could have been read, but the DTA (disk transfer area) did not have sufficient space for a full record; and if AL is 3, it signals an end-of-file with a partial record read (the record is padded with zero bytes).

Function 21 (hex 15): Write Sequential File Record

Function 21 writes a sequential record and is the companion to the previous service, function 20. Registers DS:DX point to the FCB, where the record address is stored. After reading the address, DOS takes the data from the DTA (☞ see function 26) and writes it to the disk.

After the service is finished, AL contains a return code: AL = 0 reports success; AL = 1 reports disk full; AL = 2 reports not enough space in the disk transfer segment to write the record. Note that DOS's internal disk transfer segment must have enough room to accommodate the records in our disk transfer area.

It's important to note that data is logically written by this service, but not necessarily physically written. DOS will buffer output data until it has a complete disk sector to write—at which time it will write it. Until a file is closed, there may be data in DOS's buffer that our programs consider written, but which has not yet been transferred to disk. This can be a problem if a program is terminated abnormally.

Function 22 (hex 16): Create File

Function 22 finds or creates a directory entry for a file. The service first searches the directory for a matching filename and if none is found, it searches for an empty entry. Then, when given an FCB pointer in DS:DX, the file is opened. Normally, this function is used to open an output file and function 15 is used to open an input file.

If AL is 0, it indicates a successful operation. If AL is 255 (hex FF), it signals failure, usually due to a lack of directory space. When a file is opened with this function, its length is set to 0. If we write new information to an existing file and then follow this function with function 16, which closes the file, then the old contents of the file will be lost. This would not happen if we opened the file using function 15, which sets the FCB file-size field to match the file size found in the directory.

Function 23 (hex 17): Rename File

Function 23 renames files in a modified FCB pointed to by DS:DX. For the rename operation, the FCB is specially handled. Although the drive and original filename are located in their usual positions, the new filename is placed at offset 16 in the FCB, beginning in the field normally set aside for the file size (☞ see page 291).

AL = 0 signals complete success, and AL = 255 (hex FF) signals either no files were found to rename, or the new filename is already in use.

If the new filename contains global characters, such as * or ?, they are interpreted to mean *ditto-from-old-name* and the characters in the original name that correspond to the positions of the global characters are not changed.

Function 24 (hex 18): Used Internally by DOS

Function 24 and functions 29 through 32 are used by DOS for its own internal purposes. Although there is limited information about these services available, it is unwise to use this information or spread it around. Any DOS function that is not publicly advertised as an available service cannot be relied upon to be usable in future revisions of DOS.

Function 25 (hex 19): Report Current Drive

Function 25 reports the current drive in AL, using the standard numeric code of drive A = 0, drive B = 1, etc. ☛ See function 14 for an example of how this function may be used in assembly language.

Function 26 (hex 1A): Set Disk Transfer Area

Function 26 sets the disk transfer area that will be used by DOS for file I/O. The location of the DTA is specified by the register pair DS:DX. There is a default DTA of 128 bytes available in the PSP at offset hex 80.

Function 27 (hex 1B): Get FAT Information, Current Drive

Function 27 returns key information about the disk in the current drive. Function 28 performs the identical service for any drive. Function 54, covered in the next chapter, performs a nearly identical service.

The following information is returned through this function call: AL contains the number of sectors per allocation unit (1 sector for single-sided diskettes, 2 for double-sided). CX contains the size in bytes of the disk sectors (512 bytes for all standard PC formats). DX contains the total number of allocation units (clusters) on the disk. And DS:BX points to a byte in DOS's work area containing the FAT ID (☛ see page 120 for details on the FAT). Prior to DOS version 2.00, the DS:BX register pair pointed to the complete disk FAT (which could be guaranteed to be in memory, complete), whose first byte would be the ID byte. In later DOS versions, the FAT is not necessarily present all in one place, so it's safest to assume that DS:BX only points to the single ID byte.

Beware of one dangerous possibility: This function sets DS:BX to point to the FAT ID byte, which is not located in the data segment area. This means that our current use of the data segment register (DS) will be reset by this function. Normally, this disrupts the operation of our programs, which rely on the DS register setting to remain stable. To avoid such a problem, it's best to preserve and restore the DS value around this service. Here is an example of how it might be done:

```
PUSH   DS                          ; save the DS address
MOV    AH,27                        ; ask for this function
INT    33                           ; invoke the DOS function call
MOV    AH,[BX]                      ; grab the FAT ID byte
POP    DS                           ; replace the DS address
```

This little problem is an example of how easy it is to make short-sighted mistakes in program design. If this function used the extra segment (ES) register instead of DS, then there would not be a pitfall for our programs to stumble into.

Function 28 (hex 1C): Get FAT Information, Any Drive

Function 28 works in the same way as function 27 except that it will report on any drive, not just the current drive. Before calling this service, set DL to the special drive ID number, where 0 = the current drive, 1 = drive A, 2 = drive B, etc. (Notice that we do not use the conventional drive numbering method, which specifies drive A as 0 and drive B as 1.)

Function 33 (hex 21): Read Random File Record

Function 33 reads one record from a random location in a file. After locating the FCB of the file through DS:DX, we must specify the random record we want to read by setting the random record field in the FCB. After setting the record field, data is then read into the current DTA.

AL is set with the same codes as it is for a sequential read: AL = 0 indicates a successful read; AL = 1 indicates end-of-file, with no more data available; AL = 2 means there is insufficient space in the disk transfer segment; and AL = 3 is an end-of-file, with a partial data record available.

❏ NOTE: *Our program must continually set the random record field to correspond to every random record we read. By contrast, DOS automatically increments the sequential fields, setting them to match the next record in line. Because of this, it is often more convenient to combine the two processes by following a random read with sequential reads.*

☛ Contrast this function with function 39, which can read more than one random record, or with function 20, which reads sequential records. See function 36 for more on setting the random record field.

Function 34 (hex 22): Write Random File Record

Function 34 writes one record to a random location in a file. After the register pair DS:DX points to the FCB for the file, our program must set the random record field in the FCB to correspond to the random record we want written. After the random record field is set, data is written from the current DTA.

AL is set with the same codes as it is for a sequential write: 0 indicates a successful write; 1 means the disk is full; 2 indicates insufficient space in the disk transfer segment.

❏ NOTE: *Our program must continually set the random record field to correspond to every random record we write. By contrast, DOS automatically increments the sequential fields, setting them to match the next record in line. Because of this, it is often more convenient to combine the two processes by following a random write with sequential writes.*

☞ Contrast this function with function 40, which can write more than one random record, or with function 21, which writes sequential records. See function 36 for more on setting the random record field.

Function 35 (hex 23): Get File Size

Function 35 reports the size of a file in terms of the number of records in the file. DS:DX points to the FCB of the file we want to know about. Before calling the function, the FCB should be left unopened and the record-size field in the FCB filled in. If we set the record size to 1, the file size will be reported in bytes, which is most likely what we will want.

If the operation is successful, AL is 0 and the file size is inserted into the FCB. If the file is not found, AL is 255 (hex FF).

Function 36 (hex 24): Set Random Record Field

Function 36 sets the random record field to correspond to the current sequential block and record fields in the FCB. This facilitates switching from sequential to random I/O. The DS:DX registers point to the FCB of an open file.

Function 37 (hex 25): Set Interrupt Vector

Function 37 is used to set an interrupt vector. The register pair DS:DX contains the vector address of an interrupt-handling subroutine and AL contains the interrupt number. The 4-byte interrupt vector is placed in the vector table and is called when the interrupt number is requested through the INT instruction.

While any program that knows enough to create interrupt vectors could set them itself, this service relieves us of some of the trickery necessary to set an interrupt vector safely. For vectors that point to interrupt handlers instead of pointing to tables, the segment portion would normally be our current code segment (CS), which must be transferred to DS. Again, note the poor choice of DS rather than ES, which tampers with our program users' access to data.

☞ To examine the contents of the interrupt vector, see function 53 (hex 35) in the next chapter.

Function 38 (hex 26): Create Program Segment

Function 38 is used to create a new program segment to prepare a separately loaded subprogram, or overlay, for execution. DX is used to provide the segment paragraph for the new program. The current program's program segment prefix (PSP) is copied to the first 256 (hex 100) bytes of the new segment area, creating a new PSP. This new PSP is updated with new memory and interrupt vector information. After this service sets up the PSP, we can use conventional DOS input services to read a COM-type program file into the area immediately following the PSP. With advanced versions of DOS (2.00 and later), the whole process of setting up and using overlays is much easier.

☞ See the next chapter, particularly function 75. For an explanation of the program segment prefix (PSP), see page 260.

Function 39 (hex 27): Read Random File Records

Unlike function 33, function 39 reads one or more records, starting at a random file location. DS:DX points to the FCB for the file to be read and the random record number is then taken from this FCB. CX contains the number of records desired, which should be more than 0.

The return codes are the same as they are for function 33: AL = 0 means the read was successful; AL = 1 indicates end-of-file, with no more data (if the records were read, the last record is complete); AL = 2 indicates disk transfer segment problems (often a wrap-around of the segment offset past hex FFFF, which is not allowed); and AL = 3 indicates the end-of-file, where the last record read is incomplete and padded with zeros.

No matter what the result, CX is set to the number of records read, including any partial record, and the random record field in the FCB is set to the next sequential record.

☞ Contrast this with function 33, which reads only one record.

Function 40 (hex 28): Write Random File Records

Unlike function 34, function 40 writes one or more records, starting at a random file location. DS:DX points to the FCB for the file to be written and the random record number is then taken from this FCB. CX contains the number of records desired and in this case, CX can be 0. When CX is 0, it is used as a signal to DOS to adjust the file's length to the position of the specified random record. This makes it easier for our programs to manage random files: If we have logically deleted records at the end of a file, this service allows our programs to truncate the file at that point by setting the file's length in CX, thereby freeing disk space.

The return codes are the same as they are for function 34: AL = 0 indicates a successful write and AL = 1 means there is no more disk space available. No matter what the result, CX is always set to the number of records written.

☞ Contrast this function with function 34, which writes only one random record.

Function 41 (hex 29): Parse Filename

Function 41 parses a command line for a filename with the form DRIVE:FILENAME.EXT. If a filename is found, it creates an FCB. Function 41 is particularly useful for processing the filename parameters presented to a program when it is invoked. The parsing parameters are carefully designed to make it convenient for a program to set up a default drive, a filename, and an extension, which can be overridden in a command specification. This forms the foundation for some commonly experienced program behavior.

The register pair DS:SI points to the string where the filespec string is located. The register pair ES:DI points to the memory location to be filled with an unopened FCB. Bits 0 through 3 of AL control how the filename will be parsed.

If bit 0 is 1, the function scans past the separators (for example, leading blank spaces) to find the filespec. If bit 0 is 0, the scan operation is not performed and the filespec is expected to be in the first byte location of the command line.

If bit 1 is 1, then the drive byte in the FCB will only be set if it is specified in the filespec being scanned. This allows the FCB to have its own default drive (which can be overridden), rather than using the DOS default drive.

If bit 2 is 1, the filename in the FCB will be changed only if a valid filename is found in the filespec. This allows our programs to set up a default filename, which can be overridden by the command input.

If bit 3 is 1, the filename extension in the FCB will be changed only if a valid filename is found in the filespec.

When the parsing is done, the conventional punctuation preceding, inside, and ending a filespec is recognized. If the global character * is encountered, it is translated into the more elaborate ? format.

As usual, AL reports the results: AL = 0 signals success with a single filename; AL = 1 signals success with global characters (* or ?), which alerts us to the need for find-first-find-next processing (see functions 17 and 18); AL = 255 (hex FF) signals failure (which generally means some problem in the filespec).

To facilitate repeated processing, DS:SI (just SI, really) will be updated to point past the parsed input. If the parse was unsuccessful, the second byte of the FCB (ES:DI + 1) will be blank.

As an old-style universal DOS service, this function cannot handle path names, which limits—but doesn't eliminate—its usefulness to us.

Function 42 (hex 2A): Get Date

Function 42 reports DOS's record of the current date. The date is reported in CX and DX. DH contains the month number (1 through 12); DL contains the day of the month (1 through 28, 29, 30, or 31, as appropriate); and CX contains the year (1980 through 2099).

The day of the week is reported by this service by returning a value from 0 through 6 in register AL, which signifies Sunday through Saturday. This day-of-the-week feature is something of an orphan. It has been present in DOS since release 1.10, but it was not even mentioned until DOS version 2.00. In both the 2.00 and 2.10 manuals, it is incorrectly described as a part of the get-time function and not as part of the get-date function. Starting with DOS 3.0, the manual tells it as it is. ☞ Turn to the example on page 292 to see how this service can be used.

Function 43 (hex 2B): Set Date

Function 43 sets DOS's record of the current date, in the same form as the date is reported in function 42. The date is set in CX and DX. DH contains the month number (1 through 12); DL contains the day of the month (1 through 28, 29, 30, or 31, as appropriate); CX contains the year (1980 through 2099).

☞ See function 42 for further explanation. Turn to the example on page 292 to see how this service can be used.

Function 44 (hex 2C): Get Time

Function 44 reports the time of day. The time is calculated from the ROM-BIOS clock-tick count (☞ see page 222). DOS responds to the ROM-BIOS's midnight-passed signal and updates the date every 24 hours.

The tick count is converted into a meaningful time and placed in registers CX and DX. CH contains the hour (0 through 23, on a 24-hour clock); CL contains the minutes (0 through 59); DH contains the seconds (0 through 59); and DL contains hundredths of seconds (0 through 99).

The actual rate of the clock tick is approximately .054 second, so the time cannot be reported accurately to hundredths of seconds and no event can be timed finer than to roughly 1/20 second. Nevertheless, I have confirmed that the algorithm used by DOS to calculate the hundredths does produce an even distribution of all 100 values. Because of this, it is reasonable to use the hundredths value in the seed for a pseudo-random number generator.

Contrary to what appears in the DOS Technical Reference manual, the day of the week is *not* reported by this get-time function. Instead, it is reported by function 42, the get-date function, as common sense would expect.

Function 45 (hex 2D): Set Time

Function 45 sets the time of day. The time is specified in registers CX and DX. CH contains the hour (0 through 23, on a 24-hour clock); CL contains the minutes (0 through 59); DH contains the seconds (0 through 59); DL contains hundredths of seconds (0 through 99).

Function 46 (hex 2E): Set Disk Write Verification

Function 46 controls verification of disk write operations. When verification is on, each disk write will be followed by a verify read. This does not compare the written data, but instead checks the CRC, the complex parity check of proper data recording.

When using this service, DL must be set to 0, which suggests that there are some unadvertised variations on this function. AL is set to 0 or 1, which turns verification off or on.

With DOS versions 2.00 and higher, extended function 84 (hex 54) can be used to report the current setting of the verification switch (☛ see page 319).

THE FILE CONTROL BLOCK

For the old, traditional DOS function calls, work with disk files centers around the DOS file control block (FCB), a 44-byte area that contains descriptive information about the files we are using. As we can see from many of the function calls, we not only have access to the FCB, we also have nearly complete control over it. We'll find that the new DOS function calls introduced with version 2.00 (☛ and covered in Chapter 17), keep most of the control information about a file (or other device) hidden from us. Instead, we'll work only with a simple file identification number, called a file handle—and DOS will do all the rest. But we'll save the discussion of file handles until the next chapter. Here we'll cover the format and use of the FCB.

There are two main parts to the FCB: the FCB itself, which is a 37-byte area, and the extended FCB, which is a quasi-optional 7-byte prefix to the FCB. The larger part of the FCB stores control information about the files, including the filename and drive specification, as well as record sizes and numbers. The 7-byte extension indicates that the file has special file attributes. (☛ See page 116 for more on file attributes.)

The situation with the FCB extension is more than a little peculiar. The extension is only used when we are working with files that have unconventional attributes, such as hidden or system files. Supposedly, the extension is only needed under those circumstances and if we are not using the special files, we do not need to reserve the 7-byte storage space. Ha! In practice, it is all but mandatory to set aside space for the FCB extension because the presence of the extension is signaled by the value 255 (hex FF) in its first byte. To make matters worse, if we're not using the FCB extension we have to make sure that it is marked as not being used—which means that the 7-byte memory area *is* in use, busy telling DOS that it isn't needed. This is the sort of clumsy design that drives responsible programmers wild, and makes everyone, including the DOS designers, long for the cleaner setup of the extended functions discussed in Chapter 17.

The FCB is addressed from the beginning of the main part, and all fields within the FCB are referred to in terms of their offset from this address. This places the FCB extension at a negative offset of −7. We'll follow DOS conventions and describe the various fields in these terms.

Offset (dec)	Size (bytes)	Set by	Description
−7	1	Us-1	Extension active signal: FF = yes, otherwise no
−6	5	Us-1	Nominally unused; should be set to zeros
−1	1	Us-1	File attribute, when extension active
0	1	Us-1	Special drive number
1	8	Us-1	Filename or device name
9	3	Us-1	Filename extension
12	2	Us-2	Current block number
14	2	Us-2	Record size
16	4	DOS	File size in bytes
20	2	DOS	File date (bit-coded, as in file directory)
22	10	DOS	Miscellaneous DOS control work area
32	1	Us-2	Current record number ("signed" byte, see text)
33	4	Us-2	Random record number

Figure 16-3. The file control block field descriptions

The fields shown in Figure 16-3 that are set and controlled by DOS should not be changed by our programs. The other fields should be set by us: The ones marked Us-1 should be set before the file is opened for use; those marked Us-2 should be set before the file is read from or written to. We will discuss the use and coding of the parts of the FCB in the order they appear in the table.

Offsets −7 and −6. The extension active signal must be set to 255 (hex FF) if we are using the FCB extension, or to any other value if we are not. The DOS literature indicates that the 5-byte field following it should be set to zero, though it may not matter.

Offset −1. The file-attribute field must be set to the special attributes of the file being opened. This is not needed for ordinary files, which have an attribute of 0. The attributes that must be specified are the hidden, system, and directory attributes. The label attribute is irrelevant, and the attribute specification is not needed to access a read-only file. ☛ See page 116 for more on attribute coding.

Offset 0. The special drive number in the byte at offset 0 is used to indicate which drive we wish to work with. This is not the same as the standard drive ID number, in which 0 indicates drive A, 1 indicates drive B, etc. Instead, this drive number is set up in a more flexible format, where 1 indicates drive A, 2 drive B, and so forth. The added flexibility comes from the use of 0 to indicate the current default drive, whatever that might be. Before a file is opened, we can specify the drive we want, or indicate the default drive with a 0. When the file is opened, DOS will change the 0 to the specific drive number, which we can then inspect using function 25 (hex 19). When working with this field, take care not to get the special drive values confused with the more conventional drive numbers, which are one less than the numbers used here.

Offsets 1 and 9. The two fields at byte offsets 1 and 9 give the filename and extension. Following the standard DOS conventions, these fields are left-justified and padded on the right with blanks (CHR$(32), hex 20). Also following DOS convention, either upper- or lowercase letters may be used. If the filename is a device name that DOS recognizes, such as CON:, AUX:, COM1:, COM2:, LPT1:, LPT2:, PRN:, or NUL:, DOS will use that device rather than a disk file.

❏ NOTE: *This is a reasonably good place to point out that the FCB mechanism has no provision for working with path names. Whenever we use FCBs, they always apply to the current directory in any drive. ☛ For flexible use of paths and subdirectories, see the new, extended functions in Chapter 17.*

Offsets 12 and 32. For sequential file operations, the current block and current record fields are used to keep track of the location in the file. The use of these fields is typically rather odd. Instead of using one integrated record number, the record number is divided into a high and low portion, referred to as the block and record numbers. Just to make things screwier, blocks consist of 128 records instead of the 256 records that a 1-byte record number would allow. This is why I described the record number as a "signed" byte in Figure 16-3. It actually is not signed, since negative values are not allowed; this is simply a warning that the allowed values range from 0 through 127, and not 0 through 255.

The first record of a file is record 0 of block 0. This format is designed to allow quick calculation of the location of each sequential record. With this record-locating system, DOS actually performs sequential file operations as a variation on random file operations. We set these two fields before the first sequential file operation, whether read or write. DOS automatically increments the field with each subsequent operation. We can skip around in a sequential file by modifying the fields—a tactic that is dandy for an input file, and dicey for an output file.

Offset 14. The record-size field, beginning at byte offset 14, gives the size in bytes of the logical records of the file. When our programs ask DOS to read or write a record, the logical size of the record is the number of bytes transferred between DOS's disk buffers and our program's data area. This value has nothing to do with the file as seen by DOS or with the file stored on disk; it indicates how this program wishes to view the file at this time.

The same file data can be worked on under a variety of record sizes. Unless a file is actually built of fixed-length records, we normally treat the file as though it has a record length of one byte in order to conserve space. It is customary for some of the common text-editing programs to use a record size of 128 bytes for ASCII files. This reduces the number of DOS function calls that are needed to work with the file to less than a hundredth of what they would be with a declared record size of one byte. Naturally, there is a small price to pay for this trick: The file size recorded by DOS can be too high by as much as 127 bytes, and these programs must do a little extra footwork to keep the data straight. When a file is opened through function 15, DOS sets the record size to 128 bytes by default. If we want another size, such as 1 for single-byte operations, we must change it *after* the file is opened.

Offset 16. The file-size field at byte offset 16 indicates the file size in bytes. The value is taken from the file's directory entry and is placed in the FCB when DOS opens a file. For an output file, this field is changed by DOS as the file grows. When the file is closed, the value is placed in the file's directory entry. Changing this field can give us some last-minute control over the size of an output file, but be careful when doing this. If we attempt to read a subdirectory as a file (which requires the use of the FCB extension to indicate a directory's file attribute), this field will be 0 when the file is opened because a subdirectory's directory entry indicates a zero length. To read the subdirectory successfully, we need to set this field to some arbitrarily high value. And here's something else to keep in mind: When using the rename operation (function 23), the new filename will be placed at offset 16, exactly where the file-size field is located.

Offset 20. The file's date is coded in a 2-byte field in the same form as the file directory entries, using the MM/DD/YY format. This field is set by DOS when the file is opened, with information taken from the file directory. (☞ See page 118 for more on date coding.)

Offset 33. The random record field is used during direct or random read and write operations, just as the current record and block numbers are used during sequential operations. This field is in the form of a 4-byte, 32-bit integer, which can easily be broken down into bytes or words. Records are numbered from 0, which makes it easy to calculate the file offset to any record by multiplying the random record number by the record size. We must set this field before any random file operation. DOS leaves it undisturbed.

AN EXAMPLE

For our assembly-language example in this section, I've chosen something rather interesting and foxy. It's a routine that I developed for use within my own Norton Utility programs, so you'll be seeing some actual production code, modified only to enhance the comments.

The purpose of this routine is to calculate the day of the week for any day within DOS's working range, which is stated to be from Tuesday, January 1, 1980, through Thursday, December 31, 2099. Occasionally, it's valuable for a program to be able to report the day of the week, either for the current date, or for any other date that may be in question. For example, DOS keeps track of the date and time each file was last changed. Since we often use this information to find out when we last worked with a file, it can be handy to know the day of the week as well. In fact, the day of the week is often more immediately meaningful than the actual date.

Although there are several interesting and clever algorithms published for calculating the day of the week, the actual work of writing a day-of-the-week program is usually rather tedious. It seems we rarely have these published algorithms on hand when we need them, and if we do they are often expressed in a language that is unsuitable for our purposes. Beginning with release 2.00, DOS incorporated a day-of-the-week calculation, which can spare us the chore of writing our own. DOS's program is only available to us in a form that reports the current day of the week, but that is no obstacle: We can temporarily change DOS's date to the date we're interested in and then have DOS report the day of the week. That is what the following assembly-language routine does for us.

Besides being slightly foxy, this routine is interesting because it illustrates the use of three DOS function calls operating together to produce one result. It also nicely illustrates the minor intricacies involved in saving and restoring things on the stack. As we will see here, stack use occasionally has to be carefully orchestrated so that different values don't get in the way of each other.

This particular subroutine, named WEEKDAY, is set up in the form needed for use with the Lattice/Microsoft C compiler. The routine is called with three integer variables, which give the month, day, and year we are interested in. The routine returns the day of the week in the form of an integer in the range of 0 through 6 (signifying Sunday through Saturday). This conforms nicely to the C language convention for arrays, providing an index to an array of strings that give the names of the days. Therefore, we could use this subroutine in this way:

```
DAY_NAMES (WEEKDAY (MONTH,DAY,YEAR))
```

It is important to note that this routine works blindly with the date, checking neither for a valid date nor for the range of dates accepted by DOS. Also, note that this routine requires DOS version 2.00 or higher. Here is our subroutine:

```
          PGROUP  GROUP PROG
          PUBLIC  WEEKDAY
PROG      SEGMENT BYTE PUBLIC 'PROG'
          ASSUME  CS:WEEKDAYS
WEEKDAY   PROC    NEAR
```

```
; Strategy: get and save old date
;          set new date
;          get date, which reports day of week
;          reset old date
                PUSH    BP
                MOV     BP,SP

                MOV     AH,2AH      ; get date (to save)
                INT     21H         ; DOS function call

                PUSH    CX          ; save old date...
                PUSH    DX          ; ...on the stack

                MOV     CX,[BP+8]   ; year
                MOV     DL,[BP+6]   ; day
                MOV     DH,[BP+4]   ; month
                MOV     AH,2BH      ; set date temporarily
                INT     21H         ; DOS function call
                MOV     AH,2AH      ; get date, to get day-of-week
                INT     21H         ; DOS function call
                POP     DX          ; restore old date...
                POP     CX          ; ...from the stack
                PUSH    AX          ; save weekday on stack
                MOV     AH,2BH      ; reset old date
                INT     21H         ; DOS function call
                POP     AX          ; regain weekday from stack
                MOV     AH,0        ; clear high part so OK as integer
                POP     BP
                RET
WEEKDAY         ENDP
PROG            ENDS
                END
```

17

New DOS Functions

Having focused on the DOS interrupts in the last chapter, in this chapter we'll discuss the DOS functions that are new to the advanced versions of DOS, version 2.00 and beyond. According to DOS terminology, the "old" or "universal" services covered in Chapter 16 are the *traditional* functions, and the "new" services covered in this chapter are the *extended* functions.

The extended functions of DOS 2.10 are identical to those of DOS 2.00. DOS version 3.00 introduced some changes to a few of the existing functions and also added six new functions. In this chapter, you will find each DOS-2 function described in detail, with the DOS 3.00 enhancements described wherever they occur. The new DOS 3.00 extended functions are described in detail at the end of the chapter.

☞ See Chapter 15 for the DOS interrupts, which are the services and related items that are *not* categorized as function calls. Then see Chapter 16 for the traditional DOS function calls that can be used with any release of DOS.

DOS-2 ENHANCEMENTS

With almost every DOS upgrade, there are changes in the way DOS operates and in the number of services it provides to programmers. The introduction of DOS 2.00 brought about the most dramatic changes: It added 33 new services to the existing 42; it changed the way we access file information as a result of these new services; and it made it possible to adapt DOS to work with almost any hardware device through the use of programs called installable device drivers. Before discussing the extended functions in detail, we'll briefly cover how some of these enhancements affect our programming practices.

Enhancements to the Extended DOS Functions

Many of the extended services introduced with DOS 2.00 and DOS 3.00 have three important new features that directly affect the way we use the services. First, most of the functions return a set of standard error codes in the AX register. Second, all of the functions that use string input require a special string format known as the ASCIIZ format—a string followed by a byte of zeros. And third, many of these extended DOS functions use a 16-bit number called a *file handle,* instead of an FCB, to keep track of the files and I/O devices that a program communicates with. We'll discuss each of these enhancements in turn on the next few pages.

The Standard Error Codes

Many of the new extended DOS functions return a standard set of binary error codes, called *return codes,* when the service has finished operating. These are listed in Figure 17-1. Generally, the return codes signal that a service has failed for some reason. They can be used by our programs to determine the nature of the problem and the appropriate action that should be taken.

The standard return codes are reported in the AX register (though a single half-register could be used, since all the codes have values that are well under 255). The carry flag (CF) is used to signal an error—at least that's what it's for in theory; I have discovered by experimenting with these services that you cannot depend on CF to signal conditions that you or I might think call for an error signal. Fortunately, the standard return codes are reliable and you can count on the values shown in Figure 17-1 to be used whenever a function returns an error. Whether or not you can expect to use the CF flag as a signal is another matter. I would advise that you either test the function experimentally to see what happens with the CF flag, or else completely ignore the flag and just test for the specific codes that might occur in the AX register. In the descriptions of the functions that supply return codes, you'll find a short list of the codes that are most likely to be returned by a function error.

❏ NOTE: *DOS 3.00 offers not only the standard error codes, but also more extensive error codes through function 89.* ☞ *See page 320.*

Error Code			Error Code		
Dec	Hex	Meaning	Dec	Hex	Meaning
1	1	Invalid function number	10	A	Invalid environment (see SET command of DOS)
2	2	File not found	11	B	Invalid format
3	3	Path not found	12	C	Invalid access code
4	4	No handle available: all in use	13	D	Invalid data
5	5	Access denied	14	E	Not used
6	6	Invalid handle	15	F	Invalid drive specification
7	7	Memory control blocks destroyed	16	10	Attempt to remove current directory
8	8	Insufficient memory	17	11	Not same device
9	9	Invalid memory block address	18	12	No more files to be found

Figure 17-1. The standard error codes returned in register AX after an unsuccessful function operation, and their assigned meanings

The ASCIIZ String

Whenever any of the extended functions require variable length strings, such as a path name, we use a format known as an ASCIIZ string. An ASCIIZ string consists of a series of conventional ASCII characters followed by a zero byte, which marks the end of the string. A typical path-name string may have a form something like this:

```
A:\DIRECTORY1\DIRECTORY2\FILENAME.EXT(BYTE OF ZEROS)
```

The drive specifier is optional and either the forward slash or backslash are accepted as path separators.

The ASCIIZ string format is commonly used by both the UNIX operating system and the C programming language; it is just one of many new elements with a C/UNIX flavor introduced with the DOS-2 versions.

File Handles

The new extended functions of DOS deal with files in a more internal way than the traditional DOS services. The traditional services make use of a file control block (FCB), which we have access to and nearly complete control over. The extended services keep most of the control information about a file (or device) quite private and hidden from us.

In the traditional services, we indicate which file we are working with by pointing DOS to an FCB. We use the same services to perform routine file management tasks, such as locating the file, pointing to the file's data, and determining the file size. In contrast, in the extended services we work with a file handle, which is nothing more than a simple 16-bit number returned through the AX register. This number identifies the file or device we are working with and automatically performs most of the routine file management operations.

DOS maintains complete control over the file handles, and issues the handle numbers to us whenever we create or open a file. There are five standard handles, numbered 0 through 4, which are automatically available to every program (☞ see Figure 17-2). Other handles, with higher handle numbers, are issued by DOS as they are needed.

The traditional functions allow up to 99 files (and file FCBs) to be open at the same time using the FILES command in DOS (**AT** 255 are allowed in the AT). However, the extended functions, operating under DOS-2 versions, issue a maximum of 20 file handles to any one program, thereby limiting the number of files that a program can actually open. On request, DOS 3.00 provides more handles, but defaults to the DOS-2 limit of 20 files. This limitation in the extended functions is likely to affect only highly complex programs that require a large number of open files at one time.

Handle	Use	Default Setting
0	Standard input (normally keyboard input)	CON:
1	Standard output (normally screen output)	CON:
2	Standard error output (always to the screen)	CON:
3	Standard auxiliary device (AUX: device)	AUX:
4	Standard printer (LPT1: or PRN: device)	PRN:

Figure 17-2. The five standard handles available to every file

Installable Device Drivers

Two additional features that were introduced with DOS 2.00 also deserve some attention: the installable device drivers, and specifically, the ANSI driver (usually called ANSI.SYS), a device driver that comes standard with many adaptations of DOS.

The DOS device drivers are programs that we create to link hardware devices to our computer system without rewriting the BIOS. A device driver may be a routine that supports the addition of new hardware, such as a joystick or a mouse, or it may be a routine that modifies the operation of standard hardware so that it can perform tasks that are not available through the DOS services. (The ANSI driver is an example of the latter type; it lets us modify screen output or keyboard input without using the BIOS service routines.) Since the device drivers are created as a part of DOS, our programs need not reach down to the BIOS or the hardware level to accommodate new devices, an important feature for programs that operate in windowing or multitasking environments.

The device drivers are not directly related to the extended DOS functions, so we will save a more detailed discussion of them for Appendix A. Keep in mind that by placing the discussion of device drivers at the end of the book, I in no way mean to diminish their importance. All programmers who are concerned with the range and longevity of their programs should at least be familiar with the use and operation of device drivers. ☛ See Appendix A.

SUMMARY OF THE EXTENDED DOS FUNCTIONS

All the extended DOS function calls are invoked through interrupt number 33 (hex 21). The individual functions are selected by placing the function number in the AH register. Any program that uses the extended functions should test the DOS version number first to make sure the functions are available. Extended function 48 (hex 30) provides this service.

| Function | | Group |
Dec	Hex	
47–56	2F–38	Extended function group
57–59	39–3B	Directory group
60–70	3C–46	Extended file management group
71	47	Directory group
72–75	48–4B	Extended memory management group
76–79	4C–4F	Extended function group
84–87	54–57	Extended function group
88–98	58–62	DOS 3.00 additions

Figure 17-3. The logical groups of extended DOS function calls

The functions are organized into the logical groups shown in Figure 17-3. In an effort to make the logical groupings of the function calls as clear as possible, I have organized and described them in a slightly different manner than the DOS Technical Reference manual. You may want to compare my organization with IBM's, just to make sure there is no misunderstanding. Figure 17-4 lists the individual function calls.

Function 47 (hex 2F): Get DTA Address

Function 47 returns the address of the disk transfer area, or DTA, which is currently in use by DOS. The address is returned in the register pair ES:BX. Since the ES segment register is used to return the segment portion instead of the DS register, this service will not conflict with the normal operation of a program. ☛ Contrast this with function 26, discussed on page 282.

Function 48 (hex 30): Get DOS Version Number

Function 48 returns the DOS major and minor version numbers. The major version number is in AL (for DOS version 2.10, this would be 2), and the minor version number is in AH (which would be 10 for DOS 2.10); BX and CX are both set to 0000 on return from this function. This service is new to advanced DOS versions and does not exist in DOS-1 versions. Fortunately, when function 48 is used with any DOS-1 version, a consistently identifiable result will occur: The major version number will be reported as 0 in the AL register. Unfortunately, the minor version number is not reliable in the DOS-1 versions.

Function		Description	Function		Description
Dec	Hex		Dec	Hex	
47	2F	Get DTA address	73	49	Free allocated memory
48	30	Get DOS version number	74	4A	SETBLOCK: Modify allocated memory block
49	31	KEEP: Advanced terminate-but-stay-resident	75	4B	EXEC: Load/execute program
50	32	Not used	76	4C	Terminate process
51	33	Get/set Ctrl-Break	77	4D	Get return code of subprogram
52	34	Not used	78	4E	FIND FIRST: Start file search
53	35	Get interrupt vector	79	4F	Continue file search
54	36	Get disk free space	80	50	Not used
55	37	Not used	81	51	Not used
56	38	Get country-dependent information	82	52	Not used
57	39	MKDIR: Make directory	83	53	Not used
58	3A	RMDIR: Remove directory	84	54	Get verify state
59	3B	CHDIR: Change current directory	85	55	Not used
60	3C	CREAT: Create file	86	56	Rename file
61	3D	Open file	87	57	Get/set file date and time
62	3E	Close file handle	88	58	Not used
63	3F	Read from file or device	89	59	Get extended error
64	40	Write to file or device	90	5A	Create temporary file
65	41	Delete file	91	5B	Create new file
66	42	Move file pointer	92	5C	Lock/unlock file access
67	43	CHMOD: Get/set file attributes	93	5D	Not used
68	44	IOCTL: I/O control for devices	94	5E	Not used
69	45	DUP: Duplicate file handle	95	5F	Not used
70	46	CDUP: Force handle duplication	96	60	Not used
71	47	Get current directory	97	61	Not used
72	48	Allocate memory	98	62	Get PSP address

Figure 17-4. The extended DOS function calls invoked by interrupt 33 and selected in the AH register

Any program that makes use of the advanced DOS features can use this function to determine if the appropriate DOS version is being used. The preferred test is simply to check for a major version greater than or equal to 2 (or 3, if DOS-3 services are being used). If the function reports a number less than 2 (or 3), the program should politely end.

Function 49 (hex 31): KEEP—Advanced Terminate-but-Stay-Resident

Function 49 is the advanced version of the universal DOS interrupt 39 terminate-but-stay-resident service. In addition to ending a program, function 49 allows the terminating program to report a return code, which is placed in the AL register and can be tested with the ERROR-LEVEL feature of DOS batch processing.

Any program that ends this way must tell DOS how much of itself to keep in memory and how much to throw away. This is done by passing a segment-paragraph value in DX that specifies the memory paragraph just beyond the end of the resident portion. This controls how much of the program's initial memory allotment is to be kept and how much is to be released.

A program can request additional memory by using the memory-allocation services, functions 72 through 75. Any memory that is allocated by these services is not released by the value specified in DX. DX only keeps track of the memory that DOS allocated when the program was first loaded, an allocation that is not under the program's control. Generally, we're skating on thin ice if we freely allocate memory in a resident program—but with care, it can be done.

Function 51 (hex 33): Get/Set Ctrl-Break

Function 51 either reports on or controls the state of Ctrl-Break processing. You'll recall that DOS acts on Ctrl-Break only under a limited and quirky set of circumstances (☞ see page 256). One of the nice improvements that began with DOS version 2.00 is that Ctrl-Break checking can be extended to take place during any DOS operation. For compatibility with DOS-1 versions, this extended Ctrl-Break checking must be optional. It can be controlled three ways: through the BREAK command, through the CONFIG.SYS initialization file, and through this DOS function, which lets any program do Ctrl-Break checking.

If AL is set to 0, then we can request the current break state, which is reported in DL: DL = 0 means the break check is off; DL = 1 means it is on (extra checking is in effect). If AL is set to 1, then we can set the break state using the same coding in DL: DL = 0 disables the break check; and DL = 1 enables the break check.

Function 53 (hex 35): Get Interrupt Vector

Function 53 returns the interrupt vector for the interrupt number specified in register AL. The vector is returned in the register pair ES:BX.

There are several uses for this service. The most obvious is to preserve the current interrupt vector before changing it with function 37 (hex 25), so that it can be restored later. Another use is simply to check the current vector setting; for example, we may use this function to see if the default vector setting has been changed. One particularly useful application is to find out the setting of the interrupt vectors that point to tables rather than interrupt-handling subroutines. With the vector setting in hand, it is a simple matter to access the table information.

Function 54 (hex 36): Get Disk Free Space

Function 54 provides a host of interesting and useful information about the space status of a disk—much more than just the free space that the name of the service implies. Before calling this service, we select the drive that we are interested in with the DL register: DL = 0 indicates the default drive; DL = 1 indicates drive A; DL = 2 indicates drive B; etc. Notice the difference between this notation and the more conventional 0 = drive A notation. Like all DOS services, and unlike the ROM-BIOS services, these are logical drives, not physical drives.

If there is an error—for example, an invalid drive—it is reported with hex FFFF in the AX register. Otherwise, AX contains sectors-per-allocation unit (cluster), CX contains bytes per sector, BX contains number of available clusters, and DX contains total number of clusters.

From these numbers we can calculate a lot of interesting things about the disk. For example, we can use these formulas to calculate the following:

```
CX * AX                 ' bytes-per-allocation unit (cluster)
CX * AX * BX            ' total number of free bytes
CX * AX * DX            ' total storage space
(BX * 100) / DX        ' percentage of free space
```

If S were the size of a file in bytes, then we could calculate the number of occupied sectors in this way:

```
(S + CX * AX - 1) / (CX * AX)
```

Similar formulas would give us the number of allocation units and the amount and proportion of space that is allocated to a file but not used (the "slack space").

Function 56 (hex 38): Get Country-Dependent Information

Function 56 provides an interesting service that allows programs to automatically adjust to different international currency and time format conventions by using a table of country-specific information supplied by DOS. The DOS-2 version of this service reports a very small set of country information. The DOS-3 extension reports the information for any country code in the DOS table.

Register AL must be set to 0 to get the standard country information. For DOS 3.00 or later versions, register AL can be set to a predefined country code. (The country code is the same 3-digit code used in the telephone system.) To access more than 254 country codes, AL can be set to 255 (hex FF) and the country code can be put into register BX. If the requested country code is invalid, DOS sets the carry flag (CF) and places an error code in AX. Otherwise, BX contains the country code and 32-byte area is filled in with the country-specific information shown in Figures 17-5 and 17-6; the register pair DS:DX points to the beginning of the 32-byte area. To set the current country code under DOS 3.0, set DX equal to FFFF and issue function 56 with AL equal to the country code (or if the code is greater than 254, set AL equal to 255 and BX equal to the country code); register DS will be ignored.

Programs operating under DOS-2 versions can use only the standard set of country-specific information coded into DOS, by setting AL to 0. Programs operating under DOS-3 versions can request the standard information for any country whose code exists in the table (AL = code), or they can simply go exploring for valid codes. If you want to explore the codes, you can write a fairly simple program that tests all possible country codes and displays the valid ones.

The 32-byte information area is coded somewhat differently for DOS-2 versions than it is for DOS-3 and later versions. Although the coding may appear to be similar, the two formats are not compatible.

Field	Offset	Size (bytes)	Description
1	0	2	Date and time code
2	2	2	Currency symbol string
3	4	2	Thousands separator string
4	6	2	Decimal separator string
5	8	24	Unused

Figure 17-5. The country-dependent information provided by DOS-2 versions and located in the 32-byte area pointed to by DS:DX

Field	Offset	Size (bytes)	Description
1	0	2	Date and time code
2	2	5	Currency symbol string (ASCIIZ format)
3	7	2	Thousands separator string (ASCIIZ format)
4	9	2	Decimal separator string (ASCIIZ format)
5	11	2	Date separator string (ASCIIZ format)
6	13	2	Time separator string (ASCIIZ format)
7	15	1	Currency symbol location: 1 = before; 0 = after)
8	16	1	Currency decimal places
9	17	1	Time format: 1 = 24-hour clock; 0 = 12 hour
10	18	4	Upper/lowercase map call address
11	22	2	List separator string (ASCIIZ format)
12	24	8	Reserved

Figure 17-6. The country-dependent information provided by DOS-3 versions through function 56 (hex 38) when AL = country code

Field 1 (both formats) holds an integer word whose value specifies the display format for the time and date. There are three predefined values for this word and three corresponding date and time formats (☞ see Figure 17-7). Others might be added in the future.

In the DOS-2 format, the next three fields hold three ASCIIZ strings, consisting of two bytes each: one data byte followed by the standard zero byte that ends all ASCIIZ strings.

Field 2 holds the first string, which gives the currency symbol (this is a dollar sign ($) for the United States).

Value	Use	Time	Date
0	American	h:m:s	m-d-y
1	European	h:m:s	d.m.y
2	Japanese	h:m:s	y-m-d

Figure 17-7. The three predefined time and date formats whose codes are specified in the first two bytes of the 32-byte area pointed to by DS:DX

Field 3 holds the second string, which gives the symbol used to punctuate the thousands mark in numbers (in the US, this is a comma, as in the number 12,345; other countries use a period or a blank).

Field 4 holds the third string, which gives the decimal point symbol (in the US, this is a period as in 3.00; other countries use a comma).

The remaining 24 bytes of the 32-byte information area are unused in the DOS-2 format.

The DOS-3 format begins with the same integer word that indicates the date and time format in DOS-2. Following that are the same three ASCIIZ strings that define the symbols for currency, thousands, and decimals—with one important difference: The currency-symbol ASCIIZ string in field 2 is allotted five bytes, allowing the currency symbol to be as short as a single symbol (for example, a dollar or yen sign) or as long as a four-letter abbreviation (for example, one of the currency strings used by DOS 3.00 is DKR, which stands for Danish kroner).

Fields 5 and 6 are also two bytes in length. The first gives the punctuation used in dates (for example, - as in 7-4-1985); the second gives the symbol used to punctuate time (for example, : as in 12:34).

Field 7 is a single byte that is used to indicate where the currency symbol should be placed on output. A zero places the symbol after the amount (10 DKR); a one places the symbol before the amount ($10.00).

Field 8 contains a 1-byte integer that specifies how many decimal places are used in the currency. For example, the value would be 2 for US currency (dollars and cents) and 0 for Italian currency (lire).

Field 9 is a 1-byte field that is bit-coded to specify a time format. Only the first bit (bit 0) is currently used; if the bit is 0, a 12-hour clock is used, and if it is 1, a 24-hour clock is used.

Field 10 holds a 4-byte segmented address of a subroutine that is used to determine the usage of upper- and lowercase letters.

Field 11 contains a 2-byte ASCIIZ string that gives the symbol used to separate items in a list, such as the commas in the list A, B, C, and D.

Field 12 holds the remaining eight bytes of the 32-byte area, which are reserved for future use.

Function 57 (hex 39): MKDIR—Make Directory

Function 57 creates a subdirectory, just as the DOS command MKDIR does. To invoke this service, we input an ASCIIZ string containing the path name of the new directory, followed by a zero byte to delimit the string. The register pair DS:DX points to the address of the ASCIIZ string. Errors are reported through AX in the standard format for extended commands (☛ see page 297). The possible error codes are 3 (path not found) and 5 (access denied).

Function 58 (hex 3A): RMDIR—Remove Directory

Function 58 removes (deletes) a subdirectory, just as the DOS command RMDIR does. To invoke this service, we input an ASCIIZ string containing the path name of the directory we want to remove, followed by a zero byte to delimit the ASCIIZ string. The register pair DS:DX points to the address of the ASCIIZ string. Errors are reported through AX in the standard format for extended commands (☛ see page 297). The possible error codes are 3 (path not found) and 5 (access denied).

DOS will not remove either the current directory or any directory that has files or subdirectories in it. In these cases code 5 (access denied) is signaled—or so says the DOS documentation. Common sense says that attempting to remove the current directory ought to result in the more specific error code 16 (attempt to remove current directory).

Function 59 (hex 3B): CHDIR—Change Current Directory

Function 59 changes the current directory, just as the DOS command CHDIR does. To invoke this service, we input an ASCIIZ string containing the path name of the new directory, followed by a zero byte to delimit the ASCIIZ string. DS:DX contains the address for the input string. Errors are reported through AX in the standard format for extended commands (☛ see page 297). The one possible error code is 3 (path not found).

Function 60 (hex 3C): CREAT—Create File

Function 60 opens an existing file or creates a new one, which is the standard find-or-create operation for output files. It closely parallels function 22 (☛ discussed on page 281).

To invoke this service, we provide an ASCIIZ string that contains the path name and filename, followed by a zero byte to delimit the string. The register pair DS:DX points to the address of the ASCIIZ string. CX, or really CL, contains the file attribute. (☛ See page 116 for more on file attributes and attribute bit settings.) The file handle is returned in AX.

This function opens any new or old file for read/write access, but assumes we are writing to an output file, and sets the length of any existing file to zero.

Possible return codes are 3 (path not found), 4 (no handle available), and 5 (access denied). Code 5 can indicate either that there is no room for a new directory entry or that the existing file is marked read-only and can't be opened for output. Since the AX register is used to return either the file handle or the return code, we can and must rely on the CF flag to indicate an error (☛ see page 297 for an explanation).

Function 61 (hex 3D): Open File

Function 61 is the most general-purpose way to open a file. We provide the path name and filename in the form of an ASCIIZ string, followed by a zero byte. As with all other file I/O functions, DS:DX points to this string. We also indicate how we want to use the file by placing a mode code in register AL. The eight bits of AL are divided into the four fields shown in Figure 17-8.

The open mode for DOS-2 versions is simple: Only the access bits (AAA in Figure 17-8) are used and all other bits are set to zero. The three access-code settings are defined in Figure 17-9.

DOS 3.00 uses the inheritance and sharing codes as well as the access code. DOS-3 codes are more complicated, because they must take into account the problems of file sharing (a feature introduced with DOS 3.00).

Bit 7, the inheritance bit, indicates whether or not "child processes" (programs run as semi-independent subprograms under this program) will inherit the use of this file. If bit 7 is 0, the child processes will have the use of the file. If bit 7 is 1, the file is private to this program and child processes will not have automatic access to it. (But, like any other program, they could request the program themselves, on a shared basis.)

Bits 4 through 6, the sharing-mode bits (SSS in Figure 17-8), define what will happen when an attempt is made to reopen the same file more than once. There are five sharing modes: compatibility mode (SSS = 000), deny read/write mode (SSS = 001), deny write mode (SSS = 010), deny read mode (SSS = 011), and deny none mode (SSS = 100). The sharing mode is rather complex and is best left to the DOS Technical Reference manual for an explanation.

Bit 3, marked as reserved in Figure 17-8, should be set to 0.

Notice that we do not specify either the file attribute or the record size. This service will find any existing file, including a hidden one, and sets the record size to one byte, by default.

Bit 7 6 5 4 3 2 1 0	Use
I	Inheritance flag (DOS-3)
. S S S	Sharing mode (DOS-3)
. . . . R . . .	Reserved for future use (DOS-3)
. . . . . A A A	Access code (DOS-2 and DOS-3)

Figure 17-8. The codes placed in register AL to specify the open mode for function 61

Bit 2 1 0	Use
0 0 0	Read (only) access
0 0 1	Write (only) access
0 1 0	Read or write access

Figure 17-9. The function 61 access-code settings in register AL

The possible return codes are 2 (file not found), 3 (path not found), 4 (no handles available), 5 (access denied), and 12 (invalid access code). Since the same register (AX) is used to return either the file handle or the return code, we can and must rely on the CF flag to indicate an error. (☛ See page 297 for an explanation.)

Function 62 (hex 3E): Close File Handle

Function 62 closes a file and flushes all file buffers associated with the file handle given in the BX register. BX should contain the file handle that was returned by the last open-file operation. The one possible error code is 6 (invalid handle).

Function 63 (hex 3F): Read from File or Device

Function 63 reads the file or device (which acts like a file) associated with the file handle given in BX. The CX register specifies the number of bytes to read. DS:DX points to the buffer address where the data that is read will be placed. After the function is performed, AX contains the actual number of bytes read. If this value is zero, it means the program has tried to read from the end of a file.

The possible error codes are 5 (access denied) and 6 (invalid handle). Since the same register (AX) is used to return either the number of bytes that were read or the return code, we can and must rely on the CF flag to indicate an error (☛ see page 297 for an explanation).

Function 64 (hex 40): Write to File or Device

Function 64 writes to the file or device with the file handle given in BX. CX specifies the number of bytes to be written and DS:DX points to the address of the data bytes. After the function is completed, AX contains the actual number of bytes written.

There are two ways to detect errors. One way is through a true error code signaled by CF. If CF signals an error, the possible error codes returned in AX are 5 (access denied) and 6 (invalid handle). If no overt error is detected but the function still ended in an error, it could mean there was not enough disk space to write the entire file. To test for this, see if fewer bytes are written (in AX) than were requested (in CX).

Function 65 (hex 41): Delete File

Function 65 deletes the directory entry of a file. The file is specified by an ASCIIZ string, with the path name and filename followed by a terminating zero byte. The register pair DS:DX points to the string.

Read-only files cannot be deleted by this function. To delete a read-only file, the file's attribute must be changed to 0 using function 67 (hex 43). The global filename characters ? and * may not be used.

The error codes that may be returned in AX are 2 (file not found) and 5 (access denied).

Function 66 (hex 42): Move File Pointer

Function 66 is used to change the logical read/write position in a file. To invoke this service, we load BX with a file handle and then specify the new pointer location by loading the pointer's starting location in AL and the number of bytes we want to move it in register pair CX:DX. The byte offset in CX:DX is a 32-bit unsigned long integer. CX is the high-order part of the offset (which is 0, unless the offset amount is over 65,535) and DX is the low-order part.

The starting location specified in AL is called a "method code," and there are three options. If AL = 0, the offset is taken from the beginning of the file and the pointer is moved CX:DX bytes from that point; if AL = 1, the offset is taken from the current location; if AL = 2, the offset is taken from the current end-of-file. In this last case, we usually set the offset in CX:DX to 0 to find out the current size of the file. If we set the offset to 0 and ask for method 0, we'll return to the beginning of the file.

After the function has been performed, the register pair DX:AX contains the current file pointer as an offset in bytes from the beginning of the file. The pointer is returned as a 32-bit long integer, with the high-order part in DX and the low-order part in AX.

Possible error codes are 1 (invalid function number, which refers to the method code subfunction) and 6 (invalid handle). Since the same register (AX) is used to return either part of the new location or the return code, we can and must rely on the CF flag to indicate an error (☞ see page 297).

Function 67 (hex 43): CHMOD—Get/Set File Attributes

Function 67 gets or sets the attributes of a file (☛ see page 116 for details about file attributes). DS:DX points to an ASCIIZ string, which provides the filespec of the file in question (the global filename characters ? and * may not be used). A setting of AL = 0 will return the attribute values found in CX; AL = 1 will set the attribute values found in CX. In both cases, the values are actually taken from the CL register.

The possible error codes in AX are 2 (file not found), 3 (path not found), and 5 (access denied).

Function 68 (hex 44): IOCTL—I/O Control for Devices

Function 68 performs a number of input/output control operations, mostly for devices, which are all gathered together into one rumpled package. (☛ See Figure 17-10.) AL selects one of ten subfunctions, numbered 0 through 8 and 11. (Subfunctions 8 and 11 apply to DOS-3 versions.) The file handle is specified in BX.

Subfunctions 0 and 1. These subfunctions get and set device information that is formatted in DX by a complicated set of bit coding. Bit 7 is set to 1 for devices and to 0 for disk files. For devices, bits 0 through 5 are listed as shown in Figure 17-11. For disk files, bits 0 through 5 provide the disk-drive number: A value of 0 represents drive A, a value of 1 represents drive B, and so on.

Code	Description
0	Get device information (returned in DX)
1	Set device information (from DX, DH part must be 0)
2	Read (see notes)
3	Write (see notes)
4	Read from drive (see notes)
5	Write to drive (see notes)
6	Get input status (see notes)
7	Get output status (see notes)
8	Indicates if device has removable media; DOS-3 versions only (see notes)
11	Change sharing entry; DOS-3 versions only (see notes)

Figure 17-10. The ten I/O control operations provided by function 68 through the AL register

Bit FEDCBA98	76543210	Use
. . . .	 X	1 = standard console input
. . . .	. . . . . . X .	1 = standard console output
. . . .	. . . . . X . .	1 = null device (need not do I/O)
. . . .	. . . . X . . .	1 = clock device
. . . .	. . . X	1 = special device (= 0 means device is CON: output device; will not be supported in future versions)
. . . .	. . X	1 = data is passed "raw"; 0 = data is passed processed ("cooked")
. . . .	. X	0 = end of file; 1 = not end of file (for input)
. . . .	X	1 = device; 0 = disk drive file
. . . . . . R .	. . . .	Reserved
. . . . . R . .	. . . .	Reserved
. . . . R . . .	. . . .	Reserved
. . . R	. . . .	Reserved
. . R	. . . .	Reserved
. R	. . . .	Reserved
. X	. . . .	1 = device can process control strings during read/write
R	. . . .	Reserved

*Figure 17-11. The bit settings of register DX
for subfunctions 0 or 1 of function 68*

Subfunctions 2 through 5. In all four of these functions, CX specifies the number of bytes to read or write to the drive control channel (*not* to a file within the drive), and the register pair DS:DX points to the data area. For subfunctions 4 and 5, BL contains the special drive number (0 = default, 1 = drive A, 2 = drive B, etc.).

Data can only be read and written using these subfunctions if the device or disk drive can process control strings. The read/write status is indicated by bit E (bit 14) in the DX status bits.

Subfunctions 6 and 7. For these subfunctions, the input or output status is reported in the AX register. If AX = 255 (hex FF), the device/drive is ready for I/O; if AX = 0, it is not ready.

Subfunction 8. This subfunction, which applies only to DOS-3 and later versions, indicates whether a device has removable media or not (the floppy diskettes in a diskette drive are removable; the hard disk in a fixed disk drive is not). Subfunction 8 can be extremely useful because it lets a program know if it has to check for a disk change or if it can rely on the same disk always being there. A removable device is indicated with AX = 0, a fixed disk is indicated with AX = 1, and an invalid device code is indicated with AX = 15 (hex F).

Subfunction 11 (hex B). This subfunction only applies to DOS-3 and later versions, and is used to control the attempts that are made to resolve file-sharing conflicts. Problems in sharing a file can be very transitory, since some programs use files only briefly. DOS can try more than once to gain access to a shared file before reporting a conflict, in the hope that, in the mean time, the access blockage has gone away. This subfunction sets the number of times that DOS will retry, which we specify in register DX, and the time interval between tries (in some unspecified unit), which we indicate with a count value in register CX.

Function 69 (hex 45): DUP—Duplicate File Handle

Function 69 duplicates an open file handle and returns a new handle number that refers to the same file or device. All actions performed with one handle will be automatically reflected in the other handle—the new handle does not act independently in any way. See function 70 for a related service.

The BX register contains the old file handle and AX returns the new file handle. The possible error codes are 4 (no handle available) and 6 (invalid handle). This function effectively opens a file without knowing its name. Having two handles to one file lets you refer to the same sectors on a disk as if they were two different files; you can open, read, write, close and, most importantly, position them independently. Just be careful when you do this; make sure one routine knows how the other is changing the file.

Function 70 (hex 46): CDUP—Force Handle Duplication

Function 70, similar to function 69, duplicates a file handle. However, in this case, we provide an existing second handle (one that has presumably been used for some other purpose), instead of having DOS create a new handle. If the second handle refers to an open file, the file is closed before any action occurs. Once this function is invoked, all actions that are performed with one handle are automatically reflected in the other handle, so the new handle does not act independently in any way.

The BX register contains the old file handle and CX contains the second handle. When the operation is complete, the file handle in CX will refer to the same device or file as BX. The only possible error code is 6 (invalid handle).

Although this service seems rather peculiar, it does have some clear uses. For example, a program can redirect any of the standard I/O devices (☞ see page 299 for a list and description) by using the following method. Let's suppose that the program wishes to dynamically redirect printer output to a file. First, the file is opened, which returns a handle in BX. Then this handle can be duplicated onto the standard printer handle by loading handle number 4 into CX. After this, any standard printer output will actually go to the file that was opened. To restore the normal direction of the printer but maintain the handle for later use, we need to save the normal printer handle by duplicating it using function 69 before we copy the new file handle onto the printer handle. If you followed that, consider yourself qualified to try it. ☞ See function 75 (hex 4B) for one use of this technique.

Function 71 (hex 47): Get Current Directory

Function 71 reports the current directory in the form of an ASCIIZ string. We specify the drive number in DL (0 = default, 1 = drive A, 2 = drive B). The register pair DS:SI points to a data area that contains the full path name, which can be up to 64 bytes long. DOS returns the full path name of the current directory for the specified drive, including the root directory. The path name is always followed by a zero byte—the ASCIIZ string delimiter.

Although this function returns the entire path name, the name does not include either the drive ID (as in A:) or the start-from-the-root backslash (as in A:\). By these rules, if the current directory is the root directory (a common occurrence in diskettes), then the current directory will be reported as nothing—a null string. If you want an intelligible display of the current directory, you may prefix the information returned by this function with the drive-and-root indicators (as in A:\). The only possible error code is 15 (invalid drive specification).

Function 72 (hex 48): Allocate Memory

Function 72 dynamically allocates memory. We request the number of paragraphs (16-byte units) we want allocated in BX. On return, AX points to the segment paragraph of the allocated memory block.

The possible error codes are 7 (memory control blocks destroyed) and 8 (insufficient memory). If the function fails to allocate memory, the BX registers will return the size of the largest available block.

Function 73 (hex 49): Free Allocated Memory

Function 73 returns memory to DOS that was allocated by function 72. The ES register points to the segment address of the block that is being returned. This is the same value that function 72 (hex 48) returns in register AX.

The possible error codes are 7 (memory control blocks destroyed) and 9 (invalid memory block address).

Function 74 (hex 4A): SETBLOCK — Modify Allocated Memory Block

Function 74 is used to increase or decrease the size of a block of memory that was allocated by function 72. Register ES points to the segment address of the block that will be changed. Register BX contains the new size of the block in paragraphs (units of 16 bytes).

If a request for increased space cannot be fulfilled, then BX returns the size of the largest available block of memory (in paragraphs).

The possible return codes are 7 (memory control blocks destroyed), 8 (insufficient memory), and 9 (invalid memory block address).

Function 75 (hex 4B): EXEC — Load/Execute Program

The EXEC function allows a program to load a subprogram into memory and, optionally, execute the subprogram. The register pair DS:DX points to an ASCIIZ string with the path name and filename of the file to be loaded. The register pair ES:BX points to a parameter block that contains the control information for the load operation. AL specifies whether the subprogram is to be executed after it is loaded.

If AL is 0, the subprogram is loaded, a program segment prefix (PSP) is created, and the program is executed. At this time, control passes to the subprogram, and only returns to the program when the subprogram ends. If AL is 3, the subprogram is loaded, no PSP is created, and the program is not automatically executed, although we can jump to it. The AL=3 variation is normally used to load a program overlay. It is also a simple and effective way to load data into memory.

When AL is 0, the block pointed to by ES:BX is fourteen bytes long and contains the information shown in Figure 17-12 on the following page. When AL is 3, the block pointed to by ES:BX is four bytes long and contains the information shown in Figure 17-13.

Offset	Size (bytes)	Description
0	2	Segment address of environment string
2	4	Segmented pointer to command line
6	4	Segmented pointer to first default FCB
10	4	Segmented pointer to second default FCB

*Figure 17-12. The information in the EXEC
control block that is pointed to by ES:BX
when AL = 0. Each of these items relates to
the information built into the PSP of the
program that is being loaded.*

When a program is loaded and executed, any file handles that are
currently active are available to the subprogram. As mentioned under
function 70 (hex 46), a program can redirect the standard I/O handles,
and use this technique to influence the operation of a subprogram. For
example, we can invoke the standard sort filter program to sort a set of
files, and leave its output, messages, and error messages wherever we
want them.

Before using this function, we must make sure there is sufficient
memory to load the program by using function 74 (hex 4A). Since the
program-loading process is performed by part of the command interpreter, the semi-resident portion of the interpreter must be intact, or
must be reloaded from the disk if it has been disturbed.

Among the programs that we can load and execute is the DOS command interpreter. If we wish, we can load it and pass it a command
string, which in turn could invoke a batch file—a batch file that our original program might well have constructed dynamically. This batch file
could invoke its programs and then perform the EXIT command, which

Offset	Size (bytes)	Description
0	2	Segment address where file is to be loaded
2	2	Relocation factor for program (applies only to EXE-format programs)

*Figure 17-13. The information in the EXEC
control block that is pointed to by ES:BX
when AL = 1*

would end the execution of the secondary command interpreter. At that point, our original program would be back in control. This facility opens up vast and complicated possibilities.

❑ WARNING: *The load-and-execute function clobbers all of the registers except CS. Therefore, the only place to save needed registers before making this call is in your code segment, so make sure to reserve space.*

The possible return codes from this function are 1 (invalid function number), 2 (file not found), 5 (access denied), 8 (insufficient memory), 10 (invalid environment), and 11 (invalid format).

Function 76 (hex 4C): Terminate Process

Function 76 ends a program and passes back a return code. If the program was invoked as a subprogram, the return code can be found through function 77. If the program was invoked as a DOS command, then the return code can be tested in a batch file using the DOS ERROR-LEVEL option. The return code is reported in register AL.

When this function is performed, DOS automatically closes any files that were opened with function 61 (hex 3D)—and presumably with function 60, as well.

Function 77 (hex 4D): Get Return Code of Subprogram

Function 77 goes and gets the return code of a subprogram that was invoked with function 75 and that has ended. There are two parts to the information returned. AL reports the return code issued by the program. AH reports how the program ended and has four possible results: AH = 0 indicates a normal voluntary end; AH = 1 indicates termination by DOS due to a Ctrl-Break; AH = 2 indicates termination by DOS due to a critical device error; and AH = 3 indicates a voluntary end using the terminate-but-stay-resident function 49 (hex 31).

Function 78 (hex 4E): FIND FIRST—Start File Search

Function 78 searches for the first matching file or files that match a filespec. We set DS:DX to point to an ASCIIZ string that gives the path name and filename we want to search for. The filename may contain the global filename characters ? and *. The CX register (CL, really) gives the file-attribute specification that will be used to search for the file. If a file is found, DOS formats 43 bytes of information about it in the current disk transfer area (DTA). (☞ See Figure 17-14.)

The ASCIIZ string at the end of the information area stores the filename in its conventional notation, including a period between filename and extension. If the extension is blank, the period does not appear.

This service is similar to the traditional DOS function 17 (hex 11). The use of the file attributes in this search function are the same as they are in function 17 (☞ see page 279).

The attribute search follows a particular logic. If we specify any combination of the hidden, system, or directory attribute bits, the search will match normal files and also any files with those attributes. If we specify the volume-label attribute, the search will only match a directory entry with that attribute. The archive and read-only bits do not apply to the search operations. The directory, volume-label, archive, and read-only attributes do not apply to versions of DOS before 2.00.

The error codes normally returned in AX are 2 (file not found) and 18 (no more files to be found). CF is not set to signal the error.

Offset	Size (bytes)	Description
0	21	Area used by DOS for find-next (see function 79)
21	1	Attribute of file found
22	2	Time stamp of file (see page 118)
24	2	Date stamp of file (see page 118)
26	4	File size in bytes
30	13	Filename and extension (ASCIIZ string)

Figure 17-14. The information returned in the DTA after invoking function 78 (hex 4E)

Function 79 (hex 4F): FIND NEXT—Continue File Search

Function 79 continues the file search that was begun by function 78 or continued by a previous function 79. It relies on the information formatted at the beginning of the DTA, which should not be disturbed.

The one normal error code is 18 (no more files to be found). For this code, CF is not set to the error signal.

☞ See also function 78.

Function 84 (hex 54): Get Verify State

Function 84 tells us the current state of the verify switch, which controls whether or not the disk write operations are verified. AL = 0 indicates that they will not be verified; AL = 1 indicates that they will be. Function 46 (hex 2E) sets the verification switch (☞ see page 288).

This function brings up an annoying inconsistency in DOS services: While some get/set service pairs are integrated into one function (like the following function 87), others are split into two separate functions, like function 84 and function 46.

Function 86 (hex 56): Rename File

Like the standard DOS RENAME command, function 86 changes the name of a file. But, it can also move a file's directory entry from one directory to another. The file itself is not moved, just the directory entry, which means the new and old directory paths must be on the same drive. This is a truly fabulous and useful feature, and it is rather disappointing that it's not a part of the RENAME command.

The function needs two inputs: the filespecs for both the old and the new filenames. These can be full-blown filespecs, with drive and path components. The specified or implied drives must be the same, so that the new directory entry will be on the same drive as the file. The global filename characters * and ? cannot be used, since this function works on single files only.

As usual, both filespecs are supplied in the form of ASCIIZ strings, with a zero byte marking the end. The register pair DS:DX points to the old name string and ES:DI points to the new string.

The possible error codes are 2 (file not found), 3 (path not found), 5 (access denied), and 17 (not same device).

Function 87 (hex 57): Get/Set File Date and Time

Function 87 gets or sets a file's date and time. Recall that each file is marked with the date and time it was created or last changed. AL is used to select the operation: AL = 0 gets the date and time, and AL = 1 sets the date and time.

The file is selected by placing the file handle in BX, which means that this service applies only to files that have been opened using the extended DOS functions covered in this chapter. Note, therefore, that setting a file's time stamp with this service will only take effect if the file is successfully closed.

The date and time are placed in registers CX and DX in the same format as they are stored in the disk directory entries, though in a slightly different order. In this function, the time is placed in CX and the date in DX.

Contrary to what the DOS documentation says, the time and date information is placed in its conventional format, with the high-order parts in CH or DH and the low-order parts in CL and DL.

The date and time can be built or broken down using the following formulas:

```
CX = HOUR * 2048 + MINUTE * 32 + SECOND / 2
DX = (YEAR - 1980) * 512 + MONTH * 32 + DAY
```

The possible error codes for this service are 1 (invalid function number—based on the subfunction selected in AL, not the main function number) and 6 (invalid handle).

DOS 3.00 ADDITIONS

So far in this chapter, we've discussed the new DOS functions that were introduced with DOS 2.00. DOS 3.00 brought enhancements to a few of the DOS-2 functions and brought five new functions to the extended function family.

Function 89 (hex 59): Get Extended Error Code

Function 89 is used after an error has occurred. It provides detailed information about the errors that occur under these circumstances: inside a critical-error interrupt handler; after a DOS function call invoked with the standard interrupt 33 (hex 21) has reported an error by setting the carry flag (CF); and after the old-style FCB file operations that report a return code of 255 (hex FF). It will not work with DOS functions that do not report errors in CF, even though they may have ended in an error.

This service is called in the standard way, by placing function code 89 (hex 59) in register AH. To allow for the inevitable changes that occur in this sort of function, we must also specify a version code in the BX register. For DOS 3.00, we set this code to 0.

Four separate information signals are returned on completion of this service: AX contains the extended error code; BH indicates the class of error; BL gives the code of any suggested action that our program should take; and CH gives a locus code, which attempts to show where the error occurred.

The error codes reported in AX are organized into three groups: Codes 1 through 18 are used for function-call errors (interrupt 33 functions), codes 19 through 31 are used for critical-error handler errors (from interrupt 36), and codes 32 through 83 are used for errors that are new to DOS-3 services. A code of 0 indicates that there is no error for this service to report on.

☛ Figure 17-15 lists the extended error codes, Figure 17-16 lists the error classes, Figure 17-17 lists the action codes, and Figure 17-18 lists the locus codes.

Code	Meaning	Code	Meaning
1	Invalid function number	20	Unknown unit ID
2	File not found	21	Disk drive not ready
3	Path not found	22	Command not defined
4	No handle available	23	Disk data error
5	Access denied (e.g. attempt made to write a read-only file)	24	Bad request structure length
		25	Disk seek error
6	Invalid handle	26	Unknown disk media type
7	Memory control blocks are invalid	27	Disk sector not found
8	Not enough memory	28	Printer out of paper
9	Invalid memory block address	29	Write error
10	Invalid SET command strings ("environment")	30	Read error
		31	General failure
11	Invalid format (of what, we aren't told)	32	File sharing violation
12	Invalid file access code	33	File locking violation
13	Invalid data	34	Improper disk change
14	Reserved	35	No FCB available
15	Invalid drive specification	80	File already exists
16	Requested removing current directory	81	Reserved
17	Not same device	82	Cannot make directory entry
18	No further files to find	83	Critical-error interrupt failure
19	Disk write protected		

Figure 17-15. The extended error codes returned in register AX following execution of function 89 (hex 59)

Code	Meaning	Code	Meaning
1	Out of resource: no more of whatever we asked for	7	Application software error: it's our fault
2	Temporary situation: try again later	8	Item requested not found
3	Authorization: we aren't allowed; someone else might be	9	Bad format (e.g. unrecognizable disk)
4	Internal error in DOS: not our fault	10	Item locked
5	Hardware failure	11	Media error (e.g. disk reports CRC error)
6	System software error: other DOS problems	12	Already exits
		13	Error class is unknown

Figure 17-16. The error classes returned in register BH following execution of function 89 (hex 59)

Code	Meaning	Code	Meaning
1	Try again now	5	Shut down immediately: don't try to clean up
2	Try again later, after waiting	6	Ignore the error: it doesn't matter
3	Ask the user to fix it (e.g. change the disk); see also code 7	7	Retry after user action; see also code 3
4	Shut down the program, but OK to clean up (close files etc.)		

Figure 17-17. The suggested action codes returned in register BL following execution of function 89 (hex 59)

Code	Meaning	Code	Meaning
1	Unknown: sorry	4	Serial device error (e.g. printer)
2	Block device error (e.g. disk drive)	5	Memory error
3	Reserved		

Figure 17-18. The locus codes returned in register CH following execution of function 89 (hex 59)

Function 90 (hex 5A): Create Temporary File

Function 90 creates a file for temporary use, presumably, taking care of the chore of finding a filename that does not conflict with any existing file. We provide two parameters: the file attribute, placed in the CX register, and the path name of the directory where the file will be created. If we don't want to specify a particular path, we can give DOS a null string, which tells it to use the current directory of the current drive.

The path name must be an ASCIIZ string and is pointed to by the register pair DS:DX. The path-name string must be ready to have the filename of the created file appended to it: This means that the string must end with the backslash character that is used to punctuate directory paths (if we give an explicit path string). We must also add 12 bytes to allow enough room for DOS to add a filename to the string.

On return, if there is an error in this operation, the carry flag (CF) will be set and the error code will be in AX. Also, the filename will be appended to the path string we provided.

This service is called "create temporary file" only to suggest its intended purpose. Actually, there is nothing temporary about the file that is created since DOS does not automatically delete it; our programs must look after that chore.

Function 91 (hex 5B): Create New File

Function 91 is similar to function 60 (hex 3C), which is (inaccurately) called the create-file function. Function 60 is actually designed to find a file, and to create one if the requested file does not exist. By contrast, function 91 is a pure create-file function and will fail if the file already exists.

As with function 60, the CX register is set to the file attribute and DS:DX points to the address of the path name and filename (which is stored as an ASCIIZ string). On return, if CF = 0 then AX = file handle for the new file; if CF = 1 then AX contains the error code.

There are many circumstances when a program will use a standard filename, intending to reuse a file with that name if it exists or to create a file with that name if it doesn't exist. This is the sort of situation that function 60 is best suited for. However, there are other circumstances when a program may not wish to disturb existing files, but only to open a file that does not already exist. This is the sort of situation function 91 is best suited for.

Function 92 (hex 5C): Lock/Unlock File Access

Function 92 is used to lock certain parts of a file so that it can be shared by several programs without one program interfering with the operations of another. If one program locks one part of a file, it can use or change that part of the file while it is locked, safe in the knowledge that no other program will be able to use that part while it remains locked. As you may have guessed, file locking is used only in conjunction with file-sharing operations.

There are six parameters that determine what portion of a file will be locked. AL indicates whether we are locking (AL=0) or unlocking (AL=1) a portion of a file. BX gives the file handle. CX and DX together are treated as a 4-byte long integer that specifies the byte offset into the file of the locked portion. SI and DI also form a 4-byte long integer that specifies the length of the locked portion. The first register in each of these register pairs (CX or SI) gives the high-order part of the integer.

We are not allowed to unlock file portions piecemeal, or in combination; an unlock request should exactly match a previous lock request. We are warned that locks should be removed before closing a file; contrary to what we might hope, closing a file will not necessarily clean up the locks that remain in our file.

Function 98 (hex 62): Get PSP Address

Function 98 gets the address of the program segment prefix and returns it in BX as a segment paragraph address.

In the conventional world of DOS, programs place their PSP in the first 256 bytes of the code segment. This means that the paragraph address of the PSP is the same as the code segment (CS) register contents. However, as personal computers and DOS become more complex, it may not always be this simple. For example, in the protected mode of the 80286 microprocessor in the AT, the segment registers are treated in an exotic new way. This service exists to provide (we can hope) a permanent and reliable way to touch the segment registers in the future.

18

DOS
Service Summary

T his chapter is a summary of the DOS service routines and is designed to be used as a quick reference guide. For details about the specific operation of each service and some comments about their operation, see Chapters 15 through 17. Once you understand the DOS services, these tables should provide you with all the programming information that you will need.

SHORT SUMMARY

Nine DOS interrupts are called by their interrupt numbers. Five of these interrupts are listed in Figure 18-1. The four interrupts not shown in the table are used for specialized purposes: Interrupt 33 (hex 21) is the function-call interrupt that is used to invoke one of the 80 DOS functions; and interrupts 34 through 36 are address interrupts that are used to point to special subroutines. ☞ See Chapter 15 for more information.

The DOS universal functions, shown on the next page in Figure 18-2, are called through interrupt 33 (hex 21); the function number is placed in the AH register. The universal functions can be used with any version of DOS. ☞ See Chapter 16 for more information.

The new, extended DOS function calls can only be used with DOS versions 2.00 or higher. They are called through interrupt 33 (hex 21) and the function number is placed in the AH register. ☞ See Chapter 17 for more information. Figure 18-3 lists all the new DOS functions, including those that were introduced with DOS version 3.00. (These functions cannot be used with earlier versions.)

Interrupt		
Dec	**Hex**	**Description**
32	20	Program terminate: come to a normal ending
37	25	Absolute disk read
38	26	Absolute disk write
39	27	Terminate-but-stay-resident
47	2F	Print spool control (DOS 3.00 and higher)

Figure 18-1. The five main DOS interrupts

Function			Function		
Dec	**Hex**	**Description**	**Dec**	**Hex**	**Description**
0	0	Terminate: end program	21	15	Write sequential file record
1	1	Keyboard input with echo	22	16	Create file
2	2	Display output	23	17	Rename file
3	3	Serial input	25	19	Report current drive
4	4	Serial output	26	1A	Set disk transfer area
5	5	Printer output	27	1B	Get FAT information, current drive
6	6	Direct keyboard/display I/O	28	1C	Get FAT information, any drive
7	7	Direct keyboard input without echo	33	21	Read random file record
8	8	Keyboard input without echo	34	22	Write random file record
9	9	Display string	35	23	Get file size
10	A	Buffered keyboard input	36	24	Set random record field
11	B	Check keyboard input status	37	25	Set interrupt vector
12	C	Clear keyboard and do function	38	26	Create program segment
13	D	Reset disk	39	27	Read random file records
14	E	Select current drive	40	28	Write random file records
15	F	Open file	41	29	Parse filename
16	10	Close file	42	2A	Get date
17	11	Search for first matching file	43	2B	Set date
18	12	Search for next matching file	44	2C	Get time
19	13	Delete file	45	2D	Set time
20	14	Read sequential file record	46	2E	Set disk write verification

Figure 18-2. The universal DOS functions

Function			Function		
Dec	Hex	Description	Dec	Hex	Description
47	2F	Get DTA address	70	46	CDUP: Force handle duplication
48	30	Get DOS version number	71	47	Get current directory
49	31	KEEP: Advanced terminate-but-stay-resident	72	48	Allocate memory
			73	49	Free allocated memory
51	33	Get/set control break	74	4A	SETBLOCK: Modify allocated memory block
53	35	Get interrupt vector			
54	36	Get disk free space	75	4B	EXEC: Load/execute program
56	38	Get country-dependent information	76	4C	Terminate process
57	39	MKDIR: Make directory	77	4D	Get return code of subprogram
58	3A	RMDIR: Remove directory	78	4E	FIND FIRST: Start file search
59	3B	CHDIR: Change current directory	79	4F	FIND NEXT: Continue file search
60	3C	CREAT: Create file	84	54	Get verify state
61	3D	Open file	86	56	Rename file
62	3E	Close file handle	87	57	Get/set file date and time
63	3F	Read from file or device			

DOS 3.00 Functions

Function			Function		
Dec	Hex	Description	Dec	Hex	Description
64	40	Write to file or device	89	59	Get extended error code
65	41	Delete file	90	5A	Create temporary file
66	42	Move file pointer	91	5B	Create new file
67	43	CHMOD: Get/set file attributes	92	5C	Lock/unlock file access
68	44	IOCTL: I/O control for devices	98	62	Get PSP address
69	45	DUP: Duplicate file handle			

Figure 18-3. The new DOS functions
available with DOS 2.00 and later versions

LONG SUMMARY

In the last section, we briefly listed all the DOS services, so that individual services can be found by their function number. In this section, we have expanded the listing to show the register settings for the input and output parameters.

Since every new version of DOS introduces a few functions that cannot be used with earlier versions, we have included the DOS version number in this table. The DOS versions are coded in the following manner:

DOS1   Function may be used with all DOS versions

DOS2   Function may be used with DOS versions 2.00 and up

DOS3   Function may be used with DOS 3.00 and up

Service	Function (hex)	Register Input	Register Output	Version

Program Control Functions

Service	Function (hex)	Input	Output	Version
Terminate: end program	0	AH = 00		DOS1
Create program segment	26	AH = 26 DX = segment address		DOS1
KEEP: Advanced terminate-but-stay-resident	31	AH = 31 AL = return code DX = segment address of memory to free	AX = return code	DOS2
Get/set control break	33	AH = 33 AL = 00 to get AL = 01 to set DL = code if set	AX = return code DL = current state: 00 = off; 01 = on	DOS2
EXEC: Load/execute program	4B	AH = 4B AL = subfunction code (see page 316) DS:DX = pointer to ASCIIZ string ES:BX = pointer to control block	AX = return code	DOS2
Terminate process	4C	AH = 4C AL = return code		DOS2
Get return code of subprogram	4D	AH = 4D	AL = return code AH = ending code	DOS2
Get PSP address	62	AH = 62	BX = segment address of PSP	DOS3

Keyboard Control Functions

Service	Function (hex)	Input	Output	Version
Keyboard input with echo	1	AH = 01	AL = input character	DOS1
Direct keyboard input without echo	7	AH = 07	AL = input character	DOS1
Keyboard input without echo	8	AH = 08	AL = input character	DOS1
Buffered keyboard input	A	AH = 0A DS:DX = pointer to input buffer		DOS1
Check keyboard input status	B	AH = 0B	AL = FF if character available AL = 00 if no character available	DOS1
Clear keyboard and do function	C	AH = 0C AL = function number (1, 6, 7, 8, or A)		DOS1

(continued)

Figure 18-4. A summary of the DOS services (continued)

Service	Function (hex)	Register Input	Register Output	Version
Screen Control Functions				
Display output	2	AH = 02 DL = output character		DOS1
Display string	9	AH = 09 DS:DX = pointer to output string		DOS1
Console I/O Functions				
Direct keyboard/display I/O character	6	AH = 06 DL = input character if FF, output request if 00-FE	AL = input character	DOS1
Miscellaneous I/O Functions				
Serial input	3	AH = 03	AL = input character	DOS1
Serial output	4	AH = 04 DL = output character		DOS1
Printer output	5	AH = 05 DL = output character		DOS1
Disk Functions				
Reset disk	D	AH = 0D		DOS1
Select current drive	E	AH = 0E DL = drive ID	AL = drive count	DOS1
Report current drive	19	AH = 19	AL = default drive code	DOS1
Set disk transfer area	1A	AH = 1A DS:DX = pointer to DTA		DOS1
Get FAT information, current drive	1B	AH = 1B	AL = sectors per allocation unit CX = bytes per sector DX = number of allocation units DS:BX = pointer to FAT ID byte	DOS1
Get FAT information, any drive	1C	AH = 1C DL = drive ID	CX = bytes per sector AL = sectors per allocation unit DX = number of allocation units DS:BX = pointer to FAT ID byte	DOS1
Set disk write verification	2E	AH = 2E AL = verify switch: 00 = off; 01 = on DL = 00		DOS1

Figure 18-4. A summary of the DOS services (continued)

Service	Function (hex)	Register Input	Register Output	Version
Disk Functions (continued)				
Get DTA address	2F	AH = 2F	AX = return code ES:BX = pointer to DTA	DOS2
Get disk free space	36	AH = 36 DL = drive code	AX = FFFF: Drive code in DL bad; else AX = sectors per cluster BX = available cluster count CX = bytes per sector DX = total clusters	DOS2
Get verify state	54	AH = 54	AL = verify state: 00 = off; 01 = on	DOS2
File I/O Functions				
Open file	F	AH = 0F DS:DX = pointer to FCB	AL = return code	DOS1
Close file	10	AH = 10 DS:DX = pointer to FCB	AL = return code	DOS1
Search for first matching file	11	AH = 11 DS:DX = pointer to FCB	AL = return code	DOS1
Search for next matching file	12	AH = 12 DS:DX = pointer to FCB	AL = return code	DOS1
Delete file	13	AH = 13 DS:DX = pointer to FCB	AL = return code	DOS1
Read sequential file record	14	AH = 14 DS:DX = pointer to FCB	AL = return code	DOS1
Write sequential file record	15	AH = 15 DS:DX = pointer to FCB	AL = return code	DOS1
Create file	16	AH = 16 DS:DX = pointer to FCB	AL = return code	DOS1
Rename file	17	AH = 17 DS:DX = pointer to FCB	AL = return code	DOS1
Read random file record	21	AH = 21 DS:DX = pointer to FCB	AL = return code	DOS1
Write random file record	22	AH = 22 DS:DX = pointer to FCB	AL = return code	DOS1
Get file size	23	AH = 23 DS:DX = pointer to FCB	AL = return code	DOS1

Figure 18-4. A summary of the DOS services (continued)

Service	Function (hex)	Register Input	Register Output	Version

File I/O Functions (continued)

Service	Function (hex)	Input	Output	Version
Set random record field	24	AH = 24 DS:DX = pointer to FCB		DOS1
Read random file records	27	AH = 27 CX = record count DS:DX = pointer to FCB	AL = return code CX = actual record count	DOS1
Write random file records	28	AH = 28 CX = record count DS:DX = pointer to FCB	AL = return code CX = actual record count	DOS1

Parse filename	29	AH = 29
		DS:SI = pointer to command line
		ES:DI = pointer to FCB
		AL = parsing control bits
		    (see page 286)
			DS:SI = pointer to following
			    place in command line
			AL = return code
			ES:DI = pointer to FCB
				DOS1

CREAT: Create file	3C	AH = 3C CX = file attribute DS:DX = pointer to ASCIIZ string	AX = file handle or return code If CF = 1 AX = error code else	DOS2
Open file	3D	AH = 3D AL = access code (see page 308) DS:DX = pointer to ASCIIZ string	AX = file handle If CF = 1 AX = error code else	DOS2
Close file handle	3E	AH = 3E BX = file handle	AX = return code if CF = 1	DOS2
Read from file or device	3F	AH = 3F BX = file handle CX = number of bytes to read DS:DX = pointer to DTA buffer	If CF = 0 AX = number of bytes read else AX = return code	DOS2
Write to file or device	40	AH = 40 BX = file handle CX = number of bytes to write DS:DX = pointer to DTA buffer	If CF = 0 AX = number of bytes written else AX = return code	DOS2
Delete file	41	AH = 41 DS:DX = pointer to ASCIIZ string	AX = return code if CF set	DOS2
Move file pointer	42	AH = 42 AL = method code (see 17.xx) CX:DX = offset value BX = file handle	AX = return code if CF set DX:AX = new pointer location if CF not set	DOS2

*Figure 18-4. A summary of the DOS
services (continued)*

Service	Function (hex)	Register Input	Register Output	Version

File I/O Functions (continued)

Service	Function (hex)	Input	Output	Version

CHMOD: Get/set file attributes	43	AH = 43
		AL = get/set code:
		  00 = get into CX;
		  01 = set as in CX
		CX = attribute if set used
		DS:DX = pointer to ASCIIZ string
			AX = return code if CF set
			CX = attribute if get used
				DOS2

DUP: Duplicate file handle	45	AH = 45 BX = file handle	If CF = 0, AX = file handle or return code else AX = return code	DOS2
CDUP: Force handle duplication	46	AH = 46 BX = existing file handle CX = second file handle	AX = return code if CF set CX = file handle	DOS2
FIND FIRST: start file search	4E	AH = 4E CX = attribute to search on DS:DX = pointer to ASCIIZ string	AX = return code if CF set	DOS2
FIND NEXT: Continue file search	4F	AH = 4F DS:DX = pointer to info. from FIND FIRST or previous find next call	AX = return code if CF set	DOS2
Rename file	56	AH = 56 DS:DX = pointer to ASCIIZ string (old name) ES:DI = pointer to ASCIIZ string (new name)	AX = return code if CF set	DOS2
Get extended error code	59	AH = 59 BX = 0000	AX = extended error code BH = error class BL = action CH = locus (see page 322)	DOS3
Create temporary file	5A	AH = 5A DS:DX = pointer to ASCIIZ directory path name CX = file attribute	AX = error code if CF set DS:DX = pointer to pathname with filename appended, if CF not set	DOS3
Create new file	5B	AH = 5B DS:DX = pointer to ASCIIZ file path name CX = file attribute	If CF set AX = return code else AX = file handle	DOS3
Lock/unlock file access	5C	AH = 5C AL = 0 (lock) or 1 (unlock) BX = file handle CX:DX = offset to lock SI:DI = amount to lock	AX = error code if CF set	DOS3

Figure 18-4. A summary of the DOS services (continued)

Service	Function (hex)	Register Input	Register Output	Version
Directory Functions				
MKDIR: Make directory	39	AH = 39 DS:DX = pointer to ASCIIZ string	AX = return code if CF set	DOS2
RMDIR: Remove directory	3A	AH = 3A DS:DX = pointer to ASCIIZ string	AX = return code if CF set	DOS2
CHDIR: Change current directory	3B	AH = 3B DS:DX = pointer to ASCIIZ string	AX = return code if CF set	DOS2
Get current directory	47	AH = 47 DL = drive ID DS:SI = pointer to data area	AX = return code if CF set DS:SI = pointer to full path name if CF not set	DOS2
Date/Time Functions				
Get date	2A	AH = 2A	AL = day of week: 0 = Sun; 6 = Sat CX = year (1980–2099) DH = month DL = day	DOS1
Set date	2B	AH = 2B CX = year (1980–2099) DH = month DL = day	AL = return code if date valid AL = FF if date invalid	DOS1
Get time	2C	AH = 2C	CL = minutes CH = hours DL = hundredths of seconds DH = seconds	DOS1
Set time	2D	AH = 2D CL = minutes CH = hours DL = hundreds of seconds DH = seconds	AL = 00 if time valid, FF if time invalid	DOS1
Get/set file date and time	57	AH = 57 AL = get/set indicator: 00 = get; 01 = set BX = file handle CX = time, if AL = 01 DX = date, if AL = 01	AX = extended error code if CF set CX = time, if AL = 00 DX = date, if AL = 00	DOS2

Figure 18-4. A summary of the DOS services (continued)

Service	Function (hex)	Register Input	Register Output	Version
Miscellaneous Functions				
Set interrupt vector	25	AH = 25 AL = interrupt number DS:DX = pointer to interrupt handler		DOS1
Get DOS version number	30	AH = 30	AL = major version number AH = minor version number BX = 0000 CX = 0000	DOS2 (see page 300)
Get interrupt vector	35	AH = 35 AL = interrupt number	ES:BX = interrupt vector	DOS2
Get/Set country-dependent information	38	AH = 38 DS:DX = pointer to 32-byte buffer for Get; DX = FFFF for Set AL = 00 for standard information if DOS2; AL = 00 for current country, if DOS3 AL = country code or AL = FF if country code ≥ 255 BX = country code if AL = FF	AX = return code, if CF set DS:DX = pointer to information (see page 305) BX = country code	DOS2
IOCTL: I/O control for devices	44	AH = 44 AL = sub-function code (see page 311) BL = drive number BX = file handle CX = number of bytes to read or write; of time count if AL = 0B	AX = return code, if CF set AX = number of bytes read or written, if CF not set DX = control data bits	DOS2
Memory Functions				
Allocate memory	48	AH = 48 BX = memory requested in paragraphs	AX = segment address of allocated memory, or return code, if CF set BX = largest block size available, if allocation failed	DOS2
Free allocated memory	49	AH = 49 ES = segment address of block to return	AX = return code if CF set	DOS2
SETBLOCK: Modify allocated memory block	4A	AH = 4A BX = requested size in paragraphs ES = segment address of block	AX = return code if CF set BX = maximum possible size if request to increase block size failed	DOS2

*Figure 18-4. A summary of the DOS
services (continued)*

19

Program Building

As we've stated throughout this book, the wisest approach to programming the PC family is to write nearly all of our programs in a high-level language (such as BASIC, Pascal, or C) and when necessary use the DOS or BIOS services for whatever the high-level languages don't provide. On occasion, we may also want to create our own assembly-language routines to perform specialized tasks not available from our programming language or the system services.

When creating programs within the confines of a single programming language, we really don't need to know anything more about a language than what we can find in the manuals that come with it. However, if we need to break out of the bounds of a single language to access some of the system routines, or perhaps to tie into a program that's written in a different language, we'll need to dig deeper into the technical aspects of both DOS and the programming languages—of DOS to learn how to link programs together; and of the programming languages to find out the requirements for the program interfaces that allow the different languages to communicate with each other.

This chapter presents some overall considerations that apply to the advanced use of most programming languages; that is, to building program interfaces and linking programs with the DOS LINK utility. The following chapter, Chapter 20, covers five specific types of programming language and the language translators that make them come alive. In that chapter, we will point out some of the technical characteristics of the five languages that must be considered whenever we are connecting them to assembly-language subroutines.

PROGRAM INTERFACES

A program interface is a layer of assembly-language code that makes it possible for a program written in a high-level language to communicate with an assembly-language subroutine. There are two key parts to a program interface: the control interface and the data interface.

The control interface handles the business of calling and returning; that is, of passing control of the computer from one module to another and back again without anything going amiss. The control interface, by the way, can be tricky to program. It is remarkably simple if you know how to do it right, and can create incredible messes if you get even minor details wrong.

The data interface allows the two sides of an interface to touch and correctly understand common data. Doing this successfully involves an understanding of how each side of the interface finds and works with data, and an understanding of how data is formatted so that each side can interpret it in the same way. We'll be covering these topics in more detail in the next chapter.

Designing program interfaces is only one part of the program linking process. All three program elements—the calling program, the called subroutine, and the interface—must accomplish the following in order to work together successfully:

The program must be able to find its way to the subroutine. In the 8088-based system of the standard PC family, a subroutine can be called in one of two ways: through an interrupt or through a CALL instruction. As we already know, the DOS and BIOS services are called through interrupts using the INT instruction, and the addresses of the service routines are implicit in the interrupt number. Most ordinary assembly-language programs and subroutines are called by the CALL instruction from our programming language. The addresses are associated with the program or subroutine names and established during the linking process (☛ read on for more about linking).

There are two kinds of CALL instruction: the NEAR CALL and the FAR CALL. The NEAR CALL locates a subroutine within the current 64K code segment (CS) and does not require the CS register to be changed. By contrast, the FAR CALL locates a subroutine outside of the current CS using a complete segmented address in the CALL instruction (which changes the CS setting). Some languages use both instructions and some use only one.

The subroutine must know what to do when finished. Most often a subroutine will return to the calling program using either a NEAR or FAR RETurn instruction, but there are other options—for example, we may want to terminate the program and return to DOS from the subroutine. The subroutine's RET instruction does more than just return to the caller; it also cleans the stack, as we will soon see.

The subroutine must know what supporting framework it is getting from the caller. This supporting framework involves such things as how the segment registers are set and whether there is a stack that can be used. In general, the segment registers are just as they should be: CS has the right code segment; DS points to the location of the calling program's data; and SS and SP are set up with the caller's stack.

The called subroutine can usually continue to use the caller's stack but there is no practical way to know how much working space is available. If its needs are reasonable—say, less than 64 bytes—the caller's stack space should be adequate. However, if it should need more, the subroutine should set up its own data space in memory.

If the program needs to pass information (parameters) to the subroutine, both the program and the subroutine must know how many parameters there are, where they should be placed, and whether or not they need to be changed and passed back. Most commonly, programs and subroutines work with a fixed number of parameters, although there are ways to handle a variable number of parameters in some languages. The parameters are always passed through the stack, either directly or indirectly. The direct method passes the actual value of the parameter through the stack; the indirect method passes the value's address through the stack. In either case, the called program absolutely must know which method is being used.

Which parameter-passing method is used depends primarily on the language; some languages cannot place values on the stack, only addresses. With those languages that can handle both addresses and values, we have a lot more freedom to decide which method to use, and the method we use determines how the parameters are dealt with as they are passed from one program to another. For example, if we want to protect the caller's parameters from being changed by the called subroutine, we'll want to pass the original value on the stack to make sure we maintain a copy of it. But if we want the caller's parameters to be changed by the called subroutine, we must send the address of the original value via the stack so that the subroutine will change the parameter's value by modifying what is stored at the specified address.

Parameter passing is the most complicated part of an interface routine, made even more complicated by the different ways programming languages deal with data and stack information. Because of its complexity and variability from one language to another, this is the main issue we'll discuss in our language comparisons in the next chapter.

The subroutine must preserve certain information. Although the requirements may vary in different situations, there are a few ground rules governing what information should be preserved, and what can and cannot be done when calling a subroutine. We've included some useful tips here, ☞ but you will find a few more in Chapter 3, particularly on page 39.

Interrupts can be suspended, although it is usually not a good idea, except briefly when segment registers are changed; they must be turned back on before returning. (☞ See page 48.)

If any segment register is modified, the original setting should be preserved on the stack. Another important register to preserve, under most circumstances, is the base pointer (BP) register, since it is often used to keep track of the parameters' location on the stack. By convention, a calling program does not expect its working register values to be preserved, so all the working registers, AX, BX, CX, DX, DI, and SI can be changed freely, as can all the flags. The caller's stack has to be preserved, although just how that's done is part of the clean-up process.

The stack must be cleaned up after the subroutine is finished. There are four things that might be cluttering up the stack when a subroutine is finished: some parameters; the return address from the CALL instruction; register values saved from before the CALL; and finally, some working storage from the subroutine.

Three of these leftovers are not a problem: Subroutines are expected to remove their own working storage from the stack; saved registers are removed by POP instructions; and the return address is removed by the RET instruction. It's the parameters that usually complicate the clean-up process, because the method of removal varies in different languages. Some languages expect the subroutine to remove the parameters by specifying in the RET instruction the number of bytes to remove from the stack. Other languages expect the caller to remove them. We'll point out these differences as we discuss the languages in detail in Chapter 20.

With all of these program design elements in mind, let's step back a bit farther and see how the whole process works—from creating a program or subroutine, to combining it with others.

COMBINING PROGRAM MODULES

In this section, we're going to cover the general rules for putting pieces of a program together or for combining program modules. We'll be using a standard DOS programming procedure that applies to all of the programming languages used as examples in the next chapter (except for interpreted BASIC, which always seems to be a special case). First, let's review the steps that are involved in creating a working program.

Step 1: Writing the Source Code

To begin with, we have to write our program using the commands and syntax of our programming language. This form of the program is known as the source code. For programming languages that use the standard DOS conventions, the source code must be in the form of an ASCII text file (☞ see Appendix C, page 410). Interpreted BASIC does not normally use the ASCII text file format for its source files, but it can. (To create ASCII text files with the BASIC interpreter, we use the A option of the SAVE command.)

By convention, source-code files have a filename extension that reflects the name of the programming language used, such as BAS or C.

Step 2: Translating the Source Code

On command, source files are given to our language translators, called compilers for anything other than assembly language, or assemblers for assembly language. (Again, interpreter BASIC is a special case that we are not considering here.) The translator (compiler or assembler) converts the source code into machine-language instructions; but, it doesn't convert it into a form that is ready to be executed. Instead, compilers and assemblers put their results into a form known as object code. The object-code format is designed with a particular purpose in mind: to combine separate object modules into a single larger program. Object-code files, by convention, have a filename extension of OBJ.

Step 3: Linking Programs

The next basic step is to link the programs together. The linker, or link-editor program, known as LINK in DOS, performs two main tasks: It combines separate object modules (as needed), making all the necessary connections between them; and it converts the modules from an object-code format to a loadable program in the .EXE format.

The actual combining, or linking, of program modules to create an .EXE file is the most important apect of this discussion. We'll take it up again later in this chapter, after we've covered two other steps that are involved in preparing programs.

So far, we've mentioned the three principal steps of program preparation: writing the program to produce source code; compiling or assembling the program to produce object code; and linking the program to produce a loadable program. There are two other related steps in the process: converting the .EXE format created by the LINK program to the .COM format; and using object libraries to store a number of modules.

Step 4: Converting File Formats

Programs that are stored on disk in the .EXE file format are not completely ready to go to work. When they are loaded from disk into memory, DOS performs a few last-minute operations to prepare the program for execution. These operations do such things as tell the program where it is located in memory, calculate its size, and set up a stack for it to use. But if the operating conventions of a program are sufficiently simple, and if the start-up stages of a program are sufficiently savvy, this loading preparation can be done in advance by converting the file to a .COM file format.

A .COM file is an exact image of the program as it will appear in the computer's memory. While DOS must do a good deal of work to prepare an .EXE-format program, it only has to do two things for a .COM-format program: It creates the program segment prefix (☞ see page 260); and it sets the segment registers.

We use the DOS program EXE2BIN to convert an .EXE file to a .COM file format. Not all programs can be converted to the .COM format. For those programs that qualify, we can freely convert them or leave them in the .EXE format. Either form is functionally the same, but the .COM format is more compact and loads slightly faster.

We can very simply and safely find out if a program can be converted from .EXE format to .COM format just by trying to do it. If it works, it works. If EXE2BIN or LOCATE says it can't be done, however, it can't be done.

Step 5: Creating Object-Code Libraries

Most high-level programming languages make use of dozens of prepared subroutines that support the operation of our programs. Naturally, these subroutines are in the translated, object-code form. However, it is very inconvenient to have dozens of these object files lying about on our disks. It is also inconvenient to have to determine for ourselves which ones need to be combined with our own program's object files. To solve this problem there are object libraries, which are collections of object code gathered together into one file. By convention, libraries have the file-name extension LIB.

Most high-level programming languages come with a ready-to-use library of standard supporting subroutines. Occasionally, a compiler will have several libraries that provide different versions of standard routines. For example, they may come with floating-point routines that may or may not make use of the 8087 math coprocessor.

The DOS linker is able to search through a library to find and use the subroutines that it needs in order to complete a program. Without this library mechanism, we would be faced with the annoying task of telling the linker which object files were needed. If we left any out, the link-editing would fail; if we included any that weren't actually needed, our program would become unnecessarily large. The use of a library enables us to avoid these problems.

Object libraries are mostly used to support compilers in a way that is completely out of our hands. We don't create or modify the libraries and we don't even directly select what will be used in a library. Instead, we select files from a library indirectly by using particular features of our programming language, or directly by using the LIB program.

❑ NOTE: *The LIB program is not part of every version of DOS, although it should be. The IBM versions of DOS from 1.00 through 3.1 do not include LIB. LIB is included in some non-IBM versions of DOS, and it accompanies some (but not all) compilers and assemblers. Getting your hands on a working copy of LIB is a catch-as-catch-can proposition.*

If you have a copy of LIB, you can use it for three main purposes: simply to explore the contents of existing libraries (which can be a very illuminating experience); to selectively replace modules in existing libraries if you want to change or improve the library that comes with a programming language; or to create your own libraries.

The documentation for LIB in the DOS manual will fully explain its operation, but just to give you a taste of the ways LIB can be used, we have included a few examples to try out. To create a new library named TESTLIB, enter this command:

```
LIB TESTLIB;
```

To list the contents of an existing library, directing the listing to the printer LPT1: (or to any file, or to the screen), enter:

```
LIB TESTLIB,LPT1:;
```

To add the module X.OBJ to a library, enter:

```
LIB TESTLIB+X;
```

To replace an existing module with a new version, enter:

```
LIB TESTLIB-X+X;
```

With later versions of LIB, type − +X instead of −X+X. To extract a module for disassembly or other separate use, enter:

```
LIB TESTLIB*X;
```

Our programs are usually composed of a number of subroutines. Whether or not you are likely to benefit from the services of the LIB program depends upon one basic decision that you make about the way you organize these subroutines. If you prefer to combine the source code for your subroutines into one source file, which means they will all be compiled together, then you have little need for LIB. On the other hand, if you prefer to compile your subroutines separately, which produces separate object files, then LIB performs exactly the job you need done: It gathers together and organizes your object files. I personally have no recommendation for either style of operation; I have used both of them in my PC programming and found each one practical and effective. It's mainly a matter of preference—though your choice may have some consequences if you program in Pascal (☞ see page 369).

USING THE DOS LINK PROGRAM

We're now ready to return to our discussion of combining program modules and using the LINK program. The documentation for LINK in the IBM DOS Technical Reference manual fully explains its operation, including the complexity of its control switches. Here, we'll summarize the most common and useful operations, particularly where they pertain to the programming languages discussed in the following chapter.

Just to give you some background information, the LINK program takes four parameters, which might be written like this:

```
LINK 1,2,3,4;
```

The first parameter, 1, stands for an explicit list of object modules (such as PROG1 + PROG2 + PROG3); 2 stands for the name of the finished program; 3 stands for where the linker's display output should be sent (such as to the printer or display screen); and 4 stands for an explicit list of libraries, if they are used (such as BASCOM + MYLIB).

Linking a Single Program

Now for some practical examples. To start with, let's consider a completely self-contained program, such as the BEEP program shown on page 355. To link it, we simply type:

```
LINK BEEP;
```

Linking a single program such as this simply creates an .EXE file.

Linking a Program to the Compiler Library

Next, let's consider what is surely the most common linking circumstance. Say we've compiled a program in a high-level language, such as compiled BASIC and we need to link it with its standard library. In this simple case, we're not using any interfaces or other modules that we've created. Our program's name is X and the compiler library's name is BASCOM.LIB. This is how we would write the LINK command:

```
LINK X,,,BASCOM;
```

Usually, a compiler generates an object module that goes to the library to find anything else that is needed. In the case of Lattice/Microsoft C (☛ which we cover on page 377), there is a standard start-up routine called a prefix module that must be linked ahead of our program. Supposing that the prefix module is named C, our program is named X, and the library is named MC, we would link them this way:

```
LINK C+X,X,,MC
```

Note two new items in this example. First, we explicitly asked the linker to combine two object files, C.OBJ and X.OBJ (which is the program we compiled). Second, we explicitly gave a name to the finished .EXE program, naming it X. We have to give it this name or the linker will use the name of the first object module, which is C. If we allow that to happen, all of our programs will end up with the same name, C, rather than their individual names (in this case, X). We can give the finished program any name we wish, including a name completely unrelated to any of the object-module names. In this example, however, we did the normal thing, which is to give our finished program X.EXE the same name as our object file X.OBJ.

Combining Programs

Now we're ready to illustrate how to combine program modules with the linker. First, let's consider a situation in which we have made use of a private object library to hold either our assembly-language interfaces, or our separately compiled subroutines, or both. Here is how we would link such a library using Pascal. The program is named X and our library is named OURLIB:

```
LINK X,,,PASCAL+OURLIB;
```

Next, let's consider the case where we have not created an object-module library. Instead, we simply want to combine two object files: one from our high-level language compiler and one from the assembler for interfaces to DOS and the BIOS. Here is how we would link such a program. In this example, the language is Pascal, the program is named X, and the assembly-language interface is named INTFACE:

```
LINK X+INTFACE,,PASCAL
```

There are, of course, endless variations on how program modules can be combined. However, these basic examples should provide you with the necessary core of information. Armed with the general information in this chapter, you should be ready to proceed to the next, and learn something about how the programming languages work.

20

Programming Languages

I n the last chapter, we briefly discussed the general principles of building program modules and linking them using the DOS Link program. In this chapter, we're going to discuss the programming languages we use to build the program modules, particularly those aspects of the languages that we need to be concerned with if we plan to link the modules to assembly-language subroutines.

The title of this chapter implies that we are going to discuss programming languages in general, but that's really not the case. It's all very well to discuss any topic in the abstract, but when we actually want to get anything done, we have to get down to specifics. If we want to create computer programs, we have to work with a specific programming language—and a programming language is much more specific than many people are led to believe.

First of all, there is no such thing as a generic programming language. We can only create working programs with a compiler or interpreter for a programming language that is designed for a particular machine. Although academic experts on computers would like to pretend otherwise, the practical truth is that the general definitions of programming languages lack many of the essential features that we need to create real programs that work on real computers. So, when a compiler or an interpreter is created for a particular programming language, such as BASIC, to run on a particular computer, such as the PC, the fundamental language is altered and extended to provide the things that are really needed. The alterations are often quite significant, and in every case, they create a programming language that is related to but is truly distinct from all other programming languages traveling under the same name.

This discussion is meant to set the stage for the simple announcement that this chapter does not and could not possibly cover every PC programming language that exists now or that might be created in the future. Since each compiler, in effect, creates its own unique programming language, using this chapter to cover the general aspects of the main languages would not serve our needs. We must select just a few languages, since we can't cover them all. I have chosen to discuss four popular and representative languages: assembly language, BASIC, Pascal, and C. Then, within these categories, I have selected five specific versions or implementations of these languages: IBM Macro Assembler, IBM interpreted BASIC, IBM compiled BASIC, IBM Pascal, and Lattice/Microsoft C.

My decision to choose these particular languages is guided by the past and the future. Past experience has shown me which language versions have the most widespread use in the PC family. Concern about the potential for interfacing new work and new compilers has led me to believe it is unwise to use programming languages that are not compatible with the standard DOS link editor. Unfortunately, a great many compilers and assemblers either don't produce linkable object code (for example, the admirable "cheap assembler" CHASM, Borland's Turbo Pascal, and Logitech's Modula-2), or use an object format that is not compatible with the DOS linker (for example, the Digital Research family of languages, and Computer Innovation's C-86). Personally, I am quite conservative about the matter of linking and object-code compatibility, and I fear that in straying away from the de facto standard established by DOS, we run a serious risk of encountering problems in the future, as the PC family of computers evolves.

LANGUAGE SPECIFICS

The five programming languages that I have chosen are really families in themselves. There are various versions of each one, and in most cases they are available from several sources. Fortunately, the differences between the versions are minor—minor enough that we don't need to think of them as separate languages in the same sense that BASIC and Pascal are separate languages.

Assembly language. Our discussion of assembly languages will be based on IBM's version 1.00 Macro Assembler, created by Microsoft. A number of other versions are available from Microsoft, from IBM, and from other computer manufacturers who have licensed the use of Microsoft's basic assembler. These versions vary only in their most sophisticated elements, which need not concern us here.

Interpreted BASIC. The interpreted BASIC that we'll cover in this chapter has taken on a thousand faces and minor variations. To IBM PC users, the version we'll discuss is known simply as BASIC or BASICA, and is further defined by version names such as C1.10, J1.00, and A2.10, among others. Outside the IBM world, it may be known as BASIC, Microsoft BASIC, or GW-BASIC. We're not concerned with the differences here; we're concerned with the common elements.

Compiled BASIC. For our discussion of compiled BASIC, we'll be guided by version 1.00 of the IBM BASIC Compiler. The principles we discuss will also apply to other specialized Microsoft BASIC compilers, such as Business BASIC.

Pascal. For Pascal, we'll use IBM's version 1.00 as a basis. The details we discuss will apply equally well to IBM's version 2.00 and to various Microsoft versions.

The C language. For our discussion of C, we will be using the Lattice/Microsoft C compiler version 1.04, created by Lattice. There are other closely related versions available from Microsoft, Lattice, and Lifeboat, which all share the characteristics that we will be covering. This compiler, by the way, should not be confused with the Microsoft C compiler (version 3 and above) that was created after the Lattice/Microsoft C version was released.

ASSEMBLY LANGUAGE

There are two fundamental types of assembly-language program: the assembly-language subroutine, which is called by other programs that may be written in a high-level language; and the freestanding assembly-language program. Subroutines depend largely upon the calling program to provide their structure and support, while the freestanding assembly-language programs must provide their own structure and support, and must cope with all the fundamental operating issues that stand-alone programs face. Assembler subroutines are relatively easy to construct, while assembler programs can be quite complicated. Subroutines have more immediate appeal to those of us who need to build interface routines between our high-level language and some of the system's BIOS or DOS services, while stand-alone programs are usually tackled by programmers who must accomplish something that neither their conventional programming language nor the system services provide.

In this brief discussion of assembly language, we'll be showing you some techniques that will help you figure out the high-level language interface conventions for your assembly-language subroutines. We'll also lead you through the process of creating a stand-alone assembler program. However, we will not even try to teach you how to use assembly language—that is far too large and complex a subject. If you are not particularly proficient at assembly language, one way to learn about it is to study some of the readily available sources of assembly-language coding. One dandy source is the assembler code published by computer manufacturers, such as the BIOS listings that are part of IBM's Technical Reference manuals. Another source, available with most compilers, is the assembler-like listing that the compiler can be asked to produce. This is useful both for learning how the compiler handles particular coding problems (which you can control by selecting appropriate statements in the high-level language), and also for learning the subroutine interface conventions the compiler uses. A related, but less useful way to learn about assembly language is to load an existing program using the DOS DEBUG program, and then use DEBUG's U-unassemble command to snoop through sections of the program. (The section that follows shows how to perform a related operation for snooping inside program libraries.) Each of these methods can help you learn different programming techniques and tricks. In fact, these are the methods I used to learn nearly everything that I know about assembly-language programming for the PC family.

Logical Organization

The elements of an assembly-language subroutine are easy to understand if they are laid out in the order they occur. As you may recall, the logical organization was fully explained in Chapter 8 (page 164), where we described an interface routine as five nested parts:

> Level 1: General assembler overhead
> > Level 2: Subroutine assembler overhead
> > > Level 3: Entry code
> > > > Level 4: Get parameter data from caller
> > > > > Level 5: Invoke the ROM-BIOS or DOS service
> > > > Level 4: Pass results back to caller
> > > Level 3: Exit code
> > Level 2: Finishing up subroutine assembler overhead
> Level 1: Finishing up general assembler overhead

This basic organization is one that can be followed for most interface routines written for system services, or for conventional assembly language subroutines, but the actual coding will vary with every programming language.

The standard tool for creating assembler subroutines in the PC family is the Microsoft Macro Assembler, named MASM, which is available in different versions from a variety of sources. For example, the IBM Personal Computer was introduced with a version numbered 1.00, which included both a small assembler (without macro capability) and a macro assembler. Except for advanced assembly-language work—far over our heads here—any version of the assembler will work for our purposes.

Learning About Interface Conventions

Once you have your assembly language in hand, you'll need to examine the assembly-language conventions and interface customs that apply to your programming language. Your assembly-language interface will have to know how to gain access to the parameters passed by the calling program, how to interpret the data format, and how to send the parameters back—among other things. If there is not adequate information of this sort in the language documentation, there are some rather simple ways to pry it out of the language itself.

To learn the conventions for both a calling and a called program—that is, to see both sides of the program call interface—you can study the compiler's assembler-style listing, as we mentioned earlier. You can also study the innards of the assembly-language subroutines provided with the language compiler, which may provide a somewhat different perspective from what can be learned by studying a compiler's listing. This technique not only gives you the details of the interface conventions for assembly-language routines but also gives you specific programming examples that may serve as models.

The first thing we must do is select an appropriate subroutine. The subroutines that are most accessible for study are often those that are part of the library that accompanies our compiler. Usually, it is easiest to simply choose a compiler feature that we're interested in, such as I/O, screen control, or arithmetic, and then figure out which subroutines are invoked for that feature.

Next, we have to look at the names of the library modules (which might not be the names of the subroutines inside those modules). We can do this by using the LIB program (☞ discussed in Chapter 19) to list the contents of the library. Let's assume there's a library named LANG.LIB on file. We can direct the library listing to another file named LISTING with the following DOS instruction (we could also direct it to the screen or printer):

```
LIB LANG,LISTING;
```

Looking over the library listing, we find the subroutine we're interested in and the name of the module that it's a part of; let's say it's named XMOD. Next, we ask LIB to separate XMOD out of the library, so we can work with it:

```
LIB LANG*XMOD;
```

The * operator tells LIB to create a copy of the module as a separate object file; in this case, the file will be named XMOD.OBJ.

At this point, we could try to snoop around inside XMOD.OBJ, but this file contains extraneous link-editor information that would only get in our way. Instead, we're going to turn XMOD.OBJ into a set of pure machine instructions using two steps. First we link it, to convert it into an .EXE program file:

```
LINK XMOD;
```

This gives us a file named XMOD.EXE. (Ignore any no-stack error message that the linker gives you.) Then, to get rid of the .EXE-file overhead, we convert XMOD.EXE into a .COM file like this:

```
EXE2BIN XMOD.EXE XMOD.COM
```

At this point, we have a file named XMOD.COM, which should consist of nothing but pure machine-language instructions, with all overhead removed. Now we are ready to use DEBUG to convert the instructions into a readable assembler format. First, we note the size of XMOD.COM, and then we fire up DEBUG, telling it to load XMOD.COM:

```
DEBUG XMOD.COM
```

Then we tell DEBUG to convert XMOD into a readable form with the U-unassemble command, like this:

```
U 100 L XXX
```

(The XXX is the length of the file in hex.)

All these steps may seem overly elaborate and cumbersome, but once you have learned them, they can be performed quickly and easily, and they will give you an inside look at how your own programming language uses assembly-language interface routines.

The next section will repeat the key steps of this exercise as we demonstrate the mechanics of creating a small but complete assembly-language program.

Writing and Linking Assembler Programs

To illustrate the process involved in writing and linking an assembler program, we will create an incredibly simple and yet useful program that sounds a tone on the computer's speaker. To do this on any PC family computer or any DOS computer, we just output the bell character, CHR$(7), to the screen. In this example, we'll do this by using DOS service 2, which is invoked with interrupt 33. Then we'll end the program and return program control to DOS using interrupt 32. Follow this example and you'll learn quite a bit about creating self-contained assembly-language programs. Here is the source code for this little program:

```
; DOS generic beep program
BEEPSEG    SEGMENT BYTE PUBLIC 'PROG'
           ASSUME  CS:BEEPSEG
BEEP       PROC
           MOV     DL,7              ; bell character
           MOV     AH,2              ; output character function
           INT     33                ; DOS function interrupt
           INT     32                ; return to DOS interrupt
BEEP       ENDP
BEEPSEG    ENDS
           END
```

As you see, the program is only four instructions long, filling only eight bytes. We can assemble the program with this step:

```
MASM BEEP;
```

The MASM command creates an object file that is ready for linking. In this case, we'll link the program without subroutines, libraries, or other object files, like this:

```
LINK BEFP;
```

The linker program usually expects to find a stack segment in the programs it links, but our very simple program doesn't have one—a key characteristic that makes it possible to convert it into a .COM file, as we shall soon see. The linker will complain, but we can ignore its complaint.

Linking will give us an executable program called BEEP.EXE. It is very common to write assembly-language programs in such a way that they can be converted into the more compact .COM format. We convert this simple program using the DOS command EXE2BIN, as in:

```
EXE2BIN BEEP.EXE BEEP.COM
```

Now we have a finished beeper program, that can be used on any computer that runs DOS.

It is worthwhile to pause and note what happens to the size of our program when it gets transformed from an idea to an executable .COM file. The source code for this program is approximately 378 bytes (depending upon the use of spaces in the comments, etc.). When we assemble it, we discover that just 8 bytes of working machine-language instructions are created. However, the object file, which includes some standard linker information as overhead, is 54 bytes—much smaller than our source file, but much larger than the 8 bytes of actual instruction. After linking, the 54-byte object file swells to a 520-byte .EXE file. This is because the .EXE format contains a prefix that describes how programs are to be loaded, and this prefix is created in 512-byte records—in this case, it's 512 bytes of overhead, followed by our 8 bytes of instructions. Converting the program to .COM format eliminates the 512 bytes of overhead and we end up with a .COM file that's just 8 bytes of pure machine code.

INTERPRETED AND COMPILED BASIC

To be candid and blunt, let me admit right away that I can't give you everything you need here. Working with BASIC and interfacing to BASIC are very, very complicated subjects—complex enough to fill several books just by themselves. Frankly, interfacing with BASIC is a particularly messy area, made even messier by the number of BASIC versions used with the different models of the extended PC family. Even within the IBM-made trunk of this family tree, there are more versions of BASIC than we have fingers or toes for counting them.

In this discussion, we will focus on the issues that relate to interfacing BASIC programs with external routines. The two items that we will concentrate on are BASIC's data formats (which are relevant to external routines because they need to be able to exchange data with BASIC) and the interface conventions that specify how BASIC and assembly language talk to each other.

BASIC Data Formats

BASIC uses four data formats: integers, variable-length strings, and floating-point numbers in long and short form, known in BASIC terminology as single-precision and double-precision numbers. BASIC variables can be explicitly given one of these four format types by appending an identifying suffix to the variable name: % for integer, ! for single precision (short floating point), # for double precision (long floating point), and $ for string. Numeric constants can be similarly classified. Implicit typing can be controlled with the DEF statement and defaults to single precision. For reference, here are some simple examples:

A%	Integer variable
A!	Single-precision variable
A#	Double-precision variable
A$	String variable
1%	Integer constant
1!	Single-precision constant
1#	Double-precision constant
"1"	String constant

❑ IMPORTANT NOTE: *While the three numeric data formats are the same for both interpreted BASIC and compiled BASIC, string formats are different for compiled BASIC.*

Integer Data Formats

The integer format is the standard 16-bit signed 2-byte word universally used by the PC family. The range of values is from −32,768 through 0 to +32,767. ☞ See page 23 for a general discussion of this data format. BASIC does not accommodate the standard variation on this format: unsigned 16-bit integers with a range of values from 0 through 65,535. Since the unsigned integer format is fundamental to memory addressing and address calculation in the PC, some care must be used when handling addresses. It is customary to use BASIC's signed integer format to store unsigned integer addresses; in fact, this is the preferred way to pass addresses to assembler interfaces. However, care must be exercised when displaying or calculating unsigned addresses that are stored in the signed integer format. To avoid miscalculation, it is wisest to perform address calculations in double precision, using the long floating-point format.

If you are using the BASIC integer format to hold and pass unsigned word addresses, there are some interesting points to keep in mind. In theory, a BASIC integer cannot accept any number over its range limit of 32,767; for example, we cannot assign a decimal integer a constant of 50,000 or a floating-point variable with an equivalent value. However, the hex constant format can be used to assign values from 0 through 65,535 (or &H0 through &HFFFF in BASIC's hex constant notation). This means that BASIC does not allow I% = 50,000, but it does allow the equivalent in hex: I% = &HC350. Also, BASIC provides the hex display function HEX$, making it easy for us to convert decimal values to their hexadecimal equivalents. These two features make it reasonably convenient to work with addresses in hex notation.

You can safely convert address values from integer to floating-point format, to perform simple arithmetic operations, by using this method:

```
IF I% < 0 THEN D# = I% + 65536# ELSE D# = I%
```

where I% is an integer and D# is its equivalent in double precision. To convert address values from double precision to integer, we would use this method:

```
IF D# > 32767 THEN I% = D# - 65536 ELSE I% = D#
```

The BASIC function VARPTR directly provides the offset addresses of integer variables. (☞ As we'll see shortly, it also provides them for floating-point variables; for string values, VARPTR is an indirect connection to the address of the variable values.) VARPTR gives us the offset address within BASIC's default data segment, which can then be used to PEEK or POKE at the variable's value. We can demonstrate this with the following example:

```
I% = 999 ' or any other value
I.POINTER = VARPTR (I%)
J% = PEEK (I.POINTER) * 256 + PEEK (I.POINTER + 1)
PRINT I%, J%
```

This process of using VARPTR to capture the offset address of a variable has little practical value, but it demonstrates how to find and use addresses. Examples like this one are designed to build your confidence and help you understand the use of memory addresses in BASIC—both of which are important, as you'll realize when you start creating assembly-language interfaces.

Floating-Point Data Formats

Floating-point values, both single precision and double precision, are stored in a common format that is peculiar to BASIC. Not only is BASIC's floating-point format different than that used by most other programming languages for the PC, it is also incompatible with the formats used by the 8087 and 80287 math coprocessors.

To help you make use of the BASIC floating-point data format, we'll describe its key elements. But be forewarned that the subject of floating-point formats is a complex one. The following discussion assumes that you have a strong general understanding of how computers store and use floating-point numbers.

In BASIC, the single- and double-precision data formats differ only in the number of mantissa digits. The rest of the formats, including the range of the mantissa, is the same. Single-precision data occupies four bytes and double-precision data occupies eight bytes. The mantissa is stored in the first three (or seven) bytes, with the least-significant bytes first (following the custom of the PC's microprocessor). The exponent is stored last, occupying the last byte. We could outline the four or eight bytes like this:

M7 M6 M5 M4 M3 M2 M1 E

The exponent (E) is stored as a power of 2, biased 128. This means that an exponent of 0 would be stored as 128 (hex 80) and an exponent of -3 would be stored as 125 (hex 7D).

The mantissa is stored as a normalized binary fraction, with the first, or high-order, bit implied. The high-order bit of the high-order byte (byte M1), is used to store the sign: 0 for positive values, and 1 for negative values. The sign bit occupies the place that belongs to (but isn't used by) the implied high-order mantissa bit.

The program on the next page shows how to decode a floating-point number. This example illustrates the above discussion and ought to help you understand the format if you are having trouble.

```
100 INPUT "Enter any value ",SINGLE
110 ADDRESS = VARPTR (SINGLE)
120 PRINT "The hex bytes are "
130 FOR I = 0 TO 3
140   H = PEEK (ADDRESS + I)
150    IF H < 16 THEN PRINT "0";
160    PRINT HEX$ (H);" ";
170 NEXT
180 PRINT
190 E#  = PEEK (ADDRESS + 3)
200 M1# = PEEK (ADDRESS + 2)
210 M2# = PEEK (ADDRESS + 1)
220 M3# = PEEK (ADDRESS + 0)
230 EXPONENT# = E# - 128
240 SIGN = M1# / 128
250 M1# = 128 + M1# MOD 128
260 MANTISSA# = M1# /  256 + M2# / (256 * 256)
    + M3# / (256 * 256 * 256)
270 VALUE# = MANTISSA# * 2 ^ EXPONENT#
280 IF SIGN THEN VALUE# = - VALUE#
290 PRINT "This decoded value is "; VALUE#
300 PRINT
310 GOTO 100
```

Note that lines 190 through 220 isolate the four bytes with the single-precision format, using variable names that correspond to the notation we used to represent the mantissa bytes. We stated earlier that the exponent is stored in a biased format; line 230 removes the bias, giving us an exponent ranging from -128 to $+127$. Lines 240 and 250 take care of the high-order bit of the most-significant mantissa byte: 240 records the bit setting as the sign, and line 250 puts the implied 1-bit into place. Then, line 260 puts the three mantissa bytes together into a single value, which has its decimal point (or binary point, if you will) just before the first bit place. Line 270 then factors in the exponent value, line 280 applies the sign, and—voila!—we've successfully decoded the value of BASIC's floating-point format.

With the floating-point formats done, we can now take a look at how BASIC stores strings.

String Data Formats in Interpreted BASIC

String values are stored in two parts: a string descriptor that holds the length and offset location of the string; and the string value itself, which is a series of ASCII characters.

The string descriptor is three bytes long. The first byte contains the string length, which limits the maximum size of a string to 255 bytes. The next two bytes provide the data-segment offset to the actual string value. The actual string value has no special format; it is simply stored as a series of bytes at the indicated address.

When the VARPTR function is applied to a string, it returns the off-set location of the string descriptor. From the string descriptor, we can get the offset address of the string itself. The following program demonstrates the process of finding and decoding this information:

```
100 INPUT "Enter any string ",OUR.STRING$
110 DESCRIPTOR.ADDRESS = VARPTR (OUR.STRING$)
120 PRINT "The string pointer is at hex ";
130 PRINT HEX$ (DESCRIPTOR.ADDRESS)
140 STRING.LENGTH = PEEK (DESCRIPTOR.ADDRESS)
150 PRINT "The length of the string is";
160 PRINT STRING.LENGTH
170 STRING.ADDRESS = PEEK (DESCRIPTOR.ADDRESS + 1)
        + 256 * PEEK (DESCRIPTOR.ADDRESS + 2)
180 PRINT "The string value is at hex ";
190 PRINT HEX$ (STRING.ADDRESS)
200 PRINT "The string value is ";
210 FOR I = 0 TO STRING.LENGTH - 1
220   PRINT CHR$ (PEEK (I + STRING.ADDRESS));
230 NEXT I
240 PRINT : PRINT
250 GOTO 100
```

String Data Formats in Compiled BASIC

The format for string data is quite different for compiled BASIC. While there is no difference in the *type* of string data allowed, there is a difference in the *amount* of string data allowed. In interpreted BASIC, the length of the string is recorded as an unsigned 1-byte integer, which allows a length of 0 to 255 characters. In compiled BASIC, the length is recorded as a signed 2-byte integer, which allows a length of 0 to 32,767 characters (the possible negative values are ignored).

As in interpreted BASIC, strings in compiled BASIC are accessed indirectly through a string descriptor. The memory address associated with the variable name—the address given by VARPTR (NAME$)—points to the string descriptor rather than to the string itself. The string descriptor consists of two fields containing the string length and the data-segment offset of the actual string value. The only difference between compiled and interpreted BASIC is that the length field is two bytes for compiled BASIC and only one byte for interpreted BASIC.

We can examine compiled strings with the following program. To belabor what should be obvious, note that the details of this program are peculiar to compiled BASIC and so cannot be tested with interpreted BASIC. This program differs from the interpreted BASIC program given in the previous section only in line 140 (where we pick up the string length) and in line 170 (in the PEEK offsets used to pick up the string location).

```
100 INPUT "Enter any string ",OUR.STRING$
110 DESCRIPTOR.ADDRESS = VARPTR (OUR.STRING$)
120 PRINT "The string pointer is at hex ";
130 PRINT HEX$ (DESCRIPTOR.ADDRESS)
140 STRING.LENGTH = PEEK (DESCRIPTOR.ADDRESS)
      + 256 * PEEK (DESCRIPTOR.ADDRESS + 1)
150 PRINT "The length of the string is";
160 PRINT STRING.LENGTH
170 STRING.ADDRESS = PEEK (DESCRIPTOR.ADDRESS + 2)
      + 256 * PEEK (DESCRIPTOR.ADDRESS + 3)
180 PRINT "The string value is at hex ";
190 PRINT HEX$ (STRING.ADDRESS)
200 PRINT "The string value is ";
210 FOR I = 0 TO STRING.LENGTH - 1
220   PRINT CHR$ (PEEK (I + STRING.ADDRESS));
230 NEXT I
240 PRINT : PRINT
250 GOTO 100
```

Interpreted BASIC Assembler Interfaces

In this section, we'll be covering the interface rules that apply to assembly-language interfaces called from interpreted BASIC programs. We will discuss only CALLed subroutines, not USR functions. In my opinion, USR functions involve annoying and unnecessary complications, and inherently possess special problems that may vary enormously between IBM and non-IBM members of the extended PC family. In general, I do not advise the use of USR functions.

Interpreted BASIC makes use of a standard interface convention that fits nicely into the customary pattern for assembly-language connections. Here is the essence of BASIC's interface convention:

- All parameters are passed by placing their offset addresses on the stack, a format known as call-by-name. This means that assembly-language subroutines can both access and change the values of parameters; it also means that addresses and not values appear on the stack, so accessing the values requires several steps.

- Parameters are passed in the order they are written, as they are in most other languages (except C; ☞ see page 377). This means that the first parameter is closer to the bottom of the stack and the last parameter is closer to the top.

- Subroutines are invoked by a FAR CALL and must therefore finish with a FAR RETurn instruction.

- The subroutine is responsible for removing parameters from the stack, as in most other languages (except C; ☞ see page 377). This means, among other things, that the subroutine must be passed a fixed number of parameters, which is known in advance.

- The AX register is not used to return values or error codes, unlike many other languages. Any information passed back by the subroutine must be passed by a change of the parameter data.

- BASIC sets up and maintains the segment, code, and stack registers. The other registers may be changed as needed.

We'll describe details of an assembly-language interface routine in terms of the five logical levels that we discussed earlier in this chapter and in Chapter 8 (☞ see page 165). Levels 1 and 2, the assembler overhead, can be coded like this:

```
MY_SEG      SEGMENT
            ASSUME   CS:MY_SEG
MY_PROC     PROC     FAR
            ; levels 3 through 5 appear here
MY_PROC     ENDP
MY_SEG      ENDS
END
```

The names MY_SEG and MY_PROC are arbitrary. In interpreted BASIC, we can choose any workable names to identify the subroutine, but in compiled BASIC, there are restrictions.

If you compare this routine with the general interface routine discussed in Chapter 8, you will notice two differences. First, in this example the SEGMENT statement is not followed by the classification 'CODE'; furthermore, it does not have a PUBLIC MY_PROC statement. Both of these changes, and the fact that the procedure name is irrelevant to BASIC, have to do with the fact that assembly-language interfaces are not linked with interpreted BASIC. For programs that are linked, such as the rest of the languages covered in this chapter, these items are important.

The next level to consider, level 3, provides the entry and exit code for the subroutine. The form of the code is as follows.

```
PUSH    BP
MOV     BP,SP
; levels 4 and 5 appear here
POP     BP
RET     XXX
```

All four of these instructions are standard and should be the same for all assembly-language interfaces. The one changeable item, shown as XXX in this example, represents the number of parameter bytes to be popped off the stack. The value of XXX must be twice the number of parameters that were passed when BASIC CALLed the subroutine because each parameter causes two bytes to be pushed onto the stack. So, for example, if three parameters were passed we would replace XXX with 6 to clean the stack; if there were no parameters, then we'd use a zero. Incidentally, the RET instruction used in this example is assembled into a FAR RETurn instruction based on the PROC FAR command that appeared at the beginning of the routine.

The next level, level 4, concerns accessing and changing the parameters. As we discussed on page 167, the address of the last parameter will be on the stack at the location referred to as [BP + 6], the parameter before that at [BP + 8], and so on.

By way of illustration, let's assume there are three parameters, all integers, and that we want to load them into the AX, BX, and CX registers (for whatever reason). Here is the level 4 code that would get those parameters:

```
MOV     SI,[BP+10]          ; get address of first parameter
MOV     AX,[SI]             ; get first value
MOV     SI,[BP+8]           ; get address of second parameter
MOV     BX,[SI]             ; get second value
MOV     SI,[BP+6]           ; get address of third parameter
MOV     CX,[SI]             ; get third value
```

Note that we get the parameter values in two steps: First we get the address (which we park in the SI register, just because it's a convenient place to put it), and then we use the address to get the value (which we put where we actually want it).

That illustrates just the first half of level 4; the second half concerns moving values back to the BASIC program by storing them in the parameters. We do this by getting the parameter address (again), and using that address to store the new value. For example, let's assume that we have calculated a new value and have it in the DX register. We wish to pass it back to BASIC as a new value for the first parameter. We can do it using two simple instructions.

```
MOV     SI,[BP+10]                          ; get address of first parameter (again)
MOV     [SI],DX                             ; pass value back, from DX
```

To provide a complete example, here is an assembly-language sub-routine that passes back the values of the SS and SP registers, a technique that makes it possible for a BASIC program to investigate its own stack. Normally, there would be no good reason to do that, but we might want to play with it for the simple reason that it can be very educational. The subroutine assumes that it is called with two integer parameters; it places the current stack segment (SS) and stack pointer (SP) values into these parameters. Here is our routine:

```
STACKINFO SEGMENT
          ASSUME  CS:STACKINFO
GETSTACK  PROC    FAR
          PUSH    BP
          MOV     BP,SP
          MOV     SI,[BP+8]
          MOV     [SI],SS
          MOV     SI,[BP+6]
          MOV     [SI],SP
          POP     BP
          RET     4
GETSTACK  ENDP
STACKINFO ENDS
          END
```

Compiled BASIC Assembler Interfaces

Anyone who has worked extensively with BASIC for the PC family is no doubt familiar with the sometimes maddening differences and incompatibilities between compiled and interpreted BASIC. Here we'll note only the significant difference that applies to assembly-language interfacing, and then work through an example.

In interpreted BASIC, the normal way of working with assembly-language interfaces is to stuff them into some memory location (one of the most annoying and error-prone programming chores in BASIC), set a variable to the memory offset address of the interface, then CALL the variable name.

By contrast, compiled BASIC gives us two primary methods for working with assembly-language interfaces—one that closely matches the interpreted BASIC method, and one that follows the standard conventions for compiled languages.

The first method closely follows the interpreted BASIC method in substance, although the form differs. To illustrate, we'll let LOCATION% stand for the BASIC variable name that has been set to the memory offset location of the assembly-language interface, and we'll let PARAMETERS stand for any parameters passed to the interface. With that setup, in interpreted BASIC we would invoke the interface like this:

```
CALL LOCATION% (PARAMETERS)
```

In compiled BASIC, the format used to invoke the interface would be quite different, although the net result is exactly the same. It is done like this:

```
CALL ABSOLUTE (PARAMETERS,LOCATION%)
```

One critical difference in the compiled BASIC version is that the variable LOCATION% must be an integer. In interpreted BASIC, any numeric variable is acceptable.

Some of the mechanics of this CALL ABSOLUTE operation are worth discussing. In compiled BASIC, all calls are actually conventional calls to external routines that are linked to the compiled programs. This is the standard mechanism that is used by all compiled languages. Compiled BASIC actually simulates the equivalent of interpreted BASIC's CALL LOCATION% through a library subroutine named ABSOLUTE. In other words, ABSOLUTE is not part of the BASIC language, in the sense that ON ERROR or CHAIN are parts of the BASIC language. Instead, ABSOLUTE is simply the name of an external subroutine residing in BASIC's linking library. The subroutine ABSOLUTE performs a simple operation: It uses its parameters (including the LOCATION% parameter) to simulate the CALL LOCATION% operation that interpreted BASIC performs.

Before we continue on to the other method of invoking assembly-language interfaces in compiled BASIC, we should comment on the problems involved in placing an assembly-language interface into memory. The mechanisms used to place these interfaces into memory are the same for both interpreted and compiled BASIC: It is usually done either with the BLOAD statement to load the interface from a file, or by POKEing it into memory, byte-by-byte. Although the mechanisms are the same for both compiled and interpreted BASIC, the problems of finding an appropriate memory location can be quite different, depending on circumstances and programming techniques. You will note that so far I have successfully ducked treating this topic, and I will continue to do so here. This particular subject is a messy one and really a specialty area for books on BASIC.

The other method for using assembly-language interfaces in compiled BASIC is the standard method used by all normal DOS programming languages. Modules, such as assembly-language interfaces, are separately prepared and are stored either in the form of distinct object files (with a filename extension of .OBJ) or inside an object-file library (with a filename extension of .LIB). In either case, separate modules, such as compiled BASIC programs and assembled assembly-language interfaces, are combined by the LINK program as we described in the previous chapter.

We're going to look at how this interface routine is used from both sides—from the BASIC side and from the assembly-language side. From the BASIC side, an assembly-language interface is invoked like this:

```
CALL NAME (PARAMETERS)
```

The PARAMETERS are the same as those used in the previous method or in interpreted BASIC. The NAME is the same name that appears in the assembly-language interface and identifies the desired routine.

The steps followed by the compiled BASIC code in calling a subroutine are the same as those followed by interpreted BASIC; the same interface rules apply to how the stack is used, how parameters are placed on the stack, and how the call is made (a FAR CALL, requiring a FAR RETurn). Because of this, we will use the routine from the previous section about interpreted BASIC (the one that passes back the current stack-segment and stack-pointer settings) and point out the differences:

```
STACKINFO SEGMENT
          ASSUME   CS:STACKINFO
          PUBLIC   GETSTACK
GETSTACK  PROC     FAR
          PUSH     BP
          MOV      BP,SP
          MOV      SI,[BP+0]
          MOV      [SI],SS
          MOV      SI,[BP+6]
          MOV      [SI],SP
          POP      BP
          RET      4
GETSTACK  ENDP
STACKINFO ENDS
          END
```

The one new requirement to link this sort of assembly-language interface to a compiled BASIC program is that the name of the subroutine must be made "public"; that is, it must be declared as an official name for use by the assembler. This is done in the third line of this routine, which reads PUBLIC GETSTACK. This is the one difference between this routine and the one on page 365. (Actually, the PUBLIC statement would do no harm in the previous routine but it would serve no purpose, since interpreted BASIC does not use it.)

To show the use of this sort of assembly-language interface, here is a compilable BASIC program that uses it and displays the results:

```
100 ' demonstrate the use of linked interfaces
110 '
120 I% = 0
130 J% = 0
140 CALL GETSTACK (I%,J%)
150 PRINT "In the midst of a program"
160 PRINT "  the stack segment is ";HEX$(I%)
170 PRINT "  the stack pointer is ";HEX$(J%)
180 GOSUB 200
190 GOTO 270
200 ' our go-sub subroutine
210 '
220 CALL GETSTACK (I%,J%)
230 PRINT "In the GO-SUB subroutine"
240 PRINT "  the stack segment is ";HEX$(I%)
250 PRINT "  the stack pointer is ";HEX$(J%)
260 RETURN
270 END
```

There are several things worth noting in this program. When we call the assembly-language subroutine (in lines 140 and 220), we call it by its name, GETSTACK, which is the name that appears in the PUBLIC statement of the assembly-language code. The names must agree for the linking process to work. (On the other hand, the name of the segment in the assembly-language program, STACKINFO, is arbitrary and does not matter, as long as it is used consistently inside of the assembly.) Also note that both the calling BASIC program and the called assembly-language program should agree on the number of parameters being used. The RET 4 statement, which is the last working instruction in the assembly, pops four bytes of parameters off the stack, which corresponds to two parameters with two bytes per parameter. (A sophisticated and tricky assembly-language routine can accept a variable number of parameters, but the methods are too advanced for us to do justice to here.)

This particular sample program reports on the state of the stack twice (as encountered inside the assembly-language routine): once in the linear flow of statements, and once in a GOSUB routine. The difference between the two stack-pointer values allows us to discover how the use of GOSUBs affects BASIC's stack. Run this example to learn the answer.

Here are the steps necessary to prepare and combine compiled BASIC programs and assembly-language interfaces, using the preceding programs as an example. First, assuming that we have our assembly-language source code in a file named GETSTACK.ASM, we would assemble it with this command:

```
MASM GETSTACK;
```

This would result in the creation of an object file named GETSTACK.OBJ. Next, assuming that we have our BASIC source code in a file named TEST.BAS—which must be an ASCII file, not a tokenized BASIC file—we would compile it with this command:

```
BASCOM TEST;
```

This would result in the creation of an object file named TEST.OBJ. Next, we would link the two together with this command:

```
LINK TEST+GETSTACK
```

This would result in the creation of a program file named TEST.EXE.

PASCAL

In this section, we'll discuss the IBM PC Pascal compiler and its generic cousin, Microsoft Pascal. When we discuss Pascal data formats, we will generally indicate which items are peculiar to these compilers and which are standard Pascal. If you are using any version of these compilers, the information we give here will apply in detail; otherwise, you should be able to use the discussion here as a basis for determining the specifics of your particular compiler.

You should be aware that there are a few significant differences between version 1 and version 2 of the IBM PC Pascal compiler. We will note them when discussing data formats.

Pascal Data Formats

There are three familiar data formats used by Pascal: integer, floating point (known as REAL in Pascal terminology), and string. There is also a specialty type known as set. Within the types, there are quite a few variations, particularly within the integer type.

Integer Data Formats

We'll begin with the integer type, in all its variations. Integers are stored as binary numbers and placed in memory with the least-significant byte first. Integers can be one, two, or four bytes long, either signed or unsigned. Of the six formats that this description suggests, five are actually used (4-byte unsigned is not), and several of the formats do double duty from Pascal's point of view.

Single byte integers are available in signed and unsigned forms. The signed form has a range of −128 through +127, and is called SINT (apparently for short integer) in Pascal; the unsigned form has the range of 0 through 255 and is called BYTE. Neither SINT nor BYTE are a part of standard Pascal, and since they are not discussed very much in the compiler's documentation, it's easy to overlook them.

Two-byte integers are also available in signed and unsigned forms. The signed form has a range of −32,768 through +32,767 and is called INTEGER; it is a standard Pascal format. The unsigned form has the range of 0 through 65,535 and is called WORD; it is not a standard Pascal format. The INTEGER format is, of course, the most universal one for programming languages in the PC family; for example, it exactly matches the format used by BASIC. The unsigned 16-bit WORD format also has its own special importance. All address facilities in Pascal, such as ADR and ADS, are based on the WORD format. (☞ See further notes about addresses in Pascal on page 375.) Pascal's WORD format is the same as the standard unsigned 16-bit integers used in the PC family and the same as the UNSIGNED INT format used in C.

Four-byte integers are available only in signed format and only in versions of the compiler numbered 2.0 and later. This format has the range of −2,147,483,647 through +2,147,483,647 and is called INTEGER4. (Note that there should be—and probably is—one additional negative value, although there isn't one the way the compiler defines this format. If you think that you need it, you're probably in trouble anyway.) This 32-bit integer format is not a part of standard Pascal nor is it used by many other PC languages. However, it is a part of C, where it is called LONG INT (☞ see page 378). The INTEGER4 format is not fully integrated with the other Pascal integer formats; in many circumstances where any other integer format can be used, INTEGER4 cannot.

The standard Pascal language provides for a generalization of the integer in a data type known as an enumeration data type. For all practical purposes, each enumeration data type consists of unsigned integers, from 0 up, that have been given new names. The actual data format for all enumeration data types consists of unsigned integers in either 1-byte (BYTE) or 2-byte (WORD) format, depending upon whether the number of values will fit into a byte. BOOLEAN, the most common specialty type, is simply a predeclared, two-value enumeration type. As such, it occupies one byte and takes on the values of 0 or 1 only.

String Data Formats

Standard Pascal has a character type called CHAR, which consists of a single ASCII character stored in a single byte. Depending upon our viewpoint, we can consider the CHAR data type either as a special case of the BYTE type or as an element of the string data types. However, Pascal treats CHAR as its own distinct format.

There are two string formats: One, a part of standard Pascal, is called STRING and holds fixed-length strings of ASCII characters; the other, an extension to Pascal, is called LSTRING and holds variable-length strings of characters. The majority of Pascal compilers have added variable-length strings to the standard language, but they have done it in several different ways. We will be covering the format used by the IBM/Microsoft compilers.

Fixed-length strings are simply stored as a string of bytes, with no special delimitation or format. Note that if S is a fixed-length string, then in Pascal notation, the first character of that string is S[1]. The address of a fixed-length string is the same as the address of its first character.

Variable-length strings are stored as a string of character bytes, preceded by a 1-byte length code in the form of an unsigned integer (a BYTE, in the notation of this compiler); therefore, variable-length strings can range from 0 through 255 characters. For a variable-length string, as for a fixed-length one, S[1] is the first character of the string and S[0] refers to the byte that holds the string's current length. The address of a variable-length string is the address of its length byte (S[0]), rather than of its first data byte (S[1]).

❏ NOTE: *The length of any string must be declared in Pascal. For a fixed-length string, the length matches the number of bytes in the string; variable-length strings use one additional byte.*

The SET Data Format

The SET type is a specialty item for Pascal, something not shared with most other languages. Sets must be based on an enumeration data type, and the enumeration type must have no more than 256 elements. The data format for sets assigns one distinct bit for each element in the underlying enumeration data type. If the element in the enumeration type is in the set, then the corresponding bit is set to 1. The size of set data depends upon how many bits are needed; that is, on how many elements are in the enumeration data type. However, unlike what you might expect, set data is sized in 2-byte units, so a set of eight elements occupies two bytes, rather than the single byte that it could be stored in. The minimum size of set data is two bytes (used for sets with from one to sixteen elements); the maximum is 32 bytes (used for sets based on an enumeration data type of from 241 through 256 elements).

The bits in set data are assigned from left to right and the bit coding corresponds to the order of the elements declared in the enumeration data type. For example, the first element in the enumeration type corresponds to the high-order bit of the first byte (in hex, 80); the next element in the enumeration type is the next bit (in hex, 40), and so on. Unused bits—which round the size of the data to two bytes, or 16 bits—are set to 0, as you might expect.

Floating-Point Data Formats

Floating-point data formats, called REAL in Pascal terminology, present some interesting complications. There are three formats that we must consider. The first format applies to version 1 of the compiler and it exactly matches the format used by BASIC for single-precision numbers; for this discussion only, we'll call this format *old-real*. The other two formats apply to version 2 (and later versions) of the compiler; these formats correspond to a standard form also used by the 8087 math coprocessor. These two formats are known, in the terminology of this Pascal compiler, as REAL4 and REAL8; for this discussion, we'll call them *new-real*.

❑ NOTE: *There is no good, uniform way to convert data between the old-real format used by the old compiler and the new-real formats used by the new compiler.*

We'll first discuss the old-real format briefly, so we can compare it with the other two formats. ☞ For more detailed coverage, see the discussion of BASIC's single-precision format on page 357 since the two formats are the same. We assume you are familiar with both floating-point arithmetic and the general data formats used to store them; we will be covering the particulars of these floating-point data formats, not the basic principles of floating-point numbers.

The old-real format is stored in four bytes, which we can summarize like this:

M3 M2 M1 E

where the M bytes are the mantissa, stored with the least-significant bytes first. The high-order bit of M1 contains the sign of the value (1 indicates negative); in place of the sign bit is an implied high-order mantissa bit. The E byte contains the binary exponent in excess-128 form (that is, $E - 128$ gives us the true exponent). The mantissa is treated as a fraction; that is, the "decimal" point (binary point, really) is to the left of the implied high-order bit.

The new-real formats differ in all essential details from the old-real. Between themselves, they follow the same design and only differ in the number of bits given to each part.

Each format consists of three fields: a sign, an exponent, and a mantissa. They are stored in that order, with the least significant bits first. In other words, the high-order bit of the last, or rightmost, byte contains the sign, followed by the high-order bit of the exponent, and so forth. Following this pattern, the least-significant bits of the mantissa will be found in the first, or leftmost, byte.

The sign field, for both formats, is one bit, with 1 indicating negative numbers and 0 positive numbers.

The exponent field is in the form of an excess-notation integer. In the case of REAL4, the exponent fills eight bits and is in excess-127 form (that is, subtracting 127 from the apparent exponent value will give the true exponent value). In the case of REAL8, the exponent occupies 11 bits and is in excess-1,023 form. Therefore, the range of exponents for REAL4 is from -127 through $+128$, and for REAL8 is from $-1,023$ through $+1,024$. Note, by way of comparison, that the old-real format (which is also used by BASIC) is in excess-128 form, instead of 127 as we see here. The new-real formats give slightly more dynamic range for very large numbers, while the old-real format gives more dynamic range to very small numbers. Note that, unlike BASIC's single- and double-precision formats, REAL4 and REAL8 differ in the dynamic range of their exponents as well as in the precision of the mantissa.

The mantissa field is in the form of a binary fraction, with the high-order 1-bit implied (as it is with the old-real format and with BASIC). The logical decimal (or binary) point is located to the right of the implied high-order bit of the mantissa. For REAL4, there are 23 mantissa bits (plus the implied high-order bit), and for REAL8, there are 52 mantissa bits (plus the implied bit).

The parts of REAL4 add up to 32 bits, or four bytes; those of REAL8 add up to 64 bits, or eight bytes. Note, however, that unlike old-real and the BASIC formats, the parts of REAL4 and REAL8 do not fit neatly into bytes. Here is a crude diagram of these two formats:

REAL4	REAL8
M3 M2 E2M1 SE1	M7 M6 M5 M4 M3 M2 E2M1 SE1

The mantissa bytes, M2 through M7, are pure mantissa bits. The other bytes contain a mixture of fields and parts. The bytes labeled SE1 in both formats contain the sign bit and the first seven bits of the exponent, like this:

Bit								Description
7	6	5	4	3	2	1	0	
S	.	.	.	.	.	.	.	Sign bit
.	E	E	E	E	E	E	E	High-order exponent bits

The bytes labeled E2M1 contain the remainder of the exponent bits (one bit for REAL4, four bits for REAL8), and the first seven or four bits of the mantissa, like this:

REAL4 Bit								REAL8 Bit								Description
7	6	5	4	3	2	1	0	7	6	5	4	3	2	1	0	
E	.	.	.	.	.	.	.	E	E	E	E	.	.	.	.	Low-order exponent bits
.	M	M	M	M	M	M	M	.	.	.	.	M	M	M	M	Mantissa bits

Note that while these two new-real formats and the old-real format operate on the same principles, they differ in nearly every detail: order and size of parts, exponent excess notation, and byte boundaries.

Earlier in this chapter, as an aid to understanding BASIC's single-precision floating-point format (which is the same as Pascal version 1's old-real format), we showed a program that decodes the bits of a number and constructs the value that they represent. The same exercise can be performed in Pascal version 1 to interpret old-real, or in Pascal version 2 to interpret REAL4 and REAL8 formats. The principles are the same for all three formats, though the details are more complicated for REAL4 and REAL8 because the fields do not fit so neatly within byte boundaries.

For compatibility reasons, note that version 1 of the compiler has a floating-point format compatible with BASIC, and that version 2 has formats compatible with most other languages, including IBM/Microsoft Fortran and Lattice/Microsoft C, and with the 8087 and 80287 math co-processors.

Pascal Assembler Interfaces

Here we will cover important details needed for using parameters in Pascal. We will borrow from the Pascal-specific example shown on page 199, stripped down to its key components:

```
1     INTERFACE SEGMENT  'CODE'
2               PUBLIC   SEGREAD
3     SEGREAD   PROC     FAR
4               PUSH     BP
5               MOV      BP,SP
6               ...
7               POP      BP
8               RET      10
9     SEGREAD   ENDP
10    INTERFACE ENDS
11              END
```

In line 1, the name INTERFACE is arbitrary; however, the classification 'CODE', in single quotes, is necessary to link this routine successfully to this Pascal compiler.

In line 2, the name of any routine, such as SEGREAD, must be declared PUBLIC in order for the linker to connect it to the routines that use it. In line 3, the PROCedure must be declared FAR because Pascal makes far-type calls to external routines.

Lines 4 and 5, and 7 and 8 represent the standard entry and exit code, which maintains the stack. The value 10 in line 8 represents the amount of stack space the parameters used, a subject we'll discuss next.

In the standard calling conventions for the PC family, subroutine parameters, in one form or another, are placed on the stack. There are two basic approaches that programs can take to placing parameters on the stack: Either the parameter value can be placed on the stack, or a pointer to the value in memory can be placed on the stack. There are advantages to both approaches; the first allows easier access to values; the second allows a subroutine to pass data back by modifying parameter variables. Pascal uses both methods, and within limits, allows us to choose which is used. (By contrast, BASIC only uses the second method, placing the address of the parameter on the stack.)

If, when we define a subroutine, we specify a parameter as VAR or VARS, we are instructing Pascal to place the address of that parameter on the stack. (From the point of view of Pascal, using VAR or VARS is giving a subroutine permission to change the value of a variable; in practice, it means we're giving the subroutine the address of a variable.) If we specify VAR, then the address is passed as a data-segment offset, a single 2-byte word. If we specify VARS, then the address is passed as a fully segmented address, with segment-paragraph and relative-offset portions, occupying two 2-byte words. The difference is of considerable importance because it affects the number of parameter bytes to be removed from the stack in a RETurn statement.

On the other hand, if we do not specify VAR, Pascal will defend the parameter value from being permanently modified by the subroutine. This can be done in two ways, and it matters greatly which is used. If the value is of the right type and can be placed on the stack (integers, for example), then the value itself is placed on the stack; otherwise, a safe copy of the value is made in memory and the address of the copy is placed on the stack. The difference is very important for two reasons: one is that the called routine will access the parameter differently, either getting the value off the stack or getting the value through an address on the stack; the other is that getting the value through an address on the stack is much less efficient for the calling program.

When setting up an assembly-language interface routine, it is important to know which parameter method is in effect. You may find out by using the same simple method that I have used: taking the available information and using common sense to figure out what you think is happening for any given set of parameters. Or you might run tests, either by running a couple of trial programs or by inspecting the compiler's pseudo-assembler listing of the code it generates.

If you are uncertain, you can force all parameters to be passed through simple addresses by declaring them as VAR. Using VAR uniformly has the advantage of producing a simple, consistent pattern of parameter handling. In fact, about the only advantage of not using VAR for simple variables is that VARS can save two machine-language instructions, a very minor benefit.

A subroutine can return a value if it is declared as a FUNCTION in Pascal. If the subroutine returns a sufficiently simple value, then the calling Pascal routine expects the return value to be placed in the AX register. Otherwise, the value is returned by storing it in memory at an offset address that is placed on the stack following the function's parameters.

In effect, Pascal creates one additional VAR-type parameter for the function subroutine, and the subroutine's function value is then returned into that parameter.

To show how parameters are obtained through the stack, let's create an example. Suppose an assembly-language interface routine is declared in Pascal like this:

```
PROCEDURE  EXAMPLE (I : INTEGER; VAR J : INTEGER);
EXTERNAL;
```

The assembly-language subroutine would find that the first parameter, I, was on the stack at an offset of [BP + 8]. To put that value into the AX register, we would code this instruction in assembly language:

```
MOV    AX,[BP+8]
```

On the other hand, the second parameter, J, has its address placed on the stack at an offset of [BP + 6], since it's the next parameter. So to put that value into the AX register takes two steps: one to get the address from the stack, and the other to get the value of J, like this:

```
MOV    BX,[BP+6]
MOV    AX,[BX]
```

Modifying the value of J would reverse that process:

```
MOV    BX,[BP+6]
MOV    [BX],AX
```

The value of I can't be modified by our subroutine, since we don't know where I is: we only know that a copy of its value was placed on the stack.

These principles, together with intelligence and some research into the particulars of your situation, should provide you with all you need to successfully create assembly-language interfaces for use with Pascal.

THE C LANGUAGE

Our discussion of C will center around version 1.04 of the Lattice/Microsoft C compiler and the other related compilers (some of which are available under the Lattice and Lifeboat names). As with our discussions of other languages, the specific information that we give here is based on this particular compiler, but also applies, in varying degrees, to other versions and to completely different compilers.

It is worth pausing to note that the Lattice/Microsoft C compiler uses what is called the small memory model, which means that a program's code and data are restricted to segments no larger than 64K each.

By contrast, the medium memory model uses segmented code addresses (which allows program code to grow to any size, while leaving data restricted to 64K), and the large memory model uses segmented addresses for both code and data (which allows both to grow to any size). The compiled BASIC and Pascal discussed earlier both use the medium model (although Pascal makes limited use of segmented addresses for data, so it has some aspects of the large model). Later versions of the Lattice C compiler (a close relative of the compiler we are discussing) can use any of the three memory models, at our option. The availability of three memory models in one compiler greatly complicates the discussion of interfaces (a complication that we will avoid here). Instead, we will concentrate on the small model.

The use of the small model limits the size of program code and data, but it is the most efficient format. We'll see the effects of the small model in the data address format, ☞ mentioned on page 379, in subroutine entry and exit, and in parameter access, ☞ mentioned on page 382.

C Data Formats

There are three main classes of data for C: integer, floating point, and string. For the Lattice/Microsoft C compiler, there are four distinct integer formats and two floating-point formats.

Integer Data Formats

We'll begin with the four integer formats: CHAR, INT, UNSIGNED, and LONG. The CHAR format occupies one byte and is treated as an unsigned integer whose values can range from 0 through 255. The INT format occupies a 2-byte word and is treated as a signed value, so it can range from −32,768 through +32,767. The UNSIGNED format (also known as UNSIGNED INT in more formal C terminology) occupies a 2-byte word. It is treated as an unsigned value and can range from 0 through 65,535. The LONG format occupies four bytes and is treated as a signed value, so it can range from −2,147,483,648 through +2,147,483,547.

While these four integer formats seem to be fairly straightforward, there are several things worth discussing about them. First, we should note that the general definition of the C language allows for LONG and SHORT, and signed and UNSIGNED versions of most of the fundamental data types. With this compiler, SHORT INT is a 2-byte signed value (the same as INT), and there is neither an UNSIGNED version of the 4-byte LONG, nor a signed version of the 1-byte CHAR. Address values appear in the form of offsets to the data segment. As you would expect, they are stored in the 16-bit UNSIGNED INT format.

The C language, in general, is a little fuzzy about the relationship between characters and numbers, and particularly about the similarities and differences between CHAR and INT. For this compiler, CHARs are strictly numbers occupying one byte, with a range in value of 0 to 255. However, CHARs can also be expressed in character form. For example, the character constant Q translates into the numeric value 81; but if we were to write 81 in a C program, it would be considered a type INT and not a 1-byte CHAR—unless we did something to force it into CHAR format. Because C does not make a firm distinction between characters and numbers (unlike Pascal), we are able to convert values between integer formats (such as INT or UNSIGNED) and character formats (CHAR, or elements of strings).

String Data Formats

Strings are handled in C in a way that reflects the ambiguous treatment of characters as either characters or numbers. In C, a character string is an array of CHARs followed by a zero character, which marks the string's end. Using a zero character to end a string means that strings can have any length, since there isn't an explicit length indicator (as there is in Pascal or BASIC) that could set a limit to the maximum size. But because there is no length indicator, the string must be scanned from beginning to end to find the length of a string. And since the string ends in a zero character, the zero character, CHR$(0) in BASIC's notation, cannot be part of a string—hardly a loss at all. Using a zero character to end a string also means that there is no distinction in form between fixed- and variable-length strings.

The C compiler takes on the task of adding the ending zero byte to any string that we show as a literal value; we don't have to put it there. For example, if we write *abc* in a program, the C compiler creates a 4-byte string which consists of the three bytes we wrote, followed by the zero byte. Be aware that, although the C compiler will add the zero byte to any string constant and the standard C string-handling subroutines will take care of the zero byte as needed, the zero byte doesn't appear by magic. If we write any string-handling programs of our own—a common thing to do—we need to take this byte into account, looking for it and creating it as needed.

Floating-Point Data Formats

There are two floating-point formats used by this compiler: FLOAT and LONG FLOAT (or DOUBLE). The FLOAT format is four bytes long; the LONG FLOAT format is eight bytes long. They follow the standard format used by the 8087 and 80287 math coprocessors and by many programming languages. In this discussion, we'll just outline the two formats. They are described in greater detail on page 373 under the names REAL4 and REAL8.

The two floating-point formats are easiest to understand if we view them as a string of bits (32 bits for FLOAT, 64 bits for LONG FLOAT), stored "back-words," with the most-significant bits in the last bytes. We'll describe the floating-point formats in bit order, starting with the most-significant bit.

The first, most-significant bit is a sign bit: 0 for positive, 1 for negative. The next group of bits (eight for FLOAT, eleven for LONG FLOAT) specifies the binary exponent in excess notation: excess 127 for FLOAT, excess 1,023 for LONG FLOAT. If we take the unsigned binary integer of the exponent bits and subtract the excess value (127 or 1,023), we obtain the true exponent value. The remaining bits (23 or 52) are the mantissa, or fractional portion. An implied high-order 1-bit belongs before the rest of the mantissa bits. The decimal point (binary point, really) belongs between the implied high-order bit and the remaining mantissa bits. ☞ On page 374, there is a table showing the layout of the sign, exponent, and mantissa bits in the four or eight bytes of these two formats.

C Assembler Interfaces

The general rules for the five-level approach to interface programming apply to our C compiler, just as they do to the other compilers we've discussed. To demonstrate the basic structure of an interface routine that will be used with the C compiler, we'll borrow a program from a previous chapter and strip it down to show just the key elements. The original program, listed on page 293, was designed to calculate the day of the week by using the DOS date and time services.

```
1              PGROUP  GROUP PROG
2     PROG     SEGMENT BYTE PUBLIC 'CODE'
3              PUBLIC  WEEKDAY
4              ASSUME  CS:PROG
5     WEEKDAY  PROC    NEAR
6              PUSH    BP
7              MOV     BP,SP
8              ...
9              POP     BP
10             RET
11    WEEKDAY  ENDP
12    PROG     ENDS
13             END
```

Line 1 is needed to help coordinate the assembly-language interface with the linking conventions used by the C compiler. In line 2, the name PROG and the classification 'CODE', in single quotes, are also needed to satisfy the linking conventions.

In line 3, the name of any routine, such as WEEKDAY, must be declared PUBLIC in order for the linker to connect it to the routines that use it. In line 4 the ASSUME is necessary to assemble this NEAR procedure, even if we are not doing any program address references. In line 5, the PROCedure must be declared NEAR because this particular C compiler makes near-type calls to external routines. This feature is unlike most other languages, and it is the first of three important departures that this C compiler makes from the most common interface rules.

Lines 6, 7, 9, and 10 represent the standard entry and exit code, which maintains the stack.

You will note that in line 10 there is no value following the RET instruction. Subroutine parameters are placed on the stack by the caller and may be removed from the stack by either the called subroutine or the caller (after the subroutine returns control). As we have seen, most programming languages have the called subroutine perform this task; we specify the number of parameter bytes to be removed in the RET instruction. However, this C compiler has the calling subroutine remove parameters from the stack, so our RET has no number following it. This is the second of three ways that C departs from conventional interface rules.

You should note that C also allows a subroutine to be called with a variable number of parameters; this is a standard part of the C language and is needed, for example, by the often-used PRINTF routine. A called routine can determine how many parameters were pushed onto the stack by checking the stack pointers and BP values.

Lines 11 through 13 are the standard items used to finish an interface routine.

Parameter Passing in C

Parameters are placed on the stack directly or indirectly. Our C compiler places parameters on the stack in reverse order from the way they are written, so that the first parameter is pushed onto the stack last and is thus nearest; that is, it has the least offset from the BP register. This is opposite from the convention used by most languages, and it's the last of the three unusual things about C interfaces.

As we've discussed elsewhere, parameters can be passed either by placing their value on the stack or by placing their address on the stack.

Unless we instruct it otherwise, our C compiler will attempt to place the value on the stack, rather than the address. This statement may be slightly deceptive because C considers many things to be addresses that we might not. For example, if we have a string variable named S, C considers the value of the name S to be an address of a string—not a string. If S is a string variable and I an integer variable, calling a subroutine with this instruction:

```
SUBR (S,I)
```

will cause the values of both S and I to be placed on the stack; the value of I is an integer, but the value of S is an address (of a string value).

In C, we can force an address to be passed as a parameter by prefixing the variable name with &, like this:

```
SUBR (S,&I)
```

which would pass the address of the variable I. In this example, the subroutine SUBR would receive two addresses, each pointing to a value. If we'd made the mistake of writing SUBR (&S,&I), we'd be passing the address of the address of a string—probably not something we'd want to do.

Newcomers to C can easily be confused by parameter passing. In my experience, it is one of the greatest sources of mistakes in the use of assembly-language interfaces with C. Use common sense and test your routines thoroughly to make sure that what is actually happening with interface parameters is what you think is happening.

For comparison with Pascal, using & in C before a subroutine parameter is equivalent to declaring the parameter VAR in Pascal: It causes an address to be passed on the stack and not a value.

Parameters are accessed from the stack and parameter values are modified in the customary way, through parameter addresses placed on the stack. The main peculiarity we need to discuss regarding C-specific interfaces is that the stack offsets will be different than those we usually encounter. Since subroutines are accessed with a NEAR call instead of a FAR call, the closest parameter on the stack will be at offset [BP+4] instead of the more customary [BP+6]; also, as we've mentioned before, the closest parameter will be the last one written, rather than the first one.

To provide a concrete example of accessing and modifying parameters, let's consider a subroutine that is called with two integers like this:

```
SUBR (&I,J)
```

and whose job is to place the value from the second parameter into the first one, making the subroutine the equivalent of the assignment statement I = J. The working code to do this would be as follows:

```
MOV     AX,[BP+6]                ; get J value
MOV     BX,[BP+4]                ; get I address
MOV     [BX],AX                  ; put J value into I
```

In C, all subroutines normally return an integer value, even when a return value isn't meaningful to us. The value can be used or ignored by the caller. (Again, C is peculiar in this regard—most other languages make a clear distinction between subroutines that do or do not return a value.) Following the usual convention, C expects this return value in the AX register. If we have a value to return, we place it in AX; if not, and we wish to be meticulous, we might want to set AX to zero before we return, to ensure that we return a consistent, non-accidental value.

A PARTING COMMENT

Although this has been a brief analysis of a very small number of programming languages, we hope it has helped put their features in perspective. To compare the merits of every language used in the PC family would be ideal, but impossible in a book of this nature. However, you may find that the criteria we used to compare our five languages can help guide you in examining other languages.

A

Installable
Device Drivers

T wo features that were introduced with the DOS-2 versions call for special discussion: the subject of installable device drivers in general, and the ANSI driver (also called ANSI.SYS) in particular. These subjects are related by their common introduction in DOS version 2.00 and by the fact that the ANSI driver is itself an installable device driver, but they are radically different topics from our programming perspective. We'll begin by looking at the device drivers in general and then move on to discuss the ANSI driver in more detail.

GENERAL OVERVIEW

DOS has the built-in capability to work with most common computer devices, such as ordinary disk drives, communications lines, printers, and, of course, the keyboard and display screen. However, many other kinds of devices can be attached to our computers. All these attachments generally require is some additional software support—called device drivers—that connect them to DOS and to DOS programs.

Since the release of version 2.00, DOS has been able to incorporate into its own operations any device driver that follows a standard set of integration rules. The device driver program is read from disk and integrated into DOS during DOS's start-up process. A disk file named CONFIG.SYS tells DOS when there is a device driver to be loaded. The name and file location of the device driver are identified by the command line DEVICE = *filespec* in the CONFIG.SYS file. For each such command, DOS locates the program file, loads it into memory, and goes through the series of steps necessary to welcome the device driver into the DOS fold.

Typically, a device driver supports a new kind of device in an old kind of way. For example, a device driver that supports a disk drive whose detailed control commands are new to DOS but whose overall features are similar to other kinds of disk drives, will most likely follow the program format laid down by its more common predecessors. Likewise, a device driver that supports the addition of a mouse or joystick may treat them as keyboard-like devices.

On the other hand, device drivers can perform functions that have little or nothing to do with the addition of new hardware devices to the computer; witness the ANSI device driver, which we'll be discussing in the following section. The ANSI device driver doesn't *add* new hardware to the computer; instead, it *modifies* the operation of the computer's standard hardware (the keyboard and the display screen).

All the technical details of writing a device driver really belong in a book specializing in DOS systems programming, but we can give you the main points here.

The device driver file itself has a nearly standard program format with some driver-specific identifying information added. There are two kinds of device drivers: those for *character devices,* which, like the keyboard, display screen, printer, or communications port, work with a serial stream of characters, and those for *block devices,* which, like a disk drive, read and write random blocks of data identified by some form of block address. Character devices are identified by their own names (similar to the names LPT1: or COM1:) and can be treated like files. Block devices are identified by a drive letter that DOS assigns and that are identical to the drive ID letters A, B, C, etc.

The device-driver program file must provide DOS with several entry-point addresses where the driver will be invoked for various purposes: for initialization, for servicing command requests, and for performing strategy work. The driver program must be prepared to handle a standard set of commands that DOS calls on all drivers to perform, and to report the device status to DOS.

Writing a device driver is akin to writing the BIOS programs that are at the heart of DOS and at the heart of the computer's built-in ROM-BIOS. It is among the most sophisticated and intricate programming that is ever undertaken.

THE ANSI DRIVER

One example of an installable device driver that comes as an optional part of DOS is the ANSI driver, a program that greatly enhances the handling of keyboard input and screen output. For our IBM versions of DOS, the ANSI driver is only active when we deliberately introduce it into DOS through the CONFIG.SYS file that DOS loads during the start-up operation. The specific command in the CONFIG.SYS file that is used to activate the ANSI driver is:

```
DEVICE = ANSI.SYS
```

It is worth noting that while the ANSI driver is an optional part of the IBM versions of DOS, the driver is an integral part of the DOS used on some computers that are similar to (but not fully compatible with) the IBM PC family. For example, both the Texas Instruments Professional computer (commonly called the TI Pro) and the NEC Advanced Personal Computer III (the NEC APC-III) automatically include the ANSI driver in their DOS-2 versions.

The ANSI driver monitors both the screen output and the keyboard input that pass through the standard DOS screen and keyboard services. (It's important to note that any keyboard or screen data that bypasses DOS is never seen or processed by the ANSI driver.)

In monitoring the screen output, the ANSI driver looks for special codes that identify commands for the driver. The driver takes note of anything it recognizes as a command and then removes it, so that the special command codes do not appear on the display screen. In effect, this aspect of the driver acts as a two-way switch: It inspects output that is headed for the display screen and passes on anything that is not a driver command, while passing anything that is a driver command into its command-processing part.

Commands for the ANSI driver are identified by a special 2-byte code: The first byte is the "escape" character, hex 1B or CHR$(27), and the second is the left-bracket character [, hex 5B or CHR$(91). Following these identifying bytes are the command parameters and finally the command code itself. The command parameters are either numbers (in the form of ASCII numeric characters interpreted as decimal digits) or strings of ASCII characters enclosed in quotes, like this: "a string parameter". If there is more than one parameter, they are separated by semicolons. The command code itself, which completes the ANSI driver command, is always a single alphabetic character. The case of the command letter matters; for example, lowercase *h* is one command and uppercase *H* is an entirely different one.

To show you what these commands look like, here are two examples, one simple and one complex (the asterisk stands for the escape character, hex 1B):

```
*[1C
*[65;32;66;"Re-mapped B"p
```

The ANSI driver recognizes a large number of commands, but they all fall into two broad categories: screen control commands and keyboard translation commands. Let's look at screen control first.

ANSI Screen Control

Although the BIOS services for the PC let us move the cursor anywhere on the screen and do other things that give us full-screen control, the standard DOS services do not. In fact, the DOS screen output services are completely oriented to TTY (or teletype) output—output that only encompasses the sort of things that can be done with a printer. This, of course, ignores the richer potential of a display screen. It's the lack of full-screen output in DOS that forces most programs to bypass the DOS services and use lower-level services, such as the BIOS services.

The screen control commands of the ANSI driver remedy this situation by providing a set of full-screen commands that can be used to do nearly anything that the display screen is capable of doing. The commands include moving the cursor, clearing the screen, setting the display attributes (color, underscore, blinking, etc.), and changing the mode from text to graphics and vice versa. As a further level of sophistication, there are commands that can save the current cursor location, so that the cursor can be moved to display information and then returned to its original position.

ANSI Keyboard Control

The other type of command accepted by the ANSI driver is a keyboard translation command. When one of these commands is given to the driver, the driver monitors keyboard input and replaces one key character with another single character or even a whole string of characters. This allows the ANSI driver to act as a crude but effective substitute for popular keyboard-enhancer programs, such as ProKey (☞ see page 129).

Note that these two types of ANSI driver commands are very different in their purpose and use, but they are both passed to the driver the same way—through a stream of screen output characters.

The Pros and Cons of the ANSI Driver

As I see it, there are two main ways to look at ANSI driver commands: from the perspective of the user, who can use the ANSI driver to perform a few beneficial tricks, and from the perspective of the programmer, who can use it as an aid to program development. This is a programmer's book, but let me comment briefly on some common user's tricks with the ANSI driver.

As far as I know, users most often regard the ANSI driver as a poor man's ProKey and as a DOS command-prompt enhancer. By using the keyboard translation commands, as we mentioned earlier, it is possible to roughly simulate the ProKey program. Usually the keyboard commands are activated by placing them in a text file and sending them to the screen (and therefore to the ANSI driver) with the TYPE command. By embedding ANSI driver commands into the prompt string, it is possible to launch the DOS command prompt into the fourth dimension. Such a fancy prompt might move the cursor to the top of the screen, display the date and time in reverse video, and then return the cursor to its regular position, or—to get really fancy—even clear the screen and then paint a complete menu display. The possibilities are endless (and also a little silly, in my opinion).

From a programmer's point of view, the ANSI driver looks quite different. Use of the driver presents a programmer with two main benefits, both of which can be quite important. For programmers who do not have the skills and tools necessary to build assembly-language interfaces into the BIOS services, the ANSI driver makes the most crucial BIOS-type services available to any programming language. Furthermore, it can be a great benefit to programmers who want to write programs that are not tied to the PC family, but instead will work on any DOS computer using the ANSI driver.

Despite these apparent advantages, I generally believe that the use of the ANSI driver commands in our programs is not a good idea. For one thing, it requires that the ANSI driver be installed in any computer that our programs are used on, which adds considerably to the instructions that we have to prepare to accompany the programs. It is difficult enough trying to explain the setup and use of our programs to both novices and experts, without adding extra layers of complexity, such as the explanation of how to install the ANSI driver.

A further argument against the use of the ANSI driver is that it is not available under all circumstances. For example, IBM's windowing system, Topview, does not support the features of the ANSI driver, so programs that require the driver cannot be used with Topview. This may well turn out to be true with other windowing environments as well.

But most important of all is the fact that, compared to other methods that are available, the ANSI driver is pathetically slow in generating full-screen output. You can get a direct comparison of the relative speed of the ANSI driver, the PC BIOS services, and direct-to-memory screen output by playing with the NU program that's in version 3 of my Norton Utilities set. The NU program contains three screen drivers that use these three output methods. If you try them all, you'll quickly see how much slower the ANSI driver is. Unless there is very little screen output to be displayed, the ANSI driver is just too slow to be satisfactory.

B

Hexadecimal Arithmetic

H exadecimal numbers crop up in computer work for the simple reason that everything a computer does is based on binary numbers, and hexadecimal notation is a convenient way to represent binary numbers.

Hexadecimal numbers are built on a base of 16, just as ordinary decimal numbers are built on a base of 10; the difference is that hex numbers are written with sixteen symbols while decimal numbers are written with ten (0 through 9). (From here on, we'll use the terms "hexadecimal" and "hex" interchangeably.) In hex notation, the ten symbols 0 through 9 are used to represent the ten values zero through nine, and the remaining six values, ten through fifteen, are represented by the symbols A through F (☞ see Figure B-1).

The hex digits A through F are usually written with capital letters, but you may also see them with the lowercase letters *a* through *f*; the meaning is the same.

Hex numbers are built out of hex digits the same way that decimal numbers are built. For example, when we write the decimal number 123, we mean:

$$\begin{array}{rr} 1 \text{ times} & 100 \quad (10 \text{ times } 10) \\ +2 \text{ times} & 10 \\ +3 \text{ times} & 1 \end{array}$$

If we use the symbols 123 as a hex number, we mean:

$$\begin{array}{rr} 1 \text{ times} & 256 \quad (16 \text{ times } 16) \\ +2 \text{ times} & 16 \\ +3 \text{ times} & 1 \end{array}$$

There does not seem to be a standard way to write hex numbers and you may find them expressed differently in different places. BASIC uses the prefix &H to identify hex numbers and this notation is sometimes used elsewhere, as well. Occasionally the prefix # or 16# is used,

Hex	Dec	Hex	Dec	Hex	Dec	Hex	Dec
0	Zero	4	Four	8	Eight	C	Twelve
1	One	5	Five	9	Nine	D	Thirteen
2	Two	6	Six	A	Ten	E	Fourteen
3	Three	7	Seven	B	Eleven	F	Fifteen

Figure B-1. The decimal value of the sixteen hex digits

but more often a hex number is simply followed by an *H*. However, the most common way to express hex numbers, especially in reference information, is without any special notation at all. You are expected to understand from the context when a number is written in decimal notation and when it is written in hex. When you see a number in any technical reference information that seems to be a decimal number, check carefully: It may actually be in hex. In this book we have usually identified hex numbers by adding *hex* in front of them.

When you need to work with hex numbers, you can use BASIC as an aid (☛ see page 398) or you can work with them by hand. Whichever method you choose, you may find the conversion and arithmetic tables located toward the end of this appendix helpful. But before we get to the tables, we'll first explain why hex numbers and binary numbers are so compatible. Then we'll describe one of the most common uses of hex numbers in programming: segmented addressing.

BITS AND HEXADECIMAL

Hex numbers are primarily used as shorthand for the binary numbers that our computers work with. Every hex digit represents four bits of binary information (☛ see Figure B-2). In the binary (base 2) numbering system, a 4-bit number can have sixteen different combinations, so the only way to represent each of the 4-bit binary numbers with a single digit is to use a base-16 numbering system, which is why hex arithmetic is used with our computers. (☛ See Figure B-3.)

Hex	Bits	Hex	Bits	Hex	Bits	Hex	Bits
0	0 0 0 0	4	0 1 0 0	8	1 0 0 0	C	1 1 0 0
1	0 0 0 1	5	0 1 0 1	9	1 0 0 1	D	1 1 0 1
2	0 0 1 0	6	0 1 1 0	A	1 0 1 0	E	1 1 1 0
3	0 0 1 1	7	0 1 1 1	B	1 0 1 1	F	1 1 1 1

Figure B-2. The bit patterns for each of the sixteen hex digits

Bit	Word	Byte	Value Dec	Value Hex
0	 1	 1	1	1
1	. . . . 1 .	. . . . . . 1 .	2	2
2	. . . . 1 . .	. . . . . 1 . .	4	4
3	. . . . 1 . . .	. . . . 1 . . .	8	8
4	. . . . 1	. . . 1	16	10
5	. . . . 1	. . 1	32	20
6	. . . . 1	. 1	64	40
7	. . . . . . 1	1	128	80
8	. . . . . . 1		256	100
9	. . . . . 1		512	200
10	. . . . 1		1,024	400
11	. . . 1		2,048	800
12	. . . 1		4,096	1000
13	. . 1		8,192	2000
14	. 1		16,384	4000
15	1		32,768	8000

Figure B-3. The hexadecimal and decimal equivalents of each bit in a byte and each bit in a 2-byte word

When you're using 2-byte words, remember the reverse, or "back-words," order in which they are stored in memory. ☛ See Chapter 3, page 28.

SEGMENTED ADDRESSES AND HEXADECIMAL NOTATION

One of the most common uses of hex numbers is for memory addressing. You may recall from Chapters 2 and 3 that a complete address is 20 bits, or 5 hex digits, wide. Since the PC's 8088 microprocessor can work only with 16-bit numbers, addresses are broken down into two 16-bit words, called the segment paragraph and the relative offset. The two parts are written together as 1234:ABCD. The segment part is always written first, and both parts are given in hex.

The segment part of an address is treated as if it were multiplied by 16, which is the same as if it had an extra hex 0 written after it. The two parts, added together, yield the actual 20-bit address that they represent. For example, the segmented address 1234:ABCD converts into a complete address like this:

$$
\begin{array}{r}
1\ 2\ 3\ 4\ 0 \quad \text{(note the zero added on the right)} \\
+ \quad A\ B\ C\ D \\
\hline
1\ C\ F\ 0\ D
\end{array}
$$

If you need to calculate the actual address that a segmented address refers to, follow this formula. ☛ The addition tables on page 399 may also help.

❏ NOTE: *Be aware that the same actual address can be represented by many distinctly different segmented addresses.*

There is no one best way to break down an actual address into its segmented format. One simple way is to take the first digit of the actual address followed by three zeros as the segment-paragraph part, and the remaining four digits as the relative part. Following this rule, the address above, 1CF0D, would be separated out as 1000:CF0D. IBM's listing for the ROM-BIOS in the Technical Reference manual follows this convention, so that all the relative addresses that appear there have the (unshown) segment-paragraph part of F000.

When you are working with real segmented addresses, the segment-paragraph part will represent the actual contents of one of the segment registers and could point to nearly anywhere in memory. The relative off-sets vary with usage. Code offsets, which indicate program locations, usually begin with hex 100, since 256 (hex 100) bytes are set aside before every program for its program segment prefix. Data offsets, used for data, usually start from 0. Stack offsets are usually large numbers, since the stack works backward from within the stack segment.

To see a live example of the sort of segmented address that is in use when a program is executed, run the DOS DEBUG program. When DEBUG begins, it will give you a command prompt of -. When you enter the single-letter command D, DEBUG will display part of memory; the ad-dresses that are shown on the left are the way segmented addresses typ-ically appear.

DECIMAL-HEXADECIMAL CONVERSION

The tables on the next page show the decimal equivalent of each hex digit in the first five digit positions, which covers the complete ad-dress-space arithmetic used in the PC. As we'll demonstrate, these tables can be used to convert between hexadecimal and decimal numbers.

First Position				Second Position			
Hex	Dec	Hex	Dec	Hex	Dec	Hex	Dec
. . . . 0	0	 8	8	. . . 0 .	0	. . . 8 .	128
. . . . 1	1	 9	9	. . . 1 .	16	. . . 9 .	144
. . . . 2	2	. . . . A	10	. . . 2 .	32	. . . A .	160
. . . . 3	3	. . . . B	11	. . . 3 .	48	. . . B .	176
. . . . 4	4	 C	12	. . . 4 .	64	. . . C .	192
. . . . 5	5	. . . . D	13	. . . 5 .	80	. . . D .	208
. . . . 6	6	. . . . E	14	. . . 6 .	96	. . . E .	224
. . . . 7	7	. . . . F	15	. . . 7 .	112	. . . F .	240

Third Position				Fourth Position			
Hex	Dec	Hex	Dec	Hex	Dec	Hex	Dec
. . 0 . .	0	. . 8 . .	2,048	. 0 . . .	0	. 8 . . .	32,768
. . 1 . .	256	. . 9 . .	2,304	. 1 . . .	4,096	. 9 . . .	36,864
. . 2 . .	512	. . A . .	2,560	. 2 . . .	8,192	. A . . .	40,960
. . 3 . .	768	. . B . .	2,816	. 3 . . .	12,288	. B . . .	45,056
. . 4 . .	1,024	. . C . .	3,072	. 4 . . .	16,384	. C . . .	49,152
. . 5 . .	1,280	. . D . .	3,328	. 5 . . .	20,480	. D . . .	53,248
. . 6 . .	1,536	. . E . .	3,584	. 6 . . .	24,576	. E . . .	57,344
. . 7 . .	1,792	. . F . .	3,840	. 7 . . .	28,672	. F . . .	61,440

Fifth Position			
Hex	Dec	Hex	Dec
0	0	8	524,288
1	65,536	9	589,824
2	131,072	A	655,360
3	196,608	B	720,896
4	262,144	C	786,432
5	327,680	D	851,968
6	393,216	E	917,504
7	458,752	F	983,040

Figure B-4. The decimal equivalent of each hex digit position

Here is how these tables can be used to convert a hex number to a decimal number. We'll use the hex number A1B2 as an example. Look up each hex digit in the table corresponding to its position and then add the decimal values, like this:

2 in the first position is	2
B in the second position is	176
1 in the third position is	256
A in the fourth position is	40,960
The total is	41,394

To convert a decimal number to hex using these tables, the process is as simple to do, but it's slightly more complicated to describe. Once again, things will be clearer if we work through an example. We'll use the decimal number 1,492.

Work from the table for the fifth position over to the table for the first. In the fifth-position table, find the biggest hex digit with a value that isn't greater than 1,492, write down the hex digit, subtract its decimal value from 1,492, and continue to the next table with the new value (that is, the difference after subtracting). Go from table to table until the number remaining is 0. The process is shown in Figure B-5. The result is 005D4, or 5D4 without the leading zeros.

Position	Largest Hex Digit	Decimal Value	Remaining Decimal Number
Starting			1,492
5	0	0	1,492
4	0	0	1,492
3	5	1280	212
2	D	208	4
1	4	4	0
Result	005D4		

*Figure B-5. Converting the decimal number
1,492 into a hexadecimal number*

USING BASIC FOR HEX ARITHMETIC

One easy way to manipulate hex numbers is to let BASIC do the work. To do this, activate the BASIC interpreter and enter any operations you want to perform using the command mode (without line numbers).

To display the decimal equivalent of a hex number, such as hex 1234, you can simply do this:

```
PRINT &H1234
```

Be sure to prefix any hex number with &H, so that BASIC knows it is a hex number. To get the best display of decimal numbers, particularly large numbers, use the PRINT USING format, like this:

```
PRINT USING "###,###,###"; &H1234
```

To display the hex equivalent of a decimal number, such as 1,234, you can simply do this:

```
PRINT HEX$( 1234 )
```

The examples so far have only used decimal and hex constants. We can just as easily have BASIC perform some arithmetic and show the result in decimal or hexadecimal. Here are two examples:

```
PRINT USING "###,###,###"; &H1000 - &H3A2 + 16 * 3
PRINT HEX$(1776 - 1492 + &H100)
```

Using variables to hold calculated results can save us from having to rekey an expression or a complicated number. Variables that hold hex numbers should always be written as double-precision variables (with a # at the end of the variable name) so that we get the maximum accuracy. For example:

```
X# = 1776 - 1492 + &H100
PRINT USING "###,###,###"; X#, 2 * X#, 3 * X#
```

HEX ADDITION

To add hex numbers, we work digit-by-digit, just as we do with decimal numbers. To make it easier, use Figure B-6, which calculates the sum of any two hex digits. To use this table, find the row for one hex digit and the column for the other. The hex number located at the row/column intersection is the sum of the two digits.

	0	1	2	3	4	5	6	7	8	9	A	B	C	D	E	F
0	0	1	2	3	4	5	6	7	8	9	A	B	C	D	E	F
1		2	3	4	5	6	7	8	9	A	B	C	D	E	F	10
2			4	5	6	7	8	9	A	B	C	D	E	F	10	11
3				6	7	8	9	A	B	C	D	E	F	10	11	12
4					8	9	A	B	C	D	E	F	10	11	12	13
5						A	B	C	D	E	F	10	11	12	13	14
6							C	D	E	F	10	11	12	13	14	15
7								E	F	10	11	12	13	14	15	16
8									10	11	12	13	14	15	16	17
9										12	13	14	15	16	17	18
A											14	15	16	17	18	19
B												16	17	18	19	1A
C													18	19	1A	1B
D														1A	1B	1C
E															1C	1D
F																1E

Figure B-6. Addition of two hex numbers

HEX MULTIPLICATION

To multiply hex numbers, we work digit-by-digit, just as we do with decimal numbers. To make it easier, use Figure B-7, which calculates the product of any two hex digits. To use the table, find the row for one hex digit and the column for the other. The hex number located at the row/column intersection is the product of the two digits.

	0	1	2	3	4	5	6	7	8	9	A	B	C	D	E	F
0	0	0	0	0	0	0	0	0	0	0	0	0	0	0	0	0
1		1	2	3	4	5	6	7	8	9	A	B	C	D	E	F
2			4	6	8	A	C	E	10	12	14	16	18	1A	1C	1E
3				9	C	F	12	15	18	1B	1E	21	24	27	2A	2D
4					10	14	18	1C	20	24	28	2C	30	34	38	3C
5						19	1E	23	28	2D	32	37	3C	41	46	4B
6							24	2A	30	36	3C	42	48	4E	54	5A
7								31	38	3F	46	4D	54	5B	62	69
8									40	48	50	58	60	68	70	78
9										51	5A	63	6C	75	7E	87
A											64	6E	78	82	8C	96
B												79	84	8F	9A	A5
C													90	9C	A8	B4
D														A9	B6	C3
E															C4	D2
F																E1

Figure B-7. Multiplication of two hex numbers

C

About Characters

There are 256 distinct characters used by the IBM personal computer family. They have numeric byte codes with values ranging from 0 through 255. Often these characters are referred to by their numeric value using the BASIC notation CHR$(0) through CHR$(255). The first 128 characters, CHR$(0) through CHR$(127) are the true, standard ASCII characters. The last 128 characters, CHR$(128) through CHR$(255) are special characters that make up an extended ASCII character set.

Generally, computers treat the true ASCII characters in a similar way, although there is some variety in the way the first 32 characters are used. (☞ See page 407 for a discussion of these characters.) The computer manufacturer decides how to use the 128 special characters.

Fortunately, all models of the IBM personal computers use the same extended ASCII character set. Computers that closely mimic the IBM personal computers use this set as well, but other computers often have their own special characters. This is important to consider when converting programs from other computers, or when writing PC programs that you plan to convert for use on other computers.

THE STANDARD AND EXTENDED CHARACTER SET

Here is a BASIC program that will display all 256 characters along with their numeric codes in both decimal and hexadecimal notation. The characters are also listed in Figure C-1, on page 404.

```
1000 ' display all the PC characters
1010 '
1020 MONOCHROME = 1
1030 IF MONOCHROME THEN WW = 80 : HH = &HB000
       ELSE WW = 40 : HH = &HB800
1040 GOSUB 2000                                    ' initialize DS register
1050 FOR I = 0 TO 255                               ' for all character codes
1060    GOSUB 3000                                  ' display the information
1070 NEXT I
1080 PRINT "Done."
1090 GOSUB 6000
1095 SYSTEM
1999 '
2000 ' initialize
2010 '
2020 DEF SEG = HH                                   ' set up DS register for poke
2030 KEY OFF : CLS                                  ' set up the screen
2040 WIDTH WW : COLOR 14,1,1
2050 FOR I = 1 TO 25 : PRINT : NEXT I
2060 PRINT "  Demonstrating all characters"
```

```
2070 GOSUB 5000                              ' periodic subheading
2080 RETURN
2099 '
3000 ' display character information
3010 '
3020 PRINT USING "  ###       ";I;
3030 IF I < 16 THEN PRINT "0";
3040 PRINT HEX$(I);"          ";
3050 POKE WW * 2 * 23 + 34, I                ' insert the character
3060 GOSUB 4000                              ' print any comments
3070 IF (I MOD 16) < 15 THEN RETURN          ' pause after each 16 characters
3080 GOSUB 6000
3090 IF I < 255 THEN GOSUB 5000
3100 RETURN
3997 '
3998 ' character comments
3999 '
4000 IF I =    0 THEN PRINT "shows blank";
4007 IF I =    7 THEN PRINT "beep (bell)";
4008 IF I =    8 THEN PRINT "backspace";
4009 IF I =    9 THEN PRINT "tab";
4010 IF I =   10 THEN PRINT "line feed";
4012 IF I =   12 THEN PRINT "page eject";
4013 IF I =   13 THEN PRINT "carriage return";
4026 IF I =   26 THEN PRINT "end text file";
4032 IF I =   32 THEN PRINT "true blank space";
4255 IF I =  255 THEN PRINT "shows blank";
4997 PRINT                                   ' finish the line
4998 RETURN
4999 '
5000 ' periodic subheading
5010 '
5020 COLOR 15
5030 PRINT
5040 PRINT
5050 PRINT "Decimal - Hex - Char - Comments"
5060 PRINT
5070 COLOR 14
5080 RETURN
5999 '
6000 ' pause
6010 '
6020 IF INKEY$ <> "" THEN GOTO 6020
6030 PRINT
6040 COLOR 2
6050 PRINT "Press any key to continue..."
6060 COLOR 14
6070 IF INKEY$ = "" THEN GOTO 6070
6080 PRINT
6090 RETURN
```

There are a few things to note about this program and the characters that it shows:

The program is designed to automatically adjust itself to a monochrome or color/graphics adapter based on the value shown in line 1020; use 1 (as shown) for a monochrome adapter; change the 1 to 0 for a

NUMBER, dec	NUMBER, hex	SCREEN	NUMBER, dec	NUMBER, hex	SCREEN	NUMBER, dec	NUMBER, hex	SCREEN	NUMBER, dec	NUMBER, hex	SCREEN	NUMBER, dec	NUMBER, hex	SCREEN	NUMBER, dec	NUMBER, hex	SCREEN	NUMBER, dec	NUMBER, hex	SCREEN	NUMBER, dec	NUMBER, hex	SCREEN
0	00		32	20		64	40	@	96	60	`	128	80	Ç	160	A0	á	192	C0	└	224	E0	α
1	01		33	21	!	65	41	A	97	61	a	129	81	ü	161	A1	í	193	C1	┴	225	E1	β
2	02		34	22	"	66	42	B	98	62	b	130	82	é	162	A2	ó	194	C2	┬	226	E2	Γ
3	03		35	23	#	67	43	C	99	63	c	131	83	â	163	A3	ú	195	C3	├	227	E3	π
4	04		36	24	$	68	44	D	100	64	d	132	84	ä	164	A4	ñ	196	C4	─	228	E4	Σ
5	05		37	25	%	69	45	E	101	65	e	133	85	à	165	A5	Ñ	197	C5	┼	229	E5	σ
6	06		38	26	&	70	46	F	102	66	f	134	86	å	166	A6	ª	198	C6	╞	230	E6	μ
7	07		39	27	'	71	47	G	103	67	g	135	87	ç	167	A7	º	199	C7	╟	232	E7	τ
8	08		40	28	(	72	48	H	104	68	h	136	88	ê	168	A8	¿	200	C8	╚	232	E8	Φ
9	09		41	29	)	73	49	I	105	69	i	137	89	ë	169	A9	⌐	201	C9	╔	233	E9	θ
10	0A		42	2A	*	74	4A	J	106	6A	j	138	8A	è	170	AA	¬	202	CA	╩	234	EA	Ω
11	0B		43	2B	+	75	4B	K	107	6B	k	139	8B	ï	171	AB	½	203	CB	╦	235	EB	δ
12	0C		44	2C	,	76	4C	L	108	6C	l	140	8C	î	172	AC	¼	204	CC	╠	236	EC	∞
13	0D		45	2D	-	77	4D	M	109	6D	m	141	8D	ì	173	AD	¡	205	CD	═	237	ED	φ
14	0E		46	2E	.	78	4E	N	110	6E	n	142	8E	Ä	174	AE	«	206	CE	╬	238	EE	∈
15	0F		47	2F	/	79	4F	O	111	6F	o	143	8F	Å	175	AF	»	207	CF	╧	239	EF	∩
16	10		48	30	0	80	50	P	112	70	p	144	90	É	176	B0	░	208	D0	╨	240	F0	≡
17	11		49	32	1	81	51	Q	113	71	q	145	91	æ	177	B1	▒	209	D1	╤	241	F1	±
18	12		50	32	2	82	52	R	114	72	r	146	92	Æ	178	B2	▓	210	D2	╥	242	F2	≥
19	13		51	33	3	83	53	S	115	73	s	147	93	ô	179	B3	│	211	D3	╙	243	F3	≤
20	14	¶	52	34	4	84	54	T	116	74	t	148	94	ö	180	B4	┤	212	D4	╘	244	F4	⌠
21	15	§	53	35	5	85	55	U	117	75	u	149	95	ò	181	B5	╡	213	D5	╒	245	F5	⌡
22	16	▬	54	36	6	86	56	V	118	76	v	150	96	û	182	B6	╢	214	D6	╓	246	F6	÷
23	17	↨	55	37	7	87	57	W	119	77	w	151	97	ù	183	B7	╖	215	D7	╫	247	F7	≈
24	18	↑	56	38	8	88	58	X	120	78	x	152	98	ÿ	184	B8	╕	216	D8	╪	248	F8	°
25	19	↓	57	39	9	89	59	Y	121	79	y	153	99	Ö	185	B9	╣	217	D9	┘	249	F9	∙
26	1A	→	58	3A	:	90	5A	Z	122	7A	z	154	9A	Ü	186	BA	║	218	DA	┌	250	FA	·
27	1B	←	59	3B	;	91	5B	[	123	7B	{	155	9B	¢	187	BB	╗	219	DB	█	251	FB	√
28	1C	∟	60	3C	<	92	5C	\	124	7C	¦	156	9C	£	188	BC	╝	220	DC	▄	252	FC	ⁿ
29	1D	↔	61	3D	=	93	5D	]	125	7D	}	157	9D	¥	189	BD	╜	221	DD	▌	253	FD	²
30	1E	▲	62	3E	>	94	5E	^	126	7E	~	158	9E	₧	190	BE	╛	222	DE	▐	254	FE	■
31	1F	▼	63	3F	?	95	5F	_	127	7F	⌂	159	9F	ƒ	191	BF	┐	223	DF	▀	255	FF	

Figure C-1. The IBM PC family character set

color/graphics adapter or its equivalent. Depending on the value in line 1020, the program makes two adjustments: one that changes where display information is POKEd into the screen memory, and another that changes the screen width to either 40 or 80 columns. For a color/graphics adapter, 40-column mode is generally used for greater clarity.

The POKE statement in line 3050 is what causes the characters to be displayed. This extra step is necessary because a few characters cannot be displayed by the ordinary PRINT statement. ☞ See page 407, "The First Thirty-Two ASCII Characters," for an explanation.

Each of the 256 distinct characters has its own unique appearance except for the two characters CHR$(0) and CHR$(255), which appear the same as the blank-space character, CHR$(32). (☞ See Figure C-1.)

The Character Format

All characters that appear on the display screen are composed of dots drawn within a grid called a character box. There are two standard grids, one for the Monochrome Adapter (and its equivalents) and one for the Color/Graphics Adapter (and its equivalents). In either case, characters are created by filling (or lighting) the appropriate dots in the grid.

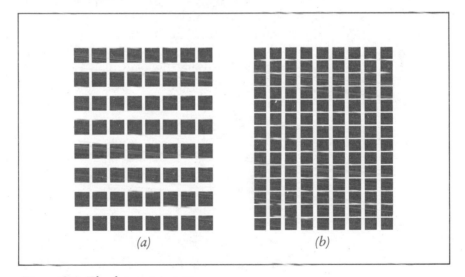

(a)   (b)

Figure C-2. The dot-matrix pattern
produced by (a) the Color/Graphics Adapter
and (b) the Monochrome Adapter

The Color/Graphics Adapter uses an 8- by 8-dot character box; the Monochrome Adapter uses a 9- by 14-dot box, which allows a more refined character drawing. Most non-IBM members of the PC family use only the color/graphics format, as does IBM's PCjr. A notable exception is the Compaq PC-compatible computers, which successfully merge both formats into the same display.

Dot-matrix printers, such as the IBM Compact printer, also draw characters with a grid of dots. However, each model of printer may have its own particular way of drawing characters that may not exactly match the screen characters dot-for-dot. On the other hand, a graphics screen dump to a graphics printer should match the screen dot-for-dot.

To see how characters appear, the three dot matrices in Figure C-3 illustrate a Y, a y, and a semicolon, using the 8-by-8 character box.

There are several rules that apply to the character drawings. For ordinary characters, the two right-hand columns are left unused to provide separation between characters. These two columns are used only by characters that are supposed to fill the entire character box, such as the solid block character, CHR$(219). The top two rows are used for ascenders (the part of a character that is above the ordinary character height). The ascender space is used for capital letters and for such lowercase letters as *b, d,* and *k.* The bottom row is used for descenders (the part of a character that drops below the line), as in the lowercase letters *g* and *y.* These general guidelines are occasionally compromised for the best overall effect. For example, the semicolon, our third example in Figure C-3, is shifted up one row from what we might expect so that it does not use the descender row.

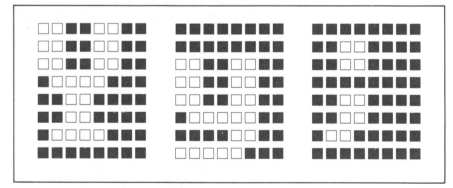

Figure C-3. The dot pattern of three characters in an 8-by-8 character box

Bit 7 6 5 4 3 2 1 0	Value (hex)
1 1 0 0 1 1 0 0	CC
1 1 0 0 1 1 0 0	CC
1 1 0 0 1 1 0 0	CC
0 1 1 1 1 0 0 0	78
0 0 1 1 0 0 0 0	30
0 0 1 1 0 0 0 0	30
0 1 1 1 1 0 0 0	78
0 0 0 0 0 0 0 0	00

*Figure C-4. The coding of the eight
character bytes for the Y character*

In graphics display modes 4 through 6 and 8 through 10 (screen modes 1 through 6 in BASIC), we can create our own character drawing tables using the above guidelines. The character drawing tables are coded with eight bytes for each character—one byte for each row in the drawing. The eight bits of each byte indicate which dots in the row are to be shown. For example, the Y character is coded in hex as CC CC CC 78 30 30 78 00. The individual bits in each byte are shown in Figure C-4 (look closely and you'll see the Y pattern again).

The First Thirty-Two ASCII Characters

The first 32 ASCII characters, CHR$(0) through CHR$(31), have two important uses that just happen to conflict with each other. On the one hand, these characters have standard ASCII meanings; they are used for both printer control (for example, CHR$(12) is the form-feed character) and for communications control. On the other hand, IBM also uses them for some of the most interesting and useful display characters, such as the card-suite characters (hearts, diamonds, clubs, and spades), CHR$(3) through CHR$(6).

Generally, all computer devices, including the printer and the display screen, act on the ASCII meaning of the characters instead of showing the character's picture. A simple way to demonstrate this is with the beep/bell character, CHR$(7), which has a dot for a picture. If we write this character to the screen in BASIC, like this:

```
PRINT CHR$(7)
```

the PC's speaker will beep. But if we put the character directly onto the screen by POKEing it into the screen buffer, like this:

```
DEF SEG = &HB800 : POKE 0, 7
```

the character's picture will appear. We can always make characters appear on the screen by POKEing them into the screen buffer. However, POKEing should be avoided whenever possible, since it makes our programs harder to adapt to changes. It is always a better programming practice to display information on the screen using ordinary methods, such as the PRINT statement in BASIC.

Most of the first 32 characters can be written to the screen, but the display characters may vary, depending upon which language is used. Figure C-5 shows some of these differences. The characters not shown, CHR$(0) through CHR$(6), and CHR$(14) through CHR$(27), can always be written to the screen with predictable results.

Character	Result In BASIC	In most other languages
CHR$(7)	Beeps	Beeps
CHR$(8)	Character appears	Backspace action
CHR$(9)	Tab action	Tab action
CHR$(10)	Line-feed and carriage-return action	Line-feed action
CHR$(11)	Cursor to top left	Character appears
CHR$(12)	Screen clears	Character appears
CHR$(13)	Carriage-return action	Carriage-return action
CHR$(28)	Cursor moves right	Character appears
CHR$(29)	Cursor moves left	Character appears
CHR$(30)	Cursor moves up	Character appears
CHR$(31)	Cursor moves down	Character appears

Figure C-5. The results when certain characters are written to the screen using different languages

The Box Drawing Characters

Among the most useful of the special extended ASCII characters are the characters that are designed for drawing single- and double-lined boxes. These characters have the codes CHR$(179) through CHR$(218). Since they are difficult to combine properly, you may find the information in Figure C-6 helpful.

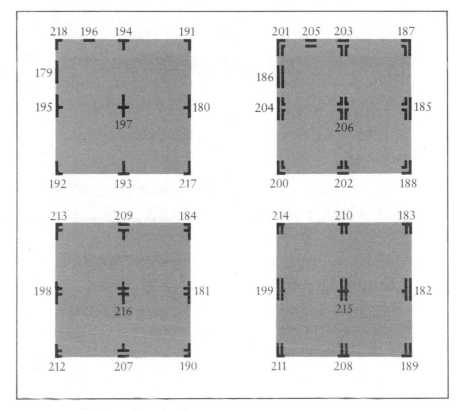

Figure C-6. The box drawing characters

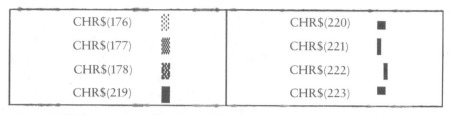

CHR$(176)		CHR$(220)	
CHR$(177)		CHR$(221)	
CHR$(178)		CHR$(222)	
CHR$(219)		CHR$(223)	

Figure C-7. The two sets of graph and block characters

The Graph and Block Characters

In addition to the box drawing characters, there are two series of characters designed for graphs and block drawings. One series consists of four characters that fill the entire character box, but are shaded in different densities. For the three that are not solid, part of the character's dots are on, or set to the foreground color, while the remaining dots are off, or set to the background color. The other series consists of block characters that provide a solid color covering half the character box. The solid character, CHR$(219), is also used with these half characters.

TEXT FILE FORMATTING CONVENTIONS

Many programs work with files of text data. As a result, most programmers have adopted some text file format conventions that make it easier for data files to be used by different programs. The formats are defined by characters embedded in the text that perform such functions as carriage returns, line feeds, or backspaces, just to name a few.

Generally, it is a good idea for programs to be very tolerant of different text data formats. It is also important to design programs that create text data with simple formats, using just a few formatting characters. This is not always possible for word-processing programs, which must be able to format the text on screen in a variety of ways. In this section, we'll first discuss the most ordinary sort of text file, and then go on to discuss word-processor files.

Ordinary Text File Formats

Ordinary text files are made up of only the standard ASCII characters and do not use any of the extended ASCII characters. In the ASCII coding scheme, the first 32 characters, CHR$(0) through CHR$(31), have special meanings: Some of them are used for formatting text data and the others are generally used for communications control. Since these characters are used to control the format of the text, they don't need to appear on a display; in fact, it's best if they do not appear, as they often have rather unusual pictures associated with them.

There is just a handful of formatting characters that are widely used in ordinary text files. They were originally developed as commands to tell a printer how to format a printed page and how to recognize when the end of the file was reached. Now their use extends to all output devices. We'll discuss each of the main formatting characters in turn.

CHR$(26) is used to mark the true end of a text file. This character may come before the end of the file indicated by the file size in the directory entry. This is because many text-processing programs typically read and write files, not byte by byte, but in larger chunks—128 bytes at a time. When they transfer data at this rate, DOS sees only the end of the 128-byte block, and does not recognize the actual end of the file delimited by the CHR$(26) character.

CHR$(13) and CHR$(10) normally divide a text file into lines by marking the end of each line with a carriage return (CHR$(13)) and a line feed (CHR$(10)), usually in that order. Many text-processing programs have difficulty with lines over 255 characters in length and some are limited to 80 character lines.

A carriage return may be used by itself. Unfortunately, this can be interpreted as either of two things: the end of a line with a line feed that is implied and automatically provided by some printers, or a return to the beginning of the current print line, which causes the entire line to be overprinted. (The backspace character, CHR$(8), is also sometimes used to make a printer overstrike a character.)

CHR$(9), the tab character, is sometimes used to represent one or more spaces, up to the next tab-set location. Unfortunately, as yet, there is no universal convention on tab settings, which makes the use of the tab character uncertain. However, one of the most common tab settings is every eight spaces.

CHR$(12), the form feed or page eject, is another format character. This character is interpreted as a command to a printer that tells it to skip to the top of the next page.

There are also other formatting characters available, such as the vertical tab, CHR$(11), but they are not generally in widespread use with personal computers.

It is possible to avoid many difficulties by having programs create text data with simple formats. The simplest formats allow lines no longer than 255 characters and use only the carriage return (CHR$(13)), line feed (CHR$(10)), and end-of-file (CHR$(26)) formatting characters. Most programming languages, including BASIC and Pascal, automatically generate these formatting characters when creating text data. Normally, they also process the characters so we only have to deal with text formatting when we have bypassed our language's usual data control.

Many programs, such as compilers and assemblers, expect to read text data that has the ordinary, plain format that we have been discussing. Often these programs cannot work with the more complex data formats that are created by some word processors.

Word-Processor Text Formats

Word-processing programs have special needs for formatting text data. The files that these programs create are rarely simple and typically have many exotic additions to the simplest ASCII format. Generally, each word processor has its own unique formatting rules; luckily there are some common features.

Many of the special format codes used by word processors are created by using an extended ASCII code that is 128 greater than a normal ASCII code. This is equivalent to setting the high-order bit of an otherwise ordinary byte. For example, a "soft" carriage return, CHR$(141), is coded by adding 128 to an ordinary carriage return, CHR$(13). Soft carriage returns are often used to indicate a tentative end-of-line, which can be changed when a paragraph is reformatted. On the other hand, an ordinary carriage return, CHR$(13), may be used to mark the end of a paragraph that isn't changed by reformatting. This kind of coding in word-processing text can cause some programs to treat an entire paragraph as one single line.

"Soft" hyphens, CHR$(173), which are 128 higher than ordinary hyphens, CHR$(45), are sometimes used to indicate where a word may be split into syllables at the end of a line. Ordinary "hard" hyphens, CHR$(45), are treated as regular characters and they cannot be used or removed by the word-processing program in the same way as soft hyphens can be.

Even ordinary alphabetic text may have 128 added to its character code. This may be done by some programs to mark the last letter in a word. For example, a lowercase *a* is CHR$(97); but when it appears at the end of a word, such as America, it may be stored as CHR$(225), since 225 is the sum of $97+128$.

Programs that are intended to work with a variety of text and word-processing data should be prepared, as much as possible, to cope with the variety of coding that these examples suggest.

INDEX

C

E

PETER NORTON

Peter Norton was raised in Seattle, Washington, and educated at Reed College in Portland, Oregon. Before discovering microcomputers, he spent a dozen years working on mainframes and minicomputers for companies including Boeing and the Jet Propulsion Laboratories. After the debut of the IBM PC, Peter was among the first to buy one. Now recognized as a principal authority on IBM personal computer technology, Peter is the author of *Inside the IBM PC* and creator of the best-selling *Norton Utilities* programs. He is also a popular featured columnist for both *PC* and *PC Week* magazines.

The manuscript for this book was prepared on an IBM Personal Computer. Submitted to Microsoft Press in electronic form, the text files were processed and formatted using Microsoft Word.

Cover design by Ted Mader and Associates.
Cover photo by Tom Collicott.
Technical illustrations by Rick van Genderen.

Text composition in Sabon, with program listings in HP Monospace. Typesetting by Microsoft Press, using the CCI system and the Mergenthaler Linotron 202 digital phototypesetter.

Other Titles from Microsoft Press

Running MS-DOS, 2nd Edition
The Microsoft guide to getting the most out of the standard
operating system for the IBM PC and 50 other personal computers
Van Wolverton $21.95

Advanced MS-DOS
The Microsoft guide for assembly language and C programmers
Ray Duncan $21.95

Supercharging MS-DOS
The Microsoft guide to high performance computing for the
experienced PC user
Van Wolverton $18.95

Windows
The official guide to Microsoft's operating environment
Nancy Andrews $17.95

CD ROM 1: The New Papyrus
The current and future state of the art, Foreword by William H.
Gates
Edited by Steve Lambert and Suzanne Ropiequet $21.95

CD ROM 2: Optical Publishing
A practical approach to developing CD ROM applications
Edited by Suzanne Ropiequet $22.95

Command Performance: Lotus 1-2-3
The Microsoft desktop dictionary and cross-reference guide
Eddie Adamis $24.95

Command Performance: dBASE III
The Microsoft desktop dictionary and cross-reference guide
Douglas Hergert $22.95

Variations in C
Programming techniques for developing efficient professional
applications
Steve Schustack $19.95

Word Processing Power with Microsoft Word, 2nd edition
Peter Rinearson $19.95

Programmers at Work
Interviews with 19 of today's most brilliant programmers
Edited by Susan Lammers $14.95

XENIX at Work
*Edited by JoAnne Woodcock and
Michael Halvorson* $21.95

Available wherever fine books are sold.